THE WINES AND VINEYARDS OF NEW ZEALAND

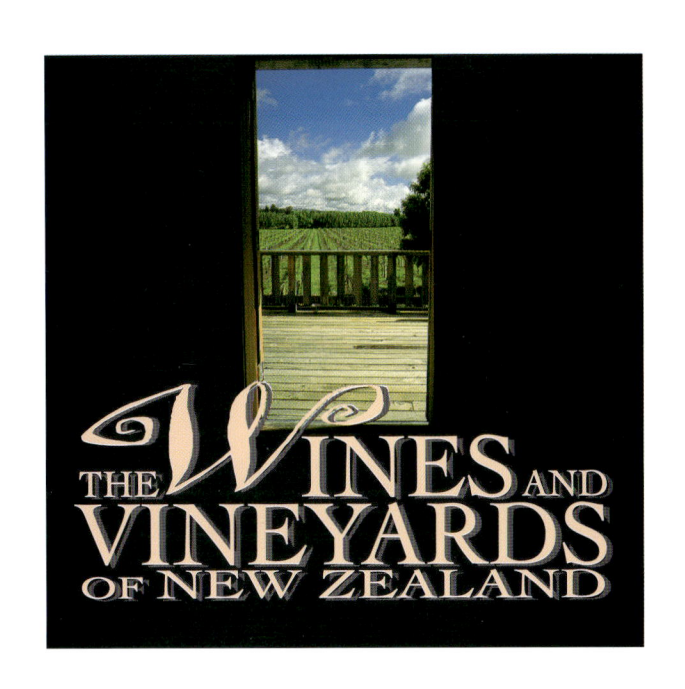

THE Wines AND VINEYARDS OF NEW ZEALAND

Text by
Michael Cooper

Photographs by
John McDermott

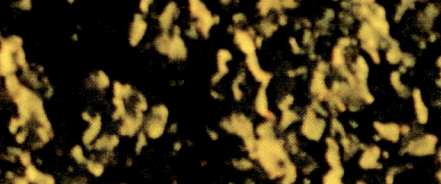

Hodder Moa Beckett

Contents

Introduction	6
A Brief History	8
Making Wine in New Zealand	12
Climate and Soils	16
Grape Varieties	18
Wineries, Winemakers and Wines	28

Northland/Auckland	30
Waikato/Bay of Plenty	72
Gisborne	82
Hawke's Bay	90
Wairarapa	114
Nelson	130
Marlborough	140
Canterbury	164
Otago	182
INDEX	190
BIBLIOGRAPHY	192

INTRODUCTION

Supercharged Sauvignon Blanc, overflowing with green-edged, zingy flavour, first ushered New Zealand wine onto the international stage in the 1980s. Now the country's burgeoning band of winemakers is also producing a glittering array of Chardonnays, Rieslings, sweet wines, bottle-fermented sparklings and reds. No one knows what will eventually emerge as New Zealand's greatest gift to the wine world.

The exciting diversity of the New Zealand wine scene in the 1990s reflects the restless, innovative spirit of the winemakers, unfettered by tradition. Over 40 per cent of the national vineyard is currently devoted to Chardonnay and Sauvignon Blanc, but Sangiovese, the noble grape of Chianti, is established in several vineyards; Malbec, a minor blending variety in Bordeaux that yields notably dark, tannin-laden wines, is stirring up interest; Syrah, of northern Rhône Valley fame, is sinking its roots around the country. And far from the major wine trails, grapevines are sprouting in such hitherto virgin wine territories as Taupo, Whakatane, Galatea in the inland Bay of Plenty, Takapau in Central Hawke's Bay and Omarama in North Otago.

The industry's growth over the past decade, especially in the south, is reflected in the successive editions of *The Wines and Vineyards of New Zealand*. When first published in 1984, the book discussed 50 wineries, including seven south of Hawke's Bay. This fifth edition features 134 wineries (with many others described briefly), of which 70 (over half) lie in the Wairarapa or south of Cook Strait.

The Introduction sets the scene, with a brief survey of the history of wine in New Zealand; a region-by-region summary of the critical influences of climate and soil; a short description of winemaking techniques; and an in-depth look at the classic grape varieties on which New Zealand's 'varietal' wines and the vast majority of its wine labels are based.

The heart of the book follows: a region-by-region, winery-by-winery tour of New Zealand from Okahu Estate in the far north to Black Ridge in the deep south. *The Wines and Vineyards of New Zealand* is a book about people, as much as wine. In New Zealand's youthful wine industry, where so much is still in a state of flux, the impact of an individual winemaker on a company's wines is often much greater than in Europe, where most winemakers face the joint constraints of geography and tradition. New Zealand's colourful community of winemakers, in past editions so memorably portrayed by the late Robin Morrison's lens, is now brought vividly to life by photographer John McDermott.

For the first time in this edition, many of the country's classic wines are examined in detail – what do they taste like? How are they made? Why are they so good? Photographs, labels and maps flesh out the picture of this notably vibrant industry.

For permission to use material first published in my articles in *North and South*, *Cuisine* and *Winestate*, I am indebted to those magazines' publishers. (A small amount of material first appeared in my 1990 book, *Michael Cooper's Pocket Guide To New Zealand Wines and Vintages*, now out of print.) Viticulture experts Dr David Jordan and Steve Smith of Villa Maria made major contributions to the section on grape varieties, and Joe Babich read the winemaking section in manuscript; my sincere thanks to all three. Kevin Judd of Cloudy Bay and Ray Bennett of Matua Valley smoothed John McDermott's path.

During the two months I spent on the road, the country's winemakers were as warm, welcoming and wonderfully generous with their wines and time as ever.

Michael Cooper

A BRIEF HISTORY OF WINE IN NEW ZEALAND

At first glance the history of wine in New Zealand appears remarkably short. Wines from classic *Vitis vinifera* grape varieties have only been widely procurable since the early 1970s; only since the mid 1980s have the new breeds of Chardonnays and Sauvignon Blancs carved out their elevated international reputation. Yet the grapevine was a common sight in the early colonists' gardens, and by the time of the signing of the Treaty of Waitangi in 1840, the first recorded New Zealand wine was already bottled. Wine in fact has had a long, tortuous and fascinating history in this country.

The first recorded planting of grapevines, at Kerikeri in the Bay of Islands, derived from the Anglican missionary Samuel Marsden's belief that Maori should be taught the civilising pursuits of agriculture and handcrafts before being converted to Christianity. In his journal for 25 September 1819 Marsden wrote: 'We had a small plot of land cleared and broken up in which I planted about a hundred grapevines of different kinds brought from Port Jackson [Sydney]. New Zealand promises to be very favourable to the vine as far as I can judge at present of the nature of the soil and climate.'

Twenty years were to pass, however, before the first recorded New Zealand wine flowed. James Busby, a Scot also acknowledged as the father of Australian viticulture, was appointed British Resident at Waitangi in 1832. Four years later a tiny vineyard sprouted between the Resident's house and the flagstaff. Visiting Busby in 1840, the French explorer Dumont d'Urville observed 'a trellis on which several flourishing vines were growing . . . with great pleasure I agreed to taste the product of the vineyard that I had just seen. I was given a light white wine, very sparkling, and delicious to taste, which I enjoyed very much.'

Although Busby's vineyard was ruined in 1845 by troops camped at Waitangi, the flame he had ignited was to be kept alight throughout the 19th century. Bishop Pompallier, the first Catholic Bishop of the South Pacific, brought French vine cuttings to the Hokianga in 1838; thereafter, wherever French mission stations sprang up, vineyards were planted to supply the Marist priests with table grapes and sacramental and table wines. At Akaroa, French peasants who planted vines in 1840 sold fresh grapes to visiting whalers and also produced a rivulet of wine for their own tables.

The honour of being the first to capitalise on winemaking's commercial potential in New Zealand, however, belongs to an Englishman. Charles Levet, a Cambridge coppersmith and his son, William, in 1863 planted a seven-acre (2.8ha) vineyard on an inlet of the Kaipara Harbour. For over four decades the Levets made their living exclusively from producing and selling wine.

Joseph Soler, a Spaniard, was equally successful. Soler made his first wine in Wanganui in 1869 and each year until his death in 1906 despatched about 20,000 bottles of wine to customers throughout the colony.

Winemaking, though, was an extremely precarious pursuit in 19th-century New Zealand. Those who laboured with peasant tenacity in isolated vineyards faced crushing odds. Oidium, a powdery mildew which covered the grapes with mould, splitting their skins and exposing their juice to fungi and insects, caused widespread havoc.

Powerful cultural factors also tethered the fledgling industry. The predominantly British-born and descended population lacked any national tradition of viticulture. Wine was also perceived as a 'class' drink, consumed not by working men and women but by the elite – who demanded true port and sherry and ignored the antipodean substitutes.

Another increasingly formidable foe was the temperance movement. The New Zealand Temperance Society was founded in 1836, and as the movement gathered momentum its call for the prohibition of all alcoholic beverages grew more insistent. The passage of more and more restrictive liquor legislation between 1881 and 1918 severely retarded the wine industry's progress and soon threatened its survival.

Before the prohibition storm-cloud burst, however, several Hawke's Bay land-owning families eager to explore new economic ventures plunged into commercial winemaking. They were encouraged by the success of William Beetham, a Wairarapa farmer, who planted his first vines in 1883 and by 1897 was making about 1850 gallons (8410L) of wine from Pinot Noir, Meunier and Hermitage (Syrah) grapes.

At Henry Tiffen's Greenmeadows Vineyard – praised by a contemporary observer as 'the premier vineyard of New Zealand' – Pinot Noir and Meunier were the principal varieties planted. The 1890s also witnessed the first recorded sales of Mission wines.

At the Te Mata station, Bernard Chambers planted his first vines as a hobby in 1892 and advanced to commercial wine production in 1896. By 1909 his 14ha vineyard of Meunier, Syrah, Cabernet Sauvignon, Riesling and Verdelho was the largest in the country, annually producing 12,000 gallons (54,552L) of wine.

An overseas expert's fervent advocacy of viticulture as an industry 'that will by far eclipse any other that has hitherto been prosecuted here' also stimulated a surge in vineyard plantings in the late 1890s. Romeo Bragato, a Dalmatian-born graduate of the Royal School of Viticulture and Oenology at Corregliano, Italy, arrived in New Zealand on loan from the Victorian Government in 1895 to assess the colony's potential for winemaking.

Bragato's far-sighted *Report on the Prospects of Viticulture in New Zealand* enthused that 'there are few of the places visited by me which are unsuitable to the vine. The land in your colony, if properly worked, should yield a very large quantity of grapes per acre from which wine of the finest quality, both red and white and Champagne could be produced. . .'. Bragato also made an identification of *Phylloxera*, a root-sucking aphid which was then devastating many of the country's vineyards.

Further impetus was given to the burgeoning industry in the 1890s when Dalmatians working in the gumfields of Northland began producing wine. Dalmatians had first planted vines at Pahi in north Kaipara in 1896. By 1907 14 miniscule vineyards at Herekino, south of Kaitaia, had an annual output of about 2000 gallons (9092L).

Another boost to the wine industry's fortunes came in 1902 when Romeo Bragato returned to New Zealand to accept the newly created post of Government Viticulturist. The Government viticultural research station at Te Kauwhata was swiftly upgraded; classic *vinifera* vines grafted onto *Phylloxera*-resistant American rootstocks were widely distributed to growers; a programme of experimental winemaking started. The wine industry looked to be on the verge of prosperity: in 1902 a Lebanese stonemason, Assid Abraham Corban, established a four-acre (1.6ha) vineyard at Henderson; in the same year Stipan Jelich made the first wine at the Pleasant Valley winery in Henderson. By 1913 some 70 winemakers were producing a total of 366,525 litres of wine per year.

The solid progress of two decades was largely destroyed as the influence of the prohibitionists began to peak. When Masterton and Eden – an electorate including part of Henderson – voted 'no-licence' in 1908, many winemakers denied the right to sell their wines locally were forced out of business. Official support began to wither away; the Viticultural Division of the Department of Agriculture was disbanded and in 1909 Bragato left the country, frustrated and disillusioned.

The New Zealand Viticultural Association was formed in 1911 and promptly petitioned the Government for aid, but the beleaguered wine-growers soon found themselves embroiled in a bitter controversy over their own winemaking standards. Prime Minister W.F. Massey, altogether untroubled by the fact that he had 'never seen the stuff', lambasted the Dalmatians' wine as 'a degrading, demoralising and sometimes maddening drink'. The Government subsequently tightened its control by setting up a new system of winemakers' licences, although accusations of adulteration continued to hound the country's winemakers until the early 1980s.

Prohibition fervour gradually went off the

Corbans counter-attack the prohibitionists at the 1919 Auckland Spring Show.

boil in the 1920s and 1930s, bringing an interval of steady although unspectacular growth in the wine industry. On the east coast, Friedrich Wohnsiedler of Waihirere, Tom McDonald of McDonald's and Robert Bird of Glenvale all entered the industry during this period. Henderson received an influx of Dalmatian wine-growers. The number of licensed winemakers soared from 40 in 1925 to 100 in 1932.

The health of their vineyards was, however, declining. Most classic *vinifera* vines had been so weakened by blight and viruses that it was popularly believed that *vinifera* varieties could not successfully be cultivated in New Zealand. Growers turned instead to disease-resistant Franco-American hybrid vines or to the extraordinary Albany Surprise, a particularly heavy-bearing clone of the American Isabella variety. The outcome: wines which at best were coarse and at worst undrinkable.

Having languished without political encouragement for three decades, the wine industry benefited greatly from Labour's ascension to power in 1935. A key ally was the Hon. H.G.R. (Rex) Mason, who as MP for Auckland Suburbs and then Waitakere strongly promoted his West Auckland wine-grower constituents' interests for a period spanning 37 years.

The Te Kauwhata research station was now expanded and upgraded and a new Government Viticulturist, B.W. Lindeman, appointed. Duties on overseas wines were raised and import licences for wine halved. Demand for New Zealand wine grew rapidly, and then further escalated during the Second World War when American servicemen flooded into the country. The wine reseller's licence created in 1948 gave winemakers a string of new retail outlets around the country.

The growers' wartime prosperity rapidly faded, however, when an easing of import restrictions in the late 1940s sent prices tumbling. George Mazuran, elected president of the Viticultural Association in 1950, was convinced that reform of the country's restrictive liquor laws held the key to the wine industry's future prosperity. His tenacious lobbying soon paid dividends. In 1955 Parliament slashed the minimum quantities that had to be sold by a wine reseller or winemaker. The Winemaking Industry Committee, set up in 1956, recommended that wine reseller licences should be much more liberally granted, and the outcome was that by 1965 the number of wine-shops around the country had doubled.

The incoming second Labour Government slashed imports of wines and spirits in 1958 and 1959 by half and slapped higher taxes on beer and spirits – but not wine. According to the 1959 Annual Report of the Department of Agriculture, 'the market position for New Zealand wines changed from one of difficult and competitive trading to a buoyant market capable of absorbing all the wine that producers could supply'.

A critical turning-point in the wine industry's fortunes had been reached. Winemakers now entered a 25-year period of unbroken growth and prosperity. Overseas funds began to pour into the industry. McWilliam's of Australia had set the precedent, establishing a winery and vineyards in Hawke's Bay between 1947 and 1950. Penfolds Wines (NZ) was founded at Henderson in 1963 by its Australian parent.

Montana's rapid expansion, which had begun in the 1960s, acquired even greater momentum in 1973 when Seagram of New York acquired a 40 per cent shareholding.

New Zealanders' attitudes towards wine were also maturing. Thousands of Kiwi soldiers campaigning in Europe were introduced to the pleasures of wine consumption. The post-war boom in overseas travel; the migration of many wine-drinking Yugoslavs, Italians and Greeks to New Zealand; the spread in the 1960s of licensed restaurants – all these factors eroded New Zealanders' traditional perceptions of local wine as 'plonk'. By the 1970s wine had even become fashionable.

Hand in hand with the community's more favourable attitudes towards wine came a proliferation of licences opening up new avenues for its sale. BYO permits allowing the consumption of wine in unlicensed restaurants, and vineyard bar licences legalising the sale and consumption of wine by the glass or bottle at wineries, were both introduced in 1976.

Wine quality, responding to the growing sophistication of New Zealanders' palates, has surged strongly ahead. During the 1970s, influenced by the views of German viticultural scientist Dr. Helmut Becker, winemakers planted countless Müller-Thurgau vines in the conviction that New Zealand in viticultural terms was a sort of Germany of the Southern Hemisphere. Light, mild and fruity white wines like Montana Blenheimer and Nobilo's Müller-Thurgau won instant popularity.

In the 1980s, though, the industry realised that most New Zealand wine regions enjoy grape-growing climates much more akin to the leading wine regions of France. Grape varieties which traditionally have excelled in France, like Chardonnay, Sauvignon Blanc, Gewürztraminer, Pinot Noir, Cabernet Sauvignon and Merlot, are now also deeply entrenched in New Zealand's vineyards. The outcome has been a stream of deep-flavoured dry white and red wines much more clearly uncovering New Zealand's wine potential.

Aiding wine quality were regulations (1983) which set a minimum 95 per cent grape-juice level for all table wines; water, hitherto commonly used to 'stretch' bulk wines, could only be added to wine in small amounts as a processing aid for legal additives. Cask wines were transformed.

Many years' negotiations finally achieved in 1976 the formation of a single, united wine organisation, the Wine Institute, to represent all New Zealand winemakers on such crucial issues as licensing laws, tariffs and taxation.

In response to the surging popularity of wine-drinking, production has leapt from 4.1 million litres in 1960 to 56.4 million litres in 1995. The sales of fortified wines (sherries and ports) which captured 88 per cent of the market for New Zealand wines in 1962, slumped to 8 per cent by 1995.

TOTAL SALES OF NEW ZEALAND WINE
(INCLUDING EXPORTS) 1960–95
(Millions of litres)

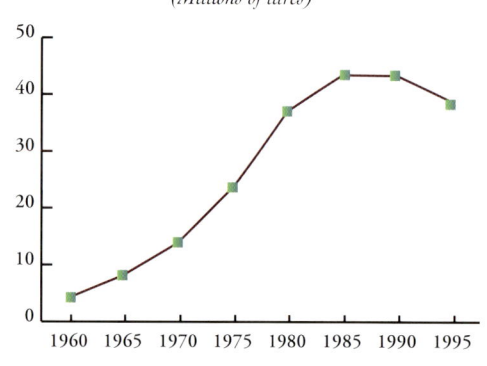

Such radical shifts in the wine styles favoured by New Zealanders have led to far-reaching changes in the country's vineyards. The three most common grapes planted in 1960 – Albany Surprise and the hybrids Baco 22A and Seibel 5455 – proved useless as raw material when the call went out for quality table wines. At the head of the list in 1995 were Chardonnay, Sauvignon Blanc and Müller-Thurgau – all classic *vinifera* varieties yielding white wines of sound to outstanding quality.

NEW ZEALAND WINE SALES
BY STYLE 1982–95
(Percentage of total sales)

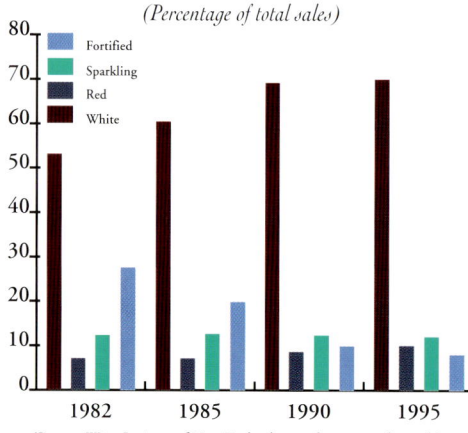

(Sources: Wine Institute of New Zealand annual reports and monthly newsletters)

The emergence of contract grape-growing and the planting of several new regions have further restructured the viticultural industry. Wine companies grew 96 per cent of their grape requirements in 1960; today they grow 32 per cent, with the balance supplied by hundreds of independent grape-growers. The location of vineyards has also shifted southwards. Vines swept across the fertile Gisborne flats in the late 1960s, into Marlborough and Nelson in the early 1970s, and during the 1980s into such promising new regions as Canterbury, the Wairarapa and Central Otago.

The wine boom of the sixties and seventies led the industry to over-enthusiastic expansion of vine plantings in the early 1980s, raising fears of a wine glut. In 1984 the Government compounded the wine-growers' difficulties by hiking the excise on fortified wines by 54 per cent and on table wines by a scorching 83 per cent. Wine prices leapt by 15 per cent, with a corresponding fall-off in sales.

The price-slashing that followed proved too cut-throat for some of the independently owned vineyards lacking corporate financial clout; by late 1985 Villa Maria and Delegat's were both in receivership.

In February 1986 the Government stepped in with an offer of up to $10 million to fund a vine-uprooting scheme. About one-quarter of the national total (1517ha of vines) was promptly destroyed. Gisborne and Hawke's Bay witnessed the heaviest vine pulls; Müller-Thurgau was the most heavily culled variety. Profitability gradually returned to the industry as its production base shrank to a size more aligned to market needs.

In the past decade, new wineries have mushroomed from Northland to Central Otago. In 1984 the Wine Institute had 97 members; in 1990, 131; in 1996, over 220. This proliferation of new wine producers has not been matched by an increase in domestic wine sales, but the wine industry is forever abuzz with the excitement of new companies, new faces, new labels.

In the mid 1990s, a flurry of new plantings again raised the over-production spectre. After the three low-cropping vintages of 1992, 1993 and 1994 – which retarded the sales of New Zealand wine at home and abroad, boosted retail prices, stimulated wine imports and forced several owners of small wineries to take jobs outside the industry – 1995 produced a bumper harvest, the second heaviest on record. In April 1996, the Wine

PERCENTAGE OF NATIONAL VINEYARD BY REGION

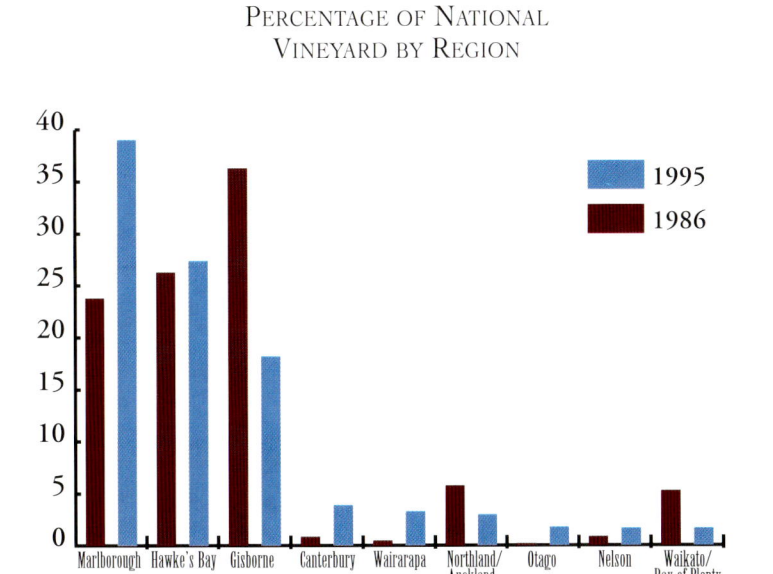

(Source: New Zealand Vineyard Surveys 1986 and 1995)

NEW ZEALAND WINE EXPORTS 1986–96 BY VALUE
($ Millions)

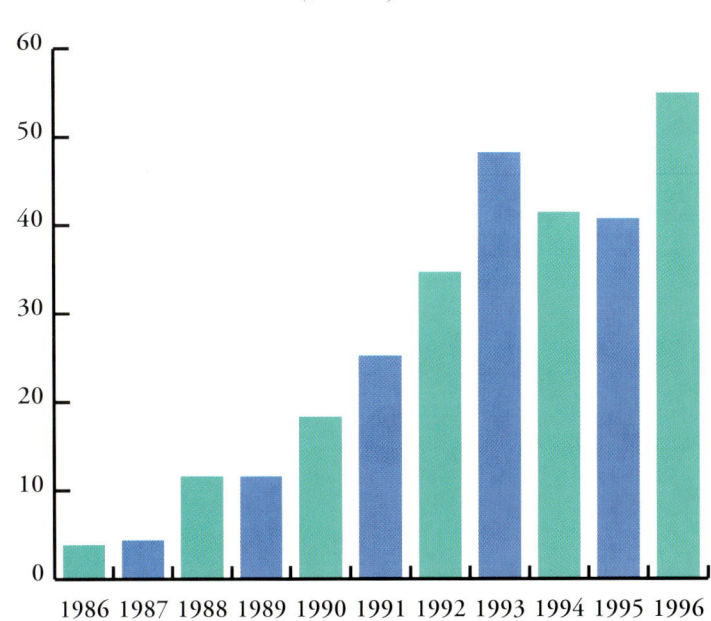

Institute suggested the 1996 crop could be the largest ever.

With the grapes from recent massive vineyard plantings coming on stream, the industry is experiencing a huge production leap. Will there be a glut? By clawing back some of the domestic market recently forfeited to imports (46 per cent of all wine sold in New Zealand in the year to June 1995 was from overseas) and expanding exports, winemakers have plenty of scope to increase their sales. If the next few vintages are lighter, production and sales may be balanced, but a series of heavy vintages could produce a huge surplus.

A highlight of the past decade has been the industry's export triumphs. A long-term strategy whereby the winemakers chose to concentrate their promotional activities on the United Kingdom market, in the belief that acceptance by the influential British wine trade would eventually bring positive sales benefits in other countries, has paid off. The value of New Zealand's wine exports to the UK skyrocketed from $0.4 million in 1985 to $7.8 million in 1990 and $27.6 million in 1995, with New Zealand Sauvignon Blanc becoming a market leader in Britain.

Outside of the UK, trade and consumer awareness of New Zealand wine is still minimal. However, New Zealand wines do have a foothold in retail outlets in Western Europe, Ireland, the United States, Canada, Japan, Australia and the Pacific Islands. Total export receipts climbed to $40.8 million in 1995, and the Wine Institute declared it had a 'very good chance' of bettering its target of $100 million in exports by the year 2000. A new era in the history of New Zealand wine – its emergence onto the international stage – is now unfolding.

TOTAL VINE AREA IN NEW ZEALAND 1960–95
(Hectares)

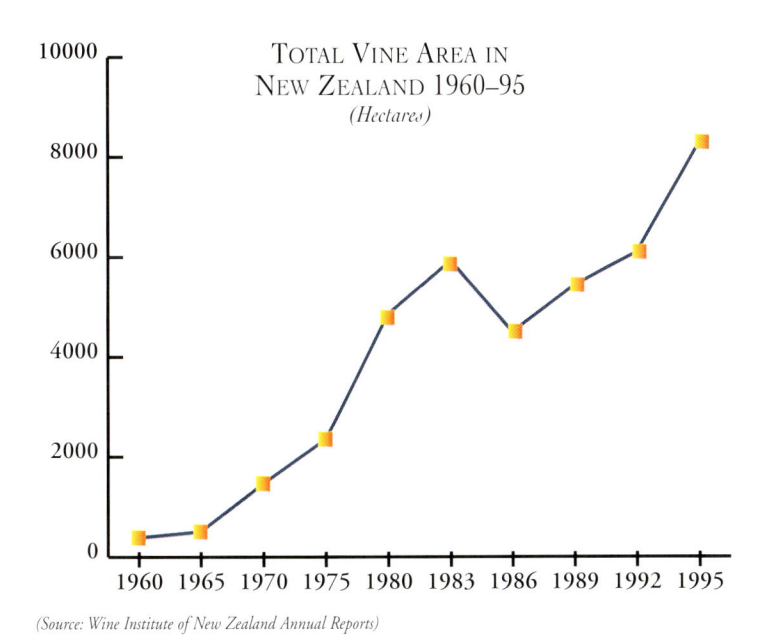

(Source: Wine Institute of New Zealand Annual Reports)

NEW ZEALAND WINE EXPORT DESTINATIONS 1995
(% of Volume)

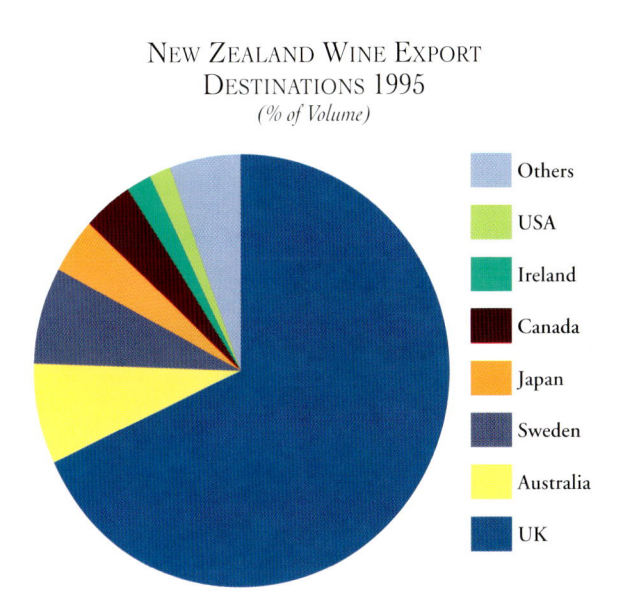

(Source: Wine Institute of New Zealand Annual Reports)

MAKING WINE IN NEW ZEALAND

Where is wine made – in the vineyard or the winery? Take a bow if you answered 'in both places'. A common saying in the wine industry is that 'you can't make good wine from bad grapes'. Although in New Zealand the media spotlight is invariably focused on winemakers rather than grape-growers, it is in the vineyards that the raw materials of wine are cultivated, and there that each wine's basic potential is set.

Climate and soil (see pages 16–17) are the two crucial factors the viticulturist evaluates before planting a new vineyard. When choosing a site on which to cultivate grapes for a wine of superior quality, viticulturists today look for a combination of adequate, but not excessive, heat; a relatively dry autumn; and well-drained soils.

THE ANNUAL CYCLE IN THE VINEYARD

Vineyard toil itself is peaceful, with fixed seasonal routines. Winter's icy-cold, damp months are devoted to pruning, the most time-consuming and costly of all vineyard jobs. In spring the buds swell and eventually burst, unfolding tender shoots, leaves and flower clusters. Tractor-towed spraying machines are soon swinging into action against fungal diseases and insects, and another battle is joined against weeds. Late in spring the flower clusters shed their caps; by early December the flowers 'set' as small, green, pea-like berries.

In mid-summer, when the vineyards reach their peak period of growth, the sides and tops of the vines are mechanically trimmed to control the shapes of their canopies. The removal of excess vegetative growth enables light to more easily penetrate the canopy, which improves fruit ripeness and reduces disease problems. Plucking (removing) the leaves around the bunches, by hand or machine, produces similar benefits. Many small vineyards have recently adopted the 'Scott Henry' vine-training system (installed on the standard New Zealand vertical trellis by adding a pair of movable foliage wires), which reduces fruit-shading problems by dividing the canopy into two separate curtains, trained both upwards and downwards.

As ripening proceeds, the fruit gradually evolves its mature skin colours – yellow-green for 'white' varieties, blue-black for 'red' varieties – and its juice composition alters markedly: acids decline and sugars soar.

The fungus, *Botrytis cinerea*, can be the winegrower's worst enemy or best friend. Late in the season warm, wet weather encourages grapes to swell with moisture and split open. *Botrytis*, which appears as a grey, fluffy mould on the bunches, causes the grapes to rot on the vines. Fine dry autumn weather can allow *Botrytis*-infected grapes to develop an intense concentration of flavour and sweetness. In New Zealand's frequently wet autumns, however, *Botrytis* can severely damage the grapes; growers rely heavily on the use of fungicides in sprays to combat it.

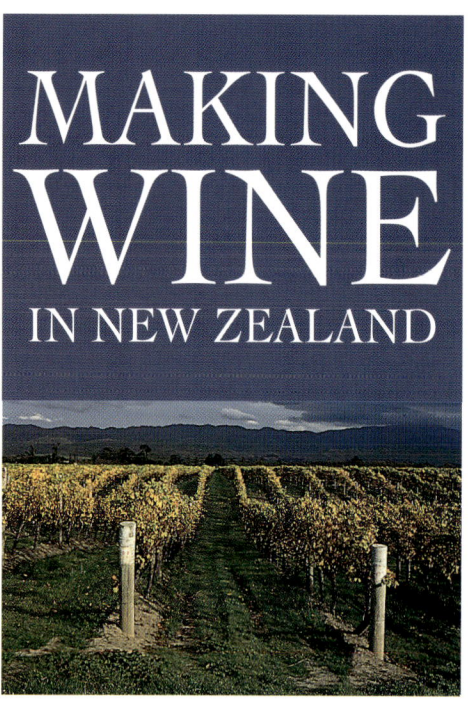

'Vintage' starts late in February or early March with the gathering-in of the early-ripening varieties: Müller-Thurgau, Gewürztraminer and Chasselas. Mechanical harvesters, which pick grapes at the speed of 80 vineyard labourers, straddle the trellises and lumber up and down the rows, slapping the berries – but not their stalks – off with fibreglass rods. The traditional hand-pickers now survive only in the most isolated, hilly or quality-orientated vineyards.

By mid May the harvest is over; the vineyards fall silent. In a flaming shower the vines shed their leaves. The annual cycle in the vineyards is now at an end. The viticulturist's job is done; the pressure is now on the winemaker to ensure that the fruit's potential is carried through into the finished wine.

WINEMAKING

New Zealand's principal wineries are heavily staffed with graduates of the famous wine school at Roseworthy Agricultural College in South Australia. Michael Brajkovich, winemaker at Kumeu River winery – and himself a Roseworthy College old boy – has argued that this strong trans-Tasman technical link has in some ways retarded the advancement of New Zealand's wine quality. 'Despite its obvious climatic differences, New Zealand has derived most of its winemaking technology and skills from warmer areas [Australia and California] simply because we all speak the same language.' One instance: the use in white winemaking of an acid-softening malolactic fermentation (traditional in Burgundy's cool climate, but less desirable in the warmer regions of the New World) was rare in New Zealand – until the launch of Kumeu River Chardonnay 1985, which underwent a total malolactic fermentation. In Brajkovich's view, 'it would have made much more sense to study and adapt the practices of a climatically similar region, such as the cooler areas of France'.

A busy programme of winemaker interchanges between New Zealand, Australia, California and France has recently exposed the industry to a far greater diversity of oenological influences. When commercial volumes of premium grape varieties like Chardonnay and Sauvignon Blanc first came on stream, few winemakers had any specialist knowledge of how to handle them. 'During the late 1970s and early 1980s, when more Chardonnay grapes became available, the winemaking procedures followed the pattern of white winemaking of that time,' recalls Kerry Hitchcock, until recently Corbans' chief winemaker. 'This involved quick separation of the juice from its skins and stainless steel fermentation at low temperatures, followed by aging in oak barrels for a short period. Then as the market became more demanding, winemakers looked at Chardonnay-making in the traditional French way, and we saw different styles being produced in New Zealand. These involved longer skin contact time to extract flavour; fermenting in oak barrels with higher solids in the juice; leaving the wine on its lees for flavour development; and a partial or complete malolactic fermentation in the traditional French way.' The relatively simple Chardonnays of the early 1980s have swiftly been transformed into the rich, multi-faceted Chardonnays of today.

The rules governing winemaking practices in New Zealand are set out in the Food Regulations 1984. Scores of permitted additives are listed: fining and stabilising agents such as bentonite and tannin; preservatives such as sulphur dioxide and sorbic acid; sweeteners such as glucose syrup. Limits are also prescribed for the amount of alcohol, sulphur dioxide and water New Zealand wines can contain.

WHITES

The transport of freshly picked grapes from vineyard to winery can itself help to make or mar the quality of the eventual wine. White wines are much more difficult to make than reds, due to the extreme vulnerability of their delicate juices to oxidation and browning. To protect the fruit, sulphur dioxide is usually added at the harvester. However, wines made from machine-harvested fruit trucked long distances reflect the inevitable 'skin contact'. The greater extraction of polyphenols – flavour compounds including anthocyanins (colouring matter) and tannins – from the skins into the grapejuice produces deeper-coloured, more strongly flavoured wines.

Upon their arrival at the winery, therefore, white-wine grapes are swiftly crushed and destemmed. Sulphur dioxide may be added to the crushed fruit ('must') to prevent oxidation and inhibit natural ('wild') yeasts and bacteria.

To separate the juice from the skins, the must is usually pumped into a 'drainer' tank with a slotted screen at its base (although modern tank presses, which allow the winemaker to more precisely control the period of skin contact, are also becoming popular). The majority of the juice is in this way able to be recovered by the winemaker without pressing; 'free-run' juice of superior quality is the result. Only the residue of pulp, pips and skins, which is still juice-saturated, is conveyed to the press to extract the coarser juices, called 'pressings'.

Although it is usual to make a swift separation of white-wine juice from the skins, this is not a hard-and-fast rule, as the period of contact depends on the style of wine being made. Where the goal is a light, delicate white, the juice is removed immediately. If a more substantial style is sought, the juice may be allowed up to 24 hours' skin contact in an effort to step up the colour and flavour of the finished wine. A precisely opposite approach to 'whole-bunch pressing' (below), the skin-contact method boosts the juice's phenols level, and is therefore well suited to delicately flavoured wines with low natural levels of phenols.

'Whole-bunch pressing' is a gentle, increasingly in-vogue technique whereby the winemaker bypasses the crusher and places bunches of hand-harvested grapes directly into the press. Whole-bunch pressing yields juices with greater flavour delicacy (due to the lack of skin contact), lighter colours and much lower levels of solids and phenols. Flavoursome grapes with high phenol levels are especially well suited to whole-bunch pressing; conversely, delicately flavoured juices with low levels of phenols tend to benefit from a greater degree of skin contact.

Prior to its fermentation, the juice is clarified to rid it of suspended particles of skin, pulp and yeast cells; its sugar and acid levels are adjusted if necessary; and finally it is normally inoculated with a selected 'pure' yeast culture (although interest is growing in fermenting with natural yeasts). A faint stirring of bubbles on the juice's surface is the first sign that the fermentation is underway. Fermentation – the conversion of sugar by yeasts into ethyl alcohol, carbon dioxide and energy – is also the happiest of miracles: the transformation of grapejuice into scented, delectable, life-enhancing wine.

The vast majority of New Zealand white wines are fermented in enclosed, stainless steel tanks at low temperatures (12–15°C). Compared to traditional, warmer fermentation methods, this long, cool fermentation technique retains much more of the juice's fragile aromas and flavours in the finished wine.

After the fermentation has subsided, the new wine is again clarified, stabilised, sweetened if necessary (usually by the addition of unfermented grapejuice, or by 'stop-fermentation', whereby the fermentation is arrested by chilling before all the grape sugars have been converted into alcohol) and then typically bottled early. Lusciously sweet white wines are produced by stop-fermenting late harvested, ultra-ripe, *Botrytis*-infected fruit, or by the 'freeze concentration' method, whereby a proportion of the natural water content in the grapejuice is frozen out, leaving a sweet, concentrated juice to be fermented.

The last of the whites to be bottled are those matured in casks: wood-aged Sauvignon Blancs, Chenin Blancs and Sémillons and the vast majority of Chardonnays. The finest wines are not just aged, but also fermented in the barrel. By fermenting a full-bodied dry white wine in the cask (most often a 225L French oak barrique), and then maturing it on its lees for a few months, yeast-related flavour complexity and a superior integration of wood and wine flavours can both be achieved.

Another technique increasingly in favour is to put full-bodied dry white wines, or at least a part of the final blend, through a secondary, bacterial malolactic fermentation. The search here is for a softer-acid style with heightened complexity.

Nets guard ripening grapes from feathered vandals.

REDS

Red wines are typically more robust than whites, with more grape 'extract' (stuffing), alcohol, and sheer flavour richness. A key difference in red and white winemaking is that, unlike white wines, reds are always fermented in contact with their skins. This enables the skins' colouring pigments and tannins – key elements in any red wine's flavour, hue and longevity – to gradually dissolve into the fermenting wine.

During fermentation the evolution of carbon dioxide gas causes the skins to rise to the surface. This dense cap is periodically mixed with the juice by plunging the skins under by hand, or by drawing off the juice below the cap and spraying it back over the skins until they are broken up. Red-wine fermentations are usually warmer than whites: 20–32°C is ideal to secure a generous extraction of colour and tannin.

The yeasts will have consumed at least the majority of the natural sugars before the fermenting juice is removed from the skins. For light, early-maturing styles, to reduce tannin levels winemakers cut down on the period of skin contact. Where the goal is a more robust red, or if the wine is naturally low in tannin, after the fermentation has subsided the winemaker may continue to macerate the new wine with its skins for up to a month. The recent trend in New Zealand red winemaking has been towards longer periods of skin contact.

Another fermentation technique, called carbonic maceration, is ideal for producing fragrant, fruity, soft reds. Instead of being immediately crushed, whole berries are piled inside a fermenting vessel. The weight of the upper layers crushes the fruit below, which commences a normal fermentation, giving off carbon dioxide which blankets the intact fruit on top. Here, enzyme activity triggers an individual fermentation within each berry, extracting both colour and flavour from the inner skins. New Zealand Pinot Noirs often display the supple mouthfeel derived from using the carbonic maceration technique for a portion of the final blend.

A pivotal aspect of red winemaking is the malolactic fermentation. This secondary fermentation – based on the bacterial conversion of malic acid to lactic acid and carbon dioxide – occurs in red wines after the initial alcoholic fermentation. New Zealand's reds gain immensely from this process because the wine becomes more palatable: malic acid has a harsh, sour taste, whereas lactic acid is a soft, warm acid that enhances red wine.

Oak comes more into centre-stage during red than white winemaking. The accent in most white winemaking is on preserving the fruit's delicacy and freshness; oak would swamp the flavour of the majority of white wines. Mouth-filling reds, by contrast, are usually much enhanced by a spell in wood, emerging from the barrel not only richer and more complex in flavour, but more soft and supple. All of New Zealand's top reds spend a year or longer in the cask, most commonly 225L French oak barriques.

Nevers (especially) and Limousin are the two principal French oaks encountered in New Zealand wineries. Tighter-grained French oaks such as Allier, Tronçais and Vosges are also winning popularity as winemakers strive for a finer balance of fruit and oak flavours.

A cheaper alternative to the French timber is American oak, which contributes more of the colour and flavour of oak to wine than does French oak, but less extract and tannin. American oak-aged wines have a lifted perfume and pungent, sweeter, more vanilla-like oak flavour, which experienced tasters can easily pick.

An even cheaper method to secure some of the flavouring effects of wood is to simply suspend oak chips in the wine.

ROSÉS

Rosés, which range in hue from pink to onion-skin, are made using primarily white-wine production techniques. The accent with rosés, as with whites, is on achieving flavour delicacy and freshness.

The best rosés are produced by giving the juice of black grapes one or two days' skin contact before or during the fermentation; the juice is then promptly separated from the skins and fermented alone. The precise duration of the skin contact determines the rosé's colour.

SPARKLINGS

The flavour delicacy and crisp acid structure of New Zealand's white wines are superbly well suited to the production of top-class sparkling wines. Low-priced, 'carbonated' bubblies are made by simply injecting carbon dioxide into the base wine. The finest sparklings, however, are all produced by the classic technique first perfected in Champagne, known as 'méthode champenoise' or (increasingly) 'méthode traditionnelle'.

By hand-harvesting and whole-bunch pressing the fruit, the winemaker can achieve a base wine with a desirably low level of phenols. Following cold settling, racking and the addition of dried 'Champagne' yeast strains, the base wine undergoes its primary, alcoholic fermentation at 10–14°C in stainless steel tanks, after which it may or may not undergo a malolactic fermentation.

The 'méthode traditionnelle' involves a secondary, bubble-inducing fermentation that takes place in the individual bottle. After sugar and yeasts are added to the base wine, it is ensconced in heavy-duty bottles and stored at 10–12°C in a temperature-controlled cellar. Following the secondary fermentation – lasting six weeks to several

Grey-blue Pinot Gris grapes, about to be whole-bunch pressed, are loaded into a Willmes press at Dry River.

The skins of red-wine grapes, steeped in the juice during fermentation, are rich in colour, tannins and flavouring substances.

months – the yeast cells gradually break down, conferring on the wine a distinctive yeastiness. The bottles are then stacked away to mature for one to three years.

'Riddling' is the next stage, in which the yeast sediment is gradually shaken from the sides of the bottle down to the cork. Small batches are still hand-riddled, but for larger production runs automatic riddling machines have provided welcome relief from the traditional wrist-wrenching labour.

Next comes the 'disgorging': the neck of the bottle is frozen, allowing the cork and plug of sediment to be removed without losing much wine. Finally the bottle is topped up, sweetened, corked and wired.

The 'transfer' method (used by Montana for Lindauer) is a modern approach to bottle-fermentation evolved to speed up the final stages. Instead of riddling and then disgorging the wine, after its fermentation in the bottle it is transferred into pressurised tanks where it is cleaned up and sweetened in bulk, before being re-bottled.

FORTIFIEDS

'Sherry' and 'port' styles reigned supreme on the New Zealand wine scene until the mid 1970s. Since then their sales have plummeted.

The base wine for a sherry style should be fairly neutral in character; it is usually fermented from Palomino, a traditional Spanish sherry variety. The wine is fortified to the desired alcohol strength (18–19 per cent by volume) before being overlaid with the classical sherry characters of wood flavour and slight oxidation. 'Port' styles are made by interrupting a red wine's fermentation before all the sugar in the must has been consumed. The sweet part-wine is fortified to the desired level of alcohol (18–19 per cent by volume), removed from the skins, fined, filtered and then transferred into oak casks to mellow. Ruby ports are bottled young, within a couple of years, and display a distinct ruby colour combined with a fruity, relatively fresh flavour. Tawny ports show the effects of longer oak aging with a tawny-brown appearance and a more mature, complex palate. Vintage ports are full-bodied, dark, deep-flavoured wines designed for cellaring.

CLIMATE AND SOILS

A cool climate is New Zealand's key viticultural asset. Anyone poring over the globe, however, could be forgiven for failing to realise that New Zealand is a cool-climate wine country. Marlborough lies in comparable latitudes to the fortified-wine region of the Douro Valley in Portugal, Auckland in parallel latitudes to southern Sicily and Greece.

New Zealand's wine regions, however, are favoured with markedly lower temperatures during the vine's growth than their latitudinal equivalents in the Northern Hemisphere. New Zealand has a temperate, maritime climate with cooler summers and milder winters than those experienced in Europe. Isolated from adjoining continents, and thus removed from the influence of continental hot-air masses, New Zealand escapes the summer heatwaves which descend on wine regions at similar latitudes in the Northern Hemisphere.

'Cool-climate' is a buzz term in both industry and wine-tasting circles. What is all the fuss about?

According to Dr David Jackson and Danny Schuster, Canterbury-based co-authors of *The Production of Grapes and Wine in Cool Climates* (1994), 'It is not yet fully understood why cool climates generally produce the best quality table wines, but the evidence suggests that it is the lower temperatures in the autumn which are of special significance. In warm climates ripening of grapes occurs early, when the weather is still warm or even hot. These hot conditions cause rapid development of sugars, rapid loss of acids and high pHs . . . and the grape appears to have insufficient time to accumulate those many chemical compounds which add distinction to the wine. A cool autumn – often with considerable diurnal [night and day] temperature variation – slows down development; better balances can be achieved and more aroma and flavour constituents are accumulated.'

The influential Californian 'heat summation' index evaluates New Zealand as a classic cool-climate wine-growing country. Because grapes must receive an adequate amount of heat to reach full ripeness, temperature is the most crucial aspect of climate for viticulture. Heat summation measures the amount of heat received during the growing season, above the minimum required for active growth. 'Region One' climates accumulate up to about 1370 'degree days', which is the sum of the growing season's mean daily temperatures above 10°C, the temperature at which the sap rises in the vine.

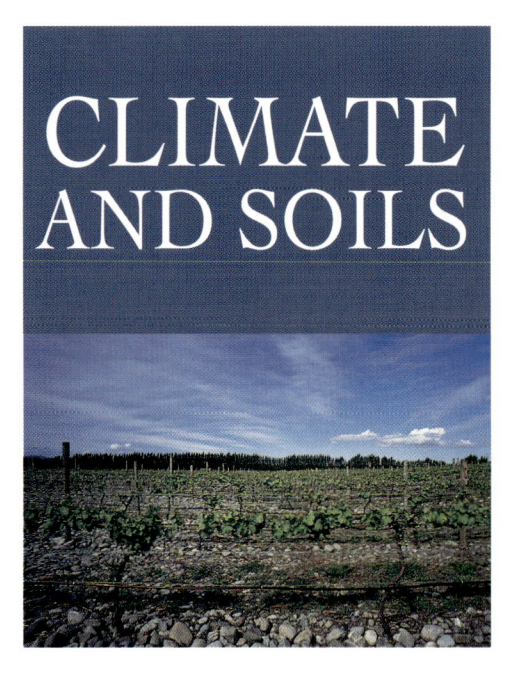

'Region One' climates are blessed with moderately cool temperatures under which ripening proceeds slowly, bringing to the fruit optimal development of its aroma and flavour components. Bordeaux, Burgundy, the Rhine and the Mosel all possess Region One climates as does every New Zealand wine region from Central Otago to Northland.

Heat summation is an imperfect method of analysis, and it has been shown to work better in California than elsewhere, but as a means of quickly comparing different regions, temperatures are a useful tool.

If moderately cool weather during the vine's growing season is New Zealand's greatest viticultural advantage, unpredictable and frequently heavy rainfall is its greatest liability. The rains descend most frequently and heavily on the west coast, leaving the drier east coast as a rain shadow area. Although most tropical cyclones peter out well to the north of the country, three or four arrive each year between December and March, bringing gale-force winds and torrential rain. In adverse vintages, heavy rains can descend on all the major regions during summer and the crucial autumn weeks leading into the harvest.

Regions on the east coasts of both islands, however – particularly Hawke's Bay, Wairarapa, Marlborough and Canterbury – enjoy much drier climates than West Auckland and the Waikato. This relative dryness (Marlborough averages only 140mm of rain during the crucial February–April ripening period, compared to Henderson's 360mm) sharply lowers the risk of disease. Growers are thus able to hang their grapes longer on the vines in pursuit of optimal ripeness and flavour development, instead of being forced to pick prematurely to avoid such wet-weather diseases as *Botrytis* and downy mildew.

Soils are crucial. The grapevine doesn't like getting its feet wet. Vines planted in damp clay soils tend to grow luxuriantly, producing a tangle of canes and leaves which retard fruit quality by casting the ripening bunches into shade. Free-draining gravels, by contrast, lead to the growth of a lighter foliage canopy, allowing the ripening grapes more exposure to sunlight.

Most New Zealand vineyards have in the past been planted in soils of high – or, as English wine writer Jancis Robinson put it, 'almost embarrassing' – fertility. However, the rich alluvial silts of the Gisborne flats and much of the Heretaunga Plains in Hawke's Bay are often poorly drained and wet. The search in recent years for sites which can both reduce vine vigour and advance fruit ripening has led growers to establish vineyards in the freer-draining, shingly soils of Marlborough, Canterbury, Wairarapa and parts of Hawke's Bay. Drip irrigation systems have been widely installed in these regions to alleviate vine stress and maintain yields during dry years. This recent trend to locate new vineyards in well-drained soils of low-to-moderate fertility is yielding major advances in wine quality.

The New Zealand wine industry is extremely regionalised: almost 85 per cent of the country's vines are concentrated in only three regions – Marlborough, Hawke's Bay and Gisborne. In view of the 1000km separating the Northland and Otago regions, it is predictable, yet still a source of endless fascination, that New Zealand wines are now displaying pronounced regional differences.

White-wine grapes have enjoyed success in both islands, whereas the majority of red-wine varieties have performed better in the warmer North Island. The most internationally acclaimed wines resulting from successful marriages of regions and grape varieties are the full-frontal Sauvignon Blancs of Marlborough and Hawke's Bay's mouth-filling, rich-flavoured Chardonnays.

NORTHLAND/AUCKLAND

Climate
(West Auckland) challenging: plentiful rain, high humidity (lead to fungal diseases); mild winters, warmth favours red-wine production.
(Waiheke Is.) hot, dry summer
Soils   heavy clays (drain poorly)
Degree Days   (West Auckland) 1300–1350°C
Feb–April Rainfall (West Auckland) 280–360mm
1995 Plantings 248ha (3% NZ total)
Major Varieties
Cabernet Sauvignon, Chardonnay, Merlot, Palomino, Pinot Noir

WAIKATO/BAY OF PLENTY

Climate
temperatures and sunshine hours high, but so are rainfall and humidity
Soils
heavy loams over clay (produce lower yields)
Degree Days   1250–1300°C
Feb–April Rainfall 260mm
1995 Plantings 137ha (1.7% NZ total)
Major Varieties
Chardonnay, Sauvignon Blanc, Cabernet Sauvignon

GISBORNE

Climate
bountiful sunshine, frequent autumn rainfall
Soils
fertile, alluvial loam, good water-holding capacity
Degree Days   1250–1300°C
Feb–April Rainfall 240mm
1995 Plantings 1514ha (18.3% NZ total)
Major Varieties
Müller-Thurgau, Chardonnay, Muscat Dr Hogg, Reichensteiner, Sauvignon Blanc

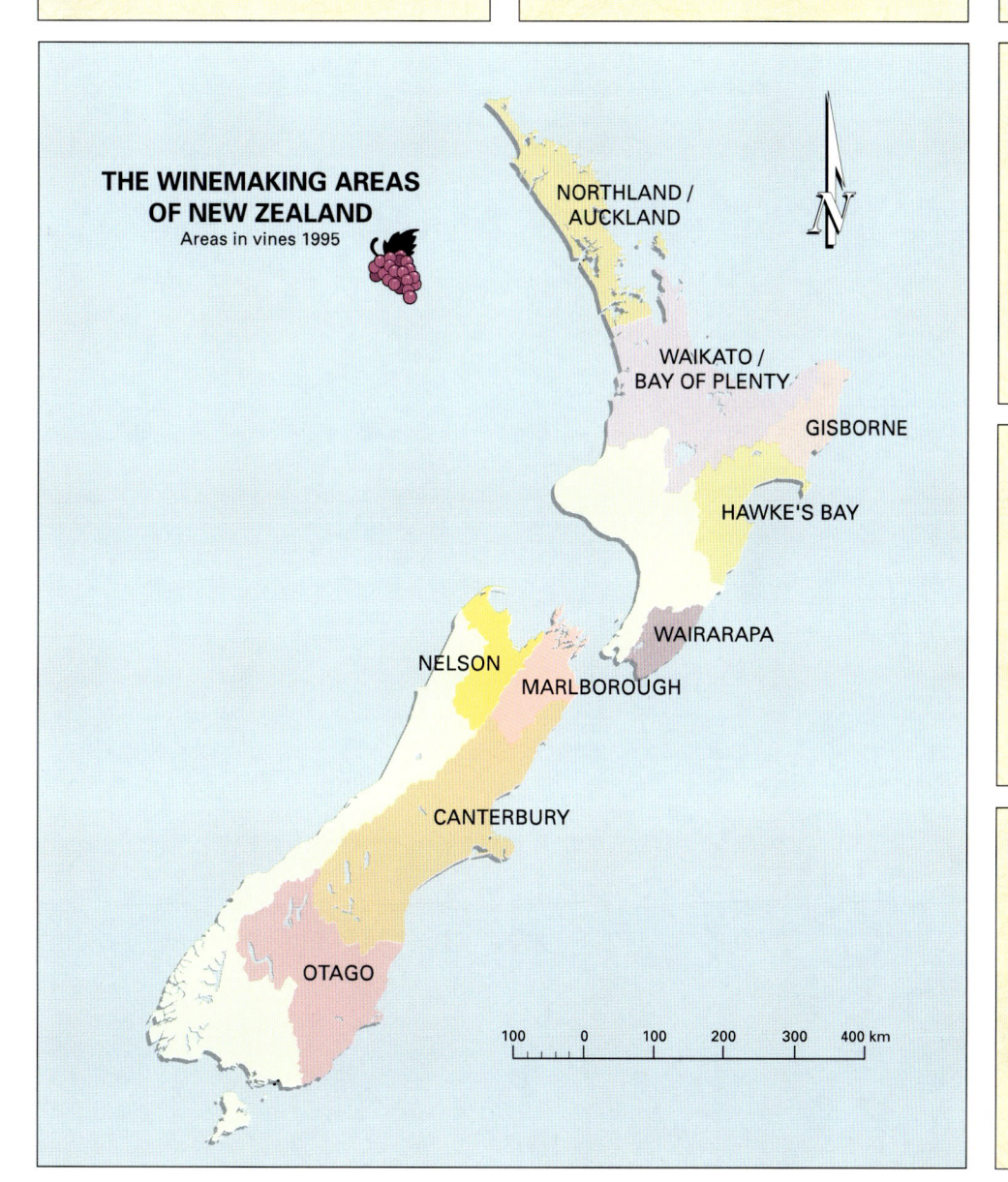

HAWKE'S BAY

Climate
very high sunshine hours, warm summer temperatures; dryish autumn
Soils
range from fertile, silty loams with high water table to freer-draining shingle
Degree Days   1200–1250°C
Feb–April Rainfall 180mm
1995 Plantings 2276ha (27.4% NZ total)
Major Varieties
Chardonnay, Cabernet Sauvignon, Müller-Thurgau, Sauvignon Blanc, Merlot

WAIRARAPA

Climate
warm summer; cool, dry autumn; wind can cause shoot damage
Soils
free-draining, shallow loam, gravelly subsoils
Degree Days   1150°C
Feb–April Rainfall 160mm
1995 Plantings 271ha (3.3% NZ total)
Major Varieties
Pinot Noir, Chardonnay, Cabernet Sauvignon, Sauvignon Blanc, Merlot

NELSON

Climate
warm summers, high sunshine hours but autumn rains
Soils
range from alluvial loams (Waimea Plains) to heavier clays (Upper Moutere)
Degree Days   1050–1100°C
Feb–April Rainfall 200mm
1995 Plantings 137ha (1.7% NZ total)
Major Varieties
Sauvignon Blanc, Riesling, Chardonnay, Pinot Noir, Cabernet Sauvignon

THE WINEMAKING AREAS OF NEW ZEALAND
Areas in vines 1995

OTAGO

Climate
hazardously low heat summation; vineyards planted in sunny meso-climates; danger of spring and autumn frosts; extremely dry autumn allows an extended ripening period
Soils
silt loams with mica and schists
Degree Days   850–1000°C
Feb–April Rainfall 100mm
1995 Plantings 152ha (1.8% NZ total)
Major Varieties
Pinot Noir, Chardonnay, Sauvignon Blanc, Riesling

CANTERBURY

Climate
dry autumn, warm days and cool nights (fruit ripens slowly, with high levels of extract and acidity); some years too cool for full ripening
Soils
free-draining, silty loams overlying river gravels; chalky loams in the north
Degree Days   900–1100°C
Feb–April Rainfall 140mm
1995 Plantings 325ha (3.9% NZ total)
Major Varieties
Chardonnay, Pinot Noir, Riesling, Sauvignon Blanc

MARLBOROUGH

Climate
warm with very high sunshine hours but cool nights; dryish autumn (a long, slow, flavour-intensifying ripening period)
Soils
variable, even within individual vineyards; less fertile, more shingly sites most sought after
Degree Days   1150–1250°C
Feb–April Rainfall 140mm
1995 Plantings 3233ha (39% NZ total)
Major Varieties
Sauvignon Blanc, Chardonnay, Müller-Thurgau, Riesling, Cabernet Sauvignon, Pinot Noir, Sémillon

Sources: Jackson, D. and Schuster, D. *The Production of Grapes and Wine in Cool Climates*, 1994, p.42; Desborough, P.G. and Horner, D.W. *New Zealand Vineyard Survey*, 1995.

THE PRINCIPAL GRAPE VARIETIES

Several basic factors influence the emergence of all wine styles – climate, the soil, grape varieties, vineyard management and the winemaker. The careful selection of soils and climates – regional and local ('meso-climate') – must be matched by the planting of suitable grape varieties. In New Zealand, the choice of grape varieties involves a very considered judgement about grape quality, hardiness and yield.

The 1995 vineyard survey, conducted by the Horticulture and Food Research Institute, like its forerunners reveals drastic changes in the varietal composition of our vineyards as well as a dramatic 36 per cent expansion in the national vineyard since 1992, from 6099 to 8293 hectares. Chardonnay has increased its dominance since 1992, and Sauvignon Blanc has surged well past the contracting Müller-Thurgau to become the second most widely planted variety. Merlot, by doubling its plantings in three years, has emerged as the latest glamour horse.

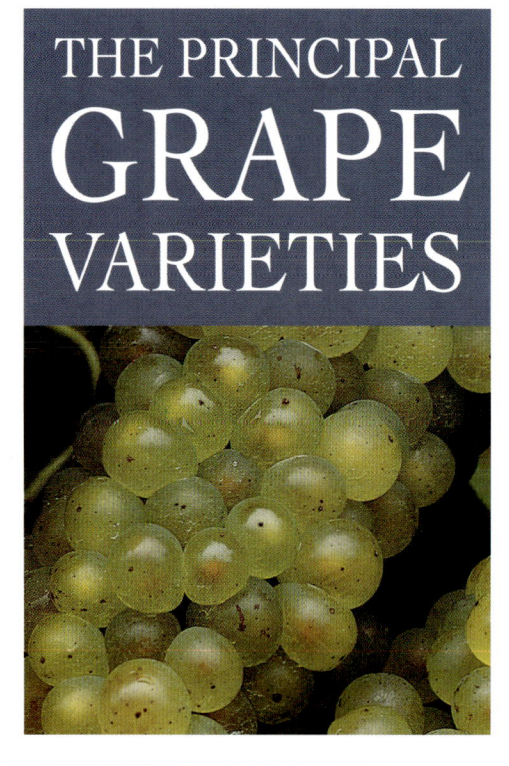

NATIONAL TOTAL AREA OF PLANTED VINES	1995 Hectares	1995 % of Total Plantings	1986 Hectares	1986 % of Total Plantings
Chardonnay	1917	23.1	394	10.0
Sauvignon Blanc	1472	17.7	254	6.5
Müller-Thurgau	992	12.0	1232	31.4
Cabernet Sauvignon	753	9.1	308	7.9
Pinot Noir	569	6.9	110	2.8
Merlot	435	5.2	55	1.4
Riesling	427	5.1	234	6.0
Sémillon	231	2.8	87	2.2
Muscat Dr Hogg	228	2.7	234	6.0
Chenin Blanc	186	2.2	245	6.2
Gewürztraminer	138	1.7	156	4.0
Cabernet Franc	113	1.4	15	0.4

WHITE WINE VARIETIES

White-grape varieties predominate in New Zealand's vineyards. Chardonnay, Sauvignon Blanc and Müller-Thurgau – the big three – account for over half of the country's total vine plantings.

The six great 'classic' white-grape varieties (Riesling, Chardonnay, Sémillon, Sauvignon Blanc, Chenin Blanc and Gewürztraminer) are all well established in New Zealand. Since 1975 the proportion of the national vineyard devoted to white-grape varieties has risen from 65.9 to 75.6 per cent. New Zealand, despite its burgeoning plantings of red-wine grapes, is still largely white-wine country.

Other varieties covering at least 25 hectares are Reichensteiner (98ha), whose wine tastes like that of one of its parents, Müller-Thurgau; Chasselas (90ha), which yields heavy crops of low-acid grapes, useful for blending; Pinotage (73ha); Palomino (72ha); Pinot Gris (38ha); Syrah (38ha); Breidecker (27ha), a crossing of Müller-Thurgau with the white hybrid Seibel 7053, which yields mild, unmemorable wine; and Sylvaner (25ha), until the 1960s Germany's most widely planted variety.

Rarer grapes which are occasionally produced as varietal wines or named on labels are Pinot Blanc, a white mutation of Pinot Noir which can yield rewardingly weighty and savoury wines; Morio-Muskat, a perfumed, slightly earthy cross of Sylvaner and Pinot Blanc; Ehrenfelser, a cross of Riesling and Sylvaner with very Riesling-like qualities; Scheurebe, another Riesling and Sylvaner cross, highly rated in Germany; and Osteiner, yet another crossing of Riesling and Sylvaner, thus far not impressive in New Zealand.

Other new vine imports are being evaluated for their potential in New Zealand. Arnsburger, a heavy-cropping German cross of two Riesling clones, with good resistance to *Botrytis* rot, has been identified as an ideal Müller-Thurgau substitute for bulk wines. For finer wines, such classic Italian varieties as Sangiovese (the great grape of Chianti) and Nebbiolo (the foundation of Barolo) are being assessed, together with Tempranillo (the basis of Spain's red Riojas), Gamay (of Beaujolais fame) and Rhône varieties such as Grenache and Viognier. These evaluations of new vine imports promise to add an exciting diversity to the New Zealand wines of the future.

CHARDONNAY

Robust and rich-flavoured, the Chardonnays of Burgundy and the New World – especially New Zealand, Australia and California – rank among the greatest dry white wines. In New Zealand, plantings of this currently most fashionable grape have outstripped those of every other variety.

Chardonnay's success here is hardly surprising: it is a versatile variety that thrives in many parts of the world. In its homeland, France, it is planted in the famous Côte d'Or of Burgundy. California and Australia, infatuated with Chardonnay, now boast wines capable of challenging the Burgundians at the highest level.

The Mendoza (or McCrae) clone of

Chardonnay, imported from Australia in 1971, is now the most widely planted in New Zealand. Relatively low-yielding because of its poor grape 'set', which produces the 'hen and chicken' (large and small berries) effect, Mendoza is nevertheless favoured by most Chardonnay producers because its smaller berries give a higher skin to juice ratio and richer flavour.

Mendoza's ascendancy (at least in area terms) is being challenged by Clone 6 (UCD6), imported from Australia and released in 1982. It has a more even berry size than Mendoza, crops more heavily, and is increasingly the basis of New Zealand's mid-priced Chardonnays. Clone 6's less powerful fruit character, compared to Mendoza, makes it more suitable for sparkling wines.

Other important clones in New Zealand are the big-bunch, heavy-cropping UCD4 and UCD5, which form the basis of the Californian industry; UCD15, which crops more heavily than Mendoza but less than Clone 6, and has yielded some high quality wines in New Zealand; MVIG1, the country's first Chardonnay clone, which crops consistently well in Marlborough with lower than average acid levels; and Bernard 95 and Bernard 96, the first Chardonnay clones imported directly from Burgundy.

Chardonnay vines are spread throughout all the major wine regions, particularly in Marlborough (over 40 per cent of vines), Hawke's Bay (where it is now the number one grape) and Gisborne. The variety is as popular in the vineyard as it is in the market, adapting well to a wide range of climates and soil types. An early bud burst renders it vulnerable to damage from spring frosts in colder regions, but the grapes ripen mid-season in small bunches of yellow-green berries harbouring high sugar levels (hence the sturdy alcohol typical of its wine).

New Zealand's Chardonnays are full-bodied, with fruit flavours ranging from crisp, flinty apples and lemons, through to the lush stone-fruit (peach and apricot) flavours of very ripe grapes. Styles produced range from fresh, unwooded wines like Nobilo Poverty Bay Chardonnay through to mouth-filling, multi-faceted wines like Neudorf Moutere Chardonnay.

The hallmark of New Zealand Chardonnays is their delicious varietal intensity. The leading wines display such concentrated aromas and flavours, supported by crisp, authoritative acidity, that they have rapidly emerged on the world stage.

Leading Labels
Ata Rangi Craighall and Dalnagairn, Babich Irongate, Brookfields Reserve, Church Road Reserve, Clearview Reserve, Cloudy Bay, Collards Rothesay, Coopers Creek Swamp Reserve, Corbans Cottage Block Gisborne, Private Bin Gisborne and Private Bin Marlborough, Cross Roads Reserve Hawke's Bay, Delegat's Proprietors Reserve, Dry River, Esk Valley Reserve, Foxes Island, Goldwater Delamore, Hunter's, Kumeu River Kumeu and Mate's Vineyard, Martinborough Vineyard, Mills Reef Elspeth, Millton Clos de St Anne, Mission Jewelstone, Montana Ormond Estate, Morton Black Label, Neudorf, Ngatarawa Glazebrook, Nobilo Reserve Marlborough, Palliser, Revington, Selaks Founders, Stonecroft, Te Mata Elston, Vavasour Reserve, Vidal Reserve, Villa Maria Reserve Barrique Fermented and Reserve Marlborough.
1995 plantings: 1917 hectares

CHENIN BLANC

At their best, New Zealand's Chenin Blancs are full in body, with a fresh, buoyant, pineappley flavour and mouth-watering acidity. At their worst, they are over-acidic, and lack charm and drinkability.

Chenin Blanc is only a workhorse variety in Australia and California – where it wins favour for its abundant yields of fresh, medium-dry wines which usefully retain an invigorating acidity – but in the Loire it achieves greatness. The finest dry Vouvrays are substantial, fruity wines with tongue-curling acidity and an ability to unfold in the bottle for decades.

In New Zealand the wine industry is less enthusiastic than it used to be about this vigorous variety, which is largely concentrated in Hawke's Bay and Gisborne. Although Chenin Blanc ripens early in warm climates, in New Zealand the grapes tend to ripen late.

Yields are high for a premium variety, at 12 to 15 tonnes per hectare. Also, Chenin Blanc's tight bunches are highly susceptible to wet weather and to *Botrytis*. Many growers have discarded their vines; plantings plummeted from 372 hectares in 1983 to 176 hectares in 1992, but rose slightly again between 1992 and 1995.

Chenin Blanc reveals its full personality only in cooler growing conditions, and should therefore feel very much at home in New Zealand. It demands careful vineyard site selection and long hours of sunshine, however, to build up its potentially high sugar levels. In New Zealand, as in France, its acid levels can often be searingly high.

Riper fruit is essential if New Zealand is to master Chenin Blanc. The vine's vigour must be controlled, crop levels reduced and the grapes exposed to maximum sunshine. By cultivating Chenin Blanc in stony, devigorating vineyards, using canopy division and leaf plucking, viticulturists are starting to achieve lower acid levels and richer, riper flavours.

Chenin Blanc's most common role in New Zealand is as a blending variety, adding body and 'spine' to its blends with Müller-Thurgau in casks; it also has a pervasive presence in many bottled dry whites. To its well-priced blends with the more slowly evolving Chardonnay, Chenin Blanc contributes a splash of vigorous fruitiness.

Only Collards and The Millton Vineyard – and to a lesser extent Esk Valley and Seibel – have consistently mastered Chenin Blanc as a strong, distinctive varietal with seductive, steely, tropical-fruit flavours. However, interest is building in this great variety's potential; New Zealand's finest Chenin Blancs are yet to come.

Leading Labels
Collards, The Millton Vineyard
1995 plantings: 186 hectares

GEWÜRZTRAMINER

Gewürztraminer, which is at its ravishingly perfumed and pungently seasoned best in Alsace, has also been a success story in New Zealand's cool climate. Our top wines burst with its heady scents and flavour-packed spiciness.

Pronounced Ge-vertz-truh-meen-uh, the name of the wine is sometimes shortened to Traminer. 'Gewürz' means spicy. In Germany it was customary to call the wine Gewürztraminer if it was spicy, Traminer if it was not. In Alsace the current practice is to label all the wines Gewürztraminer.

The variety is now established in all regions, with the heaviest plantings in Hawke's Bay (over 30 per cent of vines), Marlborough and Gisborne (the source of many champion wines). Gewürztraminer has never risen to the popularity of Chardonnay or Sauvignon Blanc, however, and between 1983 and 1995 plantings contracted by over 50 per cent.

Gewürztraminer is a grower's nightmare. The vine is notoriously temperamental, ripening its grapes easily in New Zealand with plenty of sugar and fragrance, but highly susceptible to adverse weather during flowering (which can dramatically reduce the crop) and also vulnerable to powdery mildew and *Botrytis*. To plant a vineyard exclusively in Gewürztraminer is a risk, one that few local viticulturists would contemplate. Clonal variation is marked. The country's older clones, such as UCD1 and UCD4 (imported from the USA by Bill Irwin of Matawhero in 1976), with small berries and light crops, make the best wine. Other clones (GM11, GM12 and GM14) imported from Germany in the early 1980s, crop more regularly with less concentrated flavour. Alsatian clones recently released from quarantine show promise, combining good flavour and yields.

Gewürztraminer is a wine to broach occasionally, when you're in the mood to delight in its overwhelming aroma and lingering, full-flavoured spiciness.

Leading Labels
Dry River, Eskdale, Lawson's Dry Hills, Longridge of Hawke's Bay, Martinborough Vineyard, Matawhero, Montana Patutahi Estate, Revington, Stonecroft, Vidal Reserve, Villa Maria Reserve
1995 plantings: 138 hectares

MÜLLER-THURGAU

Although New Zealanders drink oceans of Müller-Thurgau every year, this once-ubiquitous variety is rarely exported as a varietal wine and is more often packaged in casks than in bottles. Yet a cool glass of refreshingly fruity and flowery Müller-Thurgau makes delicious summer sipping.

Müller-Thurgau (pronounced Mooler-Ter-gow) is the world's most famous vine crossing, yet its parentage is uncertain. It is probably a crossing of Riesling and the more humble German variety, Sylvaner, but may be a crossing of two different Riesling clones.

The commercial value of Müller-Thurgau became apparent when the demand for white table wines escalated in the 1960s. Then the vine spread rapidly, prized for its early ripening ability and high yields. A rush of plantings in the early 1970s rapidly established it as New Zealand's leading grape variety. Over a third of all Müller-Thurgau vines were uprooted in the 1986 vinepull scheme, however, and since then plantings have shrunk by a further 19 per cent. Its strongholds are Gisborne (40 per cent of vines), Hawke's Bay and Marlborough.

Müller-Thurgau grows vigorously in New Zealand (although susceptible to wet weather and fungal diseases) and on most soils yields good crops of about 20 tonnes per hectare. The berries, yellow-green and flecked with small brown spots, ripen early, and Müller-Thurgau is generally one of the first varieties to be picked. Clonal variation is not marked, although clone GM1-1, imported from Germany in the early 1980s, is attracting interest for its ability to produce quality wine while retaining high yields.

Müller-Thurgau's future in New Zealand is question-marked. Montana and Corbans have in recent years imported cheap bulk wine from Europe, South America and Australia to help fill their wine casks. New German varieties such as Arnsburger and GM 312-53 (a vine bred from Riesling, Sylvaner and the hybrid Seibel 7053) are also viewed as promising Müller-Thurgau substitutes.

Most Müller-Thurgau wines are backblended with a small amount of unfermented grapejuice to produce a slightly sweet style. It is light-bodied, with a garden-fresh bouquet and a mild, distinctly fruity flavour. It reveals flashes of the classic Riesling variety's citric-fruit aroma and flavour, although to a less memorable degree, and lacks Riesling's acid backbone. Müller-Thurgau's natural role is as a beverage wine: an easy-drinking, enjoyable, low-priced white wine to consume anywhere, anytime.

Leading Labels
Babich, Matua, Nobilo, Pleasant Valley, Seifried, Selaks, Vidal, Villa Maria Private Bin
1995 plantings: 992 hectares

Muscat Dr Hogg

Muscat varieties form a large, instantly recognisable family of white and red grapes notable for their almost overpowering musky scent and sweet grapey flavour.

Muscat Dr Hogg, an old English table grape, is the most common Muscat variety in New Zealand, and the country's sixth most widely planted white-wine variety. Over 70 per cent of plantings are in Gisborne, with the rest virtually confined to Hawke's Bay and Marlborough.

The vines crop well in New Zealand, producing large fleshy berries with a typical Muscat aroma and flavour, although our cooler temperatures may inhibit greatness; in Gisborne, Muscat is normally the last white-wine variety to be harvested. Another, earlier-ripening Muscat variety grown in Gisborne, Early White Muscat, although very susceptible to rot, may have the potential to produce wines with more concentrated varietal character.

Often, following the German practice, Muscat is blended with Müller-Thurgau to enhance the wine's bouquet. It also gives a lift – again, often as a minor partner of Müller-Thurgau – to charmingly light and perfumed Asti-type sparklings.

Leading Label
Matua Late Harvest Muscat
1995 plantings: 228 hectares

Palomino

Palomino is the leading New Zealand 'sherry' variety. The grape is traditionally used to produce the famous sherries of the Jerez region of Spain and at first glance would appear ill-suited to New Zealand's cooler climate.

The variety was largely unknown in New Zealand until its ability to produce very large crops was demonstrated at Te Kauwhata in the early 1950s. Thereafter the vine spread rapidly through all the wine districts. Palomino emerged by 1970 as the main grape variety in the country. Today, after an 82 per cent drop in plantings between 1983 and 1995 – reflecting the plummeting demand for 'sherry' – it ranks as New Zealand's 16th most important grape variety, with the surviving vines concentrated in Hawke's Bay, Auckland and Gisborne.

The Palomino vine grows with much vigour, yielding 20 to 30 tonnes per hectare of large, thick-skinned, fleshy yellow-green grapes that make good eating. The grapes ripen mid to late season with a relatively low acidity and without the high sugars achieved in warmer climates.

Leading Labels
Cellarmans Extra Special Sherry, Henderson's Mill Flor Fino and Rare Old Sherry, Pleasant Valley Amontillado, Amoroso and Oloroso Sherry, Soljan's Pergola and Reserve Sherry.
1995 plantings: 72 hectares

Pinot Gris

An outstanding Chardonnay substitute, weighty and deep-flavoured, Pinot Gris is still rare in New Zealand vineyards. The variety belongs to the Pinot family of vines and is cultivated in Italy, Germany and various regions of France. In Alsace (where it is known as Tokay d'Alsace) Pinot Gris produces good wine: dry, full-flavoured and flinty.

Although Bragato praised the variety in 1906 ('in the far north [it] bears heavily and produces an excellent white wine'), Pinot Gris later lost favour with most growers because of its tendency to crop erratically. Now the tide has turned: plantings doubled between 1992 and 1995, with over half the vines concentrated in Canterbury and Otago.

The vines grow with moderate vigour, bearing an average crop of 7 to 12 tonnes per hectare of small, thin-skinned, reddish-pink berries. The grapes mature early with fairly low acidity and high sugar levels.

Savoury, with an earthy stone-fruit flavour, Pinot Gris offers an underrated alternative to the higher profile dry whites. With its ability to produce wines of impressive weight and flavour richness (without the assistance of oak – a major plus-point), Pinot Gris looks set to flourish in the cooler regions of New Zealand.

Leading Labels
Brookfields, Dry River, Gibbston Valley, Mission.
1995 plantings: 38 hectares

RIESLING

A few years ago, New Zealand wine lovers were so entranced by Sauvignon Blanc and Chardonnay that winemakers could hardly give their Rieslings away. Now about 100 labels are on the market, ranging in style from bone-dry to honey-sweet, and the grape's ravishing perfume and piercing, racy flavour have captured thousands of admirers. Riesling, suddenly, is fashionable.

Riesling is the greatest grape variety of Germany. In the Rheingau and the Mosel its wine is strongly scented, the flavour a harmony of honey-like fruit and steely acid. Riesling also performs well in Alsace, Central Europe, California and Australia.

The proper name of the variety is Riesling. In New Zealand it has often been called Rhine Riesling to avoid confusion with Riesling-Sylvaner (Müller-Thurgau). The current trend is towards increasing use of the classic name Riesling.

In 1975 there were just eight hectares of Riesling vines in Hawke's Bay and half a hectare in Auckland. Since then planting has gathered momentum: the area of vines nearly doubled between 1983 and 1989, stagnated for the next three years, then lifted again by over 50 per cent between 1992 and 1995. Now New Zealand's fourth most widely planted white-wine grape, almost 60 per cent of vines are in Marlborough (and over 80 per cent in the South Island), with significant plantings in Hawke's Bay and the Wairarapa.

Riesling is a shy bearer, yielding only about eight tonnes per hectare. The grapes ripen late but hang on well in the cool conditions experienced at the end of the season. The tight bunches are vulnerable to *Botrytis* rot, but the lower humidity in the South Island reduces the disease risk.

This variety needs a long, slow period of ripening to fully develop its most intricate flavours. Thus the finest Rieslings tend to be grown in cooler regions enjoying long, dry autumns – Canterbury and Central Otago are outstanding prospects. Given a good summer and settled autumn, a fragile, luscious wine emerges of unparalleled elegance and perfume.

Noble rot, a beneficial form of *Botrytis cinerea*, can transform Riesling's quality. Depending on the extent of *Botrytis* infection, the bouquet of the grape variety itself is replaced by an aroma reminiscent of honey and dried apricots. The wine tastes richer, more luscious, smoother and honeyed.

The overall standard of New Zealand Riesling has soared in the past five years, with achieving full ripeness the key to rich, expressive wines.

Leading Labels
Allan Scott, Collards Rhine Riesling and Marlborough Riesling, Coopers Creek Riesling and Late Harvest, Corbans Cottage Block Noble and Private Bin Amberley, Dry River, Grove Mill, Neudorf, Ngatarawa Glazebrook Late Harvest, Palliser, Pelorus, Rongopai Reserve Botrytised, Stoneleigh, Te Whare Ra Botrytis Bunch/Berry Selection, The Millton Vineyard Opou Vineyard, Villa Maria Reserve Noble
1995 plantings: 427 hectares

Noble rot dehydrates Riesling grapes, concentrating their sugars and flavours – perfect for making sweet wine.

SAUVIGNON BLANC

Nowhere else in the world does Sauvignon Blanc yield such breathtakingly aromatic and strong-flavoured wine as it does in Marlborough. The variety enjoys an exceptionally high profile in New Zealand – higher than in all other wine countries – and in 1995 it accounted for over 17 per cent of our vine plantings.

In Bordeaux, where Sauvignon Blanc (or Sauvignon, as the French call it) is widely planted, traditionally it has been blended with the more neutral Sémillon, to produce dry white Graves and sweet Sauternes. But in the regions of Sancerre and Pouilly in the upper Loire Valley, the Sauvignons are unblended and here the wines are assertive, cutting and flinty, in a style readily recognisable as cool-climate Sauvignon Blanc.

The vigorously growing vine yields a moderate crop (12 to 13 tonnes per hectare) of small, yellow-green berries. Grapes ripen mid to late season, harbouring adequate sugars and a high level of acidity. Viticulturists have to combat two problems, however: the vines are tough-stemmed, making the bunches difficult to harvest mechanically, and in wet weather the thin-skinned grapes are prone to split, causing rot.

Sauvignon Blanc has been grown in New Zealand for about 25 years. The clone known as UCD1, imported in the early 1970s from California, is thought to be the source of almost all the current plantings (although five new clones, including three from Bordeaux, were released in 1992). Matua Valley produced the first trial wine in 1974 and Montana issued its first Marlborough Sauvignon Blanc in 1979. By the mid 1980s, Montana's penetratingly herbaceous wine and (in smaller volumes) the riper, more subtle Cloudy Bay and Hunter's had alerted the world to the startling quality of New Zealand Sauvignon Blanc. Plantings leapt 480 per cent between 1986 and 1995, including a 72 per cent surge between 1992 and 1995. Marlborough (where Sauvignon Blanc is the number one variety) has 65 per cent of the vines; the variety also has a strong presence in Hawke's Bay and is widely dispersed throughout the rest of the country. In the North Island's warmer climate, Sauvignon Blanc yields riper, softer, less assertive wines than the forthright style typical of Marlborough.

THE PRINCIPAL GRAPE VARIETIES

Why are New Zealand's, and especially Marlborough's, Sauvignon Blancs so brimful of varietal character? The magical ingredient is an organic compound that is far easier to drink than it is to pronounce – methoxypyrazine. The green, grassy scent of methoxypyrazine is detectable in miniscule amounts by humans, and New Zealand's Sauvignon Blancs harbour about three times as much as Australia's.

Two distinct methods of handling Sauvignon Blanc are practised in New Zealand wineries. By far the most common involves bottling the wine directly out of stainless steel tanks. These wines, placing their emphasis squarely on the grape's tangy, piquant varietal character, are most often labelled as Sauvignon Blanc.

By contrast, those labelled as Fumé Blanc (or, increasingly, Oak Aged Sauvignon Blanc or Reserve Sauvignon Blanc) usually tone down Sauvignon's natural ebullience by maturing, and sometimes fermenting, the wine in oak casks. The result is a broader, potentially more complex wine, more costly to produce.

The pungent, 'nettley' bouquet of cool-climate Sauvignon Blanc, traditionally described as gunflint (the smell of sparks after a flint strikes metal) leaps from the glass with a forcefulness some criticise as unsubtle. Others adore its distinctiveness. The flavour ranges from a sharp, green capsicum character – stemming from a touch of unripeness in the fruit – through to a riper, fruity gooseberry style and, finally, to the tropical-fruit (melons and passionfruit) overtones and lower acidity of very ripe fruit.

The grower can manipulate these Sauvignon Blanc flavours in the vineyard. In Marlborough, where shaded fruit tends to yield wine with nettley aromas and flavours, markedly riper flavours can be achieved by canopy division and leaf plucking.

Leading Labels
Babich Mara Estate and Marlborough, Clearview Reserve Fumé Blanc, Cloudy Bay, Collards Rothesay, Delegat's Proprietors Reserve Oak Aged, Grove Mill, Hunter's Sauvignon Blanc and Oak Aged, Jackson, Kumeu River Sauvignon/Sémillon, Matua Reserve, Mills Reef Elspeth, Nautilus Marlborough, Nga Waka, Nobilo Marlborough, Palliser, Rongopai Winemaker's Selection, Saint Clair, Seifried, Selaks Sauvignon Blanc/Sémillon, Te Mata Cape Crest, Vavasour Reserve, Villa Maria Reserve, Wairau River
1995 plantings: 1472 hectares

SÉMILLON

New Zealand-grown Sémillon can be pungently herbaceous. Overseas, the grape gives rise to a diversity of styles ranging from the fine dry whites of Graves and Australia to the sweet, late-harvested wines of Sauternes and Barsac. Sémillon imparts softness to its blend with Sauvignon Blanc in Graves, and in Sauternes, infection of Sémillon grapes with *Botrytis cinerea* brings a distinctive, 'noble rot' character to the best wines. Although in Europe the variety is invariably blended with other grapes, Sémillon reaches its apogee as an unblended varietal in the smoky, soft, honey-and-toast flavoured 'white burgundies' of the Hunter Valley in New South Wales.

The commercial plantings of Sémillon in New Zealand initially yielded confusing results. The vines, which display vigorous growth, yield moderately high crops of 10 to 17 tonnes per hectare. Their tough-skinned, greenish-yellow berries appeared to have good weather resistance – surprising, because the compact grape cluster typical of Sémillon usually renders it highly vulnerable to bunch rot. The clone widely planted in New Zealand (UCD2) grows much looser bunches. Doubts (now proven unfounded) were expressed as to whether UCD2 is true Sémillon.

Sémillon's typical herbaceousness in New Zealand, and its apparent resistance to rot, are now known to be the result of widespread virus infection, which retards ripening. Attractive, ripe flavours are now starting to be achieved by virus-free vines and vineyard practices which expose the fruit to higher sunshine levels. Hopes are also high for a new Sémillon clone, BVRC-14, imported from the Barossa Valley in Australia. Now starting to be widely planted in New Zealand, its first wines are promisingly free of greenness.

Now New Zealand's fifth most important white-wine variety, Sémillon plantings have grown steadily over the past decade, and expanded by 37 per cent between 1992 and 1995. Sémillon's stronghold is Marlborough (half of all plantings), but 29 per cent of the vines are in Gisborne. No plantings are recorded in Canterbury or Otago.

Sémillon is often (but usually anonymously) blended in New Zealand with Sauvignon Blanc. That it is also a useful, flavour-packed blending variety in lower priced wines has been well demonstrated by such wines as Babich Fumé Vert (Sémillon, Sauvignon Blanc and Chardonnay) and Coopers Classic Dry (Sémillon and Chardonnay).

Leading Labels
Collards Barrique Fermented, Neudorf
1995 plantings: 231 hectares

> **RED WINE VARIETIES**
>
> *The range of red-wine grapes grown in New Zealand is narrower than that of white-wine varieties: of the country's 20 most widely planted grapes, only six are red. However, Cabernet Sauvignon and Pinot Noir are New Zealand's fourth and fifth most important varieties, and Merlot recently soared into sixth place.*
>
> *The 1995 vineyard survey also revealed expanded plantings of such up-and-coming red-wine grapes as Cabernet Franc, Syrah and Malbec. Between 1992 and 1995, the proportion of the national vineyard devoted to red-wine varieties rose from 22.5 to 24.4 per cent.*

CABERNET FRANC

Cabernet Franc, a happier vine in cooler regions than Cabernet Sauvignon (because it buds, and thus ripens, earlier) is one of New Zealand's most important red wine varieties. It is much valued in Bordeaux, particularly in St Émilion where, under the name of Bouchet, it is the grape primarily responsible for the esteemed Cháteau Cheval Blanc. Cabernet Franc is also widely planted in the middle Loire and in north-eastern Italy.

Cabernet Franc is expected to yield its finest wines in New Zealand in the warmest sites. Cooler vineyards most experience the problem of coulure (failure of the vine flowers to develop), and when not fully ripe, the variety can taste very green. Planted in warmer vineyards, Cabernet Franc crops more consistently with riper flavours.

Established here early this century but virtually unknown for several decades, Cabernet Franc has recently surged in popularity and is now our fourth most widely planted red-wine variety. The New Zealand industry has derived almost all its Cabernet Franc from trial vines imported in the late 1960s from California. Plantings have expanded from 15 hectares in 1986 to 113 hectares in 1995, particularly in Hawke's Bay (which has over half the vines) and Marlborough.

Cabernet Franc's wine is more genial than that of Cabernet Sauvignon, lower in tannin, acids and extract, with an instantly appealing aroma variously described as raspberries, violets and pencil shavings. By coupling a degree of the strength of claret with the suppleness of Beaujolais, Brajkovich Cabernet Franc first demonstrated this variety's ability to make a delicious varietal red in New Zealand. And as part of the encépagement (varietal make-up) of many of New Zealand's top red-wine labels, Cabernet Franc is aiding winemakers in their pursuit of Medoc-like complexity.

Leading Labels
Brajkovich, Clearview
1995 plantings: 113 hectares

CABERNET SAUVIGNON

Cabernet Sauvignon is to the red-wine world what Chardonnay is to the white: both are of impeccable pedigree and every wine lover's favourite.

Cabernet Sauvignon – often abbreviated to Cabernet – has a long history in New Zealand, arriving with Busby or with the French settlers at Akaroa, and was well known last century. Nevertheless, interest in the variety slumped during the wasted years of cheap 'plonk' manufacture. The current commercial revival dates from the early 1970s, when Cabernet Sauvignon came to be regarded as the ideal grape to upgrade the overall standard of red wines.

The arrival of Montana Cabernet Sauvignon 1973 ushered in a new era: for the first time a decent quality New Zealand red was widely available. By 1983, following a surge of plantings in the late 1970s, Cabernet Sauvignon – the aristocratic grape of the Médoc in Bordeaux – was the second most common variety in the country. The stage was set for the explosion of Cabernet Sauvignon labels over the past decade.

Between 1992 and 1995 Cabernet Sauvignon's plantings rose by 44 per cent, and although the grape is now New Zealand's fourth most widely planted vine, it is still firmly established as our most popular red-wine variety.

In cool climates Cabernet Sauvignon ripens late in the season. Despite some susceptibility to fungal diseases, with proper spray protection the grapes hang well on the vine. Often labelled a shy bearer, Cabernet Sauvignon produces between 8 and 12 tonnes per hectare of small, blue-black, tough-skinned berries tasting of blackcurrants or blackberries. In New Zealand the grapes are usually picked last, in April and even May, with high levels of tannin.

Cabernet Sauvignon performs best in the warmer summer temperatures of the North Island. Almost half of all plantings are in Hawke's Bay, where in favourable vintages the grape yields fragrant, sturdy wine of a richness and complexity only consistently rivalled by the Cabernet-based reds of Waiheke Island. West Auckland (where Cabernet Sauvignon is the most important variety), Matakana and Northland can also produce full-bodied, satisfyingly ripe and flavoursome wines.

Most of the Cabernet Sauvignons grown in Gisborne's fertile soils have veered towards blandness. In Marlborough (the second most heavily planted region) they are often rather too cool-climate in style, lacking the strength and opulence of optimally ripened fruit. Wherever they are grown, Cabernet Sauvignon vines yield the best wine when grown in dry soils, which avoid late-season vegetative growth.

Most of the early New Zealand Cabernets were thin and marred by green, unripe, excessively herbaceous flavours. Today this problem lingers, although reduced. Other common faults are lightness of colour, high natural acidity and coarse, green tannins. Unripe grapes too often yield light, simple wines, lacking aroma and flavour intensity.

Producing fine quality Cabernet Sauvignon in New Zealand is a challenge: many regions are simply too cool for the late-ripening Cabernet variety; poor site selection compounds the problem. Fertile soils, except in dry years, cause luxuriant foliage growth, which shades the grapes and causes all the deficiencies outlined above.

Other inhibiting factors include widespread leafroll, a serious viral disease which lowers yields and retards ripening.

Yet with a tiny volume of splendid Cabernets from Hawke's Bay and Waiheke Island, New Zealand has recently proved its ability to produce world-class reds. The planting and maturation of healthier, less virused vines; planting on less fertile, stonier soils; lower crop levels per vine; improved canopy management; greater appreciation of the way new oak casks enhance quality; blending with the classic Bordeaux varieties, Merlot and Cabernet Franc – these factors have all played a crucial role in transforming the quality of New Zealand's premier Cabernet-based reds.

Leading Labels
Babich Irongate Cabernet/Merlot, Benfield and Delamare, Brookfields Cabernet/Merlot, Church Road Cabernet Sauvignon/Merlot, Coopers Creek Reserve Huapai Cabernet/Merlot, Goldwater Cabernet/Merlot/Franc, Heron's Flight Cabernet Sauvignon/Merlot, Matua Ararimu Cabernet Sauvignon/Merlot, Montana Fairhall Estate, Morton Black Label Cabernet/Merlot, Ngatarawa Glazebrook Cabernet/Merlot, St Nesbit, Stonecroft Ruhanui, Stonyridge Larose, Te Mata Awatea Cabernet/Merlot and Coleraine Cabernet/Merlot, Vidal Reserve Cabernet Sauvignon and Reserve Cabernet Sauvignon/Merlot, Villa Maria Reserve Cabernet Sauvignon and Reserve Cabernet Sauvignon/Merlot
1995 plantings: 753 hectares

MALBEC

Malbec is the fourth traditional red-wine grape of Bordeaux – after Cabernet Sauvignon, Merlot and Cabernet Franc – to stir up interest in New Zealand.

Although of declining importance in Bordeaux (due partly to its great vulnerability to coulure), Malbec (or Cot, as it is also known) is still fairly common in Bourg, Blaye and the Entre-Deux-Mers region.

Jancis Robinson, in *Vines Grapes and Wines*, describes Malbec's wine in Bordeaux as 'a sort of watered-down rustic version of Merlot, mouthfilling and vaguely reminiscent of blackberries in youth but soft and fairly low in acid, and, therefore, early maturing.' The total plantings of Malbec in Bordeaux fell from 4900 hectares in 1968 to 1500 hectares in 1988.

Last century, Malbec was the foundation of the famous, flavour-crammed, tannic 'black wine' of Cahors, in south-west France (where it is still widely planted). In Argentina, where plantings outstrip those in Bordeaux by 7:1, it produces dark, muscular wines capable of lengthy aging. Malbec is also Chile's third most widely planted red wine variety, but in California and Australia plantings have recently declined.

In New Zealand, Malbec has tended to 'set' poorly, but on warmer vineyard sites it crops more generously, and a newly released French clone shows much improved yields. Malbec plantings, although still rare, have climbed steadily from three hectares in 1989 to 17 hectares in 1995; 70 per cent of all vines are in Hawke's Bay.

When planted in favourable sites in New Zealand, Malbec achieves sugar-ripeness very early, while retaining good acidity. Its large berries harbour strong tannins and rich, plummy, spicy, pruney flavour. With its brilliant colour and ripe, sweet fruit flavours, Malbec adds an extra dimension to several top claret-style reds, including Esk Valley The Terraces, Stonyridge Larose, Providence, Matawhero Bridge Estate and Ngatarawa Glazebrook Cabernet/Merlot.
1995 plantings: 17 hectares

MERLOT

A vital ingredient in classic Bordeaux, Merlot has enormous potential in New Zealand. Over the lengthy ripening season in our cool climate, Merlot is able to slowly build and concentrate its flavours. And with its early ripening nature – two to three weeks ahead of Cabernet Sauvignon – it can achieve higher sugar levels, lower acidity and riper fruit flavours before late autumn's coolness descends.

Following a 300 per cent surge in plantings between 1986 and 1992, and a further doubling between 1992 and 1995, Merlot is New Zealand's sixth most common grape, and third most widely planted red-wine variety. Hawke's Bay has 54 per cent of the vines, and it is a proven and increasingly popular variety in the North Island. Merlot's early-ripening ability is also arousing intense interest in Marlborough (with 26 per cent of vines), where Cabernet Sauvignon frequently fails to reach optimum ripeness.

Merlot flourishes in clay – precisely where Cabernet Sauvignon vines, which prefer the relative warmth of gravel, struggle to ripen their fruit. Merlot's early – compared to Cabernet Sauvignon – budding and flowering can be a problem in cooler regions prone to spring frosts. The vine grows vigorously, producing 8 to 10 tonnes per hectare of blue-black, loose-bunched berries, harbouring less tannin than Cabernet Sauvignon. Merlot's major drawback is its susceptibility to coulure (poor fruit set), which often reduces crop size.

Clonal selection can reduce, although not eliminate, the threat of coulure. Most of the early Merlot plantings in New Zealand were of the clone UCD3, imported from California and released in 1970. More popular now is clone UCD6, also from California (released 1978) which 'sets' significantly better than the older Merlot clone.

In the past Merlot has principally been used as a blending variety, adding its lush fruit flavours and velvety mouthfeel to the more angular, often leaner, predominant Cabernet Sauvignon; these wines are typically labelled as Cabernet/Merlot. Now that Merlot's status as a premium red-wine variety in its own right has been recognised by winemakers, a cluster of instantly appealing reds, simply labelled Merlot, has also recently reached the shelves.

Corbans, Babich and Collards produced unblended Merlots in the late 1970s and early

1980s, but Kumeu River Merlot 1983 was the first stylish red produced from the variety in New Zealand.

For wine lovers, Merlot's early-drinking appeal is a boon. A high quality Cabernet Sauvignon needs three to five years before it becomes a pleasure to drink; Merlot can knock your socks off in two. As Cabernet Sauvignon's bridesmaid, or increasingly as the bride, Merlot adds a lush, sensuous appeal to our reds.

Leading Labels
Clearview Reserve, Corbans Cottage Block Marlborough, Delegat's Proprietors Reserve, Esk Valley Reserve, Kumeu River Merlot/Cabernet
1995 plantings: 435 hectares

Pinotage

New Zealand's fifth most important red-wine grape, Pinotage is a South African variety, obtained by crossing Pinot Noir with a vine known in South Africa as Hermitage, but which is really the more humble Cinsaut grape of French and Algerian origin.

As a commercially grown wine variety Pinotage is unique to South Africa and New Zealand, where it yields soft, rounded reds that are often underrated.

Pinotage was established in New Zealand during the late sixties and early seventies, during the rush to replace hybrids with vinifera material. The vine grew prolifically, ripening mid season with good yields of medium-sized, thick-skinned berries. The variety was especially popular in Auckland, because of its ability to withstand humid conditions. Pinotage's plantings rose by 60 per cent between 1986 and 1992, but have not expanded since. Marlborough is the most heavily planted region, with over a third of all vines, and there are significant pockets in Hawke's Bay, Gisborne and Auckland.

A well-made Pinotage is a soft, early-maturing, peppery wine, less tannic than Cabernet Sauvignon, with a pleasant berry-like flavour and smooth finish.

Leading Labels
Nobilo, Pleasant Valley Signature Selection
1995 plantings: 73 hectares

Pinot Noir

If all the Pinot Noir grapes grown in New Zealand were processed into red wine, we'd have as much Pinot Noir as Cabernet Sauvignon to drink. The 1995 vintage yielded 4480 tonnes of Pinot Noir – a bucket or two more than Cabernet Sauvignon with 4360 tonnes.

Pinot Noir ranks behind only Cabernet Sauvignon as our second most widely planted red variety, and is our fifth most commonly planted grape overall. In the past decade the beguilingly scented and supple Pinot Noirs of the Wairarapa and several South Island regions have added an exciting new dimension to New Zealand's premium reds.

Singlehandedly responsible for the majestic, velvety reds of Burgundy, Pinot Noir tastes of strawberries and raspberries in its youth, with fairly high alcohol and often a suggestion of sweetness. Mature Burgundy can be arrestingly complex, with an array of aromas and flavours suggestive of red berry fruits, violets, rotten vegetables, coffee and fruit cake. Pinot Noir is also of pivotal importance in Champagne, where it is prized for its body and longevity; great care is taken to keep the white juice free of tint from the skins. But the vine is notoriously temperamental in its choice of residence and has not readily adapted to regions beyond Europe.

Twenty years ago, most New Zealand Pinot Noirs were pale and thin – rosé look-alikes. Yet today, New Zealand is internationally recognised as one of the world's tiny band of successful Pinot Noir producers. Burgundy stands pre-eminent, but elsewhere, only in Oregon, cooler parts of California, around Melbourne in Victoria, and in New Zealand, has this minx of a vine yielded truly distinguished reds.

The vine is a challenge to viticulturists: as an early budder, it is vulnerable to spring frosts, and its compact bunches are very prone to rot. One advantage is it ripens ahead of Cabernet Sauvignon, typically producing 6 to 12 tonnes per hectare of small berries of varying skin thickness. Compared to other classic red-wine grapes, Pinot Noir has fewer anthocyanins (colouring pigments), tannins and flavouring substances, so is very vulnerable to over-cropping; about seven to eight tonnes per hectare is regarded as the maximum yield for fine quality wine.

Several clones are being cultivated, of

THE PRINCIPAL GRAPE VARIETIES

which the best known are the well-performed AM 10/5, which yields wine with good colour and a soft, fruity palate, and Bachtobel, whose wine lacks colour and weight and is not highly regarded (except as a base for high volume bottle-fermented sparkling wines). Clone UCD5 ('Pommard') yields deep-hued, firm-structured wine. The clone previously called 'Gamay Beaujolais' (here and in California) has now been positively identified as Pinot Noir. 'It is a common belief that a single clone will not provide the final answer', says viticultural expert Dr David Jordan. Other clones will gradually add greater complexity and character, especially original selections from Burgundian vineyards.

Pinot Noir thrives in coolish climates, where the grapes are able to hang on the vines for extended periods, picking up the most subtle scents and flavours. Plantings in New Zealand virtually doubled between 1986 and 1989, and again between 1989 and 1992, and by 1995 had leapt a further 40 per cent. In the Wairarapa and Otago, Pinot Noir is now the most important variety; in Canterbury it ranks second (behind Chardonnay). Almost 40 per cent of the vines are found in Marlborough, where the majority of the crop is reserved for bottle-fermented sparkling wine. Hawke's Bay also has extensive plantings – more than any other region except Marlborough.

Nobilo set the early pace with some superb Huapai-grown Pinot Noirs in the 1970s. Later Babich at Henderson and St Helena in Canterbury shared the top show honours. The finest Pinot Noirs of today are mouth-filling, rich-flavoured reds that flourish in the bottle, gaining in complexity and subtlety for five years or longer.

Leading Labels
Ata Rangi, Corbans Cottage Block, Dry River, Gibbston Valley, Mark Rattray, Martinborough Vineyard and Reserve, Neudorf, Palliser, Rippon and Selection, Te Kairanga and Reserve
1995 plantings: 569 hectares

SYRAH

Syrah is still rare in New Zealand and the grape has not previously succeeded here because it thrives in a warm growing environment and is much less rain-resistant than Cabernet Sauvignon. But now the winemakers' interest is mounting.

Syrah is the principal black grape of the upper Rhône Valley of France and is also heavily planted in Australia. In the Rhône it is called Syrah and in Australia, Shiraz or Hermitage. Lauded in France as the foundation of such great reds as Côte Rotie and Hermitage, Syrah nevertheless constitutes less than two per cent of France's red-wine vineyard. In Australia, by contrast, Syrah is the most widely planted red-wine variety.

Regardless of the name of the vine or the location of its vineyard, Syrah typically yields robust, richly flavoured reds with a heady perfume. Top versions are almost opaque, with a characteristic spicy, black pepper aroma and flavour.

Syrah has a long history in New Zealand. Last century good wines were made, but in many areas the grapes failed to ripen, lacking sugar and colour, and remaining overly acid.

After decades of eclipse, Syrah is now enjoying a resurgence of interest. New clones and virus-indexed vines show an improved ripening performance. Syrah grows very vigorously, crops well – better than Cabernet Sauvignon – and is resistant to most pests and diseases. Its drawbacks in New Zealand are that it ripens even later than Cabernet Sauvignon, and after persistent, heavy rain its berries swell, split and rot. Careful site selection, vigour control and severe restriction of yields will be essential to produce top Syrah.

Plantings of Syrah in New Zealand doubled between 1989 and 1992, and in the next three years almost tripled to 38 hectares. Hawke's Bay has 60 per cent of vines; there are smaller plots in Marlborough and the Wairarapa. Hopes are high that Syrah will flourish on the sheltered, shingly sites inland from Hastings.

Leading Labels
Stonecroft, Villa Maria
1995 plantings: 38 hectares

WINERIES, WINEMAKERS AND WINES

The Principal Wine Regions

The New Zealand wine trail rises hesitantly in the Far North, winds busily through West Auckland and Waiheke Island, proceeds in fits and starts through the Waikato and Bay of Plenty, then runs boldly through Gisborne, Hawke's Bay and the Wairarapa. Over Cook Strait, the wine trail snakes across the Waimea Plains and Upper Moutere hills of Nelson, criss-crosses the Wairau Valley of Marlborough and plunges south from Waipara to Burnham in Canterbury, before finally ascending to the vineyards burgeoning in the majestic inland hills and basins of Central Otago.

With almost 85 per cent of the country's vines concentrated in only three regions, New Zealand wine is overwhelmingly of Marlborough, Hawke's Bay or Gisborne origin. A whopping 93 per cent of the total national grape crop was harvested in the big three regions in 1995, reflecting the high natural fertility of many Gisborne and Hawke's Bay vineyards, and the heavy-yielding bulk-wine varieties often cultivated there. Many other regions, however, now boast a sizeable cluster of vineyards. This far-flung spread of viticulture has greatly enhanced the diversity – and hence fascination – of New Zealand wine.

Clear-cut regional differences can often be discerned in the wines. Why does a Canterbury Riesling taste different from a Gisborne Riesling? Climate is the key influence: our wine-growing regions in northern latitudes are a lot warmer than those in the south. Sunshine hours, rainfall and soil types also vary from region to region. These factors influence the grape varieties suitable for each region and also the styles of wine they yield. Grapes cultivated in the cooler southern regions tend to produce delicate, mouth-wateringly crisp wines, whereas fruit grown in the warmer northern regions typically produces more mouth-filling, softer styles.

At various stages of our history, grapevines have been planted, with or without success, over most parts of the country. Bragato in 1895 encountered vines growing in Central Otago, Akaroa, Nelson, the Wairarapa, Hawke's Bay, Bay of Plenty, Wanganui, the Waikato, Auckland and Northland. Such a widespread scattering of early grape-growing and winemaking reflected the isolated, far-flung nature of the first settlements. Although, ideally, considerations of climate and soil should have been uppermost in selecting areas to establish vines, in fact it was the influence of cultural traditions and the availability of cheap land which played leading roles in the early location of the industry in New Zealand.

The early exploitation of the Auckland region was due to the scale of the available market and the presence of Dalmatians and others eager to make wine, rather than to any climatic or physical advantages. Hawke's Bay, with ideal natural conditions for grape-growing, was sufficiently distant from Auckland to compete for markets in the south. Auckland and Hawke's Bay thus remained the two centres of New Zealand wine for more than a half century. Then in the 1960s, when it became obvious that extensive new plantings would be necessary to cater for the soaring demand for table wines, vineyards spread beyond the traditional grape-growing zones into Taupaki, Kumeu, Mangatangi and, above all, Gisborne.

Corbans, Cooks and Montana encouraged contract growers in Gisborne to establish substantial areas in vines. The answer lay in the fertility of Gisborne's soils, which yield bumper crops. The more recent move into Marlborough by Montana, Corbans and others was in pursuit of another objective. Yields there are relatively light, but the region is superbly suited to the production of quality cool-climate table wines.

The 1980s brought the emergence of the Wairarapa, Canterbury and Central Otago onto the national wine map. By shifting to cooler climate zones, New Zealand winemakers are paralleling a trend overseas. The search for riper and cleaner fruit has led many newcomers to the industry to avoid the higher rainfall areas of West Auckland, the Waikato and Gisborne in favour of the long dry belt extending down the east coast of both islands from Hawke's Bay through the Wairarapa and Marlborough to Canterbury.

Numerous regional strengths have emerged, as an analysis of the results of the Air New Zealand Wine Awards in 1993, 1994 and 1995 underlines. Of the 13 gold medals won by Auckland wines, nine went to Cabernet Sauvignon and Merlot-based reds. Of Gisborne's 16 golds, 13 were won by Chardonnays. Hawke's Bay's tally of 33 golds included 14 Cabernet Sauvignon and Merlot-predominant reds, eight Chardonnays – and not a single Sauvignon Blanc. Marlborough's haul of 35 golds included eight for Sauvignon Blanc, seven for Riesling, eight for sweet whites – and only three for reds.

Each of New Zealand's wine regions has its own distinctive blend of landscapes, climates, soils, individuals and wine styles. The formation of Hawke's Bay Vintners in 1979 heralded the growing emphasis on regional identification – all wineries in the province agreed to jointly foster Hawke's Bay's image as an area which produces fine quality wines. Since then, up and down the country, other winemakers have banded together to promote their regional identities.

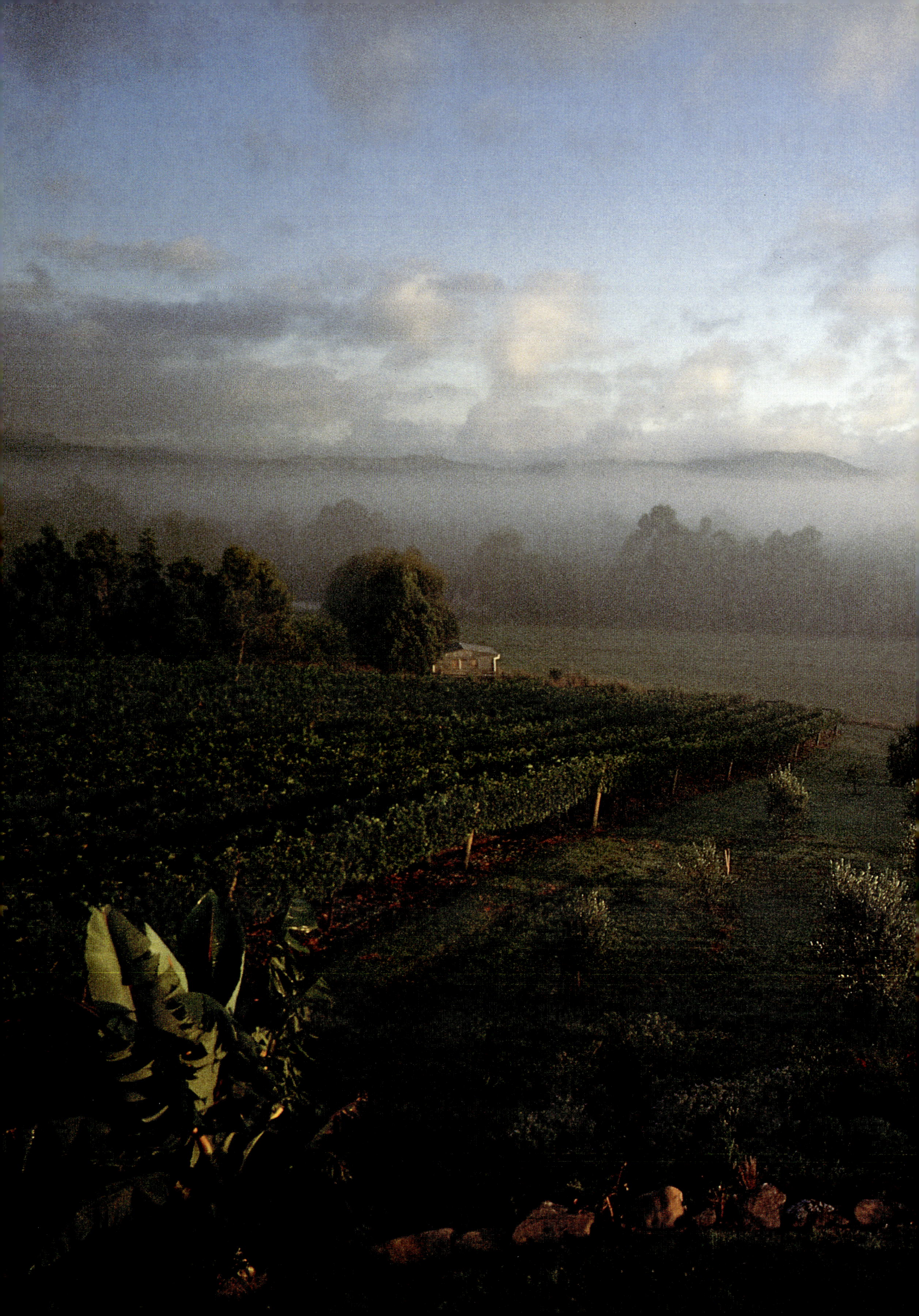

NORTHLAND/ AUCKLAND

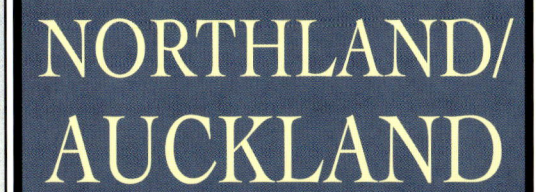

PRODUCERS

NORTHLAND
Longview Estate, Okahu Estate

MATAKANA
Heron's Flight, Providence, Te Arai Point, The Antipodean

KUMEU/HUAPAI/WAIMAUKU
Bazzard Estate, Coopers Creek, Kumeu River, Limeburners Bay, Matua Valley, Nobilo, Selaks, Waitakere Road Vineyard

HENDERSON
Babich, Collards, Corbans, Delegat's, Lincoln, Mazuran's, Misty Valley, Pacific, Pleasant Valley, Sapich, Seibel, Soljans, St Jerome, West Brook

WAIHEKE ISLAND
Goldwater Estate, John Mellars of Great Barrier Island, Peninsula Estate, Stonyridge Vineyard, Twin Bays, Waiheke Vineyards

CENTRAL AND SOUTH AUCKLAND
Montana, St Nesbit, Villa Maria

Northland

Northland's current role in the wine industry is only peripheral. The northernmost region of New Zealand stretches out over 260 kilometres of rolling hill country, but its almost subtropical climate – heavy rainfall, high humidity and relatively warm winters – is less well suited to viticulture than the cooler, drier regions to the south. Northland's main occupation is pastoral farming, yet the region currently boasts five licensed winemakers – at Dargaville, Kaikohe, Kaitaia, Kerikeri and Whangarei – with a cluster of new vineyards on the horizon.

Northland was the cradle of New Zealand wine: here Marsden planted the first vines and here, too, Busby made the first wine. After 1840 and the Treaty of Waitangi, however, the region was exploited mainly for its magnificent kauri forests and later for its gum. Descendants of Dalmatian gumdiggers and the sons and daughters of later Dalmatian arrivals until recently almost alone preserved the winemaking traditions of Busby.

Between 1976 and 1995, as demand for the traditional, fortified wines of Northland declined, the number of licensed winemakers in the region nose-dived from 19 to four. By the early 1990s, the total area under vines – 18 hectares in 1983 – had contracted to seven hectares.

Now a revival is underway. Continental Wines, established near Whangarei since 1964, recently propelled itself into a new era by changing its name to Longview Estate and releasing a stream of chunky, impressively rich-flavoured Cabernet-based reds.

The launch in early 1992 of Okahu Estate Ninety Mile Red 1989, grown near Kaitaia, heralded the arrival of a new, quality-orientated winery in the Far North. Other new vineyards have been planted at Russell and Tutukaka, and the first Cabernet Sauvignon and Chardonnay flowed from Rod McIvor's Marsden Estate, at Kerikeri, in 1995.

Matakana is part of the Auckland province, rather than Northland. However, the high standard of Matakana's full-bodied, ripe-flavoured Cabernet Sauvignon and Merlot-based reds and its recent flurry of vineyard plantings have played a key role in stimulating others to explore the wine potential of districts north of Auckland.

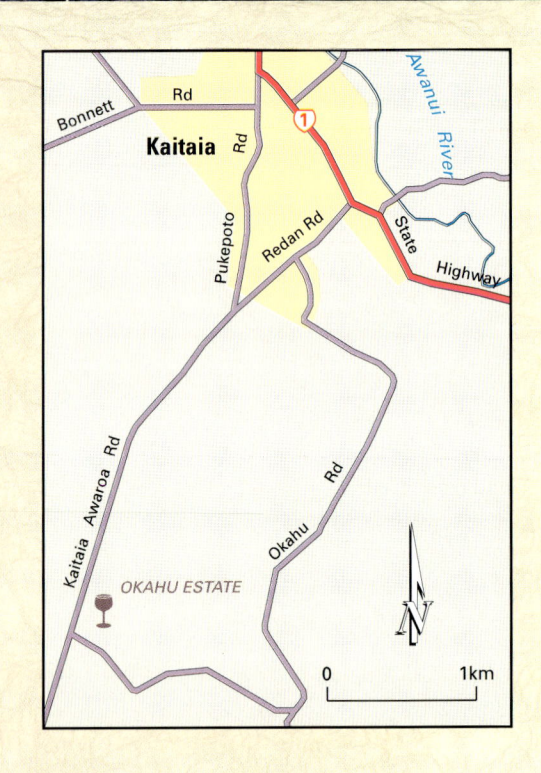

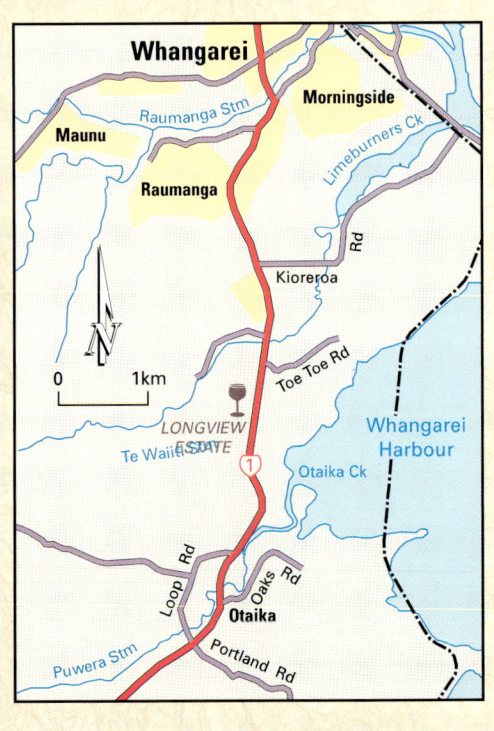

Longview is playing a vital role in the resurgence of winemaking in the north. For a long time Continental Wines (as it was known until recently) seemed content to produce sound vin ordinaire, but in recent years the fruits of a major vineyard replanting programme have come on stream and the standard of the Cabernet Sauvignon and Merlot-based reds has soared.

Now winemaker Mario Vuletich's ambition is to 'make a really good red, as good as Goldwater or Morton – it can be done here. If we really play hard at it, as good as any Australian . . .'

The pretty, terraced vineyard alongside the state highway at Otaika, just south of Whangarei, was established by Mate Vuletich who, as his widow, Milica, relates, was born under a grapevine on the family vineyard in Dalmatia. Vuletich planted his first Baco 22A and Niagara vines in 1964 to produce wine for his own medicinal purposes.

Today, Milica still works in the winery shop, alongside her son Mario's wife, Barbara. Mario Vuletich, the effusive, dark-haired, moustachioed managing director, admits he only 'really got serious about winemaking about 10 years ago – when I got married.'

The original hybrid and native American vines were uprooted and replaced with five hectares of Cabernet Sauvignon, Chardonnay, Merlot, Gewürztraminer and Müller-Thurgau.

The hill-grown clay vineyard, with its 'long view' over Whangarei Harbour to Mt Mania, is mainly laid out in east-west rows that follow the fall of the land. However, the latest plantings, on flatter terrain, run in the conventional north-south direction to maximise the vines' exposure to the sun.

'We get clean fruit here,' reports Vuletich. 'There's a steady breeze from the harbour, which promotes the circulation of air through the vines' canopies, drying them and reducing disease.' Longview's grapes are all estate-grown.

Output is low: about 2500 cases per year, all sold at the gate ('It's bedlam at Christmas') or by mail order. Production will rise as the latest plantings come on stream; Vuletich plans production to peak at about 5000 cases.

The latest releases are far superior to those of a decade ago, with ample body and rich, ripe flavour. The Gewürztraminer is richly perfumed, with exotic fruit flavours, and the Chardonnay shows good depth of crisp, citrusy, slightly buttery and nutty flavour.

Chewy, fragrant and deep-coloured, with an abundance of ripe fruit, the Scarecrow Cabernet Sauvignon and Mario's Merlot are extremely decent reds, with a string of recent awards to prove it.

If you need convincing that Northland can produce generous, satisfying reds, try these.

Longview Estate

State Highway One, Otaika, Whangarei

Owners:
The Vuletich family

Key Wines:
Scarecrow Cabernet Sauvignon, Mario's Merlot, Pinot Noir, Chardonnay, Gewürztraminer, Müller-Thurgau, Gumdiggers Port

---

Mario Vuletich's Scarecrow Cabernet Sauvignon is a satisfyingly chunky, rich-flavoured Northland red.

Strapping, seductively soft, rich-flavoured reds oozing ripe, sweet fruit are the most memorable wines at New Zealand's most northern vineyard. Okahu Estate lies near Kaitaia, on the Pukepoto Road to Ahipara Bay, a few kilometres from the sand dunes of Ninety Mile Beach.

Monty Knight, the founder, is famous in the Far North, although far more for his entrepreneurial career as a Kaitaia home appliance retailer than as a winemaker. He and his wife, Bev, live on the crest of their west-facing, two-hectare, hillside vineyard. 'We didn't come here to make wine,' he recalls. 'When I planted the first vines in 1984, the idea was just to make wine for our own consumption.' The first experimental wine flowed in 1986. After 'deciding to do it properly', in 1990 the Knights erected their iron-clad timber winery and hired Nick Chan (then at Lincoln Vineyards) as their winemaking consultant.

Cabernet Sauvignon is the major variety planted in Okahu Estate's loam-clay soils, with smaller plots of Merlot, Cabernet Franc, Pinotage, Chambourcin (one of the better French hybrids), Syrah, Chardonnay, Sémillon and Arnsburger. Knight also draws grapes regularly from a vineyard at Te Hana, near Wellsford, and is encouraging other landowners in the Far North to establish vineyards to supply Okahu Estate.

In the heat of the north, the estate-grown grapes ripen up to three weeks ahead of those in Gisborne and Hawke's Bay. The combination of high humidity and high temperatures in Kaitaia, conducive to extremely vigorous vine growth and the spread of fungal diseases, has encouraged Knight to plant thick-skinned grapes like Cabernet Sauvignon which ripen late in the season, when the humidity has started to fall.

Okahu Estate's annual output has grown from 600 cases in 1991 to over 3000 cases. 'We're still learning how to handle the fruit,' admits Knight. 'It's different from what you get in the other regions.' The red wines all display a sturdiness of body, flavour richness and soft, supple mouthfeel that clearly reflect the northern warmth.

Chunky, spicy and savoury, Ninety Mile Red is a Cabernet Sauvignon-based blend with lots of character. The dark Kaz Shiraz is succulent, smooth and soft, with a strong surge of minty, berryish, slightly peppery flavour. Shipwreck Bay Red, an oak-aged blend of Chambourcin (predominantly) and Pinotage, is a robust, well-rounded, easy-drinking red, in style reminiscent of a southern Rhône.

Clifton Chardonnay, a barrique-fermented wine made from Te Hana fruit, has been of varying quality, but the Proprietor's Reserve model, held longer in the cask, can be highly impressive. The estate-grown, barrel-fermented Ninety Mile White, a unique blend of Chardonnay (principally), Sémillon and Arnsburger, is typically a full, buttery, leesy, nutty style with rewarding flavour complexity and depth.

It's taken years for most of the locals to accept that Okahu Estate is making decent wine. 'It was widely believed that you can't grow grapes and make wine in the Far North,' says Knight. 'Sometimes I've wondered why I'm doing this when I could be in the Riviera. But now we're starting to be accepted as the genuine article; lots of people are visiting the winery and we're winning medals. I think we've got a tiger by the tail.'

Okahu Estate's notably robust and rich-flavoured Kaz Shiraz 1994 achieved a unique double at the 1996 Liquorland Royal Easter Wine Show – the first gold medal anyone can recall for a Northland wine, and the first gold ever awarded to a New Zealand Syrah.

Okahu Estate Vineyard and Winery

Okahu Road, Kaitaia

Owners:
Monty and Bev Knight

Key Wines:
Ninety Mile Red, Shipwreck Bay Red, Kaz Shiraz, Ninety Mile White, Clifton Chardonnay, Proprietor's Reserve Clifton Chardonnay, Old Brother John's Tawny Port

In the warmth of the Far North, Monty Knight produces notably robust, generously flavoured, smooth reds.

MATAKANA

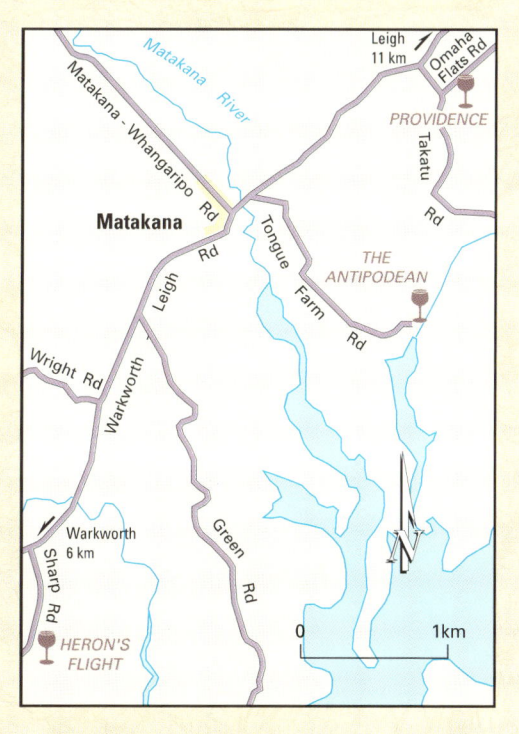

Amid the oyster farms, potteries, orchards, market gardens and beaches of Matakana, a new wine district has surfaced. An hour's drive north of Auckland, on the east coast between Warkworth and Leigh, Matakana first entered the spotlight in the late 1980s when The Antipodean winery spectacularly flared and faded. Now several new vineyards lie draped across the hills encircling this early rural settlement.

According to James Vuletic, owner of the fledgling Providence winery, Matakana – or nearby Leigh – in some years has the highest sunshine hours in the country. He is also confident that the rainfall is much lower on the coast than over the ranges to the west: 'Matakana's in the dry belt that runs down the coast from the Mangawhai Heads to Mahurangi and Waiheke Island. I can't think of anywhere else north of Auckland that's as climatically suitable for wine.'

One of the newcomers is already known to many wine lovers. A five-hectare vineyard near Warkworth is being established by Rex Soljan, until 1994 a partner in Soljans Wines in Lincoln Road, Henderson. Soljan's winemaker son, Darryl, and his wife, Bridget, are also involved in the project.

With a string of classy wines since the dark, deliciously perfumed and brambly 1991, David Hoskins and Mary Evans of Heron's Flight have proven the red-wine potential of the Matakana district first suggested in the 1980s by The Antipodean. 'We are sorting out a style which reflects this site,' says Hoskins. 'That seems to be one which is ripe, rich and round, what I call a "feminine" wine with supple tannins, approachable young, yet with sufficient structure to age.'

Hoskins is a Pennsylvania-born science and philosophy graduate who worked as a teacher and community worker before plunging into full-time winemaking. He and his wife, Mary Evans, planted their first vines on a north-facing clay slope overlooking the Matakana Valley and Sandspit Estuary in 1988. This is a maritime climate: 'When you take the bird netting off at vintage, you get salt all over your fingers,' says Evans.

Named after the white-faced herons which nest down by the river (and fly up and perch on the vineyard posts), the five-hectare vineyard is planted principally in Cabernet Sauvignon, with a hectare of Sangiovese, the great grape of Chianti (which Hoskins and Evans are pioneering in New Zealand), and smaller plots of Merlot and Cabernet Franc. The vines are widely spaced on a unique trellis system designed to maximise the fruit's exposure to the sun.

Heron's Flight's current production is about 1000 cases per year, but output is expected to rise to 1700 cases. Hoskins makes his wine in a small building that served as the original The Antipodean winery, but a new winery, cafe and function complex is on the drawing board.

The highlight of the range is the sturdy, flavourful, deliciously drinkable Cabernet Sauvignon/Merlot, which in the 1991 and 1994 vintages has been of exceptional quality. It matures gracefully; the 1991 and 1993 have blossomed in the bottle. To ensure their wine offers consistently good value, Hoskins and Evans adjust its price according to the standard of the vintage: the '92 sold ex-winery at $20, the '94 at $27.

Two Chardonnays have been produced – a fresh, drink-young wine and a more complex style fermented and lees-aged in oak barriques – but these have yet to reach the standard of the red, and following the 1996 vintage some of Heron's Flight's Chardonnay vines were top-grafted over to red varieties.

The Blush, a weighty, berryish, dry style, slightly earthy and tannic, is an ideal picnic wine. The Sangiovese, when it comes on stream, will probably be blended with Cabernet Sauvignon in the mould of many of the new wave Tuscan reds.

Mary Evans is frank about the often romanticised lifestyle of a winemaker. 'It's exhausting. It's 7am to 7pm, seven days a week. But when you reflect on it, you can see your achievements. It's a creative satisfaction: it's a beautiful vineyard, and the wines are drinking well.'

Heron's Flight Vineyard

Sharp Road, Matakana

Owners:
David Hoskins and Mary Evans

Key Wines:
Cabernet Sauvignon/Merlot, Chardonnay, Barrique-Fermented Chardonnay, Blush

David Hoskins and Mary Evans (pictured with their son Gwynn) make one of Auckland's most distinguished reds – the powerful, concentrated Heron's Flight Cabernet Sauvignon/Merlot.

In 1995 James Vuletic launched New Zealand's priciest red – the 1993 vintage of Providence at $62 per bottle. 'The price is not a statement about other New Zealand reds,' insists Vuletic. 'It reflects the cost of production and the wine's standard in international terms. Opus One and Dominus [from California] are no better, and any Bordeaux able to match its quality sells for more than $100.' A provocative statement, but as a former partner in The Antipodean, Vuletic is accustomed to controversy.

After the collapse of the original Antipodean partnership, Vuletic planted another Matakana vineyard in 1990, calling it Providence because he liked his dictionary's definition: 'a manifestation of divine care and prudent management'. A powerfully intelligent and articulate Auckland lawyer, Vuletic still lives on the North Shore site where his father once made wines under the Palomino Vineyards label.

The vineyard lies on a north-facing slope, surrounded by low hills, with a small cedar and concrete winery, built in 1995, squatting on the crest. It looks like a model small vineyard. 'I took one look at the site,' recalls Vuletic, 'and thought: "If the soil's right, that's it!"' In the iron-rich clay soils, free-draining due to the steep incline, Vuletic has planted two hectares of Merlot (70 per cent), Cabernet Franc (20 per cent) and Malbec vines.

Providence is fermented with natural yeasts in open-top vats, hand-plunged every four hours, given lengthy skin maceration, and then matured for up to two years in all-new French oak barriques. Vuletic also makes an oak-aged, weighty, dry Rosé.

So how good is Providence? I put it in a blind tasting alongside Auckland's other leading Cabernet Sauvignon and Merlot-based reds from the great (in Auckland) 1993 vintage. With its beguiling fragrance, lush fruitiness and sweet, silky, sustained finish, Providence stood up well against Matua Ararimu, Stonyridge, Goldwater and the rest, although it did not overshadow them. A voluptuous red, hugely seductive in its youth, it is clearly superior to the 1985 to 1987 vintages of The Antipodean.

Vuletic will not enter Providence in wine competitions. 'There's no point,' he believes. 'To the people who'll pay the sort of money I'm asking, a medal would be irrelevant.'

Providence Vineyard

Cnr Omaha Flats Road and Takatu Road, Matakana

Owner:

James Vuletic

Key Wines:

Providence, Rosé

James Vuletic produces a stunning, seductively scented and silky Merlot-based red at his tiny Matakana vineyard.

Other Producers

Te Aria Point Estate

About 15 kilometres (as the crow flies) north of Matakana, near the coast at Spectacle Lake, between Pakiri and Mangawhai, Mark Douglas owns a six-hectare vineyard first planted by contract grower Miles Robertson in 1981. After Douglas bought the property in 1987, he grafted Reichensteiner vines over to Cabernet Sauvignon, and is also replacing Breidecker with red-wine varieties. About a thousand cases of the impressively weighty and deep-flavoured, brambly and taut Te Arai Point Cabernet Sauvignon are produced each year, and 1996 has also brought the first white wines, based on bought-in grapes and marketed under a different label.

The Antipodean

This tiny Matakana winery, founded by brothers James and Petar Vuletic, in 1988 launched with tumultuous fanfare an attractive but extraordinarily over-priced ($93 per bottle) Cabernet Sauvignon/Merlot/Malbec 1985. However, after the brothers experienced 'a personal falling out', the company was wound up and in early 1990 all its wine stocks were sold by auction. Petar Vuletic emerged from the break-up with the majority of the vines and the right to the company's striking name. From the 1.8-hectare vineyard in Tongue Farm Road, proprietor Michelle Chignell-Vuletic (Petar's wife) currently produces The Antipodean Cabernet Sauvignon/Merlot/Malbec ($60) and several other high-priced, rarely seen wines – The Iconoclast (Syrah), Obiter (Cabernet Sauvignon), Attar (a Cabernet Sauvignon-based rosé), Pot a Pat (a non-vintage, second-tier red), and A (a barrel-fermented Sauvignon Blanc/Sémillon).

Kumeu Huapai Waimauku

Scattered across the softly undulating countryside that cradles the West Auckland townships of Kumeu, Huapai, Waimauku and Hobsonville are numerous quality-orientated wineries. The current rebirth of interest in Auckland viticulture is partly concentrated here, with the district's distance from the Waitakere Ranges giving a lower rainfall than at Henderson. The signs of success are everywhere: in the aesthetically delightful buildings at Nobilo, Matua Valley and Coopers Creek; in the burgeoning of vineyard restaurants at Selaks and Matua Valley; and, most importantly, in the wines themselves. Many are ranked among the country's best.

Kumeu-Huapai accounted for a mere 19 per cent of vine plantings in the Auckland province in 1960; by 1975 the figure had soared past 50 per cent. Henderson winemakers of the 1960s, wishing to expand to meet increasing demand, faced a serious problem in the lack of inexpensive, reasonably large blocks of land in Henderson. Expansion soon shifted to the much cheaper Kumeu-Huapai area.

Other companies, such as Nobilo and Kumeu River, have a history in the district extending over half a century. Selaks, Matua Valley and Coopers Creek are more recent arrivals who also chose to base their headquarters here.

It should be emphasised that the majority of the wines produced here are made from fruit trucked in from more southern districts, notably Gisborne, Hawke's Bay and Marlborough. However, confidence in the quality of local grapes is soaring: Kumeu River and Limeburners Bay wines are almost exclusively produced from local fruit; Waitakere Road Vineyard and Bazzard Estate wines are entirely so.

Rationalisation is underway in the vineyards as the winemakers single out the grape varieties most adaptable to the region's warm, humid summers and heavy clay soils. Red grapes are widely planted in the Auckland region: Cabernet Sauvignon is the leader, followed by Chardonnay, Merlot, Palomino and Pinot Noir. Sauvignon Blanc, Pinotage, Cabernet Franc and Sémillon are also well entrenched.

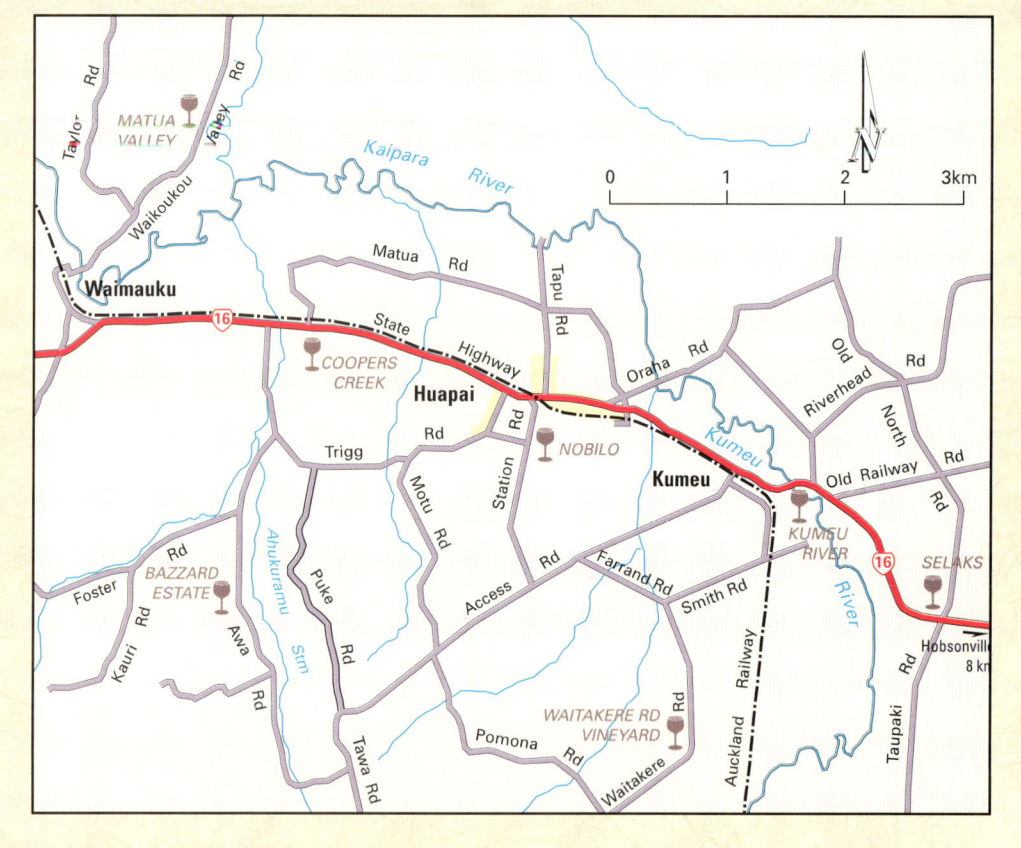

Winemakers here are also experimenting with new and healthier clones of existing varieties, use of devigorating rootstocks, 'grassing down' to reduce waterlogging of the soil, improved trellising techniques and other methods to upgrade their fruit quality.

The outcome has been some outstanding wines, both white and red. Kumeu River Chardonnay and Sauvignon/Sémillon, Matua Reserve Sauvignon Blanc, Coopers Creek Reserve Cabernet/Merlot, Limeburners Bay Cabernet Sauvignon, the reds from Waitakere Road Vineyard and Collard's Rothesay Vineyard Chardonnay have been the most eye-catching successes.

One of the iconoclasts of the Auckland wine scene, Charlie Bazzard is passionately attached to the idea of making a great Pinot Noir in a region where everyone else is focused on Cabernet Sauvignon and Merlot. Bazzard Estate is a four-hectare hillside vineyard in the wooded Awa Valley.

Bazzard is an English solicitor who in 1981 emigrated to New Zealand with his Auckland-born wife, Kay. Soon after, the Bazzards purchased the Awa Road vineyard established in hybrids and Palomino 17 years earlier by Cuthbert Woolcott. While upgrading the vineyard, between 1982 and 1988, Charlie worked as a radio operator and clerk on the Auckland waterfront.

Today Bazzard cultivates 1.6 hectares of Pinot Noir, 1.2 hectares of Chardonnay, and a 1.2-hectare plot of Merlot, Cabernet Sauvignon, Malbec and Cabernet Franc. He doesn't own a winery; the grapes are processed into wine by Kim Crawford at Coopers Creek. Bazzard reserves the Pinot Noir fruit for his own label, but sells the other grapes 'to get the cash to pay a winemaker to produce the Pinot Noir'.

The Bachtobel clone of Pinot Noir grown at Bazzard Estate usually yields pale, light wine in New Zealand, but Charlie Bazzard finds that 'on poor soils like our hard clays, you can throw away the book'. His low-yielding vines (five tonnes per hectare) produce berries harbouring a greater than usual concentration of colour and flavour.

The Pinot Noir, which is not sold at the vineyard, is distributed in New Zealand by mail order and specialist retailers, and exported to the UK and California. From the start an attractive wine with its accent on buoyant, raspberry/cherry fruit flavours, as the vintages roll by it is steadily climbing in quality, becoming tauter in structure and more satisfyingly subtle.

Bazzard Estate
Awa Road, Huapai

Owners:
Charles and Kay Bazzard

Key Wine:
Pinot Noir

Charlie and Kay Bazzard produce one of New Zealand's northernmost and rarest Pinot Noirs.

Talk Coopers Creek, and it's hard not to talk medals. The star of the 1995 Liquorland Royal Easter Wine Show was undoubtedly this small-to-medium sized winery. By scoring seven gold medals (20 per cent of those awarded) and four trophies (for champion Riesling, Cabernet/Merlot, medium-priced red and high-priced red), owners Andrew and Cyndy Hendry and their winemaker, Kim Crawford, ensured themselves a glittering awards dinner they will surely never forget.

The pink, Roman basilica-style building housing Coopers Creek's sales, administration and hospitality centre squats impressively alongside the highway just west of Huapai township. The company was founded by Andrew Hendry, a Wanganui-born accountant with a laid-back manner and ready wit, and Randy Weaver, a highly qualified Oregonian winemaker; these two first worked together at Penfolds in Henderson during the late 1970s. The winery's first vintage was in 1982. The original partnership was dissolved six years later, however, when Weaver returned to the United States, leaving the Hendrys as the principal shareholders in Coopers Creek.

From the start, Hendry set out to penetrate the burgeoning restaurant trade: 'On-premise sales was the gap when we started. Back then, restaurant wine lists were short of dry New Zealand whites; there was very little New Zealand Chardonnay available.' Today, of the company's average annual output of 45,000 cases, half is exported, principally to the UK, but also to Holland, Scandinavia, Germany, Canada, the eastern USA and Australia. Hendry predicts Coopers Creek's production will climb to around 75,000 cases over the next decade, but, he insists, 'I'm not looking for headaches'.

Winemaker Kim Crawford has enjoyed startling show success since his 1988 arrival at Coopers Creek, winning three gold medals at the 1989 Air New Zealand Wine Awards. 'Kim's pretty competitive,' notes Hendry. 'He's certainly motivated to make a good name for himself.' As a winemaking consultant to several other producers, Crawford's influence now extends well beyond Coopers Creek.

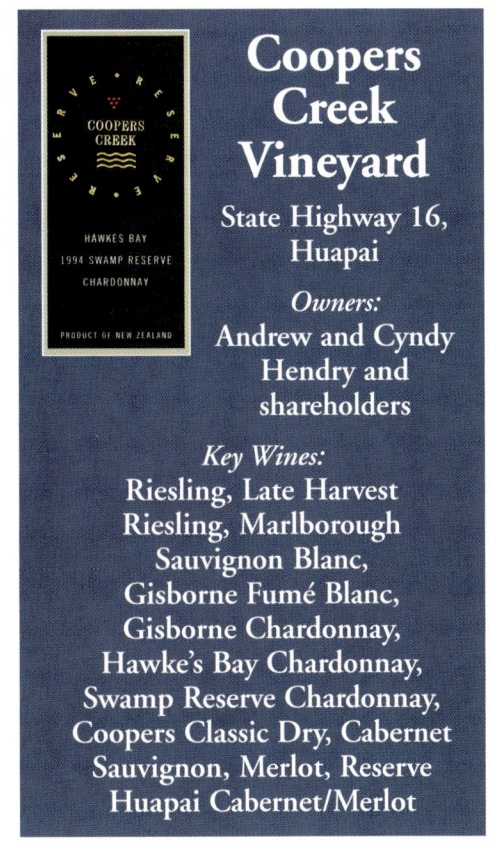

Coopers Creek Vineyard
State Highway 16, Huapai

Owners:
Andrew and Cyndy Hendry and shareholders

Key Wines:
Riesling, Late Harvest Riesling, Marlborough Sauvignon Blanc, Gisborne Fumé Blanc, Gisborne Chardonnay, Hawke's Bay Chardonnay, Swamp Reserve Chardonnay, Coopers Classic Dry, Cabernet Sauvignon, Merlot, Reserve Huapai Cabernet/Merlot

Kim Crawford works with fruit drawn from four regions. The three-hectare estate vineyard is planted in Cabernet Sauvignon, Merlot and Chardonnay; an adjoining three-hectare property bought in 1995 is also being planted in Cabernet Sauvignon and Merlot; and the company also leases another three-hectare block 'over the back' established in Cabernet Sauvignon, Merlot and Pinot Noir. The Hendrys themselves also own a six-hectare block of Chardonnay (principally) and Pinot Noir in Middle Road, Havelock North. About 85 per cent of the winery's grape intake, however, is drawn from growers in Gisborne, Hawke's Bay and Marlborough.

Riesling, Chardonnay, Sauvignon Blanc and (more recently) Cabernet Sauvignon and Merlot-based reds, are the winery's major strengths. Coopers Creek Riesling is an intensely aromatic, vibrantly fruity, penetratingly flavoured wine that in most vintages ranks at the forefront of Hawke's Bay Rieslings. Most of the region's Rieslings struggle to rival the intensity of Marlborough's. Why is Coopers Creek's so successful?

'It's partly the site,' says Hendry. 'The grapes are grown in Jim Scotland's vineyard at Clive. Good air movement close to the sea reduces the risk of disease, allowing us to hang the fruit out late. The grapes don't get wildly ripe, but they build up intense flavours. And we leave part of the block unsprayed to encourage *Botrytis*.' The equally impressive, slightly freeze-concentrated, sweet Late Harvest Riesling displays a touch of *Botrytis* influence, but places its accent on the lusher fruit flavours of late-picked fruit.

Coopers Creek Gisborne Fumé Blanc is a deep-flavoured dry wine with a penetrating, tropical fruit-like bouquet. Made with restrained oak handling, this is typically a rich, ripe wine with a long finish; one of Gisborne's top Sauvignon Blancs. The first Marlborough Sauvignon Blanc, from the 1989 vintage, collected a trophy and four gold medals. A vibrant wine with a wealth of pure, gooseberry and passionfruit-like – rather than pungently herbal – flavours, this and subsequent vintages have been classic examples of Marlborough Sauvignon Blanc at its arresting best.

Coopers Classic Dry is one of the best cheap whites on the market. In this Gisborne-grown marriage of (predominantly) tank-fermented Sémillon with barrel-fermented Chardonnay, the zesty, capsicum-like, assertive character of the Sémillon dominates.

Three styles of Chardonnay are marketed, including the Swamp Reserve Chardonnay *(see panel)*. The Gisborne Chardonnay, launch-ed from the 1990 vintage, is already the biggest seller of the trio; this is a briefly oak-matured wine with a modest price-tag. The mid-priced Hawke's Bay Chardonnay is tank-fermented and then matured for six months in American oak casks, with no malolactic influence. Using American rather than French oak, says Hendry, gives the wine 'difference and forwardness'.

Coopers Creek's reds, based on grapes grown in the estate vineyard and Hawke's Bay, have improved dramatically in recent vintages. The mid-priced Hawke's Bay Cabernet Sauvignon and Merlot are both delicious, exuberantly fruity wines with soft, easy tannins, designed for early consumption. They are overshadowed, however, by the fragrant and dark Reserve Huapai Cabernet/Merlot, a more complex, American oak-aged wine with an impressive intensity of blackcurrant and plum-like flavours. This label has recently joined the ranks of Auckland's top reds.

Andrew (left) and Cyndy Hendry, with winemaker Kim Crawford, have in the past few years built Coopers Creek into one of New Zealand's most prestigious wineries.

COOPERS CREEK SWAMP RESERVE CHARDONNAY

Mouth-filling, succulent and complex, the 1986 vintage of Swamp Road Chardonnay catapulted Coopers Creek to prominence. Still one of the jewels in Coopers Creek's range, the label was originally based on fruit grown by Fenton Kelly in Swamp Road, in the Omaranui Valley in Hawke's Bay. Congratulating them on their precise honesty in labelling, the Australian wine writer James Halliday then urged: 'Why not change the name of the road?'

The name proved popular, however – and even for a time survived the winery's swing away from using fruit grown in Swamp Road. Today, Swamp Reserve Chardonnay is based on a selection of Coopers Creek's best fruit. The early vintages were fully barrel-fermented, but to retain the fresher fruit components, a third of the wine is now tank-fermented. The barrel-fermented portion is aged on its yeast lees, with regular lees stirring. All the wine is then matured in new and one-year-old French oak barriques, with about 25 per cent malolactic influence.

Swamp Reserve Chardonnay is essentially a celebration of lush fruit flavours. Its delectably rich, grapefruit and fig-like flavours are fleshed out with subtle, nutty oak, leading to a slightly buttery, crisp, superbly sustained finish. With its accent on opulent, ultra-ripe fruit, Swamp Reserve Chardonnay drinks brilliantly within a couple of years of the vintage.

In 1994, James Suckling of the prominent American magazine, *The Wine Spectator*, was given an unidentified glass of white wine: 'Considering its lively aromas and vivid flavours of apples, vanilla and white truffles together with its refreshingly high acidity . . . it had to be one of the best Chardonnays from France's legendary Côte d'Or that I had tried in a long time.' He was wrong. The wine was Kumeu River Kumeu Chardonnay 1992.

Kumeu River's rise to international acclaim in the past decade has been founded on its rich, savoury, gloriously full-flavoured Chardonnay. Under its earlier name, San Marino, it was one of the first wineries to establish such *vinifera* grape varieties as Chardonnay and Pinotage, and also enjoyed an early reputation for hybrid quaffing wines such as its Kumeu Dry Red.

The winery is sited on the main highway, 1km south of Kumeu. Early Dalmatian settlers tended vines on the property for several decades before the Brajkovichs' arrival. When 19-year-old, Dalmatian-born Mate Brajkovich and his father bought the property in 1944, along with seven hectares of pasture, they acquired a fermenting vat, barrels and a half-hectare of Isabella and Albany Surprise vines.

The strong impact of San Marino on the Auckland wine scene of the 1950s and 1960s owed much to the Brajkovichs' legendary hospitality. Winemaking at Kumeu River is still largely a family affair. The charismatic Mate died in 1992 but his widow, Melba, is the general manager; their eldest son,

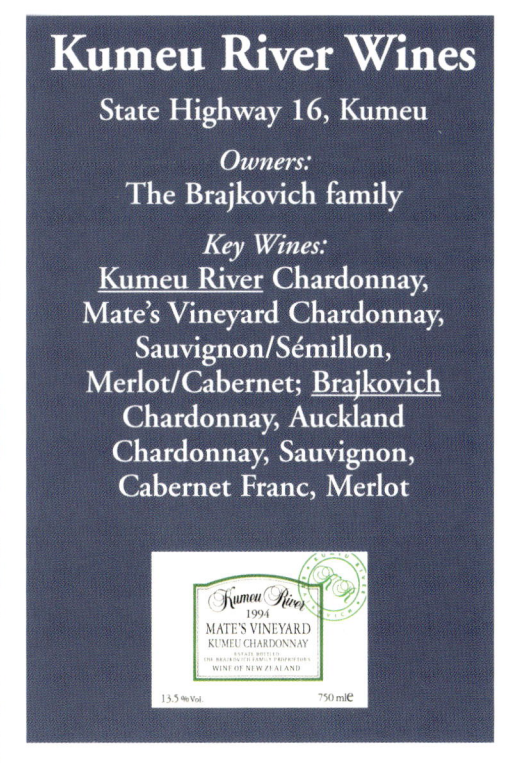

Kumeu River Wines
State Highway 16, Kumeu

Owners:
The Brajkovich family

Key Wines:
Kumeu River Chardonnay, Mate's Vineyard Chardonnay, Sauvignon/Sémillon, Merlot/Cabernet; Brajkovich Chardonnay, Auckland Chardonnay, Sauvignon, Cabernet Franc, Merlot

Michael, controls the winemaking; another son, Milan, oversees the vineyards; the youngest son, Paul, is immersed in marketing.

Michael recalls his father, who in 1985 was awarded an OBE for services to the wine industry and the community, as 'someone who could relate to anyone, from road-workers to the king of Spain. His dying was a huge shock to us all. How do you replace someone like that? The whole place *was* him.'

The Brajkovichs work largely with Kumeu fruit. 'Our best wine always comes off the home block,' says Michael. On the rise across the highway from the winery, eight hectares of Chardonnay, Cabernet Franc and Sauvignon Blanc are cultivated. Recent plantings – including the replanting of the two-hectare original block across the road from the winery, now called Mate's Vineyard – have concentrated on Chardonnay. The Brajkovichs also own a five-hectare block of Merlot vines planted by Corbans in nearby Waitakere Road in the early mid 1970s.

Auckland growers supply the rest of the winery's grapes; about 30 per cent of the total intake. Chardonnay and Sémillon are drawn from local Kumeu vineyards, and Chardonnay from Mangere.

Michael Brajkovich, a quiet, handsome man with a towering physical presence, in 1989 became the first New Zealander to succeed in the famously rigorous, London-based Master of Wine examination. After training with distinction at Roseworthy College, South Australia, he spent the 1983 vintage at Château Magdelaine, a leading premier grand cru of St Émilion.

From the start Brajkovich was convinced that Kumeu could produce fruit of outstanding quality. He points to how planting on hill sites improves drainage; to the merits of 'grassing down' between the rows as a way to reduce waterlogging of the soil; to the enhanced fruit ripeness achieved using the lyre-trellis system; and to the superior method of fruit selection with hand-harvesting. His wines have supported his conviction.

The range is marketed under three labels: Kumeu River (the premium range),

The Brajkovich family (left to right: Milan, Melba, Michael and Paul) produce powerful, lush and savoury Chardonnays of outstanding quality under the premium Kumeu River label.

Brajkovich (the middle range), and Kumeu (for everyday quaffing). New Zealand absorbs most of the winery's output, with the United Kingdom and the United States the two major export markets.

Four Chardonnays are produced. The most famous (*see panel*) is Kumeu River Kumeu Chardonnay, based on fruit grown in five local vineyards, which Michael Brajkovich likens to 'a village wine'. The most expensive, Kumeu River Mate's Vineyard Chardonnay, launched from the 1993 vintage as the first of a planned series of single-vineyard Kumeu wines, and likened by Brajkovich to 'a premier cru of the same village', is a classy, quite Burgundian wine with a seamless array of citrusy, oaky, mealy, buttery flavours, long and refined. The middle-tier Brajkovich Auckland Chardonnay (with the Kumeu River look-alike label) is grown at Mangere and Kumeu, based on low-yielding clones and fully barrel-fermented – a sort of junior Kumeu River Chardonnay. The cheapest model, Brajkovich Chardonnay, with a signature across the label and no regional designation, is based on heavier-cropping Mangere and Kumeu vines and usually not oak-aged.

Kumeu River Sauvignon/Sémillon is usually a splendidly ripe, full, rich-flavoured wine, demonstrating well the Sauvignon Blanc variety's ability when grown in Auckland to yield stylish, rather than strident, wine.

The Kumeu River label is also well known for its premium blended red. The wine started its life as a straight, varietal Merlot and later evolved into a Merlot/Cabernet, but after Kumeu River uprooted all its Cabernet Sauvignon vines in 1995, it has become a Merlot/Malbec blend. 'Merlot gives us attractive, savoury characters, even in a mediocre year,' says Brajkovich, 'whereas our Cabernet Sauvignon was usually slightly green. We find Malbec ripens earlier than Cabernet Sauvignon with great colour, sweet fruit and good tannin structure.'

This is a distinctive wine, lighter than Auckland's top Cabernet-based reds, but savoury and supple, with the medium-full body and firm structure of claret.

Under the mid-priced Brajkovich label, the non-oaked Sauvignon is fresh and tangy in a ripe, easy-drinking style. The Cabernet Franc is delectable in its youth. Fruity, yet with solid extract and an underlying firmness, this wine tastes exactly like a grape should that often is employed to soften and pacify Cabernet Sauvignon. Brajkovich Merlot is deeper and more tannic. Michael Brajkovich delights in Merlot's 'leather, tobacco and coffee' flavours. Matured for up to a year in seasoned French oak barriques, this is an excellent 'food' wine – the Brajkovichs serve it with pasta.

KUMEU RIVER KUMEU CHARDONNAY

This is one of New Zealand's most talked-about wines. A powerful, superbly constructed, deep-flavoured Chardonnay displaying intense, ripe fruit characters and a soft, seductive finish, it stands out for its distinctive, strongly malolactic-influenced buttery style and rich, mealy complexity.

The launch of the first Kumeu River Chardonnay caused a major stir. As Michael Brajkovich has written: 'In 1985 Kumeu River produced a Chardonnay that underwent a total malolactic fermentation, to the surprise of many, and certainly to the disgust of the wine judges who relegated it to the "no award" level. The style was totally foreign to that of previous New Zealand Chardonnays; it was the style of Burgundy . . .' The 1987 vintage, which earned accolades in England and the United States, became Kumeu River's first internationally successful wine.

What is the key to its consistently stunning quality? According to Michael, 'It's the vineyard, pure and simple. We manage to get the grapes very ripe. The lyre trellising system helps to control vigour and increase bunch exposure to the sun – that's where we get the flavour.'

Once at the winery, the hand-picked grapes are whole bunch-pressed to extract the most delicately flavoured juice possible. The juice is fermented with natural yeasts, which Brajkovich believes 'let the vineyard express itself more than selected yeasts'. With the wild yeasts, fermentation temperatures are high – up to 26°C. Fermented and lees-aged in Burgundy oak barriques (20–25 per cent new each year), the wine also undergoes a full malolactic fermentation, without which Brajkovich believes it would be 'unbalanced, with high acidity and a lack of its attractive, soft, milky, cheesy characters.'

One of the great New Zealand Chardonnays, the Kumeu River displays arrestingly rich, seamless, persistent flavour and a beguiling creaminess of texture. It typically offers splendid drinking at around three years old.

Limeburners Bay winery adopts a low profile: the wines are not entered in local show judgings and much of its output is sold overseas. Owned by Alan Laurenson and his Danish wife Jetta, the winery lies several kilometres to the east of Kumeu and Huapai in Hobsonville Road. Of the small selection of wines, the dark, burly, rich-flavoured and tautly structured Cabernet Sauvignon is unquestionably the star.

Limeburners Bay's grapes are usually (but not always) Auckland-grown. The two-hectare, gently sloping loam-clay vineyard adjacent to the winery is planted entirely in red grapes: 80 per cent Cabernet Sauvignon, the rest Merlot and Cabernet Franc.

In another, larger Hobsonville vineyard the Laurensons are planting six hectares of principally red grapes. Laurenson has been evaluating Sangiovese for several years and is excited by its performance: 'It could become our version of Australia's Shiraz. It ripens ahead of Cabernet Sauvignon, crops abundantly, and produces easy-drinking, low tannin wines that don't need new oak.' The winery also buys Sémillon, Sauvignon Blanc and Chardonnay from growers, usually in West Auckland.

Limeburners Bay Vineyards

112 Hobsonville Road, Hobsonville

Owners:
Alan and Jetta Laurenson

Key Wines:
Cabernet Sauvignon, Dessert Cabernet Sauvignon, Sauvignon Blanc, Sémillon/Chardonnay, Chardonnay

The Cabernet Sauvignon, estate-grown and matured for 15 months in French oak barrels – 50 per cent new each year – is the flagship wine. Dark, spicy and firm, it is chunky and concentrated, with the potential for long cellaring. In lesser vintages, the premium Cabernet Sauvignon is replaced by a lower-priced Cabernet/ Merlot.

Robust, ripe, moderately herbal and soft, Limeburners Bay Sauvignon Blanc is a good example of the style of this variety grown in Auckland's warmer climate. The Sémillon/Chardonnay marries fresh, crisp Sémillon fruit flavours with the full, savoury character of barrel-fermented Chardonnay.

The popular Dessert Cabernet Sauvignon, a sort of very full-bodied sweet red, dark and raisiny, is modelled on the vins doux naturel (fortified dessert wines) of southern France. Fractionally lower in alcohol (17 per cent) than most ports, with a liquorice-like intensity, this is a distinctive, delicious mouthful. Laurenson recommends it for the latter stages of a meal, 'when the conversation gets to sex and politics'.

Alan Laurenson is best known for his strapping, spicy, tautly structured Cabernet Sauvignon and sweet, creamy-rich Dessert Cabernet Sauvignon.

Matua Valley's handsome, octagonal winery sits on a knoll in the secluded Waikoukou Valley, just a few bends and a climb in the road from Waimauku. Matua Valley – or simply Matua, as it is often called – is one of the wine industry's greatest success stories. Here the Hunting Lodge Restaurant, in a house adjacent to the winery built in 1868, serves country-style food, emphasising lamb, beef and game.

Matua Valley – named after the original vineyard in Matua Road, Huapai – is controlled by the Spence brothers, Ross and Bill. They have winemaking in their blood: a grandfather emigrated from Dalmatia and their father Rod Spence founded Spence's Wines in McLeod Road, Henderson, in the 1940s.

Matua Valley began in 1974 in a leased tin shed near Henderson, with the brothers holding down full-time jobs elsewhere and producing their wine in the evenings and at weekends.

The present vertical-timbered winery, which crushes about 2000 tonnes of fruit annually, was still being built during the first vintage in 1978.

Today members of the Margan family also

Matua Valley Wines

Waikoukou Valley Road, Waimauku

Owners:
The Spence and Margan families

Key Wines:
Matua Ararimu Chardonnay, Judd Estate Chardonnay, Smith-Dartmoor Chardonnay, Eastern Bays Chardonnay, Gewürztraminer, Hawke's Bay Sauvignon Blanc, Reserve Sauvignon Blanc, Chenin Blanc/Chardonnay, White Hill, Late Harvest Muscat, Red Jacket, Cabernet Sauvignon/Merlot, Smith-Dartmoor Cabernet Sauvignon, Smith-Dartmoor Merlot, Ararimu Cabernet Sauvignon/Merlot, Brut; Shingle Peak Riesling, Sauvignon Blanc, Chardonnay, Cabernet Sauvignon

have a substantial shareholding in Matua Valley, and participate in decision making at board level.

In the 22-hectare, undulating estate vineyard on sandy loam soils are extensive areas of Cabernet Sauvignon, Pinot Noir, Sauvignon Blanc and Chardonnay.

Matua Valley has also recently bought two vineyards totalling 34 hectares in Marlborough, planted principally in Sauvignon Blanc, Chardonnay, Gewürztraminer and Merlot. This fruit is processed at Rapaura Vintners, formerly the contract winemaking facility known as Vintech, which Matua Valley and three other wine producers acquired in 1995.

Matua Valley also has a stake in several joint venture vineyards. According to Ross, 'If you get a part-owner operating a vineyard efficiently, with a *true* interest in what he's doing, that relieves you of a lot of pressure.' Growers in Gisborne, Hawke's Bay and Marlborough also supply about 40 per cent of the company's fruit.

Mark Robertson, a tall, fresh-faced Otago University Bachelor of Science graduate who later spent a year studying at Roseworthy College in South Australia, is in charge of the

From humble beginnings in a small tin shed, the Spence brothers, Bill (left) and Ross, have built Matua Valley into one of New Zealand's most acclaimed middle-sized wineries.

winemaking reins at Matua Valley. 'Our goal is to produce "food" wines that are fruit-driven and not aggressive in flavour,' says Robertson.

Matua Valley wines are consistently attractive and often very high-quality. Four North Island Chardonnays are produced: the luxury Ararimu model, a fat, flavour-packed, creamy-smooth wine of compelling weight and length (usually, but not always, grown in Gisborne); Smith-Dartmoor, a powerful, citrusy, deftly balanced Hawke's Bay wine that replaces the former Reserve label; the lightly oaked, straightforward Eastern Bays; and Judd Estate, for over a decade the company's white-wine flagship *(see panel)*.

Matua's non-oaked Hawke's Bay Sauvignon Blanc (for many years labelled Fumé Blanc) is a sharply priced, zesty Hawke's Bay wine with plenty of varietal character. It is overshadowed by the Reserve Sauvignon Blanc, a richer, far more subtle and complex wine made from ripe, estate-grown fruit, partly barrel-fermented; from one vintage to the next, this is one of New Zealand's most outstanding top oak-aged Sauvignon Blancs.

One of the finest value-for-money wines in the Matua Valley range is the strong-flavoured, firm Chenin Blanc/Chardonnay. Other white wines include Müller-Thurgau and Gewürztraminer (both a cut above the average) and the headily perfumed, sweet, freeze-concentrated Late Harvest Muscat. Matua Valley's bottle-fermented sparkling, which has a vintage as the key part of its name (for example, Nineteen Ninety-Two Brut), is a Pinot Noir-dominant style with powerful, yeasty, biscuity, lingering flavour.

The Shingle Peak label is reserved for Matua Valley's Marlborough wines. The Chardonnay, Sauvignon Blanc, Riesling and Cabernet Sauvignon have all deservedly been winners with their fresh, lively, incisive flavours and striking packaging.

Matua Valley's range of red wines was until recently dominated by its Smith-Dartmoor Cabernet Sauvignon. Leafy-green herbaceous characters sometimes detract from this otherwise impressively rich and robust red from Hawke's Bay. The riper-tasting Smith-Dartmoor Merlot, grown in the same vineyard, features strong, sweet red berry-fruit flavours, silky and sustained; top vintages can be outstanding.

The dark, brambly Ararimu Cabernet Sauvignon/Merlot, launched from the 1991 vintage, can also be of startling quality. The 1991, grown in Hawke's Bay, and the 1993, estate-grown at Waimauku, are exceptionally concentrated wines, awash with ripe, minty, spicy, taut and lingering flavours. This is clearly Matua Valley's flagship red.

Matua Judd Estate Chardonnay

Scented, vibrantly fruity, mealy and soft, this is a very elegant and seductive Gisborne wine. Since the 1991 vintage, its standard has soared.

Winemaker Mark Robertson explains the quality surge: 'We've settled on a style. Since the first, 1984 vintage, the wine has reflected different fashions. In the 1980s, to be competitive at shows, you had to over-oak the wine and give it too much malolactic influence. Those wines didn't mature well, but we've learned from that. Now we have a definitive style – it's back to the fruit. After all, that's New Zealand's advantage – our wines taste of fruit.'

After many years of intensive horticulture, the soils in the Judd Estate vineyard, near the hills at Patutahi, are depleted. The Chardonnay fruit, says Robertson, develops 'intense passionfruit characters'. About 40 per cent of the wine is handled entirely in stainless steel tanks. The rest is barrel-fermented, with an increasing reliance on older casks: 'We want barrel fermentation and maturation characters,' says Ross Spence, 'without oak dominance.'

Judd Estate Chardonnay is a celebration of fragrant, well-ripened, rich-flavoured fruit, overlaid with subtle oak and lees-aging characters. In its highly expressive youth, at one to two years old, of all New Zealand's Chardonnays this is one of the most irresistible.

When Nobilo celebrates, it does so with panache. Other wineries have recently marked major milestones in their history, but few with the flair Nobilo demonstrated in 1993 when 200 guests at its 50th anniversary party on the Auckland waterfront watched the company's founders, Nikola Nobilo and his wife, Zuva, step ashore from an old sailing ship to be met by swirling Dalmatian dancers and the Prime Minister, Jim Bolger.

Nobilo – or the House of Nobilo, as the company likes to be called – is New Zealand's fourth largest winery. Nobilo has recently enjoyed great export success, and its fruity, easy-drinking White Cloud is also rocketing off the shelves in New Zealand supermarkets.

Nikola Nobilo, now in his eighties, is a Dalmatian who abandoned his stonemason's toil on the island of Korcula to plant a new vineyard at Huapai in 1943. In the 1960s and 1970s, with the help of several shareholders – initially Gilbey's of England in 1966, and later Nathans, the PSIS, and the Development Finance Corporation – Nobilo grew rapidly, building a strong reputation based on quality reds and its immensely popular, slightly sweet Müller-Thurgau.

The 1985–86 wine price war caused the company severe financial problems, but soon after the Nobilo family uprooted most of its Huapai vines, sold the land, bought out its partners and regained full control. After almost a decade as New Zealand's largest family-owned winery, in 1995 Nobilo sold a 49 per cent stake to Direct Capital Limited. The $5 million paid by Direct Capital, a publicly listed investment company, is being spent to expand Nobilo's production facilities as part of a plan to more than double the company's output by 1998. A second capital injection of $5 million, perhaps involving a public share offering, is planned for 1997.

The three Nobilo brothers who have run the company for the past 30 years remain in key executive positions: Nick, the former chief executive, as executive chairman in an 'overview and strategic-planning' role; Steve as roving 'brands ambassador'; and Mark as director of viticulture. Kerry Hitchcock, for many years Corbans' chief winemaker, joined Nobilo in 1996 in the general manager's role.

Two-thirds of the company's fruit is drawn from contract growers in the Gisborne, Hawke's Bay and Marlborough regions. The eight-hectare estate vineyard at Huapai is principally established in Pinotage. A substantial vineyard has also been planted on Maori land at Mohaka,

House of Nobilo
Station Road, Huapai

Owners:
The Nobilo family and Direct Capital Limited

Key Wines:
White Cloud, Müller-Thurgau, Poverty Bay Chardonnay, Reserve Dixon Vineyard Chardonnay, Reserve Marlborough Chardonnay, Marlborough Sauvignon Blanc, Pinotage, Hawke's Bay Cabernet Sauvignon, Marlborough Cabernet Sauvignon

The Nobilo brothers (from left: Mark, Nick and Steve) are determined to build their fresh, slightly sweet White Cloud into a major international brand along the lines of Blue Nun and Mateus Rosé.

between Wairoa and Napier, in a joint venture between Nobilo and the Paroa Trust. About three kilometres from the coast, on terraces of the Mohaka River, 40 hectares of Chenin Blanc, Müller-Thurgau and Dr Hogg Muscat vines have been planted; Nick Nobilo predicts the site will also eventually produce outstanding red wines.

At Moteo, in the Dartmoor Valley of Hawke's Bay, another venture between a Maori trust and Nobilo has established 40 hectares of Chenin Blanc, Sauvignon Blanc and Müller-Thurgau. Yet another joint venture in Marlborough between Nobilo and Brian and Sheryl Blick has planted 40 hectares of vines, principally Sauvignon Blanc, in the Waihopai Valley.

After the local market turned sour in the mid 1980s, Nobilo plunged into export, with spectacular success. Nobilo now exports 70 per cent of its output – a higher proportion than any other New Zealand winery. Much of the wine is shipped in bulk to northern Europe, but Nobilo has also carved out a presence for premium varietal wines in the United Kingdom. Assaults on the Australian and American markets are being launched in 1996.

The pivotal position once held in the Nobilo range by its best-selling Müller-Thurgau is now occupied by White Cloud. The wine was initially launched overseas because the company needed to develop a new base for Müller-Thurgau, which had been highly successful for it in New Zealand in the 1970s. 'During the eighties' wine crash, we lost domestic sales,' recalls Nick Nobilo, 'so we revamped the whole Müller-Thurgau concept by blending to improve the quality, then packaging it to represent New Zealand as a generic wine. I thought: if New Zealand can produce fine Müller-Thurgau, and there are great overseas wine brands like Mateus, why can't we develop an internationally successful brand?'

The name White Cloud is based on

Aotearoa – land of the long white cloud. The wine was instantly a hit in Scandinavia, and later in the United Kingdom.

Launched locally in 1991 in eye-catching tall, frosted bottles, White Cloud recently outsold all other bottled white wines in supermarkets. Müller-Thurgau-based, with a touch of Sauvignon Blanc, Chenin Blanc and Dr Hogg Muscat to boost the flavour, it is a light, floral, fruity wine, slightly sweet (sweeter in New Zealand than in the United Kingdom) and tangy.

Twenty years ago, Nobilo's estate-grown Cabernet Sauvignon, Pinot Noir and Pinotage were the highlights of the range, and ranked among New Zealand's foremost reds. Today the spotlight has swung to white wines: 'We're market-driven,' says Nick Nobilo, 'and there's less potential in a global sense for New Zealand reds.' Two Cabernet Sauvignons, however, are still in the range – a fresh, crisp, buoyantly fruity Marlborough wine that can be delicious in its youth, and a full-flavoured and smooth but slightly green-edged Hawke's Bay red. Nobilo's Pinotage, in recent years one of New Zealand's finest examples of this variety, with loads of peppery, meaty, oaky, zesty flavour, since the 1993 vintage has evolved into a less complex, but fresher and fruitier, more Beaujolais-style red.

Chardonnay appears in the Nobilo range under five different labels. The lower-tier wine is the fresh, lemony, non-wooded Poverty Bay Chardonnay, for which Nobilo has enjoyed a lengthy contract with British Airways. Next up the ladder is Nobilo's Gisborne Chardonnay, a tank-fermented, barrel-aged, fruit-driven style for early drinking.

Of the three reserve Chardonnays, two – Dixon Vineyard and Tietjen Vineyard – are lush, ripe-tasting, highly wood-influenced, buttery-soft Gisborne styles. My favourite is Nobilo's Reserve Marlborough Chardonnay, with its powerful surge of grapefruit-like, mealy, toasty-oak flavours and steely acid spine.

After White Cloud, Nobilo's Marlborough Sauvignon Blanc is the company's biggest seller. This is a classic regional style, packed with lively melon/lime flavours and appetising acidity, and bargain-priced.

Think Selaks, and Sauvignon Blanc is the first wine that springs to mind. At the 1995 Sydney International Wine Competition, the trophy for the champion white wine of the show was scooped by Selaks' explosively flavoured 1994 Sauvignon Blanc/Sémillon.

The founder, Marino Selak, arrived in Auckland in 1906. After many years on the gumfields, he planted vines, fruit trees and vegetables at Te Atatu. The year 1934 marked the first Selak vintage in New Zealand.

Mate Selak, who as a 17 year old in 1940 journeyed from Dalmatia to New Zealand to join his winemaking uncle Marino, devoted his life to the winery that bore his family name. The firm gradually expanded in the post-war period, becoming one of the first to specialise in table wines. But in the early 1960s the north-western motorway sliced through the small vineyard. In 1965 Mate Selak re-established the company at Kumeu, with the first vintage there in 1969.

Today the Selak winery is run by Mate's sons, Ivan and Michael, with winemaker Darryl Woolley the third key figure. Ivan Selak is in charge of the day-to-day administration of the company, while Michael focuses on marketing.

The Selaks range encompasses five Sauvignon Blanc or Sémillon-based wines: the herbaceous, full-flavoured, sharply priced Marlborough Sauvignon Blanc, which constitutes over a third of the company's total sales; the very undemanding, slightly sweet Gisborne Fumé; the single-vineyard, non-oaked, magnificently scented and zingy Drylands Estate Sauvignon Blanc; the equally outstanding, wood-aged Founders Reserve Sauvignon Blanc; and the deliciously flavour-packed, subtly oaked and zesty Sauvignon Blanc/Sémillon *(see panel)*.

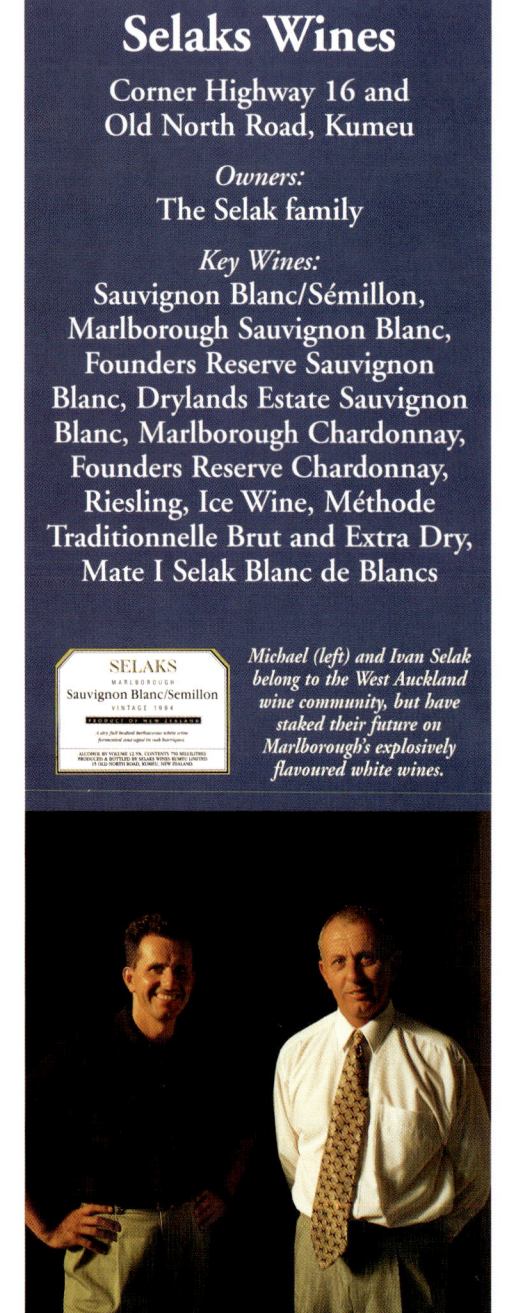

The company draws a fifth of its annual grape intake from the two-hectare estate vineyard at Kumeu, and its 16-hectare Drylands Vineyard in Marlborough, planted in Sauvignon Blanc, Sémillon and Chardonnay. John Webber's shingly Matador Vineyard, adjacent to the Drylands Vineyard, is also a key source of top quality fruit. Cabernet Sauvignon is drawn from growers in Hawke's Bay, and Sauvignon Blanc, Sémillon and Gewürztraminer from Gisborne growers.

Selaks' involvement in the Marlborough region, central to its ongoing Sauvignon Blanc success, expanded in 1996 with the opening of its Drylands Estate Winery which features a shop and 100-seat restaurant.

Selaks' Chardonnay styles have been transformed since 1991 by the company's shift in emphasis from Gisborne to Marlborough grapes. The intensely citrusy, 'standard' Marlborough Chardonnay, both tank and barrel-fermented, often shows a touch of class; the top-of-the-range Founders Reserve label, barrel-fermented and lees-aged with a strong new-oak influence, is a powerful yet refined wine with great depth.

Selaks is renowned for two bottle-fermented sparklings. The Brut, based on Marlborough Pinot Noir and Chardonnay, lees-aged for three years, is toasty, citrusy and full-flavoured; the Extra Dry is yeasty and very persistent. At around $20, both are bargains. The luxury Mate I Selak Blanc de Blancs, all Chardonnay-based, exhibits a rich, toasty fragrance and intensely yeasty, long, stylish palate.

Selaks Wines

Corner Highway 16 and Old North Road, Kumeu

Owners:
The Selak family

Key Wines:
Sauvignon Blanc/Sémillon, Marlborough Sauvignon Blanc, Founders Reserve Sauvignon Blanc, Drylands Estate Sauvignon Blanc, Marlborough Chardonnay, Founders Reserve Chardonnay, Riesling, Ice Wine, Méthode Traditionnelle Brut and Extra Dry, Mate I Selak Blanc de Blancs

Michael (left) and Ivan Selak belong to the West Auckland wine community, but have staked their future on Marlborough's explosively flavoured white wines.

Selaks Sauvignon Blanc/Sémillon

Overflowing with gooseberryish/green capsicum-like fruit and spine-tingling acidity, this is one of the most thrilling of all New Zealand's Sauvignon Blanc-based wines. Like the equally brilliant Cloudy Bay and Vavasour Reserve, it offers an extra flavour dimension rare in New Zealand Sauvignon Blancs – a touch of complexity.

Why is it so good? 'There are three key factors: the grapes, the choice of wood, and Darryl Woolley's flair for the style,' says Ivan Selak. Ever since the first, 1983 vintage, the wine has been a 60/40 blend, with the minority Sémillon adding richness and length to the palate.

To achieve the desired balance of tropical-fruit and greener-edged, herbaceous flavours, the grapes are held on the vines in Marlborough as late as possible and harvested ripe, at around 22 degrees brix, with extra body and mouthfeel. The blend is entirely fermented in French oak barriques, and wood-aged for three to four months, with regular stirring of its yeast lees, yet its breathtakingly intense Marlborough fruit flavours are never swamped.

Then there is Darryl Woolley's role. He has been a fan of Marlborough Sauvignon Blanc since he helped make the first vintage of Cloudy Bay at Corbans' Gisborne winery in 1985. 'When the Sauvignon Blanc comes in each vintage, Darryl's eyes light up,' notes Ivan Selak.

Lawyers are often attracted to the wine industry, usually as ardent imbibers, but also as owners. At Waitakere Road Vineyard in Kumeu, Tim Harris, an Auckland lawyer and *Metro* magazine wine columnist, produces some of New Zealand's most deeply satisfying, yet least-heralded, reds.

Harris and several partners bought a six-hectare block in 1986, and over the next four years close-planted it in Cabernet Franc, Merlot and Cabernet Sauvignon.

From the start, Waitakere Road Vineyard has specialised in two red wines. Both the Merlot-based Uppercase and Cabernet Franc-predominant Harrier Rise are less overtly fruity, more harmonious, subtle and complex than most New Zealand reds – and more downright drinkable.

What is the key to Harris' distinctive, distinctly European red-wine style? 'If you read French winemaking books, it's striking how for generations they've thought about their wine's structure and how best to extract colour and tannins from the skins,' he says.

Harris favours a very long period of skin contact – up to seven weeks. 'The wine starts off with an obvious fruitiness and floral characters, resembling raspberries, then develops hints of coffee. Then it becomes a lot gamier and you get distinctly organic pongs, veering towards silage. But you're looking for structure, and if you keep your nerve you end up with a red with marvellous depth of fine tannins.'

The financial side of the venture has been far from easy. Harris abandoned his legal career in June 1993 in favour of full-time winemaking, but after the 1994 crop proved 'ruinously' small (only a third of what was expected), he's now back as a full-time lawyer. The original syndicate also disbanded in 1996, with Harris and his wife, Alix, selling their personally owned vineyard, to raise the funds to buy out their partners.

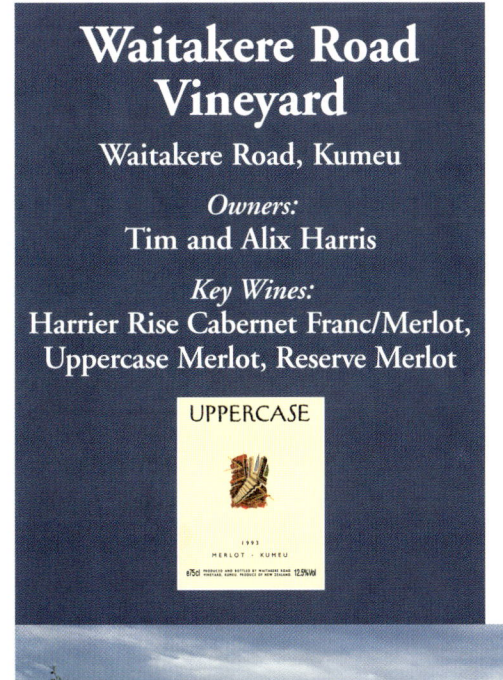

The 1994 vintage of Harrier Rise is instantly seductive with, for the first time, Cabernet Franc rather than Cabernet Sauvignon predominant. This is a robust wine with a lovely blend of power and approachability.

In Tim Harris' eyes, Kumeu is Merlot country. His strapping, dark Reserve Merlot 1993 is bursting with blackberry, spice and slightly meaty flavours, supple and lush. For drinking in its youth, it's hard to beat the Uppercase Merlot, a fleshy red with firm, well-integrated tannins and spicy, rich flavour.

Waitakere Road Vineyard

Waitakere Road, Kumeu

Owners:
Tim and Alix Harris

Key Wines:
Harrier Rise Cabernet Franc/Merlot, Uppercase Merlot, Reserve Merlot

Tim Harris makes sturdy, harmonious, smooth reds that draw you back for a second glass . . . and a third . . .

HENDERSON

In the shadow of the Waitakere Ranges are grouped several of the oldest wineries in the country. Henderson, 20 kilometres west of Auckland city, has one of the largest clusters of wineries in New Zealand; 25 winemakers based their operations here in 1996. Strung out along Lincoln Road and Henderson Valley Road, and nestled in the surrounding hills, all are small or medium-sized. (Corbans retains a head office and shop, but no winery, here.) The oldest, Pleasant Valley, produced its first wine in 1902 from vines planted last century.

A flourishing Dalmatian community has imprinted its energetic, wine-loving way of life on the district. Although winemaking in New Zealand is no longer a Dalmatian preserve, here, numerically at least, they still prevail. Winery names with a distinctively Dalmatian ring abound – Babich, Soljans, Mazuran's, Sapich, Vodanovich.

Generally, these Dalmatian vineyards began life as small mixed holdings of fruit trees, vines and vegetables. Dalmatian settlers, who had lived on peasant farms in Dalmatia, typically saved funds on the northern gumfields and then looked for self-sufficiency. Cheap parcels of land were available for purchase in the Henderson-Oratia area and the large Auckland market beckoned.

Since 1960 these holdings have shifted towards specialisation in market-gardening, orcharding or winemaking. Also there has been a gradual shift of vine plantings away from Henderson itself. Back in 1960, 80 per cent of Auckland's vineyards and orchards were in Henderson and Oratia. Later, the north-western motorway opened West Auckland up to the pressures of urban expansion and reduced the land available for viticulture.

Henderson suffers from serious physical and climatic handicaps for grapegrowing. The rainfall, rising steeply from the city westwards to the Waitakeres, is far from ideal for viticulture. The plentiful rains, in association with high humidity, create ideal conditions for fungal diseases, especially during the critical February–April ripening period. The heavy clay soils drain poorly and are slow to warm up in spring.

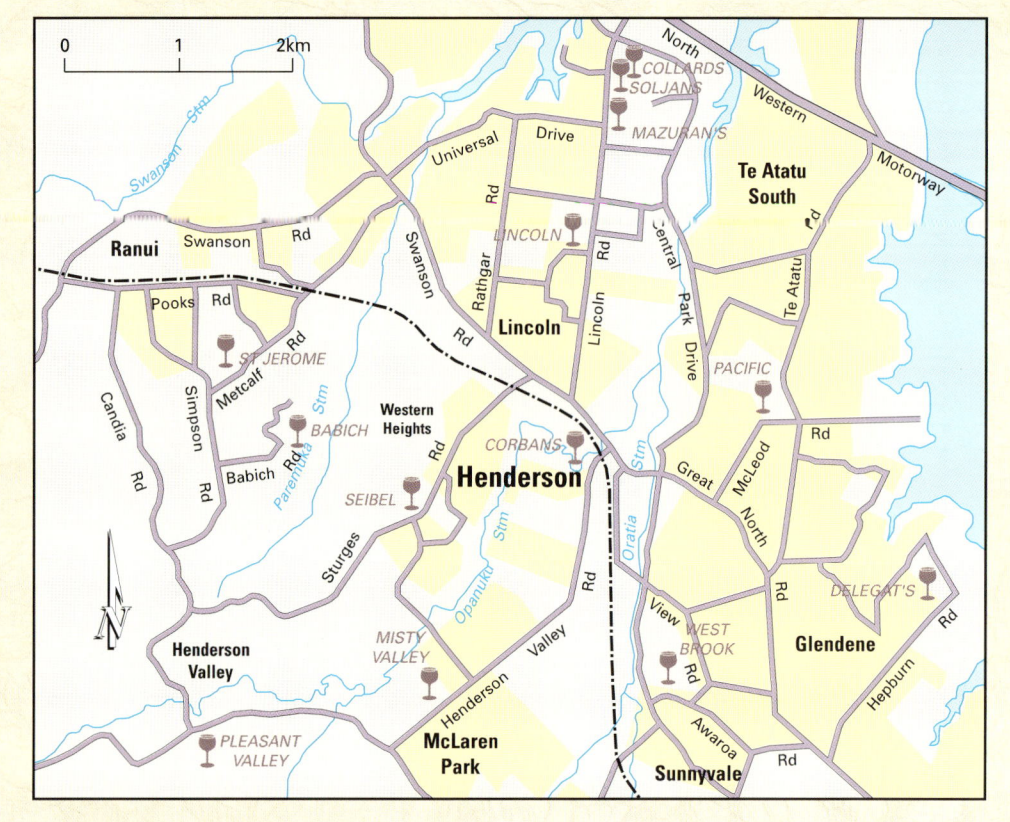

The past decade has been notable for the closure of the large Penfolds and Corbans wineries, the demise of smaller companies such as Bellamour (once called Balic Estate, and before that, Golden Sunset) and Windy Hill, and the lack of visible progress at such wineries as Mayfair, Mazuran's and Fino Valley.

Yet with three prestigious wineries – Babich, Collards and Delegat's – retaining their operations here, backed up by many other reliable producers, the Henderson wine trail still has a multitude of vinous delights for the wine lover.

Only a few of the finest wines on sale are made from Henderson grapes, but such consistently impressive estate-grown labels as Collards Barrique Fermented Sémillon, St Jerome Cabernet Sauvignon/Merlot and Pleasant Valley Signature Selection Pinotage show what can be achieved.

Babich, a long-established, middle-sized, family-owned Henderson winery, enjoys a reputation for wines of consistent quality sold at razor-sharp prices. Take the Marlborough Sauvignon Blanc. The first three vintages (1991 to 1993) won gold medals at home and abroad, yet the latest releases are priced below $13. Such bargains can obscure the fact that the top Babich wines – notably the steely, slowly evolving Irongate Chardonnay, powerful yet subtle Mara Estate Sauvignon and dark, concentrated, firm-structured Irongate Cabernet/Merlot – rank among the finest in the country.

In 1910, as a boy of 14, Josip (Joe) Babich left Dalmatia to join his four brothers toiling in the gumfields of the Far North. His first wine was produced in 1916. At Kaikino, on the last stretch of land leading to Cape Reinga, he grew grapes, trod them with his feet, and opened a wine-shop.

The shift to the Henderson Valley came in 1919. On a 24-hectare wilderness property, Joe milked cows, grew vegetables, established a small orchard – and planted classical Meunier vines. During the Second World War, winemaking slowly became the family's major business activity. Josip died in 1983, one of the 'grand old men' of the New Zealand wine industry.

Of Josip and Mara Babich's five children, three are involved in the family winery. For several decades the two brothers, Peter and Joe, neatly divided the company's tasks between them, with Peter as general manager and Joe as winemaker. Joe has recently assumed responsibility for the administration, enabling Peter, in his sixties, to ease back, although he is still actively involved in the company. Their sister, Maureen, works in the office. Neill Culley, a highly versatile Roseworthy College winemaking graduate and Master of Business Administration who has worked previously as Babich's assistant winemaker and marketing manager, now oversees the production side of the business with Joe.

The rolling loam-clay soils of the beautiful 20-hectare estate vineyard, the largest in Henderson, are planted principally in Chardonnay, Pinotage and Pinot Noir. The Babich brothers, with their minority partners in Fernhill Holdings, also own two vineyards in Hawke's Bay: a 14-hectare block in Korokipo Road, Fernhill, planted in Chardonnay, Riesling, Sylvaner, Cabernet Sauvignon and Merlot; and a 25-hectare block in Gimblett Road, where Cabernet Sauvignon, Merlot, Syrah, Cabernet Franc, Chenin Blanc, Sauvignon Blanc and Chardonnay are cultivated.

Babich, in partnership with an investor, also owns another vineyard in the stony, exceptionally free-draining Gimblett Road area, where Cabernet Sauvignon, Merlot, Pinotage and Gewürztraminer are grown. The acclaimed Irongate vineyard in Gimblett Road is also exclusively contracted to Babich.

What is the Babich winemaking philosophy? The rangy, modest Joe Babich is one of the country's most experienced winemakers, with over 30 vintages under his belt, and currently chairman of judges at the Air New Zealand Wine Awards. 'In terms of winemaker influence, I try to have a minimum input,' says Babich. 'The vineyard produces a certain style of wine; I don't try to force a style on it. For instance, our Henderson estate produces a light style of Pinot Noir, so we leave it at that. And our Chardonnays are usually fruit-driven; we don't favour heaps of buttery malolactic influence and lashings of oak.'

Joe Babich's wines are refined rather than blockbuster in style and always well balanced, with immense drinkability. Classic Dry, the popular label which has evolved from the older Dry White, is light, crisp and bone-dry. Fumé Vert ('smoky-green') a nettley, tangy, dryish blend of Sémillon, Sauvignon Blanc and Chardonnay, and the buoyant, supple Pinotage/Cabernet are also strong sellers in the sub-ten dollars market.

Babich Wines
Babich Road, Henderson

Owners:
The Babich family

Key Wines:
Irongate Chardonnay, Cabernet/Merlot; Mara Estate Sauvignon, Chardonnay, Merlot, Cabernet Sauvignon, Syrah; East Coast Chardonnay, Fumé Vert, Classic Dry, Ocean Blue, Marlborough Sauvignon Blanc, Hawke's Bay Sauvignon Blanc, Pinotage/Cabernet

Brothers Peter (left) and Joe Babich produce top-flight Hawke's Bay wines under the Irongate and Mara Estate labels.

The tank-fermented, barrel-matured East Coast Chardonnay, grown in Gisborne, Hawke's Bay and Marlborough, offers good value, and the Gisborne Gewürztraminer and Hawke's Bay Riesling are both more classy than their modest price tags would suggest. The recently launched Ocean Blue is a flavourful, fractionally sweet blended wine, citrusy and gently spicy.

Irongate wines have been a major success story, both the Chardonnay *(see panel)* and Cabernet/Merlot. The red, made in the classic claret style with rich cassis, spice and strong oak flavours, braced by taut tannins, ages gracefully; the 1987 vintage is currently perfumed and supple and the 1989 impressively rich, concentrated and complex.

Babich's heavy investment in Hawke's Bay

vineyards has borne fruit recently in the success of its Mara Estate selection of mid priced varietals. Named in honour of Mara Babich, the company matriarch who died in 1994, the wines are all dry, full-bodied, oak-matured and bottle-aged prior to release, in a style specifically designed to complement food.

The citrusy, slightly buttery, instantly appealing Mara Estate Chardonnay offers a vivid style contrast to its more austere Irongate stablemate. The mouth-filling, rich-flavoured, barrel-fermented Mara Estate Sauvignon is an arresting beauty with outstanding depth. The trio of Mara Estate reds (Merlot, Syrah and Cabernet Sauvignon) are robust and richly flavoured, even in cooler vintages, reflecting the superior ripening ability of vineyards planted in the Gimblett Road shingle country.

Most Babich wines are grown in the North Island, but Marlborough wines are also starting to flow. The sharply priced Marlborough Sauvignon Blanc is typically deep-scented, with lush, ripe fruit and racy acidity.

What lies at the root of the Babich tradition of offering fine wine at bargain prices? 'Dad's winemaking principles had integrity – he never underestimated the customer,' recalls Joe Babich. 'When New Zealand wine was still hard to sell, if he got a customer, he sought to keep him. And he never believed that wine was only for special occasions, so it had to be affordable.'

BABICH IRONGATE CHARDONNAY

Steely, intensely flavoured, lean, Irongate is one of New Zealand's most subtle, classically proportioned and long-lived Chardonnays. The first vintage, 1985, won a gold medal and the Vintners Trophy as the top-scoring current vintage dry white wine at the 1985 National Wine Competition; a feat repeated in 1987.

Shingly, arid, inhospitable – that's the first impression you get of the Irongate vineyard, planted in an old bed of the Ngaruroro River. In these bony soils, the vines develop small, open canopies of foliage, giving the ripening berries maximum exposure to the sun. The typical smallness of the berries – giving a high skin to juice ratio in the 'must' – is a key factor behind the flavour concentration in the wine.

Fermented and lees-aged for six months in predominantly new French oak barriques, the wine is typically restrained in its youth, only hinting at the richness it later unfolds. 'It's a fine, elegant wine with power that builds with age,' says Joe Babich. 'We don't normally give it a malolactic fermentation, which can be used to lower acidity or modify flavour; Irongate doesn't need either.'

The penetratingly flavoured, vigorous, beautifully balanced 1992 vintage is 'exactly the style I'm aiming at,' says Babich. 'It's got ripe fruit quality, acidity, a fair measure of alcohol, flintiness, and the oak doesn't dominate.' The wine typically peaks at around five years old, but holds its form well for a decade; the earthy 1985 and lusher, toasty 1986 are still delicious.

In 1996, Lionel Collard celebrated his 50th vintage: 'My mother always said I had the obstinacy of the weak-minded,' he chuckles. Collard's resolution and perfectionist approach to winemaking have paid rich dividends, for the family winery he heads consistently produces some of the classiest Rieslings, Chenin Blancs and Chardonnays in the country.

The Collards winery lies just off the north-western motorway in Henderson's traffic-clogged Lincoln Road. Founder John Collard, an English berry-fruit expert, came to New Zealand as an orchard instructor for the Department of Agriculture. He purchased the present Lincoln Road site in 1910, planting it in stone and pip fruits. Although grapes were cultivated at Collard's 'Sutton Baron' property – named after the village in Kent where for generations the Collard family had grown fruit and hops – initially they were for eating, not wine.

John Collard married Dorothy Averill in 1915. Between 1928 and 1963, Dorothy's brothers ran the Averill winery, just along Lincoln Road. At the urging of their uncles (the Averill brothers) in 1946 John Collard's sons, Lionel and Brian, started crushing their own wines. Until 1964, when the present Collards winery was built, Collards wines were always fermented at the Averill cellars.

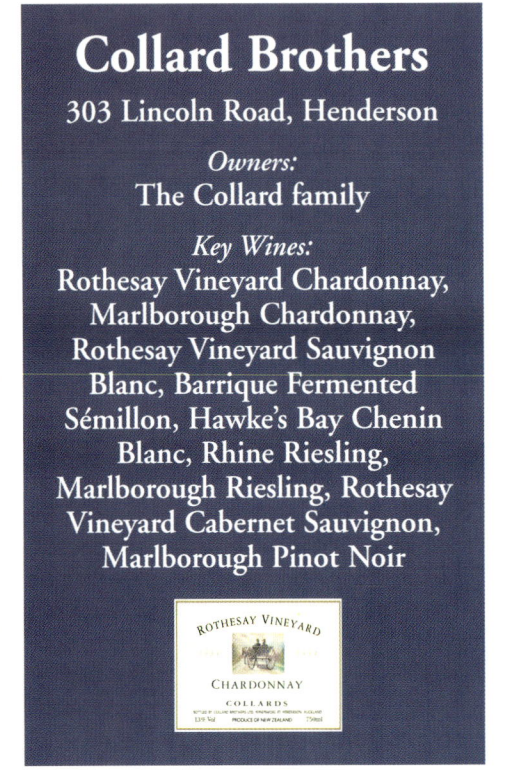

Today, Lionel and his sons, Bruce and Geoffrey, neatly divide the myriad tasks of a modern winery between them. Geoffrey, who once worked for three years in the Mosel, oversees the grapegrowing; Bruce is the talented, self-effacing winemaker; Lionel controls the company's financial administration, sales and public relations.

Steering the winery's transition from a fortified to table wine producer was the greatest challenge of Collard's career. 'In the late 1960s, I could see that we couldn't compete on the world market with golden sherry. So we selected Riesling, Gewürztraminer, Müller-Thurgau, Merlot vines and made some of the first plantings of those varieties in Auckland. My greatest thrill

Collard Brothers
303 Lincoln Road, Henderson

Owners:
The Collard family

Key Wines:
Rothesay Vineyard Chardonnay, Marlborough Chardonnay, Rothesay Vineyard Sauvignon Blanc, Barrique Fermented Sémillon, Hawke's Bay Chenin Blanc, Rhine Riesling, Marlborough Riesling, Rothesay Vineyard Cabernet Sauvignon, Marlborough Pinot Noir

was when we were awarded the first gold medal in New Zealand for a Riesling [Collards 1978]; I planted the vines myself.'

The Collard holding in Lincoln Road, originally 25 hectares, has been decimated by the construction of the surrounding roads; only two hectares are still in vines. The Collards' major company-owned plantings are now in the Waikoukou Valley, near Matua Valley, where the 15-hectare Rothesay Vineyard has yielded a string of distinguished Chardonnays and Sauvignon Blancs. About half of the winery's grapes are purchased from growers in Hawke's Bay, Te Kauwhata and Marlborough.

Chardonnay, with four labels, is a focal point of the range. The Collards style places its accent on deep, sustained fruit flavours and well-judged wood handling. Rothesay Vineyard Chardonnay, the flagship, is a powerful, robust wine with exceptionally concentrated citrusy flavours, fleshed out with quality oak. The Marlborough Chardonnay is an elegant, fruit-driven style, appetisingly crisp. The mid-priced Hawke's Bay Chardonnay is sturdy and full-flavoured, with a touch of barrel-ferment complexity. Blakes Mill Chardonnay, a bottom-tier blend of Auckland and other fruit, is fashioned in a fresh, lightly wooded, drink-young style.

Collards Rieslings are regularly in this country's top drawer. The medium Rhine Riesling, typically a three-way regional blend of Auckland, Hawke's Bay and Marlborough fruit, displays a wealth of floral/citric Riesling scents, mouth-watering sugar/acid balance and impressive flavour delicacy. The Marlborough Riesling is drier and more penetratingly flavoured. Collards are proven Riesling masters and the modest way they charge for it makes it one of this country's top value-for-money buys.

Over half a century, Lionel Collard and his family have built their Henderson winery into one of New Zealand's most highly regarded producers of Chardonnay, Riesling and Chenin Blanc.

Collards Private Bin Dry White (the original, recently resurrected name of the wine for several years called Private Bin White Burgundy) is strong in body and flavour and cheap to buy. This blend of Chenin Blanc's fruitiness and tangy acidity and Chardonnay's rich flavour and fullness is a happy one.

Collards Rothesay Vineyard Sauvignon Blanc is a robust, lush style with ripe, searching melon and lime-like flavours. It is partnered by a verdant, vigorously crisp, fresh Marlborough Sauvignon Blanc. The Barrique-Fermented Sémillon is a distinctive, estate-grown, oak-aged wine with restrained herbal flavours and lees-aging richness in a complex, subtle style.

In the past, Collards' reds lacked the distinction of the whites, but of late the standard has risen. Rothesay Vineyard Cabernet Sauvignon, launched from the 1990 vintage, is full-flavoured, spicy and firm, although slightly green-edged and austere in cooler vintages. The Marlborough Pinot Noir is a weighty style, impressively fragrant, cherryish, complex and velvety.

Collards produces about 25,000 cases per year, sold in New Zealand, the United Kingdom, Australia, Canada and Hong Kong. A small winery, it enjoys a deservedly big reputation.

COLLARDS HAWKE'S BAY CHENIN BLANC

If forced to pick one New Zealand white wine to drink every night, I'd choose Collards Hawke's Bay Chenin Blanc. From one vintage to the next, this is a delightfully rich-scented, pineappley-ripe, vibrantly fruity dry wine, with a price-tag that makes it an irresistible buy.

Obviously well-ripened fruit, grown in Hawke's Bay (predominantly) and Te Kauwhata, is fermented in stainless steel tanks and briefly matured in seasoned French oak casks. Given Chenin Blanc's chequered history in New Zealand, why is the Collard wine so consistently good?

'We encourage our growers to limit their crop, leaf-pluck and do all the things we do to our own fruit,' says Lionel Collard. 'And site selection is crucial; Chenin Blanc doesn't like too rich a soil. When it was first planted in Gisborne, it grew like a son-of-a-bitch. Someone once said they couldn't tell the difference between its brix [sugar] and acid levels.' At first grown in Forest Hill Road, Henderson, the wine was later based on fruit from Ross Goodin's vineyard in Te Kauwhata, and is now principally of Hawke's Bay origin.

Fresh-scented and zesty in its youth, after three or four years the wine softens, growing richer, toasty and honeyish. If the Chenin Blanc variety ever wins the respect in New Zealand it is accorded in other parts of the world, the Collards will deserve much of the credit.

Corbans in 1996 claimed a whopping 33 per cent share of all New Zealand wine sold in this country. A leviathan company, Corbans owns vineyards in the Hawke's Bay and Marlborough regions, wineries in Te Kauwhata, Gisborne, Hawke's Bay and Marlborough; and a headquarters and final blending, bottling and warehousing centre in Auckland. Under its key brands – Corbans, Stoneleigh Vineyard, Longridge of Hawke's Bay, Cottage Block, Robard @ Butler and Cooks – it markets a great diversity of labels: five different Sauvignon Blancs, seven different Cabernet Sauvignon and Merlot-based reds, 12 different Chardonnays.

For forty years, the adroit management of the Corban family ensured their domination of the New Zealand wine industry. From its humble beginnings as a 1.5-hectare vineyard founded by Lebanese immigrant Assid Abraham Corban at Henderson in 1902, the winery flourished through prohibition and depression and early established itself as a household name. But today the company is Corbans only in name, being a wholly owned subsidiary of DB Group Limited, itself owned by Singapore-based Asia Pacific Breweries Limited, controlled by Dutch brewer Heineken NV.

Assid Corban, a stonemason from the village of Shweir on the flanks of Mt Lebanon, inland from Beirut, arrived in New Zealand in 1892. He travelled the goldfields and mining towns of the North Island peddling ornaments and fancy goods, then set up as a dealer in Auckland's Queen Street. Two years later, he sent for his wife Najibie and sons Khaleel and Wadier to join him.

Corban's 'Mt Lebanon Vineyards' started with the 1902 purchase (for £320) of four hectares of Henderson gumland, complete with a small cottage and a few Isabella vines. His strong ambition to produce wine – a family tradition back in Lebanon – led Corban to establish a small vineyard: Black Hamburghs for the table and such classic varieties as Chasselas, Hermitage (Syrah) and Cabernet Sauvignon for winemaking; no Albany Surprise – that, said Assid Corban, was a vine suitable only for lazy winegrowers. At the first Corban vintage in the new country in 1908, the fruit was crushed by hand with a wooden club and an open hogshead used as the fermenting vat.

A small white brick building, still standing at the entrance to Corbans' headquarters, bears testimony to the marketing problems Corban immediately encountered. West Auckland voted 'dry' in 1908, denying him the right to sell his wine directly from his cellar. A railwayman's cottage, standing only a few metres away across the railway tracks in a 'wet' electorate, was pressed into service as a sales depot until 1914, when the surviving white building was erected. This was later superseded by a sales outlet in Auckland city.

By 1916 son Wadier had assumed the duties of winemaker. At the New Zealand and South Seas Exhibition 1925–26, Wadier's Corbans port won first place. Khaleel took charge of sales, travelling the length of the country in an old Dodge van, building up a strong trade in tonic and restorative wines.

Although the arrival of a rotary hoe in 1934, and a caterpillar tractor soon after, greatly eased the vineyard toil, by all accounts, until his death from a stroke in 1941, Assid Abraham Corban remained a patriarch in the Old Testament mould, and a strong believer in the virtues of hard work. Najibie, too, until her death in 1957, remained in close touch with all aspects of management.

When the wine boom began in earnest in the 1960s, Corbans' plantings leap-frogged from the Henderson Valley to Riverlea, Kumeu and Taupaki, and later contracts were negotiated with growers in Auckland and Gisborne. Alex Corban, a grandson of Assid Abraham, demonstrated a strong flair for technical innovation. As Corbans' production manager from 1952 to 1976, he was the first winemaker in the country to adopt such modern technical wizardry as cultured yeasts (1949), stainless steel tanks (1958), and pressure fermentations at controlled temperatures (Corbans Dry White 1962). Premiere Cuvée, launched in 1962, was the first 'Charmat' (tank-fermented) sparkling wine, and Corbans' 1964 vintage was New Zealand's first commercial Pinotage.

To reinforce the company's economic base, A.A. Corban and Sons admitted a 19 per cent shareholding by wine and spirit merchants. But when the powerful challenge from Montana emerged in the late 1960s, the Corban family's own financial resources proved insufficient to pay for the huge expansion necessary if the company was to retain its ascendancy. Rothmans (later renamed Magnum Corporation and then DB Group) became a shareholder and steadily increased its influence; by 1979 the Corban family had altogether lost its financial control. By selling its wine interests, historian Dick Scott has written, the Corban family

---

Corbans Wines

Great North Road, Henderson

Owner:
DB Group Limited

Key Wines:
Corbans Cottage Block Marlborough Chardonnay, Gisborne Chardonnay, Hawke's Bay Chardonnay, Marlborough Noble Rhine Riesling, Marlborough Pinot Noir, Marlborough Merlot/Cabernet Sauvignon, Hawke's Bay Cabernet Sauvignon/Franc; **Corbans Private Bin** Marlborough Chardonnay, Gisborne Chardonnay, Amberley Rhine Riesling, Hawke's Bay Pinot Noir, Hawke's Bay Cabernet Sauvignon; **Cooks Winemaker's Reserve** Chardonnay, Cabernet Sauvignon; **Huntaway** Reserve Gisborne Sémillon, Pinot Gris, Chardonnay, Merlot; **Stoneleigh Vineyard** Chardonnay, Sauvignon Blanc, Rhine Riesling, Cabernet Sauvignon; **Longridge of Hawke's Bay** Chardonnay, Oak Aged Sauvignon Blanc, Gewürztraminer, Cabernet Sauvignon/Merlot; **Corbans Estate** Gisborne Chardonnay, Gisborne Muscat, Marlborough Sauvignon Blanc, Marlborough Rhine Riesling, Marlborough Gewürztraminer; **Robard @ Butler** Gisborne Mendoza Chardonnay, Gisborne Sauvignon Blanc, Marlborough Rhine Riesling, **White Label** Chardonnay/Chenin Blanc, Sauvignon Blanc/Sémillon, Müller-Thurgau; Amadeus Méthode Champenoise, Diva Marlborough Cuvée, Waimanu; **International Cellars** Bakano, Chasseur, Italiano Spumante, Liebestraum, Montel Sauterne, St Amand, Velluto Rosso, Cellarmans sherries and ports

Under chief executive Noel Scanlan, who joined the company 22 years ago, Corbans now produces many of New Zealand's greatest wines, with a host of gold medals and trophies to prove it.

'participated in the first share-out in its history. Individual members drew on the first fruits of seventy-five years of denial.'

Corbans planted new vineyards at Gisborne in 1968 and three years later sited a second winery there. Subsequently plantings spread up the East Coast to Tolaga Bay, and also to Te Kauwhata. Rothmans, after gaining full ownership of Corbans in 1979, embarked on a multi-million dollar upgrading and expansion programme. New winemaking equipment was purchased and in 1980 the Stoneleigh and Settlement vineyards in Marlborough were planted in classic *vinifera* grape varieties. Corbans' soaring prestige in the past decade has been strongly assisted by the outstanding fruit coming on stream from these Marlborough vineyards.

In 1987 Corbans bought the assets of the ailing wine company Cooks/McWilliam's Limited for $20 million; both companies had already been subsidiaries of Brierley Investments Limited. According to Paul Treacher, who was appointed general manager of the enlarged company, Corbans' acquisition of Cooks/McWilliam's 'represented an essential major rationalisation within the local winemaking industry . . . it is essential that local large-scale winemakers become and remain as cost efficient as their counterparts abroad'.

Long one of Corbans' movers and shakers, Noel Scanlan in 1991 was promoted from marketing manager to the company's top post. Brand marketing is a Scanlan specialty. After 22 years at Corbans, he draws his greatest satisfaction from the success of brands like Stoneleigh Vineyard, Longridge of Hawke's Bay and Robard @ Butler ('they're my babies'), and the longevity of old Corbans brands such as Montel Sauterne (sic) and Velluto Rosso, 'still around and strong'.

Under Scanlan's direction, Corbans is in 'expansion mode'. In 1993 the company acquired full control of the sleek, silvery Marlborough Cellars, previously owned jointly with Mildara-Blass of Australia, and renamed it Corbans Marlborough Winery. Also in 1993, it bought out its Japanese partners in the St Niege vineyard, over the fence from the Stoneleigh Vineyard. New presses, dry goods stores and expanded oak purchases at each winery have recently absorbed millions of dollars.

About 12 per cent of Corbans' total grape requirements are company-grown. However, 50 per cent of the premium varietal grapes which avalanche into Corbans' crushers are grown in the company's own vineyards. The Stoneleigh and Moorlands vineyards (150ha), adjacent to Corbans Marlborough Winery, and the three Longridge vineyards (120ha) in Hawke's Bay – at Omarunui, Tuki Tuki and Haumoana – are the key sources of its flagship varietals. Further grapes are purchased from contract growers in Gisborne, Hawke's Bay, Marlborough and (in small volumes) North Canterbury.

Corbans' Gisborne, Hawke's Bay and Marlborough wineries all produce wine to a finished state, needing only a final filtering before being bottled in Auckland. The historic Henderson winery was sold in 1991, and its blending, bottling and warehousing operations transferred across Auckland to East Tamaki. The head office and retail shop, however, have stayed put at Henderson. The Te Kauwhata winery established by Cooks is used as a 'satellite' winery for bulk storage and blending.

For decades Corbans has been the second largest wine company in New Zealand. Vertical integration helps: DB Group owns a giant liquor production, distribution and retail empire, including Dominion Breweries, the distributor Allied Liquor Merchants, and many of the stores (others are privately owned) in the Liquorland, Robbie Burns and Green Bottle chains.

In 1993, Corbans set itself the formidable task of capturing half of the total bottled wine market in New Zealand by 1997. That goal will not be achieved, but Corbans' ambition, according to Scanlan, is still 'to dominate the bottled wine segment. We're not chasing Montana in volume terms; we're driving our sales of bottled wines, not casks.' The popular Corbans Wine and Food Challenge (for restaurateurs), Corbans Culinary Quest (for amateur chefs) and Corbans Wine Game (wine options fun for groups) reflect the company's strong commitment to educating consumers and wine retailers as a way to stimulate the sales of its premium, bottled wines.

Corbans' quality is strong throughout the various price categories, and the best wines are brilliant. The 1995 Air New Zealand Wine Awards was a Corbans bonanza. Of 12 trophies awarded, five went to Corbans: Amadeus Méthode Champenoise 1990 won the trophies for champion sparkling wine and reserve (runner-up) wine of the show; Stoneleigh Vineyard Rhine Riesling 1991 won the riesling trophy; Corbans Cottage Block Gisborne Chardonnay 1994 won the chardonnay trophy and the prestigious trophy for the champion wine of the show. Corbans also dominated the gold medal stakes, capturing 12 out of the 41 awarded.

In Corbans' diverse, recently restructured hierarchy of brands, the Cottage Block range, launched in 1994 with wines dating back to the 1991–93 vintages, sits at the top of the tree. Named after an area in Corbans' Marlborough vineyards, adjacent to an old cottage, the wines are 'handcrafted from hand-picked grapes [and] made in the true style of boutique winemaking'. Few vintages of each wine have been released, but as the summit of the Corbans range, they include some of New Zealand's greatest wines. Among the early highlights have been the arrestingly fragrant, robust and savoury Cottage Block Gisborne

Chardonnay 1994, the muscular, seductively rich and supple Cottage Block Marlborough Merlot/Cabernet Sauvignon 1994, and the ravishingly perfumed and raisiny Cottage Block Marlborough Noble Rhine Riesling 1991.

Corbans' buff-coloured Private Bin label, in the past reserved for the company's flagship wines, but now positioned below Cottage Block, is still a pointer to highly distinguished wines. Weighty, citrusy and mealy, the Private Bin Marlborough Chardonnay displays superb flavour intensity and a steely, lasting finish. The Private Bin Gisborne Chardonnay is a lusher, more forward style, deep-scented, with rich, melony, biscuity flavours. Equally classy is the Private Bin Amberley Rhine Riesling, until recently sold under the Robard @ Butler label. Grown in North Canterbury, this is a distinctively spicy and complex wine – these are rare qualities in Riesling.

Two top wines are still marketed under the Cooks label, now largely phased out in New Zealand, but widely used in the UK. Cooks Winemaker's Reserve Chardonnay, grown in Hawke's Bay, is robust, citrusy, toasty and built to last. Cooks Winemaker's Reserve Cabernet Sauvignon is a classic, concentrated Hawke's Bay claret-style red, blackcurrant-like, cedary and tautly structured.

The Huntaway label is reserved for limited edition Gisborne wines. The first two releases – an intriguingly ripe and subtle, oak-aged 1995 Sémillon and perfumed, weighty, flavour-packed 1994 Merlot – are both outstanding. The Huntaway range also features a Pinot Gris and Chardonnay.

Corbans has a much narrower range of sparkling wines than Montana. The low-priced Italiano Spumante, based on Dr Hogg Muscat grapes, is deliciously scented, light, sweet and frothy. Diva Marlborough Cuvée is a medium-dry style, floral, citrusy and invigoratingly crisp. Amadeus Méthode Champenoise, based on Hawke's Bay-grown Pinot Noir and Chardonnay, is impressively lively, citrusy, yeasty and full-flavoured. This is the best sub-$20 bubbly on the market, and is now emerging as one of the country's finest sparklings.

Of the quartet of wines marketed under the Stoneleigh Vineyard label, the leafy-green, light Cabernet Sauvignon is the least distinguished. The lemony, slightly savoury Chardonnay is very solid, but the twin peaks of the range are Stoneleigh Vineyard Sauvignon Blanc, which bursts with fresh, tangy, gooseberry and cut-grass flavours, and Stoneleigh Vineyard Rhine Riesling, with its piercing lemon/lime fruit flavours, tinged with honey, racy acidity and ability to flourish in the bottle for at least a decade.

The Longridge of Hawke's Bay quartet features a citric-flavoured Chardonnay with a delicate oak underlay; a fresh, limey, tangy Oak Aged Sauvignon Blanc; a rich, well-spiced Gewürztraminer; and a full-bodied, spicy, American oak-perfumed Cabernet Sauvignon/Merlot.

The Corbans Estate range, launched in 1995, is pitched squarely at the fastest-growing section of the wine market: varietal white wines in the $8 to $14 segment. The first five releases – Rhine Riesling, Sauvignon Blanc, Chardonnay, Gewürztraminer and Muscat – all display clearcut varietal character and a touch of class rare in their price category. Waimanu, a tangy, off-dry, slightly herbaceous blend of Sauvignon Blanc, Riesling and Chenin Blanc, is also sharply priced. A Chardonnay/Chenin Blanc, Sauvignon Blanc/Sémillon and Müller-Thurgau are sold in the even cheaper White Label range.

Corbans' subsidiary company, International Cellars, also markets a range of popular cask wines, such as Liebestraum and Chasseur, both light, fruity, slightly sweet whites; the distinctly sweet, raspberryish Velluto Rosso; and the unabashedly sweet Montel Sauterne. When the supply of suitable local grapes is low, these cask wines are often a trans-Tasman blend. Sun Country fruit juices, Blue Hawaii wine cooler, and fortified wines under the Cellarmans and Riverlea labels, are all part of Corbans' torrential output.

Since it began exporting in 1963, Corbans has shipped more than two million cases of wine overseas, and currently exports about 250,000 cases per year. The UK, the largest market, absorbs over 150,000 cases annually, principally of Cooks wines in the sub-£5 category, and Stoneleigh Vineyard wines at over £6. Other key markets are Sweden (where Stoneleigh Vineyard Sauvignon Blanc commands $NZ75 per bottle in Stockholm restaurants), Finland, the Netherlands, Belgium, Germany, Canada and the eastern seaboard of the United States.

'Walk into almost any liquor store in Manhattan,' Corbans reports, 'and you'll find Stoneleigh Vineyard and Longridge wines on the shelf.'

STONELEIGH VINEYARD RHINE RIESLING

This is a rare beast – a consistently top-flight, much-awarded wine that you can buy at any corner wine store at an irresistibly low price. Delicious in its youth, it is also a must for every New Zealand wine lover's cellar.

The Stoneleigh style of Riesling is floral and lemony, with a touch of residual sugar and a proven ability to unfold for many years, growing more honeyish and subtle with maturity. The best fruit off 16-year-old vines in the pebbly, free-draining Stoneleigh Vineyard is reserved for the label. 'The vines are well-balanced,' says Corbans' Marlborough winemaker, Alan McCorkindale. 'They're not over-vigorous and at an average of seven to nine tonnes per hectare, they certainly don't over-crop.'

When handling the wine, McCorkindale strives for the right balance on the palate between acid, sweetness and weight (alcohol and phenolics). 'That means picking the grapes at the right time, and processing them very gently, with only free-run juice (no pressings) retained.' He's given up worrying about 'noble rot' infection. '*Botrytis* makes the wine drinkable sooner – like the 1990 and 1995 vintages – but the 1994, which had no *Botrytis* influence at all, is still developing superbly.'

The top vintages, such as 1991 and 1994, take five years to reach their peak and hold it for another five years, or even longer. Now sold in the UK in Burgundy-shape bottles ('So it doesn't look German,' reports McCorkindale), this is the most stylish of the Stoneleigh Vineyard wines – and the cheapest.

Delegat's Wine Estate at Henderson produces one of the tightest ranges in the country. Winemaker Brent Marris works exclusively with four grape varieties: Chardonnay, Sauvignon Blanc, Merlot and Cabernet Sauvignon. Why not Riesling, Gewürztraminer or Pinot Noir?

'After the [glut-induced] vine-pull scheme of 1986, there was a lot of talk about 10 years ahead,' recalls Marris. 'Jim [Delegat, the company head] wanted to establish a foundation that couldn't be rocked and felt export would be the success or failure of companies in the future. In the UK, New Zealand was recognised for two wines – Sauvignon Blanc and Chardonnay. Overseas markets weren't prepared to pay for our other wines.' So Riesling, Müller-Thurgau, Gewürztraminer and the honey-sweet Auslese were axed from the Delegat's range.

Nikola Delegat, the founder of this winery, purchased land near the Whau River, an arm of the Waitemata Harbour, in 1947. Delegat first arrived in New Zealand in 1923 but later retraced his steps to Yugoslavia, before finally establishing a four-hectare plot of vines at Henderson. If you visit the property, when you step into the concrete-block shop with its exposed beams you are entering Nikola Delegat's original winery.

With Nikola's son, Jim, and daughter, Rose, now at the helm, in the early–mid 1980s Delegat's was transformed into a quality-orientated winery with a high reputation for its bold, buttery, richly oaked Chardonnays.

Rocked by the ferocious price war of 1985–86, the family admitted Wilson Neill to a majority shareholding, but in 1991 ownership of the winery reverted entirely to Jim and Rose Delegat.

Delegat's is the only large New Zealand winery owned and run by a brother and sister team. As Jim puts it: 'Rose has great empathy and an easy rapport with people which is a huge benefit to our company, whereas my strength lies more in working out where we're going to be in the next few years with our vineyards and winemaking.' Brent Marris, Delegat's winemaker for the past 11 vintages, is also an influential figure, with a string of fine wines to his credit.

Delegat's not only specialises in just four classic varieties, the company draws grapes only from regions with a proven strength in each variety and gives each region's wines a separate brand identity. The finest Hawke's Bay wines are reserved for Delegat's Proprietors Reserve label; a mid-priced range for earlier drinking is labelled Delegat's Hawke's Bay; and two Marlborough wines are marketed under the Oyster Bay label.

Delegat's holdings in Hawke's Bay are extensive: a 25-hectare vineyard in the free-draining shingles of Gimblett Road, supplying grapes for all four wines in the Proprietors Reserve range; and a 20-hectare block on State Highway 50, backing onto Gimblett Road, planted in Chardonnay, Cabernet Sauvignon and Merlot.

The Oyster Bay label burst into the limelight when the debut 1990 vintage won the Marquis de Goulaine Trophy for the best Sauvignon Blanc at the 1991 International Wine and Spirit Competition in London. The company-owned Oyster Bay vineyard in Marlborough's upper Wairau Valley, covering 55 hectares, is evenly split between Sauvignon Blanc and Chardonnay.

One of the highlights of the Delegat's range is the Proprietors Reserve Sauvignon Blanc Oak Aged. Produced from the winery's ripest Sauvignon Blanc grapes, plus some greener fruit for acid structure and balance, it is half wood-fermented and all barrel-aged for up to six months. The bouquet is a lovely amalgam of ripe tropical fruit and oak; the palate is bursting with delicious, ultra-ripe pineappley fruit flavours, fleshed out by oak.

The Proprietors Reserve Cabernet Sauvignon is typically a robust, full-flavoured red with strong, blackcurrant-and-spice, firm flavours. However, the more supple, riper-tasting Proprietors Reserve Merlot has the edge; in top vintages it displays great complexity and finesse.

Delicious in its youth, the mid-price Hawke's Bay Chardonnay is oak-matured for six months, without any barrel-ferment or malolactic influence – 'We want the fruit to do the talking,' says Marris. The Hawke's Bay Cabernet/Merlot and Hawke's Bay Sauvignon Blanc are fresh, straightforward, and easy-drinking in style.

Both the Oyster Bay Chardonnay and Sauvignon Blanc are consistently classy. The Chardonnay, 75 per cent barrel-fermented, showcases Marlborough's pure, penetrating fruit flavours, with a touch of mealiness and a crisp, zingy finish. The Sauvignon Blanc is typically chock-full of lively, tropical-fruit and cut-grass flavours.

Over a third of the total output is shipped overseas, principally to the UK and Canada, but also to 'beach-head' markets in the Netherlands, Germany and Switzerland.

Delegat's Wine Estate

Hepburn Road, Henderson

Owners:
Jim and Rose Delegat

Key Wines:
Proprietors Reserve Chardonnay, Sauvignon Blanc Oak Aged, Cabernet Sauvignon, Merlot;
Hawke's Bay Chardonnay, Sauvignon Blanc, Cabernet/Merlot;
Oyster Bay Chardonnay, Sauvignon Blanc

Jim and Rose Delegat are the only brother and sister team to head a major New Zealand winery.

DELEGAT'S PROPRIETORS RESERVE CHARDONNAY

With its glorious array of Hawke's Bay fruit flavours and deft oak handling, this is Delegat's greatest wine, with an illustrious track record in show judgings.

Winemaker Brent Marris aims for 'an elegantly assertive style in which the fruit is the hero'. Hand-picked Mendoza clone (with a small amount of clone six) grapes give 'concentrated, citrusy and tropical-fruit flavours with a very ripe, weighty, glycerol character'.

Unusually for one of New Zealand's top Chardonnays, the Delegat's Proprietors Reserve is not fully barrel-fermented. Marris believes that too high a proportion of barrel fermentation would subjugate the fruit characters he so highly prizes: 'I can still get complexity from the oak treatment and the malolactic fermentation,' he says. Half the final blend is fermented and matured in casks, with regular lees stirring; the other half is tank-fermented and then aged for nine months on its yeast lees in new and one-year-old French oak barriques.

Delegat's Proprietors Reserve Chardonnay matures gracefully; the 1989 vintage was in devastating form at five years old, with exceptional richness and subtlety, and the 1990 is currently at the height of its powers. This is one of Hawke's Bay's – and New Zealand's – most consistently classy Chardonnays.

Lincoln epitomises the West Auckland cluster of long-established, family-owned, medium-sized wineries of Dalmatian origin. Founded in 1937, it initially earned a reputation for fortified wines, especially dry sherry. Now the Fredatovich family specialises in table wines, winning a strong following for its trio of rich, citrusy, soft Gisborne Chardonnays.

Peter and John Fredatovich, the third generation of the family to produce wine in Lincoln Road, took over the reins from their father, Peter, in the late 1980s. Peter Snr – awarded an MBE in 1989 for his services to viticulture – had controlled Lincoln since the 1955 retirement of his father, also called Peter.

A third key figure is winemaker Ian Trembath, who joined Lincoln after the departure of long-term winemaker Nick Chan, who made the 1985 to 1994 vintages.

Trembath works with fruit drawn from Auckland, Gisborne, Hawke's Bay and Marlborough. The 2.5-hectare block ('The Home Vineyard') adjoining the winery is principally planted in Cabernet Sauvignon, with a smaller plot of Merlot, and Muscat vines (some over 40 years old) trained on overhead trellises.

Lincoln's most popular wines are the Gisborne Chardonnay, Gisborne Merlot and Marlborough Sauvignon Blanc (launched from the 1995 vintage). Lincoln Gisborne Chardonnay is a lightly oak-aged, easy-drinking style with ripe, citrusy and peachy fruit flavours, fresh and forward. The Marlborough Sauvignon Blanc is a verdant, full-flavoured, tangy mouthful. The Gisborne Merlot is fresh, fragrant and fruity – a drink-young style, plummy and smooth.

Parklands Chardonnay, grown in Chris Parker's Gisborne vineyard and fermented and lees-aged in American oak casks, is a consistently delicious wine: fragrant, toasty, rich-flavoured and forward, with a soft, creamy texture. The top-end-of-the-range Vintage Selection Chardonnay, also grown in Gisborne but fermented and lees-aged in French oak, is even more stylish, with very intense, citrusy, buttery flavour.

Chenin Blanc is a Lincoln specialty. The Hawke's Bay Chenin Blanc is a tart, vigorous, non-wooded wine with fresh, green apple flavours and racy acidity. The Chenin Blanc/Chardonnay is a lightly oaked blend, fleshy, ripe and rounded.

Grown in West Auckland, Lincoln Vintage Selection Cabernet/Merlot is one of the region's finest reds, with excellent depth of cassis, mint and oak flavours, long and taut. Dark and chunky, The Home Vineyard Cabernet/Merlot is an American oak-perfumed, full-flavoured wine, slightly less concentrated and stylish than its Vintage Selection stablemate. The bottom-tier, American oak-matured Hawke's Bay Cabernet/Merlot offers plenty of body and flavour at a modest price.

Lincoln produces about 45,000 cases of wine each year, and reports growing exports to the UK, Switzerland, Sweden and the Pacific Islands. The winery waited a long time for its first table wine gold medal, but has recently won two – for the Vintage Selection Chardonnay 1992 and Vintage Selection Cabernet/Merlot 1993.

Lincoln Vineyards

130 Lincoln Road, Henderson

Owners:
The Fredatovich family

Key Wines:
Gisborne Chardonnay, Parklands Chardonnay, Vintage Selection Chardonnay, Marlborough Sauvignon Blanc, Chenin Blanc, Chenin Blanc/Chardonnay, Rhine Riesling, Gewürztraminer, Merlot, Hawke's Bay Cabernet/Merlot, The Home Vineyard Cabernet/Merlot, Vintage Selection Cabernet/Merlot, Pioneer Port, Old Tawny Port, Anniversary Show Reserve Port

Peter Fredatovich (left) oversees Lincoln's production while his brother, John, controls the financial administration and marketing.

Pacific Vineyards

90 McLeod Road, Henderson

Owners: Michael and Millie Erceg

Key Wines: <u>Phoenix</u> Gewürztraminer, Chardonnay, Cabernet Sauvignon/Merlot; <u>Quail Farm</u> Chardonnay, Cabernet Rosé, Cabernet Sauvignon; Pale Dry Sherry, 10 Year Old Port

Millie Erceg and winemaker Steve Tubic in Pacific's four-hectare estate vineyard at Henderson, in summer entirely shrouded with nets to ward off birds.

Will Pacific, like the phoenix on its top labels, be a high flier again? The brewery built in 1990 at the West Auckland winery has recently been relocated. 'We're now treating Pacific as a stand-alone wine producer,' says Michael Erceg, the founder's son.

Mijo (Mick) Erceg, who died in 1983 aged 75, arrived in New Zealand in 1929. After several years' labour on gumfields, roads and the vineyards of other Dalmatians, he bought a small farm in McLeod Road, Henderson; by 1936 his own vines were in the ground.

Today, Michael – holder of an American doctorate in mathematics – is the majority shareholder and promotes Pacific wines through his liquor importing, production and distribution company, Independent Liquor. Millie Erceg, Mijo's widow, retains a minority shareholding and still runs the four-hectare estate vineyard and winery shop.

Steve Tubic, who worked at Corbans between 1979 and 1986, has been the winemaker since the 1987 vintage.

Pacific's output peaked a decade ago when production soared to 1500 tonnes, mostly made into cask wine and coolers. Now, having withdrawn from the cask wine market, each year it produces about 7500 cases of bottled wines.

Pacific's top wines are all marketed under the Phoenix brand. The star attraction is the Gewürztraminer, grown in the Thomas vineyard in Gisborne, which at its best is full-bloomed, concentrated, slightly sweet and pungently spicy.

Phoenix Chardonnay, Hawke's Bay-grown and fermented in French and American oak barriques, is a mid-priced wine of average-to-good quality. The estate-grown, French and American oak-matured Phoenix Cabernet Sauvignon/Merlot is a sturdy, slightly rustic red with spicy, green-edged, firm flavours.

Under its lower-priced Quail Farm brand, Pacific markets an unoaked Chardonnay, a light, slightly green-leafy Cabernet Rosé, and an unpretentious, estate-grown barrel-aged Cabernet Sauvignon.

Pleasant Valley Wines

322 Henderson Valley Road, Henderson

Owner: Stephan Yelas

Key Wines: <u>Signature Selection</u> Chardonnay, Sauvignon Blanc, Pinotage, Cabernet/Merlot, Brut; Gisborne Chardonnay, Gisborne Gewürztraminer, Gisborne Müller-Thurgau, Auckland Cabernet Sauvignon, Amontillado Sherry, Amoroso Sherry, Oloroso Sherry, Tawny Port, Founders Port

Pleasant Valley has the dual distinction of being not only the oldest surviving Dalmatian vineyard in Henderson, but also the oldest winery in the land under the continuous ownership of the same family.

Stipan Jelich, (Stephen Yelas), the founder, produced his first wine in 1902. Yelas' son, Moscow, ran the company from 1939 to 1984, and today his son, Stephan, is the owner.

The 12-hectare, hill-grown estate vineyard is established in Pinotage, Cabernet Sauvignon, Merlot and Chardonnay. The majority of the winery's fruit is bought from growers in the Auckland (Kumeu), Gisborne and Hawke's Bay regions.

Rebecca Salmond, handed the winemaking reins in early 1994, is a Roseworthy College graduate with experience in French, Chilean and Australian wineries.

Pleasant Valley markets a two-tier range of table wines. The top wines (formerly called Yelas Estate) are now labelled Signature Selection.

The best known wine is the estate-grown, multiple silver-medal and trophy-winning Signature Selection Pinotage, a vibrant, raspberryish, meaty, supple red, full of drink-young charm. Yelas explains the source of its quality: 'It's where it's grown – in a bowl on a steep, sunny, north-facing hillside. It's sheltered from the wind and gets really, really hot.' This is one of New Zealand's finest Beaujolais-style reds.

Stephan ('Steppie') Yelas and his wife, Ineke, outside the hugely popular café at New Zealand's oldest family-owned winery.

Other highlights of the Signature Selection are the oak-fermented, lees-aged Hawke's Bay Chardonnay, an elegant, citrusy wine that matures well; and the dark-hued, rich-flavoured Auckland Cabernet/Merlot, a classic claret style that demands cellaring.

Pleasant Valley's lower-priced table wines include a non-wooded delightful Gisborne Chardonnay; a copybook Gisborne Müller-Thurgau; and a chunky, chewy and firm Auckland Cabernet Sauvignon.

Of their traditional range of fortified wines, the barrel-matured Amontillado, Amoroso and Oloroso sherries are all impressively rich, mellow and lingering.

Flying from South Africa to his new job as Corbans' chief winemaker in 1980, Norbert Seibel was served an oxidised, almost undrinkable New Zealand wine. 'I thought: I can make a better wine than that.'

Born on the Rhine in Mainz, Germany, Seibel graduated in viticulture and oenology from the acclaimed Geisenheim Institute, where he met his wife, Silvia. Seibel then spent the 1970s in South Africa, firstly as chief winemaker for Nederburg, then as chief winemaker for The Bergkelder, before joining Corbans.

When in 1987 he launched his first releases under the Seibel label, he realised his 'long-held dream to produce a small but select range of wines which combine superior taste with a healthy composition.'

For the first few years, Seibel had no winery. In early 1993, Seibel and his wife finally acquired the historic Bellamour winery in Sturges Road, Henderson.

Seibel's output is small: about 4000 cases of wine each year. He purchases all his grapes from North Island (and occasionally South Island) growers.

The three-tier Seibel range has the 'limited edition' series at the top, several vintage-dated varietal wines in the middle, and two blended, budget-priced Long River wines at the bottom.

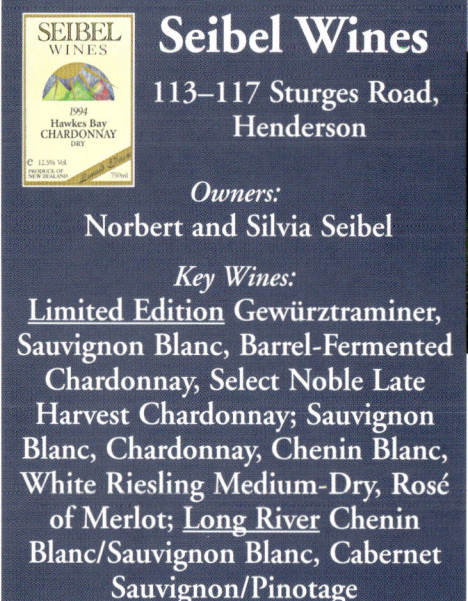

The Limited Edition range features a powerful, peachy, mealy Barrel Fermented Chardonnay from Hawke's Bay; a weighty, richly herbal and lush Hawke's Bay Sauvignon Blanc; a peppery, slightly sweet Gisborne Gewürztraminer; and a succulent, oily, honey-sweet Select Noble Late Harvest Chardonnay, made from heavily botrytised Hawke's Bay fruit.

Seibel White Riesling Medium-Dry, variously sourced from Hawke's Bay and Gisborne, is at best a compelling wine, richly scented, lively and graceful, with the ability to age well for several years. The Gisborne Chenin Blanc (Seibel made the celebrated 1976 Corbans Chenin Blanc) is a non-wooded style, typically full of zippy, tropical-fruit flavour.

Seibel Wines

113–117 Sturges Road, Henderson

Owners:
Norbert and Silvia Seibel

Key Wines:
Limited Edition Gewürztraminer, Sauvignon Blanc, Barrel-Fermented Chardonnay, Select Noble Late Harvest Chardonnay; Sauvignon Blanc, Chardonnay, Chenin Blanc, White Riesling Medium-Dry, Rosé of Merlot; Long River Chenin Blanc/Sauvignon Blanc, Cabernet Sauvignon/Pinotage

Norbert Seibel has breathed new life into the old Bellamour winery, once called Balic Estate and, before that, Golden Sunset.

Soljans, traditionally one of the best small Henderson fortified winemakers, has more recently branched out with a sound line-up of white and red varietal table wines. Bartol Soljan, grandfather of the present owner, Tony Soljan, came to New Zealand from Dalmatia in 1927, and five years later established a family vineyard in Lincoln Road. Bartol's son, Frank, bought the present site in 1937 and with his wife, Rona, established Soljans Wines. Tony Soljan's brother, Rex, maintained the vineyard and its adjacent orchard for many years, but in 1994 withdrew from the partnership.

A scene of rare beauty, Black Hamburgh table grapes trained along overhead trellises greets visitors to the Soljans winery in summer. The three-hectare estate vineyard is also planted in Cabernet Sauvignon, Merlot and Seibel 5455 (for port). Kumeu growers supply red-wine grapes, with white varieties drawn from growers in Gisborne, Hawke's Bay and Marlborough.

In the original winery, which serves today as the vineyard shop, cheerful Tony Soljan can often be found on Saturdays dispensing the fruits of his labours. Sarah Inkersell, from Hawke's Bay, has shared the winemaking duties since 1993.

This winery has long been respected as a fortified wine producer and the eight-year-old, nutty-brown, creamy-sweet Reserve Sherry, predominantly matured in totara casks, is a fine example of this wine style. The raisiny-rich, 10 to 15-year-old Pergola Sherry is even mellower, with well-aged 'rancio' complexity. The Founders Port, a 10-year-old tawny matured in small oak casks, is amber-hued, mellow, sweet and smooth.

The peaks of the table wine range are the consistently stylish, citrusy and well-balanced Barrique Selection Chardonnay, grown in Hawke's Bay; the floral, lively, semi-dry Hawke's Bay Rhine Riesling; the rich, ripe Hawke's Bay Gewürztraminer; the reward-ingly savoury and supple, meaty, lightly wooded West Auckland Pinotage; and the fragrant, French oak-matured, red berry-fruit-flavoured Cabernet/Merlot.

Tony Soljan (with winemaker Sarah Inkersell) offers contract bottling services to other wineries as well as producing his own satisfying, sharply priced wines.

Soljans Wines

263 Lincoln Road, Henderson

Owner:
Tony Soljan

Key Wines:
Barrique Selection Chardonnay, Chardonnay, Sauvignon Blanc, Gewürztraminer, Rhine Riesling, Müller-Thurgau, Pinotage, Cabernet/Merlot, Vivace Spumante, Pergola Sherry, Reserve Sherry, Founders Port

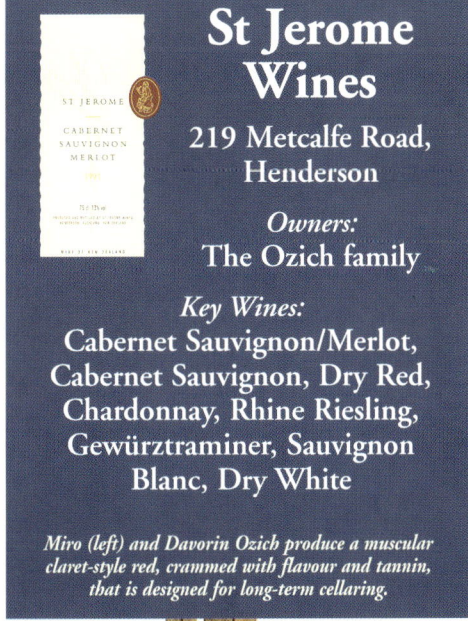

The tiny St Jerome winery lies at the top of Metcalfe Road in the foothills of the Waitakere Ranges, only a kilometre from Babich. Here, Davorin and his viticulturist brother, Miro, produce one of Auckland's finest reds: a beefy, flavour-packed, tautly tannic Cabernet Sauvignon/Merlot designed to mature well over the long haul.

The sunny, north-facing clay slope behind the winery was originally planted by Mate Ozich, Davorin and Miro's father, in the 1960s.

A pivotal step in Davorin's winemaking career came in September and October 1987 when he worked the vintage in Bordeaux, alternating his days between the fabled chateaux, Margaux and Cos d'Estournel. 'I learned that there's no magic formula in red winemaking,' recalls Davorin. 'But I came away confident about how to handle red wine.'

The eight-hectare estate vineyard is planted in 60 per cent Cabernet Sauvignon, 40 per cent Merlot. 'It's a sun-trap,' says Davorin. 'We're always a couple of brix [a measure of the grapes' sugar content] ahead of other vineyards around here.' The centre of the vineyard is bowl-shaped, protecting it from the freezing westerlies. Rain rapidly drains off the steep vineyard slope, stressing the vines in the run-up to vintage.

At the winery, the 'cap' of thick, blue-black skins is hand-plunged into the fermenting juice four times daily, and after the fermentation has subsided, the skins are kept submerged in the young wine for a further three weeks.

'We really concentrate on the skins,' says Davorin. 'During that three-week period – it's a week to a month in Bordeaux – the wine picks up a lot more colour, flavour and tannins. Then we mature the wine for a long time in oak to soften it. We've played around with cask-aging, and our best results come with increased time. The '91 spent three years in wood.'

St Jerome Cabernet Sauvignon/Merlot is the company's flagship.

The powerful tannin 'attack' typical of past vintages of the Ozich brothers' red is less evident in the more elegant and supple, but no less bold and rich-flavoured, 1991 vintage. In my experience, those previous vintages have fared better in comparative tastings with the firm, slowly evolving reds of the Medoc than the softer, more forward reds of New Zealand. Perhaps, starting with their muscular, concentrated but not austere 1991, the Ozich brothers have struck the ideal balance.

Based on grapes purchased predominantly from Hawke's Bay, St Jerome also produces a quaffing Dry White; a rounded and ripely herbal Sauvignon Blanc; a medium-dry, positively spicy Gewürztraminer; a Rhine Riesling of variable quality; a bold, barrel-fermented, peachy-ripe Chardonnay, best drunk young; a light, raspberryish, uncomplicated Dry Red; and an oak-aged, early-maturing Cabernet Sauvignon with fresh, berry-fruit flavours and soft tannins.

St Jerome Wines

219 Metcalfe Road, Henderson

Owners:
The Ozich family

Key Wines:
Cabernet Sauvignon/Merlot, Cabernet Sauvignon, Dry Red, Chardonnay, Rhine Riesling, Gewürztraminer, Sauvignon Blanc, Dry White

Miro (left) and Davorin Ozich produce a muscular claret-style red, crammed with flavour and tannin, that is designed for long-term cellaring.

The fresh, tangy, lightly wooded, melon and lime-flavoured Chenin Blanc is my favourite wine from West Brook, a small, family-owned winery in the built-up Awaroa Road area of Henderson. 'At ten dollars, it sells really well,' reports Anthony Ivicevich.

Tony Ivicevich (Anthony's father) and his father, Mick, arrived in New Zealand from their native Dalmatia in 1934. After only one year, the present property had been purchased and planted in trees and grapevines.

Today the winery is run by Anthony and his wife, Sue, who 'works more than full-time, doing the paperwork and handling sales,' says Anthony. Their son, Michael, is studying viticulture and oenology while gaining practical experience at other wineries, in preparation for his eventual return to West Brook.

The 2.5-hectare home vineyard behind the concrete-block winery is planted principally in Cabernet Sauvignon, with Merlot and a plot of Chardonnay earmarked for an estate-grown wine. White varieties are bought from growers in Gisborne, Hawke's Bay and Marlborough.

The level of production is not high – about 9000 cases of wine annually – but is gradually expanding. To symbolise the winery's switch in emphasis from fortified to table wines, Panorama, its long-standing name, was dropped in 1987 in favour of West Brook.

The label features a mill and waterfall similar to those once found in the district.

The top wines carry the Blue Ridge label, with second-tier wines called West Brook.

West Brook Winery

34 Awaroa Road, Henderson

Owner: Anthony Ivicevich

Key Wines:
Blue Ridge Sauvignon Blanc, Cabernet Sauvignon/Merlot;
West Brook Barrique Fermented Chardonnay, Sauvignon Blanc, Gewürztraminer, Riesling, Chenin Blanc, Merlot;
Panorama Aged Port

Blue Ridge Sauvignon Blanc is a briskly herbaceous, non-oaked, strongly varietal style based on Hawke's Bay fruit; Blue Ridge Cabernet Sauvignon/Merlot is an estate-grown wine, typically chunky and firm.

Chenin Blanc is one of the fastest-selling wines in the West Brook range. This is a flavoursome Hawke's Bay wine, its refreshing acidity balanced by a hint of sweetness.

The Merlot is made 'for early consumption, and as a good first step into red-wine drinking'. Estate-grown, to underline its fruitiness it is matured in seasoned French and American oak casks, and its soft tannins enhance its youthful appeal. This is typically a dark, chunky red with plenty of blackcurrant and plum-like flavours and a smooth, undemanding finish.

Other features of the sound West Brook range include: a fat, toasty, buttery-soft Barrique Fermented Chardonnay, grown in Hawke's Bay; a lightly oaked Hawke's Bay Sauvignon Blanc, designed as a more subtle, softer style than its Blue Ridge stablemate; and a characterful, slightly sweet, well-spiced Gisborne Gewürztraminer. Panorama Aged Port, a tawny style matured in totara barrels, is the most popular fortified wine.

Where to from here? 'I can see us having invested in a vineyard in Hawke's Bay by the year 2000,' says Anthony Ivicevich. 'We want to be one of the high-fliers, making some of the country's premium wines. You have to be positive.'

Anthony Ivicevich's plummy, supple West Brook Merlot is a rare beast – a red wine not just made but grown in Henderson.

Other Producers

Mazuran's

The Mazuran winery specialised in fortified wines for decades with outstanding success. It was founded in 1939 by George Mazuran, who in the 1950s embarked on a unique lobbying career designed to foster the sales of independent, family-owned wineries such as his own.

Ironically, the wine-growing bonanza that owed so much to his efforts passed his own company by. The Mazuran vineyard in Lincoln Road, today owned by George Mazuran's son-in-law, Rado Hladilo, is small (1.5ha) and the wines are sold only at the winery. The range of products, concentrated on sherries and ports – some matured for over 50 years – has barely changed for decades. The Mazuran port style is unmistakable: these are dark, almost opaque wines with an almost liqueur-like intensity – rich, treacly and creamy-sweet.

Misty Valley

Until a few years ago called Old Railway, and before that, Pechar's, Misty Valley is a small winery at 225 Henderson Valley Road, founded by Steve Pecar in 1971. Its past reputation was for low-priced, mediocre wines, but today the Chardonnay, Sauvignon Blanc and Cabernet Sauvignon are all sound and the medals recently awarded are a positive sign.

Sapich Brothers

The lovely, hill-grown Sapich vineyard in Forest Hill Road featured on the cover of the first edition of this book. Until recently, the winery's main claim to fame was 'Purple Death', a popular, bluish-purple, port-based drink labelled as 'an unusual "rough-as-guts" wine that has the distinctive bouquet of horse-shit and old tram tickets'. The gold medal won by the rare Sapich Chardonnay 1994 at the 1995 Air New Zealand Wine Awards took everyone by surprise, but several other rock-solid varietal white wines have also been marketed under the Rainbow Ridge label.

Waiheke Island

Rumours circulating in the late 1970s about the establishment of a new 'boutique' winery on Waiheke Island were met in most quarters with disbelief. Was not viticulture rapidly shifting away from the long-established Auckland region to Gisborne, Hawke's Bay and Marlborough? Few believed that outstanding red wine would soon be flowing from this lovely, sprawling island in Auckland's Hauraki Gulf.

The key to the island's wine magic is its warm, dry climate. Kim and Jeanette Goldwater have compared their consistently outstanding Cabernet Sauvignon/Merlot to fine Bordeaux: 'This may seem surprising until one considers the similarity in "terroir" between the two regions. The temperate climate combined with low summer rainfall, poor, free-draining soils and the maritime influence are the very criteria needed to produce wines with intensity of varietal flavour coupled with delicacy of natural acid and fineness of tannin.'

Although the Goldwaters at Putiki Bay pioneered the new era of Waiheke wine, they were not the first vintners the island had attracted. Old, rambling hybrid vines are tangible reminders of the Gradiska family winery, which produced both fortified and a trickle of table wines around the 1950s, until a series of personal tragedies overtook the family and winemaking ceased.

Goldwater Estate, Stonyridge Vineyard, Peninsula Estate and Waiheke Vineyards are the island's best-known producers, but a host of new ventures are getting off the ground. The Goldwaters estimate that total vine plantings on Waiheke now exceed 60 hectares, divided between 20 owners, most of whom plan to produce their own red wines.

Most of the vineyards lie in the more densely populated, western end of the island: at Onetangi (including Stonyridge, Waiheke Vineyards and Gulf Crest); Putiki Bay (Goldwater Estate); Oneroa (Peninsula Estate, Twin Bays, Delamore and Gilmour); and Church Bay, just south of the wharf at Matiatia. A five-hectare vineyard has also been planted by the Spencer family, owners of the Man O' War station near Stony Batter, at the eastern end of Waiheke Island. Their first harvest of red Bordeaux varieties was in 1996, but no winery has been built yet.

Stephen White, of Stonyridge Vineyard, is bullish about Waiheke's wine future. 'In a decade, there'll be 50 vineyards here. It'll be Auckland's most heavily planted wine district. There'll be a lot of restaurants, and Waiheke will emerge as a sort of vineyard/gourmet holiday area.'

The rivulet of fine red wine from the island is set to swell over the next few years, raising doubts about whether all the newcomers, especially those on less favourable sites, will be able to command the high prices of the established big names. However, no other district in New Zealand – including Hawke's Bay – produces top quality Cabernet-based reds with the vintage-to-vintage consistency of Waiheke.

Goldwater Estate for several years basked in the limelight as the only red wine producer on Waiheke Island, but now it's a several-horse race and the rivalry is mounting. Yet at a recent tasting of the leading Auckland reds from the great 1993 vintage, the most concentrated, complex, tautly structured, Bordeaux-like wine was Goldwater Estate.

The modern flush of viticultural enthusiasm on the island was triggered in 1978 when Kim Goldwater – a former engineer and fashion photographer – and his wife Jeanette planted their first experimental vines in poor, sandy clay soils on the hillside overlooking Putiki Bay.

Under the initial guidance of viticultural expert Dr Richard Smart, the Goldwaters have established a six-hectare vineyard of classic Bordeaux varieties: 47 per cent Cabernet Sauvignon, 47 per cent Merlot and six per cent Cabernet Franc. Chardonnay is purchased from Nick Delamore's vineyard at Oneroa, and Chardonnay and Sauvignon Blanc from Marlborough.

Goldwater Estate's output is growing fast. The 1993 vintage yielded only 2000 cases, but by 1999 the Goldwaters expect to produce 3500 cases of red wine and a larger volume of Marlborough Chardonnay and Sauvignon Blanc. Why the rapid expansion and diversification into Marlborough wine? 'Our agent in England asked us for some Marlborough white wines to supplement our red,' says Jeanette Goldwater.

Martin Pickering, who works for part of each year at Flora Springs winery in California, has been the assistant winemaker since 1992 and in 1995 Gretchen Goldwater, a lawyer, joined her parents in the company.

Although principally celebrated for its Cabernet/Merlot *(see panel)*, Goldwater Estate's white wines can also be of startling quality. The estate-grown Sauvignon Blanc was dropped from the range after the 1992 vintage, but has been replaced by the much classier Delamore Chardonnay, a fat, complex, barrel-fermented Waiheke wine that typically overflows with succulent, peachy ripe, buttery, mealy, biscuity flavour; this is a truly exciting mouthful. The lower-priced, more fruit-driven, citrusy and crisp Marlborough Chardonnay affords a clear style contrast.

Goldwater wines are exported to the UK, USA, Canada and Australia. 'I spend half my time in gumboots, the other half in a suit', says Jeanette.

Goldwater Estate

Causeway Road,
Putiki Bay,
Waiheke Island

Owners:
Kim and Jeanette Goldwater

Key Wines:
Cabernet Sauvignon/Merlot, Delamore Chardonnay, Marlborough Chardonnay, Dog Point Sauvignon Blanc, Rosé

Kim and Jeanette Goldwater pioneered winemaking on Waiheke, and still produce one of the island's most stunning reds.

GOLDWATER ESTATE CABERNET/MERLOT

Goldwater is an aristocratic red – a consistently robust wine with a bold tannin attack in its youth, masses of blackcurrant, spice and oak flavour, and the proven ability to flourish in the bottle for many years.

Kim Goldwater explains the evolution of his wine's style since 1982: 'The rough edges have been knocked off. To begin with we were preoccupied with enormity; now we aim for elegance.'

The vineyard is clearly at the root of the wine's quality. 'It's a combination of "terroir" and our intensive work with the vines', says Jeanette. 'We get lots of sun and little rain. The soil is poor and free-draining, and with the gentle influence of the sea we don't suffer from extremes of heat or cold.'

The vinification, says Kim Goldwater, is based on 'classic Bordeaux techniques used by the top chateaux'. The fermenting juice is pumped over its skins, rather than hand-plunged. The young wine is held on its skins for 15 to 25 days after the fermentation to soften its tannins, and then matured for 12 to 18 months in French Nevers oak 225-litre barriques, typically half new.

Kim Goldwater enjoys drinking his reds young, 'while they're exuberant and tannic and gutsy and brilliantly hued'. To broach them at less than five years old, however, is to ignore their strong cellaring potential.

With its bold, brambly, tannin-laden 1993 and 1994 vintages, Peninsula Estate has emerged as one of the heavyweights of the Waiheke Island wine fraternity.

On their breathtakingly beautiful, wind-buffeted site on Hakaimango Point, overlooking Big Oneroa Beach, Doug and Anne Hamilton produce a muscular, deep-flavoured red in the classic Waiheke mould.

Doug Hamilton was raised in Pukekohe and spent his early career as a mechanic. Anne, his wife, is a life-long Waiheke Island resident. The Hamiltons planted their first vines in 1986; three years later Peninsula Estate's first vintage was ensconced in bottles.

The 2.5-hectare, sloping vineyard of friable clays over broken rock is planted in Cabernet Sauvignon, Merlot, Cabernet Franc and Malbec. Further grapes will come on stream in 1997 from a 2.5-hectare vineyard of Chardonnay, Syrah and red Bordeaux grapes owned by the Hamiltons' neighbours, Robert and Emerald Gilmour (a sister of Peter Cowley, winemaker at Te Mata Estate in Hawke's Bay).

Peninsula Estate

52 Korora Road, Oneroa, Waiheke Island

Owners:
Doug and Anne Hamilton

Key Wines:
Peninsula Estate Cabernet Sauvignon/Merlot, Oneroa Bay Cabernet/Merlot

In the winery Doug Hamilton built in 1987, the annual output is currently only about 1300 cases of wine. Hamilton's full-time winemaker, Christopher Lush, hand-picks the fruit; macerates the skins in the wine for a lengthy (three weeks or longer) period following the fermentation, and then matures the red for a year in French oak barriques, one-third new each year. The wine is lightly fined with egg whites, but not filtered.

'Peninsula Estate is one of the island's cooler vineyard sites,' says Lush. 'It's not a heat trap; we don't get any excessive heat build-up so our harvest is typically two weeks behind most of the others. So long as we miss bad weather, we see that as an advantage. And it's certainly better for working in!'

Peninsula Estate is a big, generous red, savoury, spicy, tannic and ideal for cellaring. A chunky, full-flavoured, softer red with greater drink-young appeal is marketed under the Oneroa Bay label.

Doug and Anne Hamilton's bold, flavour-packed Waiheke Island red has risen sharply in quality in recent vintages.

The magical 1994 vintage of Stonyridge Larose sold out in less than three days. Produced in tiny quantities, Larose is one of the most celebrated reds in the country and – in Auckland at least – the most fashionable of all.

Stephen White, the driving force behind this high-flying Onetangi winery, is an Aucklander who graduated with a Diploma of Horticulture from Lincoln University. After working in vineyards in Tuscany and California, and at Châteaux d'Angludet and Palmer in Bordeaux, White returned to New Zealand to pursue his high ambition: 'to make one of the best Médoc-style reds in the world.'

Stonyridge, named after a nearby 100-metre high rocky outcrop, lies only one kilometre from the sea. White planted his first vines here in 1982 on poor, free-draining clay soils saturated with manganese nodules.

The Stonyridge vineyard runs to 4.5 hectares of north-facing vines, over half Cabernet Sauvignon, with smaller amounts of Merlot, Cabernet Franc, Malbec, Petit Verdot (described by White as 'like a supercharged Cabernet: very high in tannin, colour, alcohol and acidity'), Syrah, Montepulciano (a well-respected red-wine

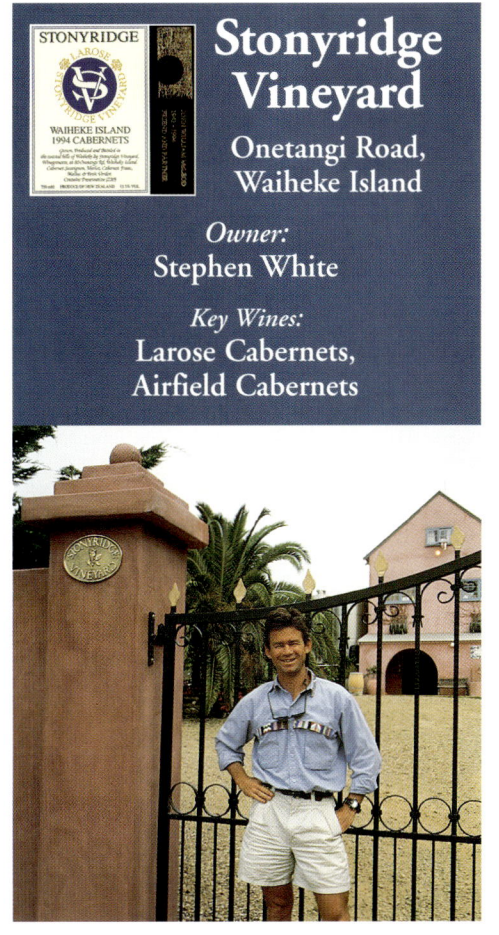

Stonyridge Vineyard

Onetangi Road, Waiheke Island

Owner:
Stephen White

Key Wines:
Larose Cabernets, Airfield Cabernets

grape of central Italy) and Chardonnay. The vines yield only about five tonnes of grapes per hectare, well below the New Zealand average for the chosen varieties.

In his elegant terracotta concrete and timber winery, with its three processing levels and underground barrel cellar, White concentrates on the production of claret-style reds. 'From the start I deliberately sought to produce a Bordeaux-style blend using low cropping, long skin maceration, a second label to allow "selection", barrique-aging and selling "en primeur". Many of these were firsts for New Zealand.'

The second-string label, Airfield, named after a nearby landing strip, is used 'as a back-up for poorer-performing rows, or for a poor year'. An impressive red in its own right, oozing exuberant, ripe fruit flavours in a more forward, supple style than Larose (see panel), it was recently based on fruit grown in the Fenton vineyard, but from the 1995 vintage onwards is estate-grown. Stonyridge's total annual output has recently ranged between 500 and 1100 cases.

The future will include a small volume of Chardonnay and a Rhône-style red.

Stephen White's arrestingly perfumed and flavourful Stonyridge Larose is one of New Zealand's most sought-after wines.

Stonyridge Larose Cabernets

Larose is a strapping, voluptuous red, richly perfumed and awash with lush, seductively ripe, almost sweet-tasting, blackcurrant-like flavour. 'If we put the Larose label on a bottle,' says Stephen White, 'it's got to have big, dark, ripe berry fruits – that's what Larose is all about. It's got masses of colour, concentrated fruit and soft tannins, yet it's still a cool-climate style, and avoids going over the top into non-varietal jammy characters.'

Why is Larose so successful? White points immediately to Waiheke's high sunshine hours, summer heat (up to 36°C in the shade), and low rainfall compared to the mainland. During the warm, dry summer of 1993, he wrote, 'the cracks in the ground got so big that dining guests [at Stonyridge's Verandah Cafe] fell into them and disappeared'. He also believes his site's northern aspect is very important: 'If you're going to maximise everything, why choose a southern aspect?'

Clay soils boost the wine's body, the rocks promote drainage, and the adjacent ridge protects the vines from cooling westerlies. A lot of time is spent manicuring the vineyard: shoot positioning, leaf plucking, crop thinning.

Matured for a year in 70 to 100 per cent new French oak barriques, Larose is a consistently powerful yet stylish red, dark hued and massive in superior vintages, and even in lesser years attractively scented and ripe. When does it peak? 'Winemakers usually like to drink their wines young,' says White, 'because they spend their lives with their nose in a barrel. Larose takes five years to reach its plateau, and stays there for a further five to ten years.'

As executive officer of the Wine Institute from 1976 to 1990, Terry Dunleavy campaigned on behalf of all New Zealand winemakers. Now he crusades on behalf of 'the best red-wine area in New Zealand – Waiheke Island'. The exceptional 1993 and 1994 vintages of Te Motu Cabernet/Merlot, the flagship red from the Dunleavy and Buffalora families' Onetangi vineyard, can only lend weight to Terry Dunleavy's claim.

Te Motu is an abbreviation of the Maori name for Waiheke Island, Te Motu-Arai-Roa (the island-sheltering-long).

Waiheke Vineyards Limited was formed in 1988. A 12-hectare goat farm separated from Stonyridge Vineyard by a 60-metre-wide airstrip was purchased in 1989, and within months the first vines were in the ground.

The key tasks of running Waiheke Vineyards are divided between three Dunleavys. 'I oversee everything on the island,' says John Dunleavy, who lives on-site. 'Paul, as managing director, looks after the financial side, and Dad takes charge of distribution and promotion.'

The four-hectare vineyard, on gently undulating land only half a kilometre from the coast, includes Cabernet Sauvignon (80 per cent), Merlot (15 per cent) and Cabernet Franc. Crushed, fermented and pressed at the vineyard, the wine is then transported to West Auckland to be barrel-matured, processed and bottled by winemaking consultant (and Matua Valley winemaker) Mark Robertson. An on-site winery is planned within the next two or three years. Output in the first three vintages averaged 900 cases.

The 1993 vintage Te Motu Cabernet/Merlot, matured in American and French oak barriques, was a superb debut – dark, concentrated and long – and is aging gracefully. The 1994 is even classier, with an exciting intensity of brambly, complex, spicy, nutty flavours underpinned by taut tannins. The 1995 vintage also brought a vibrantly fruity, plummy and supple, but relatively straightforward, wine labelled Dunleavy Merlot/Franc, sold in the island's wine shops and cafés.

Waiheke Vineyards
Onetangi Road, Waiheke Island

Owners:
The Dunleavy and Buffalora families

Key Wine:
Te Motu Cabernet/Merlot

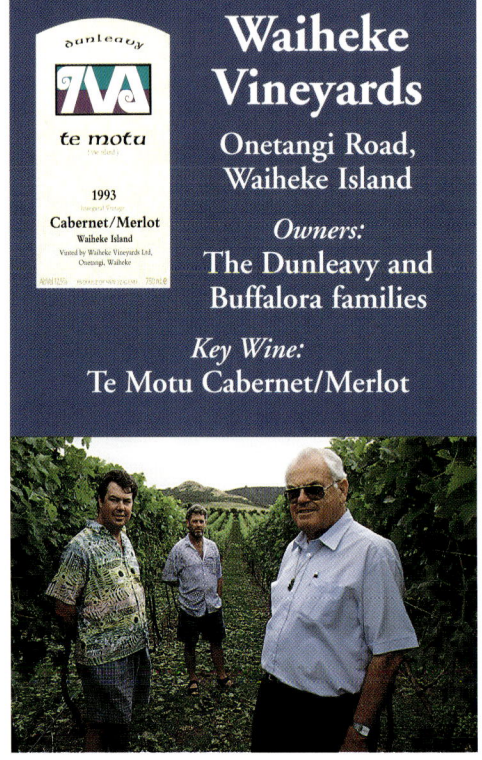

The complementary skills of Paul (left), John (centre) and Terry Dunleavy contributed to the instant success of Te Motu Cabernet/Merlot.

Other Producers

Twin Bays

Barry and Meg Fenton's Twin Bays vineyard at Oneroa, near Peninsula Estate, is sited on a headland flanked by two bays. The property, purchased in 1988, now has 2.5 hectares of Cabernet Sauvignon, Merlot and Cabernet Franc vines. The 1993 and 1994 vintages of Twin Bays were vinified by Stephen White at Stonyridge Vineyard (with some of the grapes used for Stonyridge's second-tier label, Airfield) but of late the wine has been made by consultant winemaker, Kim Crawford, at Peninsula Estate. With its classic bouquet of blackcurrants and cedarwood and bold, concentrated, supple palate, this is an impressive, although little known, Waiheke wine.

John Mellars of Great Barrier Island

The viticultural potential of Great Barrier Island, further out in the Hauraki Gulf, is also being explored. John Mellars gave up a 20-year career in computer consultancy to plant Cabernet Sauvignon and Merlot vines on a steep hill overlooking Okupu Bay. The one-hectare vineyard yielded just 156 bottles of auspiciously robust, rich-flavoured and rounded Great Barrier Cabernet in 1993, but the 1995 vintage, despite the ravages of rain and wasps, produced about 100 cases.

CENTRAL AND SOUTH AUCKLAND

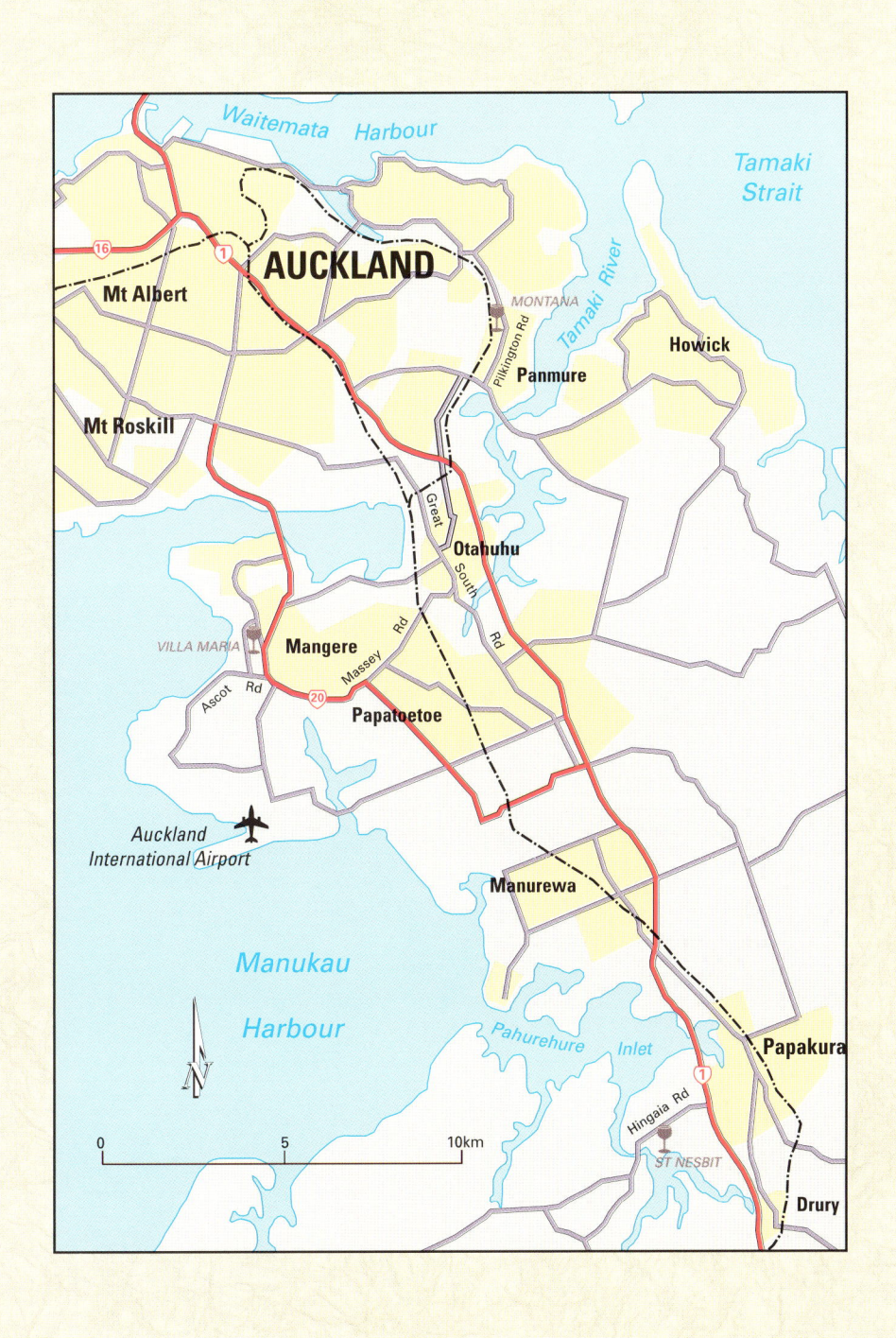

Montana is the Croatian word for mountain – a strikingly apt name for the colossus of New Zealand wine. The company's headquarters are in Auckland, but it also owns vineyards in Hawke's Bay, Gisborne and Marlborough, and a quartet of wineries located in those four regions. Its range of labels, rock solid in quality and unrivalled for their value for money, in 1996 commanded a massive 44 per cent share of the domestic market for New Zealand wine.

Although the dominant force in New Zealand wine, Montana is not a huge winery in international terms. 'Our domestic market share is very high,' says Peter Hubscher, Montana's managing director since 1991, 'but we're still only about one-fifth the size of Southcorp [the Australian giant] and slightly smaller than Mildara-Blass. If we weren't as big as we are, we wouldn't have the critical mass to compete with Australia.'

Ivan Yukich, founder of the company, arrived in New Zealand from Dalmatia as a youth of 15. After returning to his homeland, he came back to New Zealand in 1934, this time with a wife and two sons. After years devoted to market gardening, Yukich later planted a fifth-hectare vineyard high in the bush-clad folds of the Waitakere Ranges west of Auckland. 1944 saw the first Montana wine on the market.

Under the direction of sons Mate (the viticulturist) and Frank (winemaker and salesman) the vineyard grew to 10 hectares by the end of the 1950s. The company then embarked on a whirlwind period of expansion unparalleled in New Zealand wine history. To build up its financial and distribution clout, Montana joined forces with Campbell and Ehrenfried, the liquor wholesaling giant, and Auckland financier Rolf Porter. A new 120-hectare vineyard was established at Mangatangi in the Waikato and in the late 1960s Gisborne farmers plunged into grapegrowing at the Yukichs' urgings. A gleaming new winery rose on the outskirts of Gisborne in 1972 and a year later Montana absorbed the old family firm of Waihirere.

Although production was booming the company at this stage earned a reputation for placing sales volume goals ahead of product quality. The launch-pad for Montana's spectacular growth was a series of sparkling 'pop' wines – Pearl, Cold Duck and Poulet Poulet – which briefly won a following.

The real force behind Montana's rise was the ambitious, ruthless and far-sighted Frank Yukich. He early perceived the trend away from sherry to white table wine and was the first to adopt aggressive marketing strategies. 1973 was a momentous year. The giant multinational distilling and winemaking company Seagram obtained a 40 per cent shareholding in Montana, contributing money, technical resources and marketing expertise.

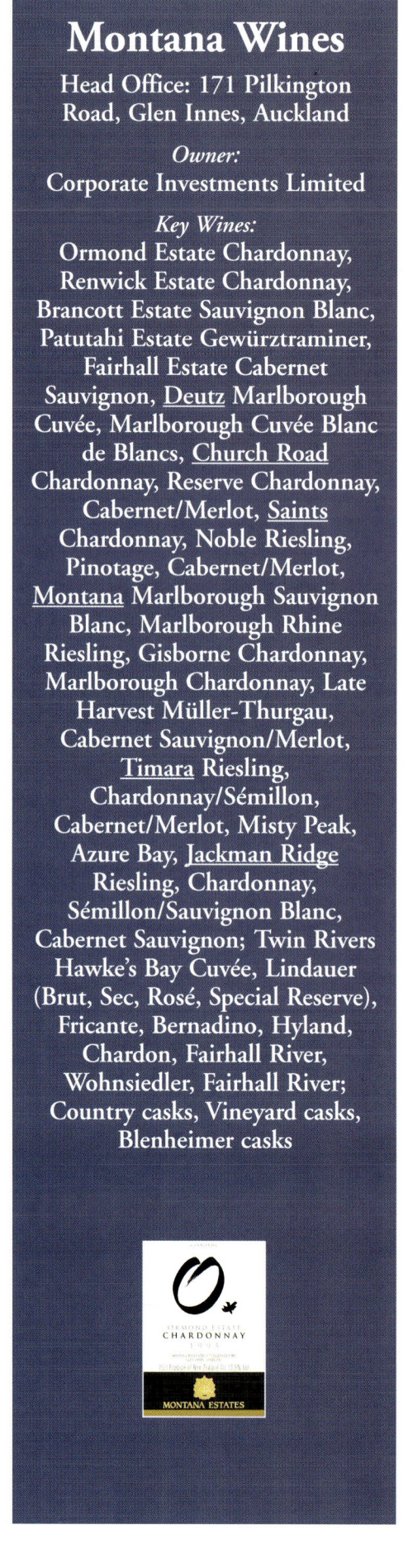

The same year, Montana made an issue of 2.4 million public shares. Seagram's investments, shareholders' funds and independent loans together provided $8 million over the next three years for development purposes.

Also in 1973 came the pivotal move into Marlborough, as part of a major vineyard planting programme. Wayne Thomas, then a scientist in the Plant Diseases Division of the DSIR has related: 'Although plenty of suitable land was available in both the Poverty Bay and Hawke's Bay regions, my own impression was that it was too highly priced for vineyards'. Thomas suggested the Marlborough region as an alternative, and the area's wine-grapegrowing suitability was independently confirmed by the Viticulture Department at the University of California, Davis.

The first vine was planted in Marlborough on 24 August 1973: a silver coin, the traditional token of good fortune, was dropped in the hole and Sir David Beattie, then chairman of the company, with a sprinkling of sparkling wine dedicated the historic vine. The first grapes were harvested on 15 and 16 March 1976; 15 tonnes of Müller-Thurgau were trucked aboard the inter-island ferry at Picton and driven through the night by Mate Yukich to Montana's Gisborne winery. A 'token' picking of Cabernet Sauvignon followed in April.

Montana was moving swiftly to rectify its quality problems. The standard of the 1974 and subsequent vintages soon lifted the company into the ranks of the industry's leaders. Still pursuing the mass market, the company now shifted its emphasis to non-sparkling table wines. Bernkaizler Riesling (later called Benmorven) began to open up a huge market for slightly sweet white wines later developed with Blenheimer, still one of New Zealand's most popular cask wines.

A year after the pivotal moves of 1973, Frank Yukich, the key visionary behind Montana's rapid rise, was gone – the loser when his relationship with Seagram turned sour. Soon after, the company also severed its link with the old Yukich vineyard at

---

Montana Wines

Head Office: 171 Pilkington Road, Glen Innes, Auckland

Owner:
Corporate Investments Limited

Key Wines:
Ormond Estate Chardonnay, Renwick Estate Chardonnay, Brancott Estate Sauvignon Blanc, Patutahi Estate Gewürztraminer, Fairhall Estate Cabernet Sauvignon, Deutz Marlborough Cuvée, Marlborough Cuvée Blanc de Blancs, Church Road Chardonnay, Reserve Chardonnay, Cabernet/Merlot, Saints Chardonnay, Noble Riesling, Pinotage, Cabernet/Merlot, Montana Marlborough Sauvignon Blanc, Marlborough Rhine Riesling, Gisborne Chardonnay, Marlborough Chardonnay, Late Harvest Müller-Thurgau, Cabernet Sauvignon/Merlot, Timara Riesling, Chardonnay/Sémillon, Cabernet/Merlot, Misty Peak, Azure Bay, Jackman Ridge Riesling, Chardonnay, Sémillon/Sauvignon Blanc, Cabernet Sauvignon; Twin Rivers Hawke's Bay Cuvée, Lindauer (Brut, Sec, Rosé, Special Reserve), Fricante, Bernadino, Hyland, Chardon, Fairhall River, Wohnsiedler, Fairhall River; Country casks, Vineyard casks, Blenheimer casks

Managing director Peter Hubscher joined Montana in 1973, the year the first vines were planted in Marlborough.

Titirangi. The 20-hectare vineyard site and substantial winery was unsuited to further development and the company chose instead to expand elsewhere. The old winery was dismantled and most of the equipment sent to Blenheim.

Montana's costly move into Marlborough contributed to the company's depressed financial condition from 1974 to 1976. But the subsequent recovery represented a major business success story. After two years of losses, Montana showed a small profit in 1975/76 and by 1978 had paid its maiden dividend.

In late 1985 Corporate Investments Limited took control of Montana, by adding Seagram's 43.8 per cent stake to its own already substantial shareholding. Seagram pulled out when the industry's fortunes turned sour: in the year to 30 June 1986 the company recorded a loss of almost $1.6 million. The principal shareholder in the listed Corporate Investments is its chairman, Peter Masfen, who has served as a director of Montana for over 20 years.

Masfen is one of New Zealand's wealthiest men, and his wife, Joanna, is the daughter of Rolf Porter, Montana's early financial backer. An accountant, Masfen owns a string of private businesses in addition to his Corporate Investments holding. 'Our company tends to buy into out-of-favour sectors and does well out of them,' observes Masfen.

Following its acquisition of Penfolds Wines (NZ) Limited in late 1986 from Lion Corporation Ltd, Montana moved back into the black, posting a $5.14 million profit for the year ending 30 June 1987. Later that year, Corporate Investments secured a 100 per cent shareholding in Montana and then de-listed the company from the stock exchange.

Montana's sales (including excise) for the year to June 1995 totalled $143.7 million, with earnings before interest and tax of $24.3 million.

In Gisborne, where the Montana and former Penfolds wineries have been linked under the road by five three-inch (7.6 cm) pipelines, in 1995 Montana crushed 10,200 tonnes of grapes — 13.7 per cent of the country's total grape harvest. About 10 per cent of the grapes are grown in the company's 88 hectares of vineyards at Ormond, Te Arai and Patutahi. Grape processing is now all at the old Penfolds winery, with tank storage (19 million L) at the original Montana winery. The old Waihirere winery in the Ormond Valley, still bearing a sign, 'F. Wohnsiedler's Cellars', is used for maturing fortified wines. A multi-million dollar cooperage was opened in 1995 at Montana's Gisborne winery, designed to accommodate several thousand barrels.

Montana's Marlborough winery at Riverlands, a few kilometres on the seaward side of Blenheim, was the first and is by far the largest in the region. Towering 550,000-litre insulated tanks have been installed to store reserves of wines in optimum condition. The 'tank farm' here, of 200 separate tanks, has the capacity to store up to 20 million litres of wine. During vintage up to 500 tonnes of fruit avalanches in each day from contract vineyards and the company's own plantings covering 500 hectares at Brancott, Renwick, Fairhall and Woodbourne.

From Blenheim and Gisborne much wine then rolls north in bulk rail tankers to Auckland for blending and bottling. All finishing and maturing of bottled wines is carried out at the Glen Innes complex in Auckland, where chief winemaker Jeff Clarke is based.

Montana now has 'management control' over 1000 hectares of grapes (12 per cent of the national vineyard) in Gisborne, Hawke's Bay and Marlborough. 'We sold 250 hectares of the company's vineyards in 1995, but leased them back for 60 years,' says Hubscher. 'That freed up capital for further vineyard investment. Over the next two or three years, we'll extend our vineyards annually by about 100 hectares.'

Montana grows about half of its grape requirements, and sources much of the rest for its blended bottle and cask wines from local growers and countries like Australia and Spain. However, about 75 per cent of the fruit for the company's premium wines is drawn from its own vineyards.

In 1988 Montana made a crucial decision: to expand its share of the premium (over $15 per bottle) market, where traditionally it has not been a major force. Previously, geared to crush huge tonnages, it simply wasn't able to handle small, superior batches of wine. Now it has three locations reserved for small-scale, premium wine production: separate flow systems at the Gisborne and Marlborough wineries for hand-picked fruit, and The McDonald Winery at Taradale.

Exports currently account for about 12 per cent of the company's sales by value. Montana has focused its export efforts on the UK and Europe, where its sales are showing rapid growth. 'We're selling over 250,000 cases per year in Britain,' says Hubscher.

How good are the wines? Those carrying the Montana Estates, Deutz Marlborough Cuvée and Church Road labels rate among New Zealand's finest. Montana's wines often match the boutiques on quality and out-perform them in the value-for-money stakes.

The Estates range is designed as the crown of Montana's varietal wine portfolio. The selection features a weighty, stylish Ormond Estate Chardonnay from Gisborne with great depth of lush, citrusy, mealy flavour; an intense, nutty, markedly steelier Renwick

Estate Chardonnay from Marlborough; a pick-of-the-crop, partly barrel-fermented Brancott Estate Sauvignon Blanc from Marlborough with lush, incisive tropical-fruit flavours fleshed out with subtle oak; a mouth-filling, musky, rich, pungently peppery Patutahi Estate Gewürztraminer from Gisborne; and a lovely, fragrant, delicately flavoured Fairhall Estate Cabernet Sauvignon that proves (in favourable vintages) Marlborough's ability to produce top class claret-style reds. Dressed in labels featuring a bold single letter ('O' for Ormond, 'P' for Patutahi, and so on), this is a striking quintet.

The string of impressive Chardonnays and Cabernet/Merlots produced under the Church Road label at The McDonald Winery are discussed on page 110. The black-label Saints range, launched in 1995, offers several mid-priced wines of high quality. Saints Chardonnay, grown in Gisborne, is scented, robust and packed with toasty, buttery-soft flavour. Saints Pinotage, from Hawke's Bay, confirms this unfashionable variety's ability to yield dark, chunky, meaty, smooth reds with great drink-young appeal. Saints Cabernet/Merlot, also grown in Hawke's Bay, displays good depth of cassis and mint flavours wrapped in sweet-tasting American oak. Saints Noble Riesling is a luscious, intense, richly botrytised Marlborough dessert wine, raisiny and honey-sweet.

In terms of sheer volume, and value-for-money, the company's key varietals are the long-popular wines marketed under the Montana brand: Marlborough Sauvignon Blanc, Marlborough Rhine Riesling, Marlborough Chardonnay, Gisborne Chardonnay, and Cabernet Sauvignon/Merlot.

Montana's range of Marlborough white wines has fully justified the company's faith in the region. Since the first 1979 vintage, Montana's Marlborough Rhine Riesling has stood out – a fragrant, flowery, polished, slightly sweet wine with abundant fruit flavour and lively acidity.

If any wine could sum up Montana, its immersion in the Marlborough region and the consistent quality and value of its wines, it is surely the famous Marlborough Sauvignon Blanc, of which 135,000 cases were produced in 1995 *(see panel)*.

The popular Gisborne Chardonnay is a light, fresh style, placing its accent on soft, peachy, citrusy fruit flavours. Until a few years ago it had no wood treatment, but now a 'portion' is oak-aged, and malolactic fermentation is also used to add a touch of complexity. This is an easy-drinking, drink-young style.

Montana Marlborough Chardonnay is a richer-flavoured, more complex style than its Gisborne stablemate, its strong grapefruit-like fruit flavours enhanced by spicy, buttery, toasty characters derived from barrique fermentation, lees aging and malolactic fermentation. Nutty, mealy and soft, this is a classy wine, bargain-priced.

For many years, the pick of Montana's commercial range of reds was the American oak-aged, flavoursome, but green-edged Marlborough Cabernet Sauvignon. This wine has been superseded since the 1994 vintage by a Cabernet Sauvignon/Merlot based on Marlborough and Hawke's Bay fruit. By adding Merlot and Hawke's Bay grapes, Montana has succeeded in producing a markedly darker, richer, riper-flavoured red.

New Zealand's greatest array of sparkling wines – from the bargain-priced Bernadino Spumante to the widely underrated Lindauer and the prestigious Deutz Marlborough Cuvee – flows from Montana.

Lindauer, launched in 1981, and sold in Brut (dry) Sec (medium), Rosé and Special Reserve versions, was this country's first widely released bottle-fermented sparkling. The Brut, the best-known of the quartet, is based on four grapes – Pinot Noir, Chardonnay, Chenin Blanc and Riesling – grown in Gisborne and Marlborough, and matured on its yeast lees for at least 18 months.

The quality of Lindauer Brut has soared in recent years, reflecting the guidance of the Champagne house of Deutz and a rising content of Marlborough grapes. With its subtle yeastiness and lively, lemony, slightly nutty, lingering flavour, this is a very stylish wine, offering exceptional value. The Special Reserve – a blend of Pinot Noir (principally) and Chardonnay, grown in Hawke's Bay and Marlborough and lees-aged for up to three years – is fuller, broader, richer and creamier.

Montana's flagship sparkling wine is clearly its outstanding Deutz Marlborough Cuvee, produced since 1988 under a joint agreement between Montana and the Champagne house of Deutz and Geldermann. The partners' ambition, says Peter Hubscher, is 'to produce the best sparkling wine outside Champagne itself'.

The hand-picked, Marlborough-grown Chardonnay and Pinot Noir grapes on which Deutz Marlborough Cuvee is based are pressed in a computer-controlled French Coquard Champagne press which yields juice of great delicacy. After each vintage, the wine is blended in Blenheim under the guidance of Deutz, and then shipped to Auckland to be bottled and matured on its yeast lees for two years in a specially built, $800,000 climate-controlled cellar.

The initial result was a rich style, bolder and riper-tasting than the true Champagnes with which it is inevitably compared. Of late, the wine has become less overtly fruity, more refined and flinty. The Chardonnay-dominated Deutz Marlborough Cuvee Blanc de Blancs is also super-stylish, with loads of biscuity, vigorous, creamy-smooth flavour.

The largest of the tanks at Montana's Gisborne winery can store the equivalent of 300,000 bottles of wine.

MONTANA MARLBOROUGH SAUVIGNON BLANC

This wine has introduced more overseas wine lovers to the soaring standard of New Zealand wine than any other. It is that rare combination: a world-class wine that is nonetheless freely available and affordable.

The focus is on the flavour explosion of slow-ripened Marlborough fruit. 'The wine *is* the fruit,' says Peter Hubscher. Grown and machine-harvested in Montana's sweeping Brancott vineyard, the unfermented grapejuice is initially held in contact with the skins to boost its flavour, and then slow-fermented at cool temperatures in stainless steel tanks. Oak plays no part in its fermentation or maturation.

Montana Marlborough Sauvignon Blanc is full of distinctive herbal varietal character. It is unmistakably Sauvignon Blanc in its youth, with a zesty, assertive capsicum-like aroma and flavour and mouth-watering crispness. After a couple of years, the wine starts to soften, acquiring more mellow, complex, toasty, bottle-aged characters.

Since the debut 1979 vintage, the wine has proved its top-flight quality over 18 years. The 1989 won the Marquis de Goulaine Trophy for the champion Sauvignon Blanc at the 1990 International Wine and Spirit Competition in London; the 1991 vintage was crowned the champion white wine of the 1992 Sydney International Winemakers' Competition.

When the 1995 vintage was released, overseas buyers immediately placed orders for 46,000 cases.

St Nesbit Winery

Hingaia Road, Karaka

Owner: Dr Tony Molloy Q.C.

Key Wine: St Nesbit

Dr Tony Molloy, a distinguished lawyer, also produces a rare claret-style red of great delicacy and breed.

'The truth about vineyards,' says Tony Molloy, 'is that the generation which plants them is sowing something which only later generations will be able to fully reap.' With his own vines under brutal assault by rabbits, birds and viruses, Molloy is talking from experience. The release of the 1991 vintage of St Nesbit in 1997 will mark Molloy's last red-wine release until the year 2001 or 2002.

St Nesbit has been one of the few Cabernet Sauvignon or Merlot-based reds made outside Hawke's Bay or Waiheke Island able to foot it in the quality stakes with the top wines of those acclaimed red-wine regions. The release of the first 1984 vintage, with a gold medal under its belt, heralded the arrival of tax lawyer Tony Molloy as a force to be reckoned with among this country's red-winemaking fraternity.

St Nesbit is a small winery tucked away on a southern arm of the Manukau Harbour in Hingaia Road, Karaka, only a couple of kilometres from Auckland's southern motorway. After buying a 14-hectare dairy farm here in 1980, a year later Molloy planted his first vines in Karaka's fertile, loamy soils.

The vineyard is planted on a cool site by Auckland standards; the grapes have been harvested up to six weeks later than Waiheke's. The three-hectare vineyard is planted in Merlot (70 per cent), Petit Verdot (a dark, peppery, traditional Bordeaux grape which Molloy introduced to New Zealand), Malbec and Cabernet Franc.

After the main block of Cabernet Sauvignon, planted in the early 1980s, showed symptoms of leafroll virus, it was levelled with a chainsaw. The vineyard has recently been extensively replanted to reflect Molloy's experiments with different rootstocks, row orientations, closer vine spacing, altered heights, and alternative varieties to the late-ripening Cabernet Sauvignon. These new plantings, on a more sheltered, warmer block of land, will take several years to come into full production.

In pursuit of Molloy's goal of 'greater flavour concentration', since 1989 at least a quarter of the bunches have been cut from the vines before flowering. With their average yield between 1989 and 1991 of about 215 cases per hectare, St Nesbit's vines cropped at about one-third the New Zealand average for the planted varieties.

Molloy makes the wine himself, and to enhance St Nesbit's individuality, he ferments his wine with natural 'wild' yeasts. To allow the wine to reflect the season, he does not chaptalise (add sugar to boost the alcohol level). Only a tiny amount of sulphur dioxide is used, and none at all until bottling.

New oak has played a key role in St Nesbit; all of the 1984 to 1991 vintages, with the single exception of the 1985, were matured wholly in new or newly shaved barrels, typically for three years. Molloy then bottle-ages his wine for a further two years before it is released at five or six years old; much older than almost any other red wine in the country.

In Molloy's eyes, the 1989 to 1991 vintages are at a much higher level of intensity, weight and richness than any previous vintage. I agree. The Merlot-predominant 1989 is a dark beauty with an arresting depth of spicy, chocolate-rich, complex, supple flavour and an overall lushness and generosity that sets it apart from most New Zealand reds. The Cabernet Sauvignon-predominant 1990 and 1991 vintages are less voluptuous than the '89 but intense, subtle and firm, in a style highly reminiscent of true claret.

Villa Maria's headquarters at Mangere, near Auckland International Airport, is a strictly utilitarian building with no frills. 'This reflects our total focus on making the best wine,' says owner and managing director, George Fistonich. 'We put our emphasis on the production areas.'

Villa Maria's empire includes three wineries: Villa Maria itself, and Esk Valley and Vidal in Hawke's Bay. Overall the country's third-largest wine company, it claims a 9 per cent share of the total domestic market for New Zealand wine, and over 20 per cent of the still (non-sparkling) bottled wine market.

The origins of Villa Maria lie in a tiny operation called Mountain Vineyards, which was run as a hobby by Dalmatian immigrant Andrew Fistonich, who arrived in New Zealand just before the Depression. Fistonich worked on the gumfields, then later made a few bottles of wine for himself and friends before becoming a licensed winemaker in 1949. When illness slowed him down, his son George leased his father's vineyard, formed a new company, and bought a press, barrels and pumps from Maungatapu Vineyards at Tauranga. In 1961, Villa Maria Hock nosed out into the market.

The winery initially made its presence felt at the bottom end of the market. The slogan 'Let Villa Maria introduce you to wine' associated with the sale of sherries and quaffing table wines, created an image the company for years struggled to overcome. But in recent times the company has established an illustrious record in wine competitions.

With his quiet manner and slow drawl, it would be easy to underestimate George Fistonich. He also avoids the limelight, happily stepping back in favour of his winemaking team. Yet the entrepreneurial Fistonich ranks among the wine industry's most powerful figures.

Villa Maria expanded rapidly through the 1970s – absorbing Vidal in 1976 – and early 1980s, emerging as a fierce rival of the largest wineries such as Montana and Corbans. To throw off its old image, recalls Fistonich, 'around 1980 we changed the label by introducing the red "V", and decided to focus on quality and gold medals.' John Spencer of the Caxton group of companies was then a silent but substantial shareholder.

At the height of the wine industry's price war late in 1985, Villa Maria slid into a much-publicised receivership. With its limited capital reserves, the winery was simply unable to survive in the heavy loss-making trading environment created by its larger rivals. It was rescued by a capital injection from its new part-owner, Grant Adams, then deputy chairman of the investment company Equiticorp. Barely a year later, Villa Maria astounded observers by absorbing the Bird family's ailing Glenvale (now Esk Valley) winery. Villa Maria was on the comeback trail.

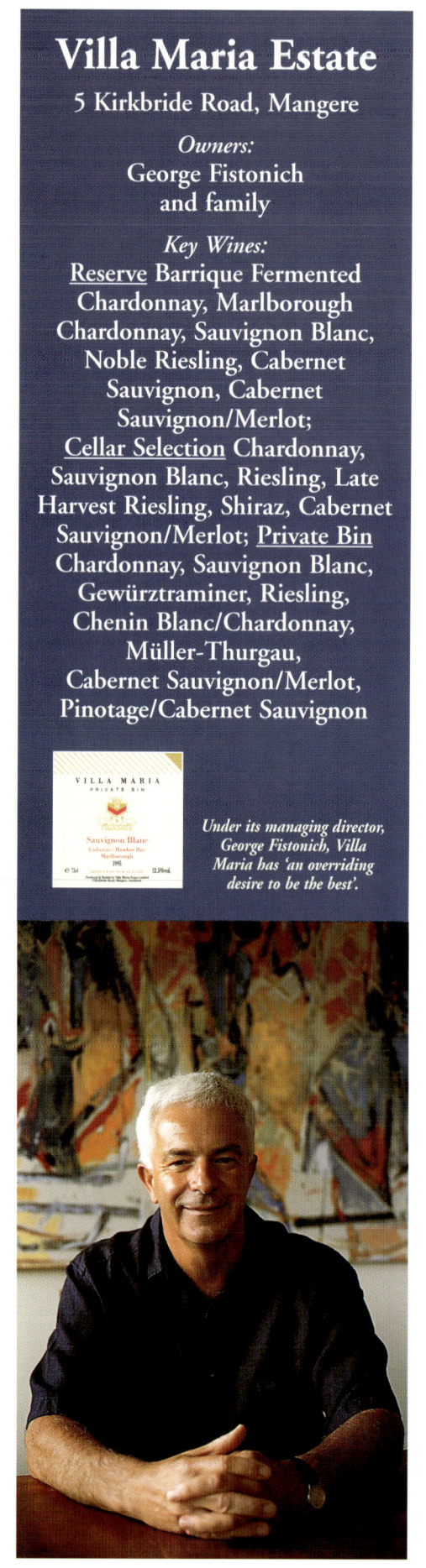

In 1991 Grant Adams sold his 50 per share in Villa Maria to Mangere grapegrower Ian Montgmerie. In 1996 Montgomerie sold his shares to the Fistonich family.

Villa Maria crushed around 6000 tonnes of fruit in the early to mid 1980s. Today, the company still processes about 6000 tonnes each vintage, but is no longer entrenched in the price-sensitive, bulk cask-wine market, having switched its focus to the more profitable, bottled wine market.

Steve Smith, who trained under viticultural guru Dr Richard Smart, liaises closely with the company's grapegrowers in a bid to constantly raise the quality of their fruit, with full-time viticulturists assisting him in Gisborne, Hawke's Bay and Marlborough.

Villa Maria relies on contract grapegrowers for the vast majority of its fruit. However, it does own Esk Valley's estate vineyard, and in 1992 planting began at a gravelly vineyard on State Highway 50, near Gimblett Road, inland from Hastings. About 20 hectares have been planted in Cabernet Sauvignon, Merlot, Cabernet Franc, Malbec, Syrah and Chardonnay, with a further five hectares to be planted each year over the next decade. The vines (1.6m apart, with 1.8m between rows) are planted at twice the normal density in New Zealand, which enables the company to reduce cropping levels per vine without sacrificing yield per hectare. In future, this vineyard will supply the grapes for at least half of Villa Maria's Reserve reds.

Villa Maria's intake of Marlborough grapes will also rise steeply from 1998, when the first fruit comes on stream from 42 hectares of Sauvignon Blanc, Chardonnay and Riesling planted by Seddon Vineyards on a north-facing terrace on the banks of the Awatere River, 12 kilometres inland from Seddon. The vineyard, funded by hundreds of small investors, is being established and managed by Villa Maria, and the company is also committed to purchase the vineyard's grapes.

Villa Maria's top wines, marketed under a

Villa Maria Estate

5 Kirkbride Road, Mangere

Owners:
George Fistonich and family

Key Wines:
Reserve Barrique Fermented Chardonnay, Marlborough Chardonnay, Sauvignon Blanc, Noble Riesling, Cabernet Sauvignon, Cabernet Sauvignon/Merlot; Cellar Selection Chardonnay, Sauvignon Blanc, Riesling, Late Harvest Riesling, Shiraz, Cabernet Sauvignon/Merlot; Private Bin Chardonnay, Sauvignon Blanc, Gewürztraminer, Riesling, Chenin Blanc/Chardonnay, Müller-Thurgau, Cabernet Sauvignon/Merlot, Pinotage/Cabernet Sauvignon

Under its managing director, George Fistonich, Villa Maria has 'an overriding desire to be the best'.

Reserve label, have of late enjoyed a phenomenal run of gold-medal and trophy-winning successes. Its Reserve Chardonnays, sweet Rieslings and Cabernet Sauvignon-based reds are indisputably among New Zealand's most outstanding wines. Their quality is matched by the top-flight Reserve wines from the two other wineries in the Villa Maria group's stable, Esk Valley and Vidal.

The winemakers in the three wineries are encouraged to strive to outperform each other. For marketing reasons, however, it is important that each label has a consistent style. Take Sauvignon Blanc: the Villa Maria Private Bin Sauvignon Blanc is designed to be 'light and racy'; Vidal wine is a medley of herbaceous and riper fruit flavours; the Esk Valley version places its accent firmly on ripeness and richness.

Andrew Phillips, formerly of Brown Brothers in Victoria, was appointed chief winemaker of the Villa Maria/Vidal/Esk Valley group in late 1995. Directly beneath the chief winemaker in the Villa Maria production pyramid are a trio of winemakers based at Mangere, Vidal and Esk Valley. The Vidal and Esk Valley winemakers prepare their wines to a 'ready for bottling' state, before they are tankered by road to Villa Maria for their final filtering and bottling.

Villa Maria's top end of the range Chardonnays, the Reserve Barrique Fermented *(see panel)* and the Reserve Marlborough, afford an absorbing style contrast. The slowly evolving Reserve Marlborough Chardonnay is a leaner, more fruit-driven style with intense lemony, figgy, slightly nutty flavours, underpinned by authoritative acidity.

Two other white wines carry Villa Maria's prestigious Reserve label (a tight, restrained, delicately spicy Reserve Gewürztraminer has also been made, but the 1994 vintage was the last). The Reserve Sauvignon Blanc, made from the ripest Marlborough fruit with a deft touch of oak, is fresh, pure, penetrating and zingy. The Reserve Noble Riesling, launched from the 1991 vintage and usually – not always – grown in Marlborough, is a ravishingly beautiful wine: succulent, honey-sweet, gloriously perfumed. This is New Zealand's most highly awarded sweet white.

The second-tier Cellar Selection wines place their accent on fruit quality – the grapes are sourced from some of Villa Maria's top vineyards – with markedly less oak influence than the Reserve range.

The quality of Villa Maria's third-tier Private Bin range has improved sharply in recent vintages. At its best, the low-priced Private Bin Müller-Thurgau is a delightfully floral, light wine with a perfect balance of slight sweetness, fruitiness and acidity. As an aperitif, this is hard to beat. With its enjoyable melon-like flavours, freshness and crisp finish, the gently oaked Private Bin Chenin Blanc/Chardonnay is an ideal everyday-drinking dry white.

The Private Bin Gewürztraminer, usually (but not always) Gisborne-grown, is perfumed, well-spiced and flavourful. Garden-fresh, herbal and zesty, the Private Bin Sauvignon Blanc has lately been blended from Hawke's Bay, Gisborne and Marlborough fruit.

With its straightforward, citrusy flavours and light oak influence, the Private Bin Chardonnay, usually grown in Gisborne, is a no-fuss style designed for early consumption. The Private Bin Riesling is a deep-scented, impressively flavour-packed wine, partly or wholly Marlborough-grown, its hint of sweetness balanced by vigorous acidity.

Under its St Aubyns, Forest Flower and Old Masters labels, Villa Maria also produces an array of low-priced white, red, sparkling and fortified wines.

The distinctive black labels of Villa Maria's reserve range are a key force among New Zealand's top reds. The Reserve Cabernet Sauvignon has captured a formidable string of gold medals. Based on Hawke's Bay fruit, it is typically matured for 20 months in a mix of new and one-year-old French, American and German oak barriques. This bold, dark hued, full-flavoured red exhibits a rich, toasty fragrance, great depth of spicy, cassis-like flavours and a tight tannin grip. Its Reserve Cabernet Sauvignon/Merlot stablemate is equally rich and complex, with mouth-encircling, spicy, plummy flavours and the firmness of structure to flourish long term in the bottle. These are very distinguished wines – a match for any reds in the land.

A vibrantly fruity, rich-flavoured red, sometimes principally based on Cabernet Sauvignon, at other times Merlot-predominant, is marketed under the Cellar Selection label. Villa Maria also produces a promisingly dark, weighty and supple Cellar Selection Shiraz, grown in Marlborough.

The Private Bin Cabernet Sauvignon/Merlot is a sturdy, flavoursome, oak-matured red, principally grown in Hawke's Bay, that in riper vintages delivers good value for money. This claret-style red has recently been partnered by a low-priced, ruby hued, fresh, berryish and supple Pinotage/Cabernet Sauvignon, designed for early consumption.

Twenty per cent of Villa Maria's output is exported, to the UK (especially), Sweden, Norway, Canada, Hong Kong, Fiji and the Cook Islands. In the future, says Fistonich, Villa Maria will not grow a lot bigger. 'We want to add more value to the wines, more sophistication.'

VILLA MARIA RESERVE BARRIQUE FERMENTED CHARDONNAY

This multiple gold medal and trophy-winning Chardonnay is powerful, mealy, creamy and rich. In the past based on Gisborne fruit, it now varies in origin according to the vintage.

'We're looking for a big, full-flavoured style based on super-ripe fruit off low-cropping vines, with lots of new wood (currently averaging 70 per cent, in the past 100 per cent) but more elegance than the rich, oaky wines of the late 1980s,' says viticulturist Steve Smith. The 1994 vintage was the first to be hand-harvested and whole bunch-pressed.

A 1994 vertical tasting of the 1986 to 1993 vintages proved the wine's ability to mature well (which, given its precocious, early-drinking appeal, some had doubted). The first 1986 vintage was bright, light gold, with an inviting, toasty bouquet, ripe citrus/lime flavours and an almost Burgundian power and richness. The bold, very ripe and deep-flavoured 1989 vintage was still ascending.

The latest releases are slightly more restrained in their youth, with a lovely harmony of grapefruit-like flavours and spicy oak, subtle lees-aging characters, creamy texture and long, crisp, succulent finish.

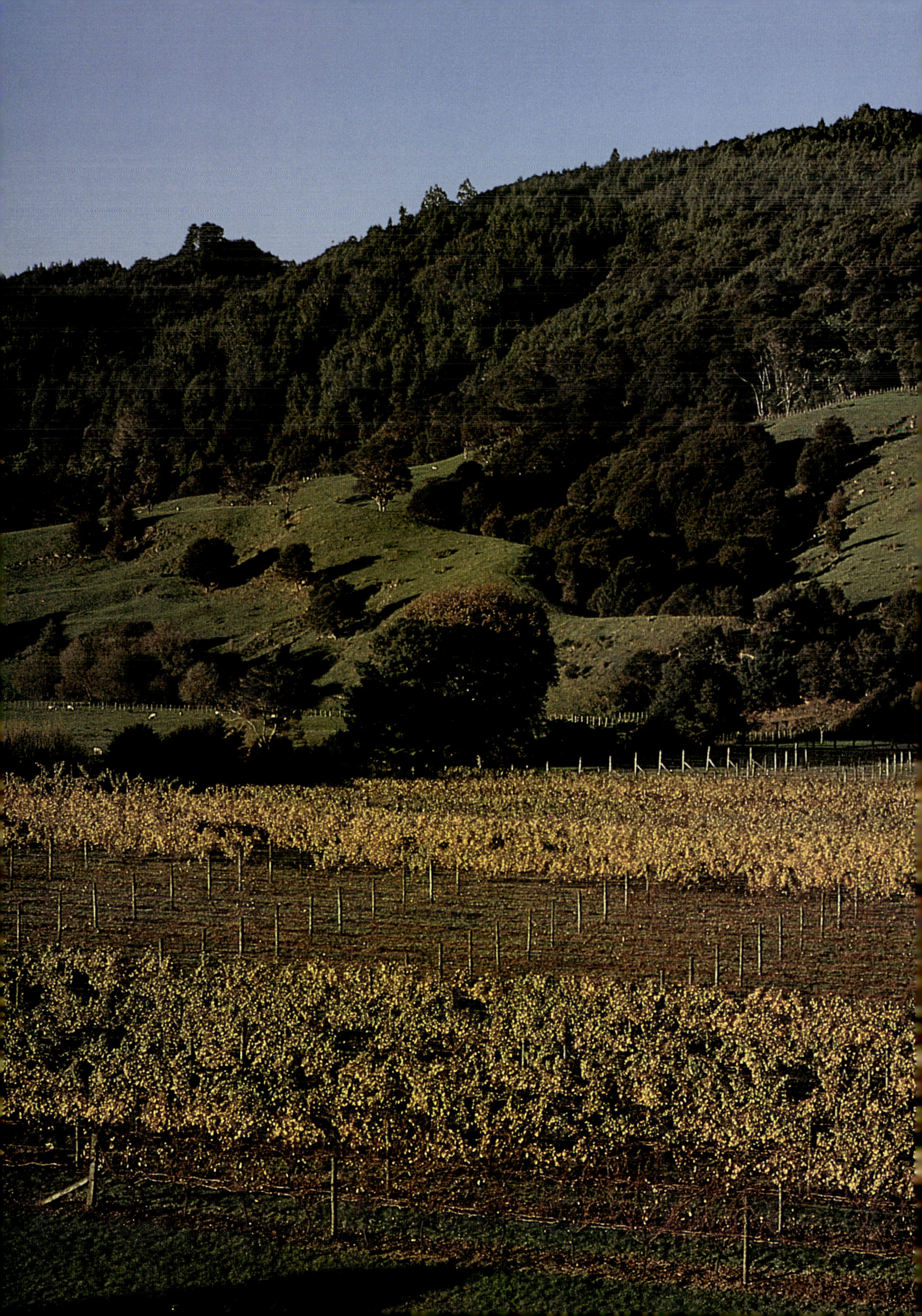

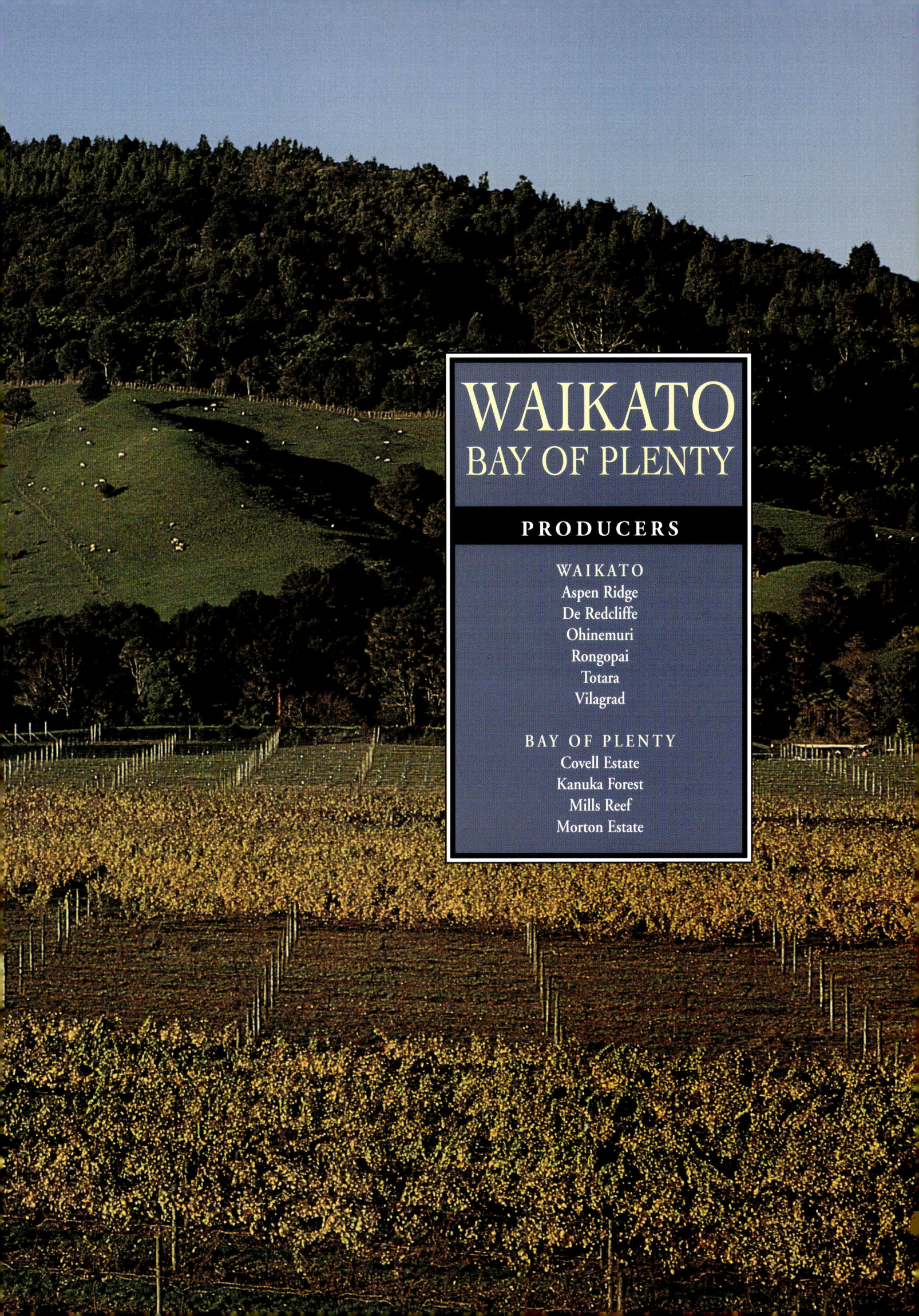

WAIKATO
BAY OF PLENTY

PRODUCERS

WAIKATO
Aspen Ridge
De Redcliffe
Ohinemuri
Rongopai
Totara
Vilagrad

BAY OF PLENTY
Covell Estate
Kanuka Forest
Mills Reef
Morton Estate

WAIKATO

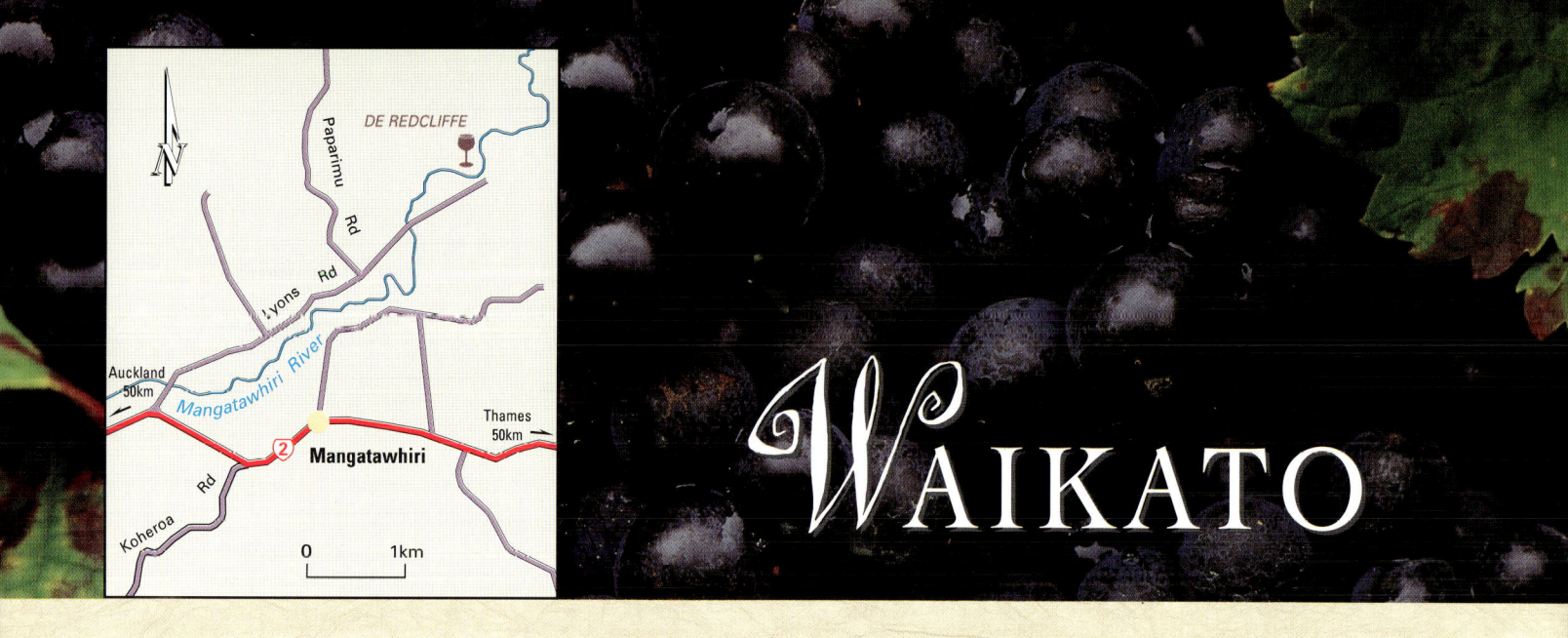

Wineries are scattered thinly across the Waikato and Bay of Plenty regions, yet several high-fliers are based there.

If you are driving from Auckland to Tauranga, stop at the secluded Hotel du Vin and its attached De Redcliffe Estate vineyard and winery at Mangatawhiri; the mouth-filling, savoury De Redcliffe Mangatawhiri Chardonnay is great value. Rongopai, just off the main highway at Te Kauwhata, is famous for its opulent, oily sweet whites. At Ohinemuri Estate, between Paeroa and Waihi, Horst Hillerich produces a slightly sweet, penetratingly flavoured Riesling.

In the western Bay of Plenty, Morton Estate produces consistently brilliant Chardonnays. From the Preston family's new Mills Reef winery at Bethlehem, flow rich, toasty, wood-aged Chardonnays and Sauvignon Blancs under the premium Elspeth label and one of the country's finest sparkling wines.

Yet the Waikato and Bay of Plenty are languishing as grapegrowing regions. With the southwards drift of viticulture, the area in vines has plummeted; in 1995 only 137 hectares of vines (1.7 per cent of the national vineyard) were planted there.

Grape yields are lower in the Waikato's clay soils than in the fertile Gisborne plains. The region also shares West Auckland's climatic disadvantages: temperatures and sunshine hours are high, but so is the average rainfall and humidity. Chardonnay, Sauvignon Blanc and Cabernet Sauvignon are the most extensively planted grape varieties, followed by Albany Surprise (grown for eating, rather than winemaking, purposes) and Chenin Blanc.

The outlook is bleak for the Waikato's viticultural future. The Viticultural Research Station closed several years ago and now serves as the Rongopai winery. The 'space age' winery erected at Te Kauwhata by Cooks in the early 1970s is now used by Corbans for bulk wine storage, but its surrounding vineyards have been uprooted.

In the Bay of Plenty to the east, the area under vines is tiny, but Morton Estate and Mills Reef are no longer the only winemaking outposts. The 1991 emergence of Covell Estate at Galatea, followed in 1993 by Kanuka Forest, near Whakatane, has doubled the number of wineries in the region.

In the high altitude heart of the North Island, in 1995 the Pukawa Wine Company planted a vineyard on the southern shores of Lake Taupo.

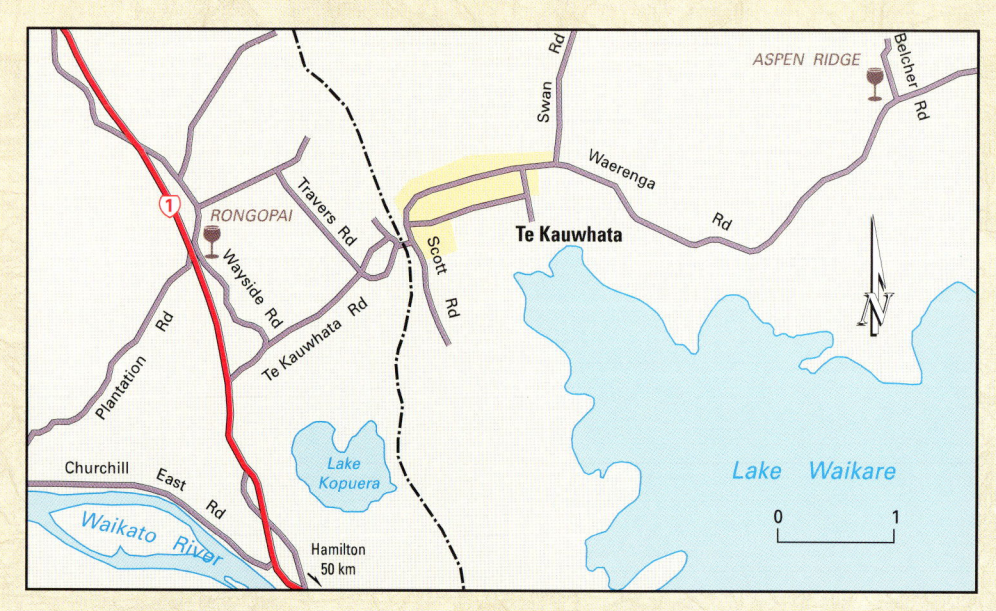

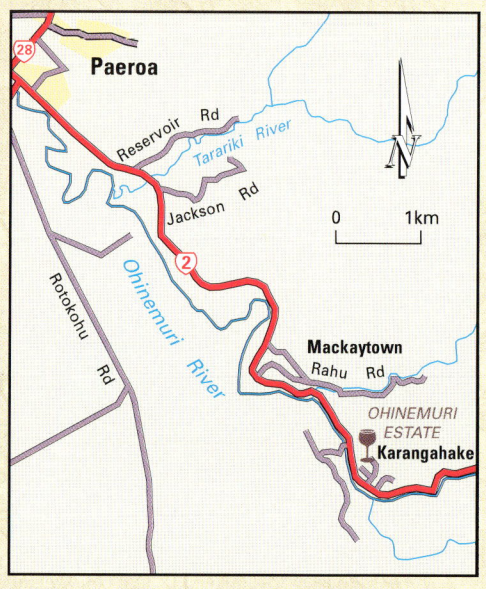

The lovely, hill-ringed De Redcliffe vineyard and winery lies in the Mangatawhiri Valley, 45 minutes by road from Auckland, 'much less by helicopter'. Here, long-term winemaker Mark Compton produces a steadily improving array of wines, including two attractive Sémillon-based whites.

Redcliffe – chosen as a title in the early nineteenth century by an ancestor of Chris Canning, the founder of the De Redcliffe winery – rises prominently above the wine-trading city of Bristol, England. The name was an obvious choice when Canning began planting his vineyard in the solitude of the Mangatawhiri Valley in 1976.

Canning admits he did not establish De Redcliffe as 'a man of destiny who had to make wine. The reason I bought the place was to escape foreign capital gains tax'.

Canning's entrepreneurial talents, and those of his wife Pamela, were again demonstrated in the late 1980s by the rise at De Redcliffe of the $8 million Hotel Du Vin, an accommodation and conference complex set (with top-class restaurant) amid native trees. To fund this major development, De Redcliffe Group Limited, incorporating the vineyard, winery and hotel, was floated on the stock exchange in 1987, with Canning the majority shareholder.

Following early financial difficulties – including a $485,000 trading loss in the year to 30 June 1989 – the De Redcliffe Group was purchased by a Japanese-owned company, Otaka Holdings (NZ) Limited, which also owns the Hyatt Auckland Hotel.

The six-hectare estate vineyard, on river silts with a gravel base, is principally planted in Chardonnay, with smaller blocks of Pinot Noir and Sémillon. The majority of the winery's fruit, however, is drawn from growers in Auckland, Waikato, Hawke's Bay and Marlborough.

To lift its production and maximise its control over grape quality, De Redcliffe has recently entered three vineyard projects on a joint-venture basis. An eight-hectare vineyard in Marlborough has been planted in Sauvignon Blanc and Chardonnay, and in Hawke's Bay, two vineyards in Gimblett Road and at Roy's Hill, totalling 15 hectares, will supply both white and red-wine varieties.

Until the 1986 vintage De Redcliffe wines were crushed and fermented elsewhere but barrel-aged at the vineyard. In late 1990 rose a handsome, spacious stone-walled winery. Viewing gantries and informative story boards permit self-conducted tours along the mezzanine floor. This stunning, extremely visitor-orientated winery is unlike any other in New Zealand.

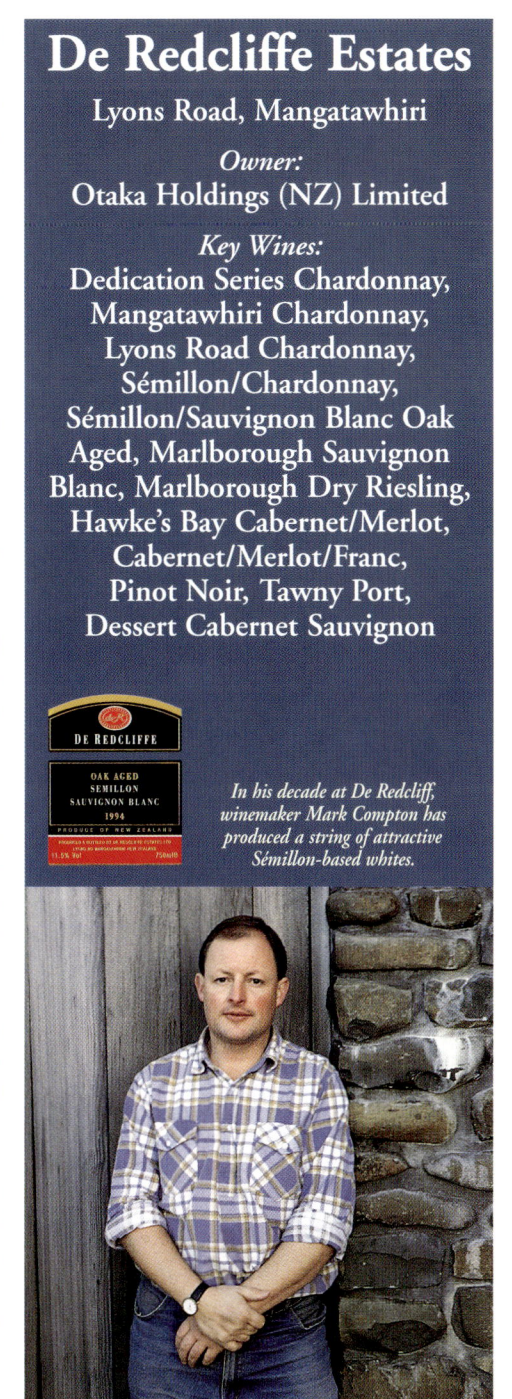

Mark Compton, a Wellington-born BSc, followed his three-year winemaking stint in Australia with a long period at Montana, overseeing bottling and the production of Lindauer, before he joined De Redcliffe in 1987. 'It's been a dynamic decade,' says Compton, 'going from a farm shed to a very modern winery with great equipment.'

With its recent plantings, De Redcliffe is poised for a big leap in production. Compton expects the winery's output to exceed 30,000 cases by 1997, and eventually climb to 45,000.

A feature of the De Redcliffe range is its pair of Sémillon-based whites. 'Sémillon is a major grape for us,' says Compton. 'The ripest fruit is reserved for the Sémillon/Sauvignon Blanc Oak Aged, and the rest goes to our "commercial" dry white – the Sémillon/Chardonnay.' The Sémillon/Sauvignon Blanc Oak Aged is a lively wine with good depth of lemon and capsicum-evoking flavours, lightly seasoned with oak. The lower-priced Sémillon/Chardonnay is a medium-bodied dry wine in a crisp, easy-drinking style.

Three styles of Chardonnay are produced. The new Dedication Series Chardonnay (the first of a new set of top-end-of-the-range wines), is grown in Hawke's Bay, fully barrel-fermented and lees-aged for nine months; this is the most distinguished of the trio, complex, mealy and deep-flavoured. The estate-grown, barrel-fermented and lees-aged Mangatawhiri Chardonnay has gone from strength to strength in recent vintages, offering lots of lively, citrusy, slightly buttery flavour and fine value in the mid-price range. Lyons Road Chardonnay is a lightly oaked Hawke's Bay wine designed for early consumption.

Two highlights of the De Redcliffe range are the Marlborough-grown Sauvignon Blanc and Dry Riesling. The Sauvignon Blanc is a medley of riper and early-picked fruit with penetrating verdant flavour and bracing acidity. The Dry Riesling is awash with lemon-and-lime varietal aromas and flavours.

The quality of De Redcliffe's white wines overshadows the reds. The flagship Cabernet/Merlot – of which the delightful, estate-grown 1980 vintage first established De Redcliffe's reputation – is now grown in Hawke's Bay. An enjoyable, supple but light wine, lacking concentration, it can be expected to improve sharply when the new Gimblett Road vineyard starts cropping in 1997. The lower-tier, slightly green-edged Cabernet/Merlot/Franc is a berryish, drink-young style. The Pinot Noir, in the past solid but unspectacular, from the 1995 vintage is wholly Waikato-grown.

Two fortified wines complete the De Redcliffe range. The seven-year-old, Cabernet Sauvignon-based, American oak-aged Tawny Port is perfumed, raisiny and creamy-smooth; one of the better New Zealand tawnies. The dark, purple-flushed Dessert Cabernet Sauvignon, fortified with 25-year-old spirit, is rich, smooth, sweet and pruney.

De Redcliffe Estates

Lyons Road, Mangatawhiri

Owner:
Otaka Holdings (NZ) Limited

Key Wines:
Dedication Series Chardonnay, Mangatawhiri Chardonnay, Lyons Road Chardonnay, Sémillon/Chardonnay, Sémillon/Sauvignon Blanc Oak Aged, Marlborough Sauvignon Blanc, Marlborough Dry Riesling, Hawke's Bay Cabernet/Merlot, Cabernet/Merlot/Franc, Pinot Noir, Tawny Port, Dessert Cabernet Sauvignon

In his decade at De Redcliff, winemaker Mark Compton has produced a string of attractive Sémillon-based whites.

'Save Water – Drink Rongopai Wine' urged the bumper stickers on countless cars during Auckland's recent water crisis. No other winery in the Waikato can match Rongopai for the diversity and quality of its locally grown wines: white, red, bone-dry and thrillingly sweet.

Rongopai winery in Te Kauwhata was founded in 1982 by Dr Rainer Eschenbruch and Tom van Dam, who worked together at the Te Kauwhata Viticultural Research Station. Three years ago, however, Eschenbruch withdrew from the company.

Faith van Dam, a director and shareholder, is involved on a part-time basis in marketing their growing output. A third shareholder, who lives overseas, has a one-third stake in the company.

Rongopai Wines

Wayside Road,
Te Kauwhata

Owners:
Tom and Faith
van Dam and
partner

Key Wines:
Winemakers Selection
Chardonnay, Sauvignon Blanc,
Syrah, Pinot Noir, Merlot;
Reserve Botrytised Riesling,
Reserve Botrytised Chardonnay,
Botrytised Reserve, Riesling,
Sauvignon Blanc, Chardonnay

Chardonnay and red-wine grapes.

The twin peaks of the Rongopai range are the gloriously nectareous Reserve Botrytised Riesling and Reserve Botrytised Chardonnay. The Reserve Botrytised Riesling is ravishingly perfumed, with steely acidity and thrillingly intense *Botrytis* character. The Reserve Botrytised Chardonnay (promoted as 'the ultimate aphrodisiac'), is a weightier style, peachy, treacly, oily and succulent. Both wines rank among New Zealand's most stunning sweet whites. The blended Botrytised Reserve is a lighter style, all sweetness and delicacy.

Chardonnay and Sauvignon Blanc are the mainstays of Rongopai's dry wine range. The Winemakers Selection Te Kauwhata Chardonnay, oak-aged for six months, is a

When Tom and Faith van Dam bought the former Viticultural Research Station at Te Kauwhata, they acquired a host of old casks dating back to the First World War.

In 1994 Rongopai purchased the historic Viticultural Research Station's winery in Te Kauwhata Road. The rambling (1600 square metres), white-walled winery, with ancient casks and a three-storey-high copper pot still, works on a three-level, gravity-feed system, with the crusher at the top and the barrels at the bottom. The 1996 vintage was Rongopai's first to be entirely processed at the 'Station' winery.

On loam-clay soils sloping gently to the north in Waerenga Road, Rongopai has a two-hectare vineyard of Riesling, Chardonnay, Cabernet Sauvignon, Bacchus and Scheurebe (the latter two for late harvest styles), densely planted to lower the vines' vigour. Rongopai also owns another two-hectare vineyard in Swan Road. On a joint-venture basis, a five-hectare vineyard across the road from the winery has been planted in Sauvignon Blanc and Chardonnay, and a larger vineyard in Hawke's Bay is being established in weighty, ripe, rich-flavoured and skilfully balanced wine with a long, soft finish. Fat and creamy-soft, with ripe tropical-fruit rather than strongly herbal flavours, the oak-aged Winemakers Selection Te Kauwhata Sauvignon Blanc is a very distinctive style – a world apart from the rapier-like Sauvignons of Marlborough.

The wines are sold from the company's shop near the main highway in Wayside Road, Te Kauwhata.

The rearing, bush-tangled slopes of the Karangahake Gorge, between Paeroa and Waihi, are an extremely unlikely site for a winery. The terrain is too precipitous, the rainfall too persistent, for grapegrowing. Yet amid these rugged hills Horst and Wendy Hillerich have established their distinctive, charming chalet-style winery – Ohinemuri Estate.

Horst Hillerich was born near Frankfurt in Germany and served his winemaking apprenticeship between 1976 and 1978 at Weingut Hulbert, a six-hectare family estate in the Rheingau. After two years' study at Veitshochheim University in Franconia, he graduated with the equivalent of a BSc in viticulture and winemaking.

After coming to New Zealand in 1987, Hillerich spent his first few months working for James and Annie Millton in Gisborne, and later that year met his Nelson-born wife, Wendy. From 1988 until early 1990 he worked under winemaker Gilbert Chan at Totara Vineyards. In 1989, while still working at Totara, he crushed and fermented the first wines under his own Ohinemuri Estate label.

Ohinemuri Estate is a winery, not a vineyard. Most of the grapes are bought from Gisborne and Hawke's Bay.

The property is delightful. A replica of a Latvian chalet, built on the banks of the Ohinemuri River in 1985, the buildings originally served as a house, stables and hayloft. The Hillerichs fell in love with the complex at first sight and have lovingly preserved its atmosphere. Customers in the winery shop call for service with the aid of an Austrian cow-bell.

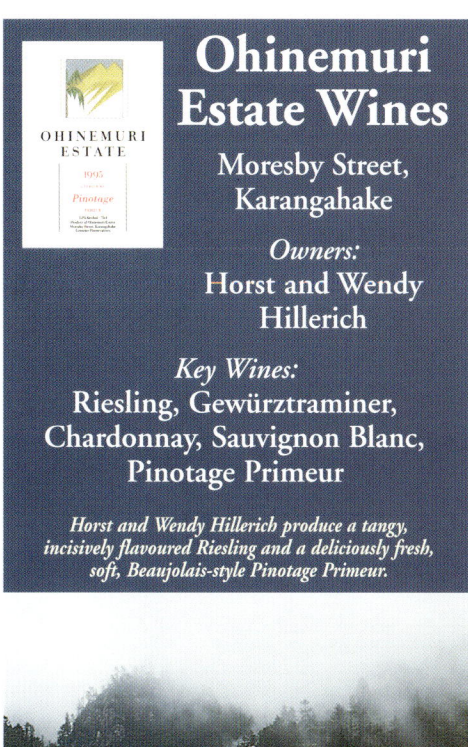

Ohinemuri Estate Wines

Moresby Street, Karangahake

Owners:
Horst and Wendy Hillerich

Key Wines:
Riesling, Gewürztraminer, Chardonnay, Sauvignon Blanc, Pinotage Primeur

Horst and Wendy Hillerich produce a tangy, incisively flavoured Riesling and a deliciously fresh, soft, Beaujolais-style Pinotage Primeur.

The first wines were crushed and fermented in Auckland but matured in the Karangahake Gorge. For the 1992 vintage, the Hillerichs converted their garage into a temporary winery. A new and larger winery, using gravity-feed systems, was built prior to the 1993 vintage; with its high-pitched roof, locals call it 'the church'.

Ohinemuri Estate is a very small company; each year it produces only about 1500 cases. 'We aim to sell 95 per cent directly to the public from the winery,' says Hillerich. 'Why grow any bigger?'

Hillerich's wines are of sound quality and often distinctive. The Riesling, which – unusually for New Zealand – is briefly aged on its yeast lees for 'extra body', is typically deep-scented and fruity with strong lemon/lime flavours, tangy acidity and a fresh, off-dry finish. The Sauvignon Blanc, also lees-matured, is a ripely herbal, crisp and flavourful wine with a touch of complexity.

The Gewürztraminer is perfumed, weighty and well-spiced in a crisp, off-dry style. The Chardonnay, barrel-fermented, has varied in quality and style.

The Pinotage Primeur is a delicious Gisborne 'nouveau' style in which strong, fresh, raspberryish fruit flavours hold sway. About 35 per cent of the grapes are whole bunch-fermented – using the traditional Beaujolais technique – giving the wine its fruity, supple charm.

Ohinemuri Estate's cafe is open every day from Labour Weekend to Easter, with wine-tasting all year round. 'It is Mediterranean cuisine served with New Zealand scenery, atmosphere and wines,' says Wendy Hillerich.

Other Producers

Aspen Ridge

Aspen Ridge is a small winery with a five-hectare vineyard in Waerenga Road, east of Te Kauwhata township. The company was established in 1963 by Alister McKissock. Aspen Ridge markets highly regarded grape jellies and varietal grape juices, but the grape wines have not been impressive.

In 1996, Aucklander Toby Cooper and his wife, Jenny Gander, in partnership with Toby's sister, Nikki Cooper and her husband Peter West, acquired Aspen Ridge, with the intention of upgrading the wines.

Totara

Out on a limb near Thames, at the base of the Coromandel Peninsula, Totara is New Zealand's only predominantly Chinese-owned winery.

Founded by Stanley Chan in 1950, the company has struggled to make an impact in recent years, and is no longer widely regarded as a producer of quality wine. Yet it occasionally springs a big surprise – its Winemakers Reserve Chardonnay 1990 won the top Chardonnay trophy at the 1992 Air New Zealand Wine Awards.

Vilagrad

Another small winery with a local following is Vilagrad, founded by Ivan Milicich at Ngahinepouri, just south of Hamilton, in 1922. Pieter and Nelda Nooyen, the third generation of the family, have a five-hectare vineyard. The top range, labelled Nooyen Reserve, includes a Pinot Noir and Cabernet/Merlot/Malbec – both slightly green-edged – and a barrel-fermented Chardonnay which in some vintages (particularly 1992) has reached a high standard, but is usually consumed at the winery.

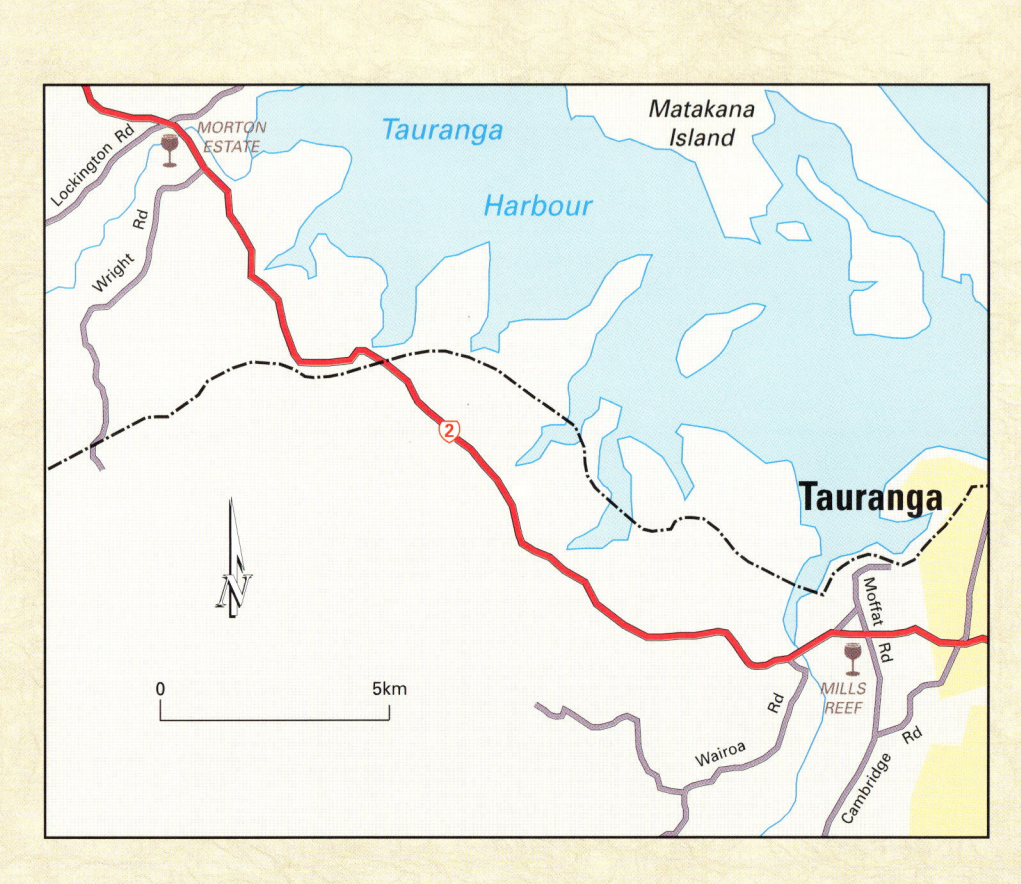

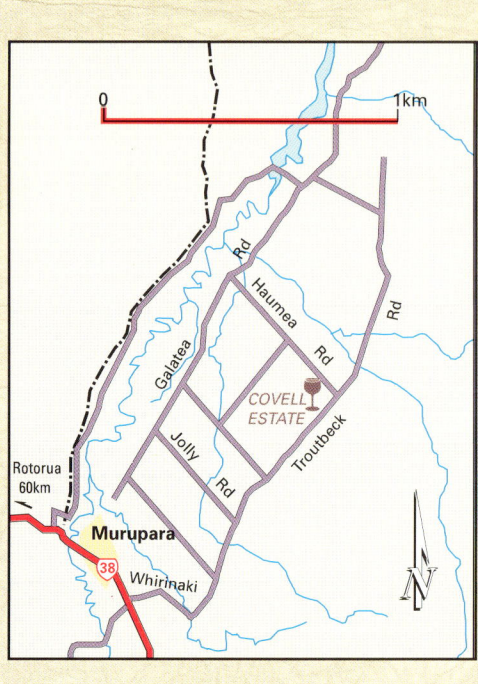

Bay of Plenty

Is this New Zealand's most remote winery? Covell Estate lies hard up against the flanks of the Ureweras at Galatea, near Murupara in the inland, eastern Bay of Plenty.

'Spring frosts are a hazard here,' admits Bob Covell, a cultured, genial beef and pig farmer turned winemaker who planted his first vines in 1981. Two years out of five, cold fronts spill down over the mountains in late September or early October, after the vines' buds have burst, causing heavy crop damage. A wind machine and mobile gas heaters mounted on a tractor can reduce, but not eliminate, the losses.

Bob and his wife, Des, are the principal shareholders in Covell Estate, with their son, Robert, and his wife, Diane, also involved. The vineyard is planted on the family's 80-hectare Birchwood Farm. 'As dairy farmers we're price takers, so we looked for a caper where we could set the price,' says Bob. The first 20 bottles of experimental wine flowed in 1987 and the first commercial vintage in 1991.

The organically cultivated five-hectare vineyard – 200 metres above sea level – is planted in 20cm of topsoil overlying pumice and a deeper layer of volcanic clay. Pinot Noir and Chardonnay are the key varieties, with smaller areas devoted to Gewürztraminer, Riesling, Cabernet Sauvignon and Merlot. 'We get ripeness in sugar terms, but the grapes always retain high acidity,' says Bob Covell.

Only a rivulet of wine flows from Covell Estate. The 1993 vintage, for instance, yielded 220 cases of Pinot Noir and 130 cases each of Chardonnay and Dry Red, made by the Covells in their small but well-equipped, on-site winery. The wines are sold at the gate and a few shops in the Bay of Plenty.

Covell Estate Chardonnay, fermented and lees-aged for 18 months in new Nevers oak barriques, is a slightly austere style with lots of citrusy, appley, yeasty flavour and a freshly acidic finish. The Pinot Noir, oak-aged for two years, is typically light in colour and body, but attractively savoury, oaky and mellow. Both wines are clean, well-made and distinctive.

With $350,000 invested in Covell Estate so far, excluding the cost of the land and labour, 'there can be no turning back,' says Bob Covell. 'We know it can be done.'

Covell Estate
Troutbeck Road, Galatea

Owners: The Covell family

Key Wines: Pinot Noir, Chardonnay

One of New Zealand's rarest Pinot Noirs flows from Bob and Des Covells' tiny winery, far from the major wine trails on the frost-prone flanks of the Ureweras.

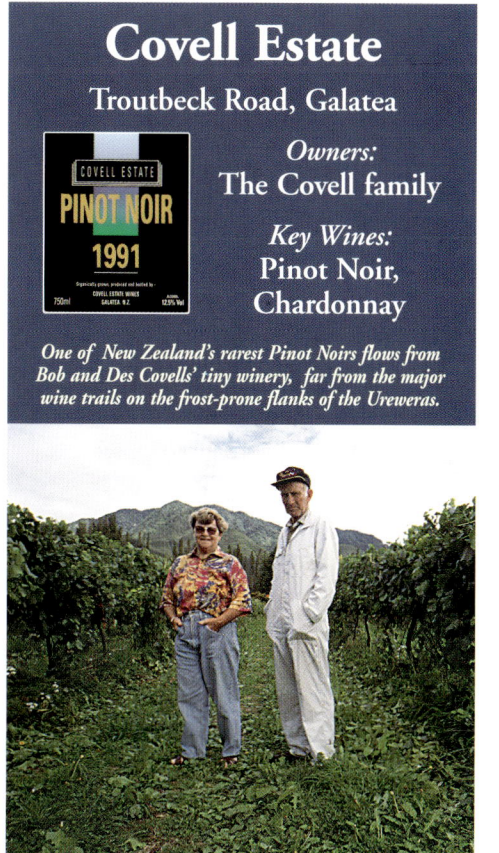

Mills Reef is making waves. Warren 'Paddy' Preston is a quiet, unassuming personality – not the sort of winemaker to pursue the limelight. Yet his glowing results in comparative tastings, here and abroad, prove this former builder and champion kiwifruit winemaker now ranks among New Zealand's finest grape winemakers.

One of the most striking wineries in the country recently rose on the outskirts of Tauranga. With its stylish architecture and sumptuous feel, Mills Reef's new winery is sure to become a mecca for wine lovers and a wine industry showpiece.

Upstairs lie the company's offices and boardroom. Italian ceramic tiles run through the public areas and onto a deck which runs almost right around the building. The deck flows to a paved and grassed area which includes three petanque (French bowls) courts.

The elegant winery restaurant seats about 75. From the spacious wine-tasting room, which has large viewing windows into the bottling and labelling areas, stairs lead down to a cellar with traditional vaulted ceilings and older vintages of Mills Reef wines for sale. Huge wooden doors lead into a spacious cellar for barrel maturation.

Mills Reef Winery
Moffat Road, Bethlehem

Owners: The Preston family

Key Wines: <u>Elspeth</u> Chardonnay, Riesling, Sauvignon Blanc, Cabernet/Merlot, <u>Reserve</u> Chardonnay, Riesling, Sauvignon Blanc, Pinot Noir, Cabernet Sauvignon, <u>Mere Road Selection</u> Chardonnay, Riesling, Sauvignon Blanc, Pinot Blush, Pinot Noir, Cabernet Sauvignon; Mills Reef Traditional Method, Charisma

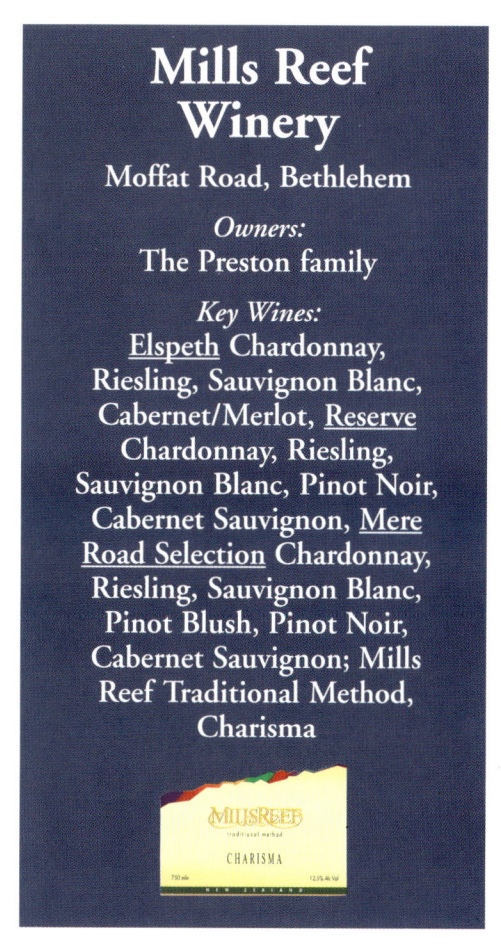

Paddy Preston came to the Bay of Plenty from Wellington in the late 1970s to make wine – from kiwifruit. The Preston family soon dominated the Fruit Winemakers of New Zealand competition, and their current output of kiwifruit wine under the Preston's label (much of it exported to Japan and Taiwan) is still not much less than their grape wine production.

Mills Reef is truly a family-run winery. Paddy is general manager and head of the grape winemaking operation; his oldest son Warren controls the marketing; Tim oversees production; Melissa is the office manager. Helen, Paddy's wife, is also involved.

Mills Reef's annual output has recently soared from 12,000 to 25,000 cases, making it a large 'small' winery by New Zealand standards. Grapes are drawn from its own eight-hectare vineyard in Mere Road, near the Stonecroft winery, and other growers concentrated in Hawke's Bay.

Mills Reef produces a three-tier range, with those labelled Elspeth (after Paddy Preston's mother) at the top, followed by a mid-priced range of Reserve wines and everyday-drinking varietals under the Mere Road Selection label.

Chardonnay and sparkling wines are the twin highlights of the Mills Reef range. Mere Road Chardonnay, partly fermented and matured in oak, is a fresh, full style with slightly nutty, buttery flavours, offering crisp, attractive drinking. The Reserve Chardonnay is more complex and savoury. The flagship Elspeth Chardonnay is a superbly well-crafted, highly concentrated wine; a powerful, mealy style with layers of peachy-ripe fruit, a deliciously creamy texture and a long, rich finish.

By fermenting and maturing his base wine in barrels, rather than stainless steel tanks, Paddy Preston produces two distinctively full-flavoured, subtle and stylish sparklings. The top wine, labelled Mills Reef Traditional Method and vintage-dated, is a Chardonnay-predominant style, bottle-aged for two years on its yeast lees before it is disgorged. In the past a celebration of rich, creamy, Chardonnay fruit flavours, it has lately evolved into a more restrained and refined style, nutty and yeasty, tight and lingering. Charisma, a non-vintage style, Pinot Noir-predominant and disgorged after 12 to 18 months lees-aging in the bottle, displays well-subdued fruit characters and a yeasty, flinty complexity that is very Champagne-like.

Riesling is another feature of the Mills Reef range, especially the perfumed, poised Elspeth Riesling with its beautiful balance of rich, citrusy flavours, slight sweetness and racy acidity. Also memorable is the partly barrel-fermented Elspeth Sauvignon Blanc, chock-full of ripely herbal and creamy oak flavours.

Warren ('Paddy') Preston produces an outstandingly rich Elspeth Chardonnay and very stylish bottle-fermented sparklings at Mills Reef's opulent new winery at Bethlehem.

Morton Estate Winery

State Highway 2,
Aongatete,
via Katikati

Owners:
John and Alison Coney

Key Wines:
<u>Black Label</u> Hawke's Bay Chardonnay, Cabernet/Merlot, Méthode Champenoise, <u>White Label</u> Hawke's Bay Chardonnay, Sauvignon Blanc, Pinot Noir, Cabernet/Merlot, <u>Mill Road</u> Hawke's Bay Chardonnay, Sauvignon Blanc, Müller-Thurgau, Cabernet/Merlot, <u>Stone Creek</u> Marlborough Riesling, Sauvignon Blanc, Chardonnay; Brut, Méthode Champenoise

The recent sale of Morton Estate and the departure of its founding winemaker have opened a new chapter in the history of this illustrious Chardonnay producer.

John and Alison Coney's purchase of Morton Estate in mid 1995 was the final act in the unravelling of the ill-fated Appellation Vineyards venture, which briefly merged Morton Estate, Cellier Le Brun and Allan Scott but never proceeded with its planned public share float. The Coneys are Kiwis who divide their time between New Zealand, Australia and Canada. John Coney, a new face to the industry, is described by former Morton Estate marketing manager Paul Treacher as 'a property developer and financier with a real enthusiasm for New Zealand wine'.

For several years after its first vintage in 1983 the Bay of Plenty winery sold all its output with impressive ease. The gold medal success of its 1983 White Label Chardonnay spurred interest, the striking Cape Dutch-style winery on the highway at Aongatete, near Katikati, attracted widespread attention, and South Australian winemaker John Hancock had already built a cult following during four spectacularly successful vintages at Delegat's.

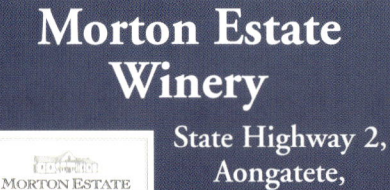

Hancock's move to Morton Estate met with immediate show success. 'We hit the Chardonnay market at the right time and grew with it.'

During his latter years at Morton Estate, as general manager John Hancock was largely immersed in paper work and public relations, with assistant winemaker Steve Bird, who arrived at Morton Estate in 1985, handling the day-to-day production. Following Hancock's departure in 1996 (to set up a new winery, Gimblett Estate, in Hawke's Bay), Bird, a Roseworthy College graduate with winemaking experience in France and China, assumed full control of the production arena.

The sloping, one-hectare vineyard behind the winery produces Pinot Noir fruit used in the bottle-fermented sparkling. However, the company-owned Riverview vineyard on terraces of the Ngaruroro River at Mangatahi, inland from Ngatarawa in Hawke's Bay, is far more important.

Here Morton Estate has planted 70 hectares of vines: 35 hectares of Chardonnay, 12 hectares each of Sauvignon Blanc and Pinot Noir, and smaller blocks of Cabernet Sauvignon, Merlot, Meunier and Syrah. A relatively late-ripening vineyard, Riverview has yielded a string of brilliant Chardonnays and highly promising Pinot Noir, Cabernet Sauvignon and Merlot. A grape-processing facility arose there prior to the 1996 vintage, enabling Morton Estate to crush and press its white-wine grapes before sending the juice to the Bay of Plenty for fermentation. Some of the Chardonnay is barrel-fermented and the red wines are fermented on-site at Riverview.

In the nearby Colefield vineyard, Morton Estate is planting 25 hectares of vines. Mill Road, a 17-hectare Haumoana vineyard, is planted in Cabernet Sauvignon, Chardonnay, Sauvignon Blanc and Müller-Thurgau (the last to be replaced by Pinot Noir).

Morton Estate also has a presence in Marlborough, as a result of acquiring the Stone Creek vineyard in Rapaura Road. The 41-hectare site is planted principally in Chardonnay, Sauvignon Blanc and Pinot Noir, with a small block of Riesling.

The Hawke's Bay wines are marketed as Black Label (the top tier), White Label (middle tier) and Mill Road (everyday wines). The Stone Creek label is reserved for Marlborough wines, not necessarily grown in the Stone Creek vineyard.

Mouth-filling and complex, the Black Label Chardonnay is one of New Zealand's most illustrious wines (see panel).

The White Label Chardonnay, which shows much of the class of its big brother, is a great buy in the mid-price range. Grown at Riverview, and fermented and matured for nine months in French oak barriques (25 per cent new), in top vintages it is rich-flavoured, with concentrated citrusy, mealy, biscuity characters and a seductive creaminess of texture. The Mill Road Chardonnay is a non-wooded style, fresh and uncomplicated.

John and Alison Coney are new faces to the wine industry who now control one of its most prestigious Chardonnay producers.

Morton Estate's vintage-dated Méthode Champenoise is a consistently classy wine. It is partnered by Morton Brut, a lower-priced, non-vintage bottle-fermented sparkling.

Of Morton Estate's Sauvignon Blancs, the White Label model is an off-dry Hawke's Bay wine, fresh, tangy and gently herbaceous. Its Marlborough stablemate, carrying the Stone Creek label, is a punchier style with rich, long gooseberry/capsicum flavours. The Stone Creek selection also features a dryish, delicate, appley, lemony Riesling and a fruit-driven style of Chardonnay.

The standard of Morton Estate's red wines has soared in recent years. The White Label Pinot Noir, Riverview-grown, is a deliciously flavour-packed and supple red; one of the finest value Pinot Noirs on the market. There is also a dark, Black Label Pinot Noir that is strikingly weighty and dense-flavoured.

Mill Road Cabernet/Merlot is a decent, flavoursome but not intense red, priced right. The White Label Cabernet/Merlot, French oak-matured, is an elegant, medium-to-full-bodied wine with good depth of blackcurrant, spice and plum flavours.

The Black Label Cabernet/Merlot, grown at Riverview and French oak-aged for 18 months, is seductively rich, spicy and soft – a smashing red to drink in its youth.

Other Producers
Kanuka Forest

This tiny winery sits right on the coast at Thornton, 15 kilometres west of Whakatane. Tony Hassall and his wife, Julia, planted their first vines there in 1988 and by 1993 had bottled their first commercial wines. 'We could see that the public are keen on visiting vineyards and there are no other wineries in this area,' says Hassall.

The sandy, three-hectare vineyard is principally planted in Cabernet Sauvignon, Merlot, Sauvignon Blanc and Chardonnay. The initial releases included an assertively oaked Fumé Blanc and a lemony, savoury, woody Chardonnay. The Cabernet Sauvignon/Merlot is a decent red with pleasing depth of blackcurrant and red berry flavours, oak richness and firm tannins.

MORTON ESTATE BLACK LABEL HAWKE'S BAY CHARDONNAY

This is a justly celebrated wine. Once golden, very substantial and huge in flavour, its style has changed in recent vintages, with greater emphasis on flavour delicacy, tightness and longevity.

The debut 1984 vintage was one of the first New Zealand Chardonnays to be barrel-fermented and lees-aged. 'I'd been influenced by wines like Louis Latour Corton-Charlemagne '79 and Domaine des Comtes Lafon Meursault Clos de la Barre '82 – mealy, biscuity wines with hazelnut characters,' recalls John Hancock. 'I went to Burgundy in 1981 and enquired about their techniques. I remember saying to Morton Brown when we made the 1984 vintage: "If it doesn't sell, we'll drink it ourselves."' It won a gold medal and streaked out of the winery.

Hancock attributes the much greater finesse evident in the 1991 and subsequent vintages to the quality of the Riverview vineyard. 'We'd previously sourced most of the fruit from a grower in Mere Road. At Riverview we could be far more selective, by using only the best blocks of grapes, and the vineyard gave a different character: more intense grapefruit flavours and better acid balances, eliminating the need for a softening malolactic fermentation in good vintages.'

One hundred per cent new oak has been a key ingredient in the Black Label recipe, right from the start. Lees-stirred since 1991, and hand-picked since 1993, the wine is also whole bunch-pressed and oak-aged for 15 months.

This is a refined, weighty, tight-structured wine with a lovely array of grapefruit and melon-like, mealy, oaky flavours and a long, rich finish. The 1991 vintage is currently at the peak of its powers.

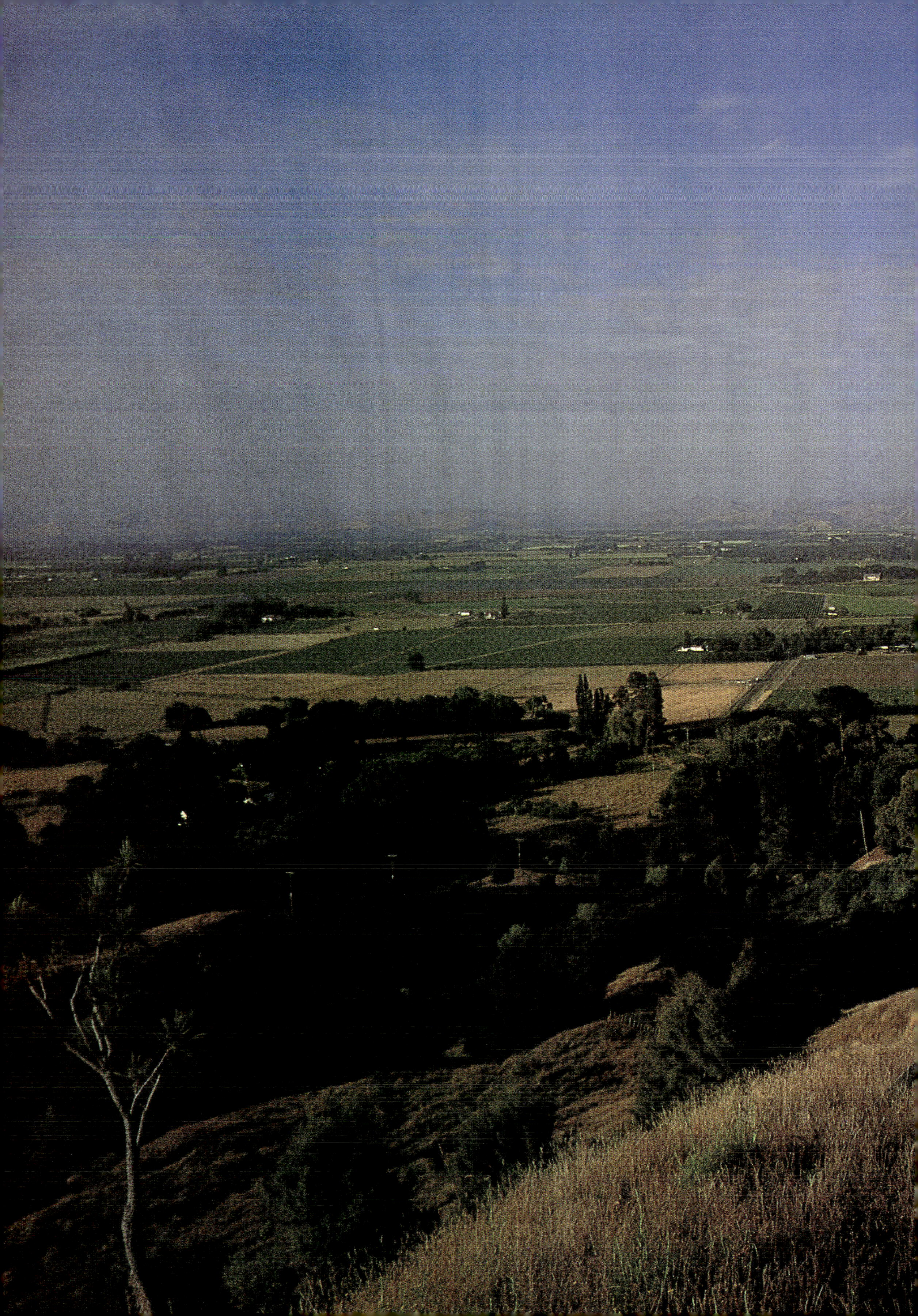

GISBORNE

PRODUCERS

Harvest Wine Company
Landfall Wines
Matawhero Wines
Parker Méthode Champenoise
Pouparae Park
Revington Vineyard
Shalimar Estate
Tai-Ara-Rau
The Millton Vineyard

GISBORNE

Almost one-third of the country's wine flowed from Gisborne in the 1995 vintage, yet the area does not enjoy the powerful profile of New Zealand's two other key wine regions, Marlborough and Hawke's Bay. Much of the Gisborne crop is utilised for low-priced wines like Montana's Wohnsiedler Müller-Thurgau and Bernadino Spumante, and with only six wineries open to the public, the Gisborne wine trail is remarkably short.

What does Gisborne do best? Chardonnay and Gewürztraminer, above all else. Gisborne's warm, sunny climate produces fragrant, ripe-tasting, well-rounded Chardonnays that can be delicious at a year old, and the best improve for several years.

Gisborne Müller-Thurgau can be a flowery, fruity, charming mouthful at just three months old. At its best – from Revington Vineyard, Montana Patutahi Estate and Matawhero – the Gewürztraminer is the most richly perfumed and flavour-packed in the country. Even the much-maligned reds are showing signs of improvement; some of the chunky, rich-flavoured and supple Merlots would not be out of place in a line-up from Hawke's Bay.

The East Cape, dominated by the Raukumara Range, has only limited lowland areas suitable for viticulture. Grapegrowing is confined to the Poverty Bay flats around Gisborne, which form the largest of the coastal alluvial plains, and to smaller ones further north at Tolaga Bay and Tikitiki, and to the south near Wairoa.

Friedrich Wohnsiedler pioneered winemaking in Gisborne after a false start by Marist missionaries, who landed by mistake at Turanganui (Gisborne) in 1850 and planted vines there before departing for their original destination, Hawke's Bay. Wohnsiedler, born on a tributary of the Rhine, arrived in New Zealand around the turn of the century. When patriots laid waste his Gisborne smallgoods business during the First World War, Wohnsiedler moved out and onto the land, planting vines at Ormond in 1921. His first vintage, a sweet red, was labelled simply as 'Wine'.

When Wohnsiedler died in 1956, his Waihirere vineyard covered only four hectares. (His name lives on, of course, on the labels of Montana's Wohnsiedler range.) In 1961, a rapid expansion programme began which, after a series of financial restructurings, saw the Wohnsiedler family eventually lose control. By 1973 Montana had completely absorbed Waihirere.

From a paltry acreage of vines supplying the old Waihirere winery, since 1965 viticulture has swept the Gisborne plains. Corbans and Montana between them have three large wineries in the area, not open to visitors. In 1995 Gisborne was New Zealand's third most heavily planted wine region, with 18.3 per cent of the country's total vines – a steep drop from 36 per cent in 1986, reflecting the recent vineyard expansion in less fertile, drier regions to the south.

Gisborne is white-wine country. Müller-Thurgau and Chardonnay total one-half of all plantings, followed by Dr Hogg Muscat, Reichensteiner, Sauvignon Blanc, Sémillon, Chenin Blanc and Golden Chasselas. Here the later-ripening red varieties have tended to become swollen, at the cost of flavour and colour intensity: with the odd exception, Cabernet Sauvignon has not performed well in Gisborne.

The few established winemakers believe that Gisborne's grapegrowers will not set up their own wineries to the extent growers have further south. 'Most of the grapegrowers are farmers at heart,' says one winemaker. 'A lot of them have the attitude: grapes are just another crop. They're not interested in wine quality; it's a tonnage game.' And several of the winemakers themselves are only involved in wine production on a part-time basis.

The doubts over grape quality centre principally on the fact that although the vines get ample amounts of sunshine and heat, the highly fertile soils and plentiful autumn rains combine to produce both excessively dense vine-foliage growth and bumper crops. The rainfall during the critical February-April harvest period averages 70 per cent higher than in Marlborough, and 33 per cent higher than in Hawke's Bay.

Some vineyards, however, are employing a variety of techniques to achieve fruit quality far above the norm. By selecting devigorating rootstocks; planting more *Phylloxera*-resistant vines (the bug has made rapid inroads into Gisborne's vineyards since its discovery there in 1970); planting new, improved clones; planting virus-free vines; plucking leaves to reduce fruit shading; later harvesting to advance ripening; and a range of other approaches, Gisborne viticulturists have of late been exploring more fully their region's fine wine potential.

As winemakers explore sites on the fringes of the plains, away from the most fertile alluvial silts, the flow of exceptional Gisborne wines is sure to rise. 'The biggest difference we see is between Patutahi, where we get very elegant fruit, and the Ormond Valley, where the clay soils produce big, fat wines,' says Steve Voysey, Montana's Gisborne winemaker.

More new wineries are needed if Gisborne is ever to rival the wine profile of Hawke's Bay and Marlborough. However, the increasing array of top Gisborne wines from Montana and Corbans is a step in the right direction.

REVINGTON VINEYARD
Ormond Valley Rd
0 1 2 3km
N
MONTANA ORMOND
Snowsill Rd
Waihirere
Waimata Hokoroa Rd
Back Ormond Rd
Taruheru River
Lavenham Rd
Waipaoa River
Tucker Rd
Bushmere Rd
Patutahi
Wharekopae Rd
POUPARAE PARK
SHALIMAR ESTATE
36
2
Makaraka
TAI-ARA-RAU
Mangapapa
Bell Rd
Matawhero
GISBORNE
Riverpoint Rd
MATAWHERO
PARKER
THE MILLTON VINEYARD
Papatu Rd
MONTANA
CORBANS
HARVEST WINE CO
Manutuke
Karaua Rd
Poverty Bay
LANDFALL
Saddler Rd
Beach Rd

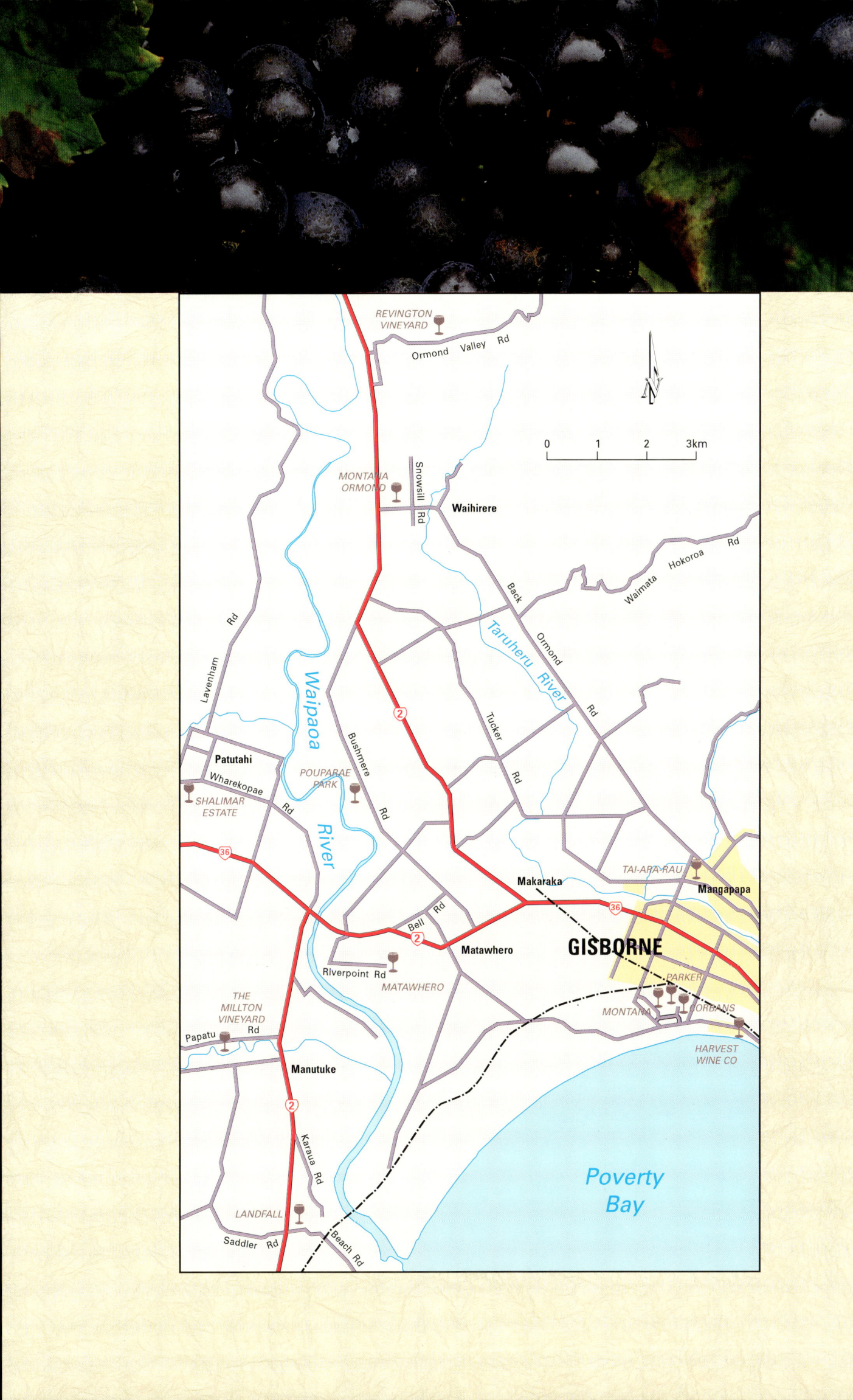

The Landfall winery, home of wines marketed under the Landfall and Longbush labels, is owned by brothers John and Bill Thorpe. Sited on the main highway at Manutuke, south of Gisborne, the winery's name commemorates the nearby landfalls of early Maori canoes and Captain Cook.

Landfall has changed tack several times during its short history. The founding partners were John Thorpe and Ross Revington. Revington, a lawyer, formed the Landfall partnership (originally called White Cliffs) with Thorpe in 1989, and for several years the wines grown in his own Revington Vineyard were marketed by Landfall. Revington, however, withdrew from the partnership in 1993. In the latest move, John and Bill Thorpe (who previously owned the Longbush range of wines, made by John at the Landfall winery) in 1995 formed a new partnership to jointly produce and market Landfall and Longbush wines.

The silty eight-hectare estate vineyard, planted in Pinot Noir and Gewürztraminer, has transitional Bio-Gro status. Landfall also buys fruit from other growers in the region.

The roomy, corrugated-iron winery started life as a packing shed, to which the partners have added a Mediterranean-inspired café. About 10,000 cases are produced each year.

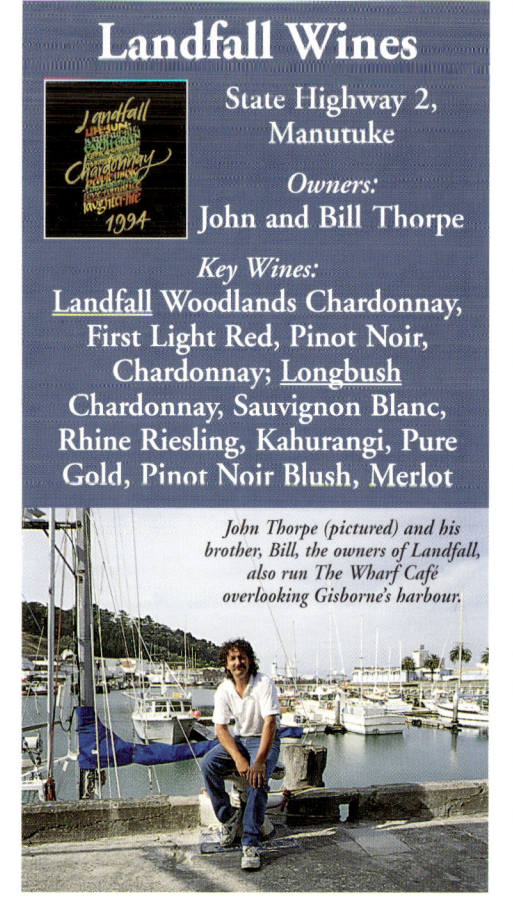

Winemaker John Thorpe has two specialties. 'Chardonnay is one of Gisborne's strengths, and constitutes half our output. Then there's Pinot Noir; we grow that and really want to develop it as a variety.'

The flagship Woodlands Chardonnay, which is fully barrel-fermented and lees-matured, and the lower-priced, partly barrel-fermented Landfall Chardonnay are both up-front, soft wines full of peachy-ripe, toasty, buttery flavour.

In the past, Landfall Pinot Noir was light, raspberryish and straightforward, but the latest vintages display greater concentration and complexity. First Light Red, a light, supple Pinot Noir, is a charmingly fresh, raspberryish red, soft and vibrantly fruity.

The Longbush range includes a crisp, vigorous, strong-flavoured Rhine Riesling that ages gracefully for several years; Kahurangi, a slightly sweet, very fruity blend of Müller-Thurgau and Muscat; the golden, sweet and treacly Pure Gold Late Harvest Riesling; and the impressively supple, spicy and rich-flavoured Merlot.

Landfall Wines

State Highway 2, Manutuke

Owners:
John and Bill Thorpe

Key Wines:
Landfall Woodlands Chardonnay, First Light Red, Pinot Noir, Chardonnay; Longbush Chardonnay, Sauvignon Blanc, Rhine Riesling, Kahurangi, Pure Gold, Pinot Noir Blush, Merlot

John Thorpe (pictured) and his brother, Bill, the owners of Landfall, also run The Wharf Café overlooking Gisborne's harbour.

'In a "Woman's Weekly" world, I'm doing Hemingway,' claims Denis Irwin, the proprietor of Matawhero and one of the great individualists of the New Zealand wine scene.

Over a decade ago, Matawhero enjoyed a reputation second to none for its handling of Gewürztraminer. Today, the winery's star has dimmed, but the wines flowing from the end of Riverpoint Road can still be absorbing. Irwin's rollercoaster career has reflected his unique personal blend of innovative winemaking, entrepreneurial business style – and love of letting his hair down.

Matawhero's 30-hectare vineyard surrounding the winery is planted predominantly in Gewürztraminer and Chardonnay, with smaller plots of Sauvignon Blanc, Chenin Blanc, Cabernet Sauvignon, Merlot, Malbec, Syrah and Pinot Noir. The nearby two-hectare Bridge Estate vineyard is entirely planted in red-wine varieties.

So far, Matawhero's success has hinged primarily on Gewürztraminer. The Gewürztraminer at its best is everything that wine of this variety should be: pungent, very aromatic, unmistakably spicy in taste. Recent vintages have been more restrained in spiciness than their ebullient predecessors, but still distinctive wines: musky, substantial, honeyish and soft.

'There are a lot of more pungent, obvious Gewürztraminers on the market than mine now,' says Irwin. 'That's great – there's no challenge for me in that. I want structure, subtlety, complexity. Varietal character is the last point I'm interested in, although it does come as the wines age.'

Two Chardonnays are produced: a tank-fermented, oak-aged Reserve Chardonnay in a slightly oxidative, fat, figgy, ripe-tasting and robust style; and a fresher, broad, rounded Estate Chardonnay that offers satisfying, smooth drinking. The oak-matured Sauvignon Blanc, a world apart from the pungent Marlborough style, offers plenty of ripe, toasty, buttery-soft flavour.

Matawhero's red wines, more than any other winery's, have disproved the theory that Gisborne cannot produce fine quality reds. The dark Cabernet Sauvignon/Merlot is spicy, gutsy and tannic, in a rich-flavoured and characterful style. Bridge Estate, a single-vineyard blend of Merlot, Malbec, Cabernet Sauvignon and Cabernet Franc, is equally bold, with concentrated, plum-like flavours and spicy/leathery nuances.

Matawhero Wines

Riverpoint Road, Matawhero

Owner:
Denis Irwin

Key Wines:
Gewürztraminer, Reserve Chardonnay, Estate Chardonnay, Sauvignon Blanc, Cabernet Sauvignon/Merlot, Estate Cabernet, Pinot Noir, Bridge Estate

Denis Irwin first entered the limelight in the mid-late 1970s with a string of arrestingly fragrant and flavour-crammed Gewürztraminers.

'Smash Palace' squats among Gisborne's factories – an 'oasis in the industrial desert'. This popular tavern features an old DC3 positioned as if about to crash-land, with the towering tanks of Corbans' Gisborne winery a stone's throw away.

Phil Parker, the handsome, charismatic owner of Smash Palace, is also a winemaker specialising in a range of high quality bottle-fermented sparkling wines. Parker made his first experimental wines in 1987. 'The business started as a winery,' recalls Parker. 'I opened Smash Palace as a wine bar, to generate cash-flow for the winery, but the local workers highjacked it and turned it into a tavern. Now the tail wags the dog.'

In his little winery behind Smash Palace, Parker's annual output is low – a few hundred cases – which allows him to offer customers what he terms 'designer sparkling wines'. 'If you would like me to add more or less sugar, more or less cognac (I add about one ml. to each bottle) please state it with your order and I will oblige.'

Parker has a flair for promotion: at a function to launch his first releases in 1989, a toy yacht was smashed across a six-litre bottle of Parker Classical Brut 1987. The Classical

Parker Méthode Champenoise

91 Banks Street, Gisborne

Owner: Phil Parker

Key Wines: Classical Brut, Dry Flint, Rosé Brut, First Light Red

Brut is his flagship. Its style has vascillated between a Chardonnay and Pinot Noir-predominant blend (the 1990 and 1991 vintages are 50 to 60 per cent Pinot Noir) but this is consistently a classy wine – light, with impressive flavour delicacy and length. The Classical Brut spends an exceptionally long period on its yeast lees; still fresh and lively, the slightly austere, bone-dry, strongly yeasty 1989 vintage was still being disgorged in 1995.

Parker's non-vintage Dry Flint is a herbal, strong-flavoured, tangy sparkling, based on an unusual blend of Sémillon and Chenin Blanc. The Rosé Brut, blended from Pinotage, Pinot Noir and Chardonnay, is a serious style with an engaging salmon-pink hue and robust, bone-dry palate.

First Light Red (aptly named, Gisborne being close to the international dateline) is Parker's 'cash-flow' wine. Released each year only a few weeks after the harvest, this Pinot Noir-based red is produced by the 'carbonic maceration' or 'whole-berry fermentation' technique perfected in Beaujolais. This is a buoyant light red, its accent on fresh, strong, supple, raspberryish flavour.

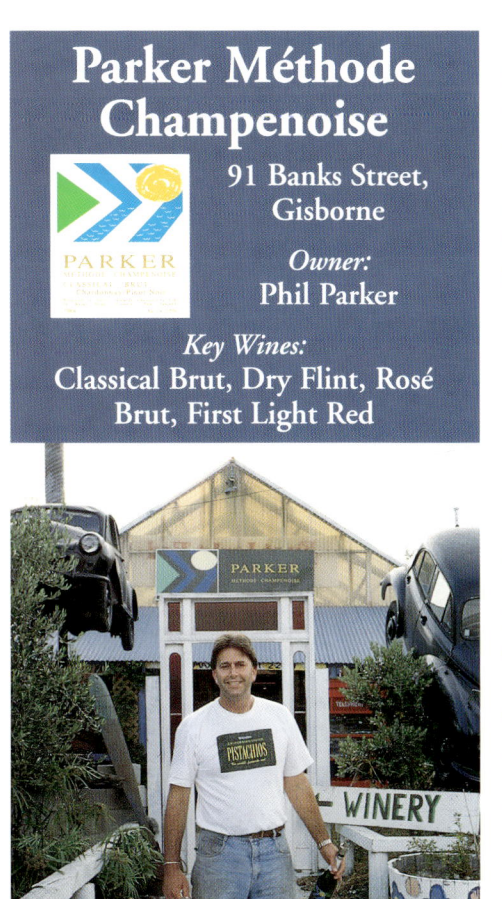

Phil Parker, a sparkling wine specialist, also dreamed up the idea of First Light Red – Gisborne's answer to Beaujolais.

From a small, hill-flanked vineyard tucked away in Gisborne's Ormond Valley, north of the city, flows one of New Zealand's most spellbinding Gewürztraminers and a consistently top-class Chardonnay.

Lawyer Ross Revington grew up in the Bay of Plenty. Revington came to Gisborne in 1982 ('partly influenced by Matawhero's success') and in 1987 he and his wife, Mary Jane, purchased what is now called Revington Vineyard – which previously had supplied the fruit for several gold medal-winning Cooks Chardonnays and the gold medal Cooks Dry Gewürztraminer 1983. 'Kerry Hitchcock, the winemaker, used to say "the fairies live there",' recalls Revington.

Today four hectares of Chardonnay (principally) and Gewürztraminer vines are planted in flat, sandy loams over clay. The vineyard is managed organically and has been awarded transitional Bio-Gro status.

The Revingtons own a vineyard, but no winery. The first 1988 wines were made by David Pearce at Corbans' Gisborne winery. The 1989 vintage (in the first instance of North Island fruit being trucked to the South Island, a reversal of the usual direction), was again processed by Pearce, now based at the

Revington Vineyard

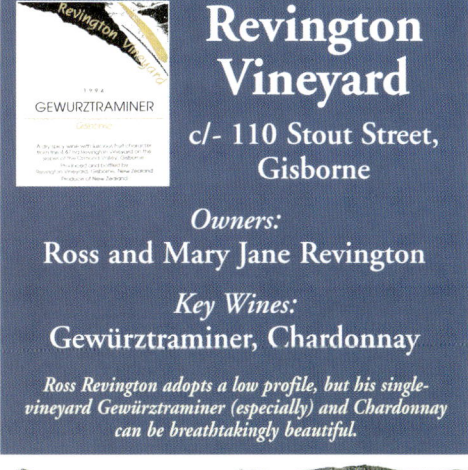

c/- 110 Stout Street, Gisborne

Owners: Ross and Mary Jane Revington

Key Wines: Gewürztraminer, Chardonnay

Ross Revington adopts a low profile, but his single-vineyard Gewürztraminer (especially) and Chardonnay can be breathtakingly beautiful.

Grove Mill winery in Blenheim. For several years, while Ross Revington was a partner in Landfall, the wine was made there by John Thorpe. Now the grapes are crushed in Gisborne and the juice is again trucked to Marlborough to be fermented and matured.

Revington Vineyard wines are high-fliers on the show circuit. The 1988, 1989 and 1994 Chardonnays have all won gold medals; the 1989 vintage also scooped the champion Chardonnay trophy at the 1990 Air New Zealand Wine Awards. The glorious, gold medal 1994 Gewürztraminer also won the trophy for champion Gewürztraminer at the 1995 Liquorland Royal Easter Wine Show.

Revington Vineyard Chardonnay is a very stylish and rich-flavoured wine, its ripe, citrusy fruit flavours overlaid with subtle, mealy characters from barrel-fermentation and lees-aging, leading to a long, crisp finish. This elegant, classically proportioned wine flourishes in the cellar for several years.

At its best (as in 1991 and 1994), the Gewürztraminer is brilliant. With its great weight and powerful, richly spicy, slightly earthy, lingering flavour, this is a dry, distinctly Alsace-like wine – truly memorable drinking.

'We want to pooh-pooh the idea that Gisborne can't grow quality red wine,' says Kerryanne Stuart, daughter of Shalimar Estate's owners. With a sunny, terraced vineyard at Patutahi and her father, Alec's, long grapegrowing experience, the Stuart family may well achieve their ambition.

Gisborne's newest winery lies on the western edge of the plains, close to Montana's Patutahi vineyard. The name Shalimar (also the name of the family farm) is derived from the title of a book, *The Oasis of Shalimar*, that is a favourite of Alec's wife, Helen.

Born and bred in Patutahi, Alec Stuart grew grapes for Montana from 1969 until the vinepull scheme of early 1986. He grew cash crops for Wattie for a few years, but hankered to establish a winery. 'I sold some land to free up the capital to pay for a winery, then built it myself,' says Stuart.

The first vines in the family's new vineyard were planted in 1992; the first vintage, based entirely on bought-in grapes, followed in 1994. The four-hectare vineyard, draped over flat land and a terraced hillside, is planted in a wide mix of varieties: Cabernet Sauvignon, Merlot, Pinotage, Sauvignon Blanc, Chardonnay, Pinot Gris, Sémillon and Riesling.

Shalimar Estate
Wharekopae Road, Patutahi

Owners:
Alec and Helen Stuart

Key Wines:
Chardonnay, Sauvignon Blanc, Sémillon, Pinot Gris, Rock Face White, Merlot

Alec Stuart and his daughter, Kerryanne, are determined to boost Gisborne's modest red-wine reputation.

Stuart is convinced he can grow fine quality red-wine grapes. 'Lower rainfall is the basic factor. The Patutahi area is recognised as a dry part of Gisborne. That's vital in reducing the vines' vigour and getting riper fruit.'

Shalimar Estate wines are made by Stuart ('Stu') and Kerryanne, who has completed two polytechnic courses in winemaking. 'We don't want to get into the rat-race and go past boutique size,' says Alec. 'We plan to sell all the wine here or by mail-order.'

Shalimar Estate has got off to a quiet start, with unexceptional but sound white wines from the first two vintages. However, the dark, chunky, flavourful 1994 Merlot must have intensified the Stuarts' red-wine aspirations.

At Britain's 1993 National Organic Wine Fair, The Millton Vineyard Chardonnay Barrel Fermented 1992 headed off 140 other wines from around the world for the trophy for the Best Wine of the Show. Millton wines also took second and third places.

Yet, proprietors James and Annie Millton feel that overall their wines are bought 'largely for their quality, rather than as organic wines'.

Strikingly rich, honeyish Chenin Blancs and exquisitely floral, vibrant Rieslings are the twin peaks of The Millton Vineyard's range. Gisborne's most acclaimed small winery lies on the banks of the Te Arai River at Manutuke, 16 kilometres south of the city.

James Millton initially spent two years with Montana before leaving to pursue his wine career overseas. After working on a small estate in the Rheinhessen, he returned to a vintage with Corbans and then went to work for John Clark, Annie's father, who first planted vines at Opou, in Manutuke, in the late 1960s.

Now the Milltons' four vineyards have spread out over 22 hectares in the Manutuke and Matawhero districts. In the original, loam-clay Opou Vineyard at Manutuke, 10

The Millton Vineyard
Papatu Road, Manutuke

Owners:
James and Annie Millton

Key Wines:
Riesling Opou Vineyard, Te Arai River Sauvignon Blanc, Chenin Blanc Dry, Chardonnay Barrel Fermented, Clos de Ste Anne Chardonnay, Estate Chardonnay, Riesling Late Harvest Individual Bunch Selection, Tête de Cuvée, Cabernet Rosé, Te Arai River Cabernet/Merlot

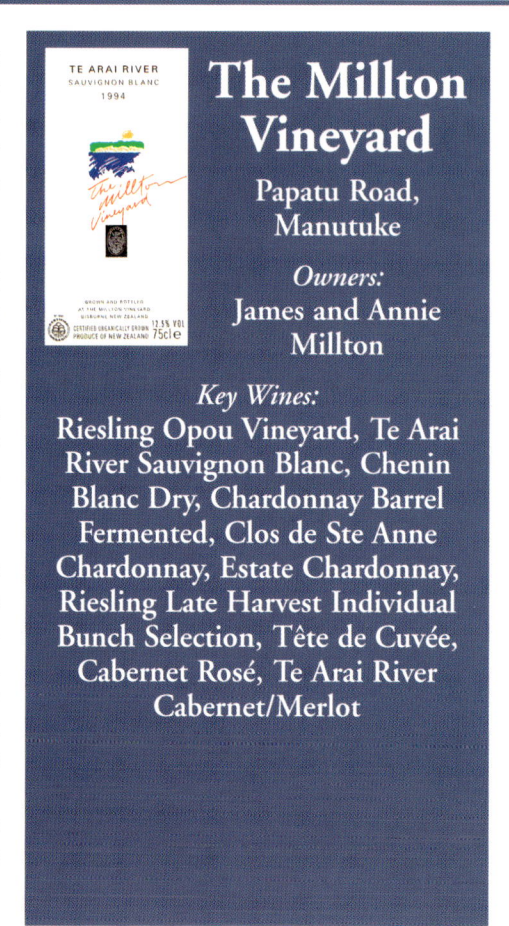

hectares of Sauvignon Blanc, Riesling, Chardonnay and Cabernet Sauvignon are cultivated. The silty, three-hectare Winery Vineyard is planted in Chardonnay, Chenin Blanc, July Muscat, Gewürztraminer, Malbec and Merlot. In the silt loams of the seven-hectare Riverpoint Vineyard – along the road from Denis Irwin in Riverpoint Road, Matawhero – the Milltons have planted Chardonnay vines. Naboths Vineyard is a two-hectare Manutuke planting of Chardonnay and Pinot Noir on a steep north-east facing hillside. None of the fruit from these vineyards is sold to other wine companies and no grapes are bought in.

In the conviction that 'we are what we eat', the Milltons have set themselves the difficult task of making organically grown wines in commercial volumes. The Millton Vineyard's Bio-Gro status (dropped for the 1995 vintage wines) affirms that it does not use herbicides, insecticides, systemic chemicals or artificial fertilisers.

James Millton readily agrees that Gisborne's warm, moist climate is not well suited to organic viticulture: 'But we can do it.' For fungus control, a limited amount of copper sulphate and sulphur is sprayed on the vines, supplemented by waterglass, seaweed extract and vegetable oils. 'Most importantly, we use bio-dynamic herbal preparations applied to the soil, compost and liquid manures.' Parasites and predators are also used to biologically control insect pests. Weed control is by mechanical means. Sulphur dioxide is added to the wine as a preservative, in controlled amounts.

The Milltons erected their coolstore winery in the summer of 1983–84. James oversees the vineyard and the winemaking, while Annie 'keeps in contact with labelling, despatch and marketing'.

The Millton Vineyard's Chenin Blanc Dry vies with Collards' as the finest in the land. 'I want honey and acidity and almond flavours,' says Millton – and he gets them. The grapes are hand-harvested at three different stages of ripening, culminating in the final picking of *Botrytis*-affected fruit. Fermented in stainless steel tanks and seasoned French oak barrels, this is a delectable, lush, fractionally off-dry wine, robust and brimming with rich, complex, pineappley, slightly honeyish flavours.

With its ravishing perfume, and intense citric-fruit and honeyish flavours underpinned by lively acidity, the medium-sweet Opou Vineyard Riesling is equally outstanding. It is partnered in some vintages by a botrytised, gorgeously scented Riesling Late Harvest Individual Bunch Selection with a thrillingly nectareous flavour. 'Sauternes' style', robust, oak-matured, botrytised sweet whites of exciting quality, labelled Tête de Cuvée ('top selection of the harvest') are also produced from such varieties as Chenin Blanc and Sémillon.

James and Annie Millton (pictured with their daughter Monique, and son, Sam) produce organic wines of an exceptionally high standard.

Millton prefers 'tropical, guava' flavours in Sauvignon Blanc-based whites. His Te Arai River Sauvignon Blanc displays appealing, ripe melon-like flavours with a gentle herbal undercurrent and a beguiling hint of honeysuckle.

Four Chardonnays are produced. The easy-drinking, citrusy Estate Chardonnay places its accent on fresh, ripe fruit, with a 'kiss' of oak. The Barrel Fermented Chardonnay (hand-picked, fermented in oak barriques – 30 per cent new – and lees-stirred every full moon), is typically a vibrantly fruity wine with good depth of citrusy, oaky flavour.

Naboths Vineyard Chardonnay, launched from the 1994 vintage, is a single-vineyard, barrel-fermented wine that does not undergo a softening malolactic fermentation. Millton expects this to be 'a leaner style, but capable of developing complexity'. His flagship Clos de Ste Anne Chardonnay, another single-vineyard wine, is fermented with natural yeasts in all-new barrels and given a full malolactic fermentation. Only produced about one year in three, this is a delicious, fat, peachy-ripe, nutty, mealy wine with a buttery-soft finish.

Don't overlook the Cabernet Rosé: a Cabernet Franc-based beauty with a bright, copper-pink hue and delicate, strawberryish flavours, crisp and lively, long and delicious. As a summer thirst-quencher, it's hard to beat.

Other Producers

Harvest Wine Company

Renowned for its cider, this Gisborne winery also makes a trickle of grape wine. The company is owned by the Wi Pere Trust (a group of farmers whose assets include 54 hectares of vineyards contracted to Corbans) and general manager Brian Shanks. The first releases include Riesling and Chardonnay.

Pouparae Park

Keen to diversify beyond kiwifruit, in 1994 Alec Cameron purchased grapes and had his first 1994 vintage processed at the Landfall winery. The wines, sold at Cameron's Bushmere Road property, include a forward, lightly oaked Chardonnay, a ripe, juicy, slightly sweet Rhine Riesling, and First Light Red.

Tai-Ara-Rau

Wines bearing the Tai-Ara-Rau ('confluence of many paths') label are made by students enrolled in the one-year, full-time Wine Industry Certificate course run by the Rural Studies Unit of Tairawhiti Polytechnic in Stout Street, Gisborne. The unit has its own 2.5-hectare vineyard and a small winery with the capacity to handle up to 15 tonnes of grapes – equivalent to just over 1000 cases of wine per year. I have tasted a light, American oak-aged, attractively leathery and gamey 1994 Merlot, a very forward, savoury and supple 1995 Pinot Noir, and a clean, easy-drinking, 50 per cent oak-fermented 1994 Chardonnay with fresh, citrusy, slightly mealy and buttery flavours.

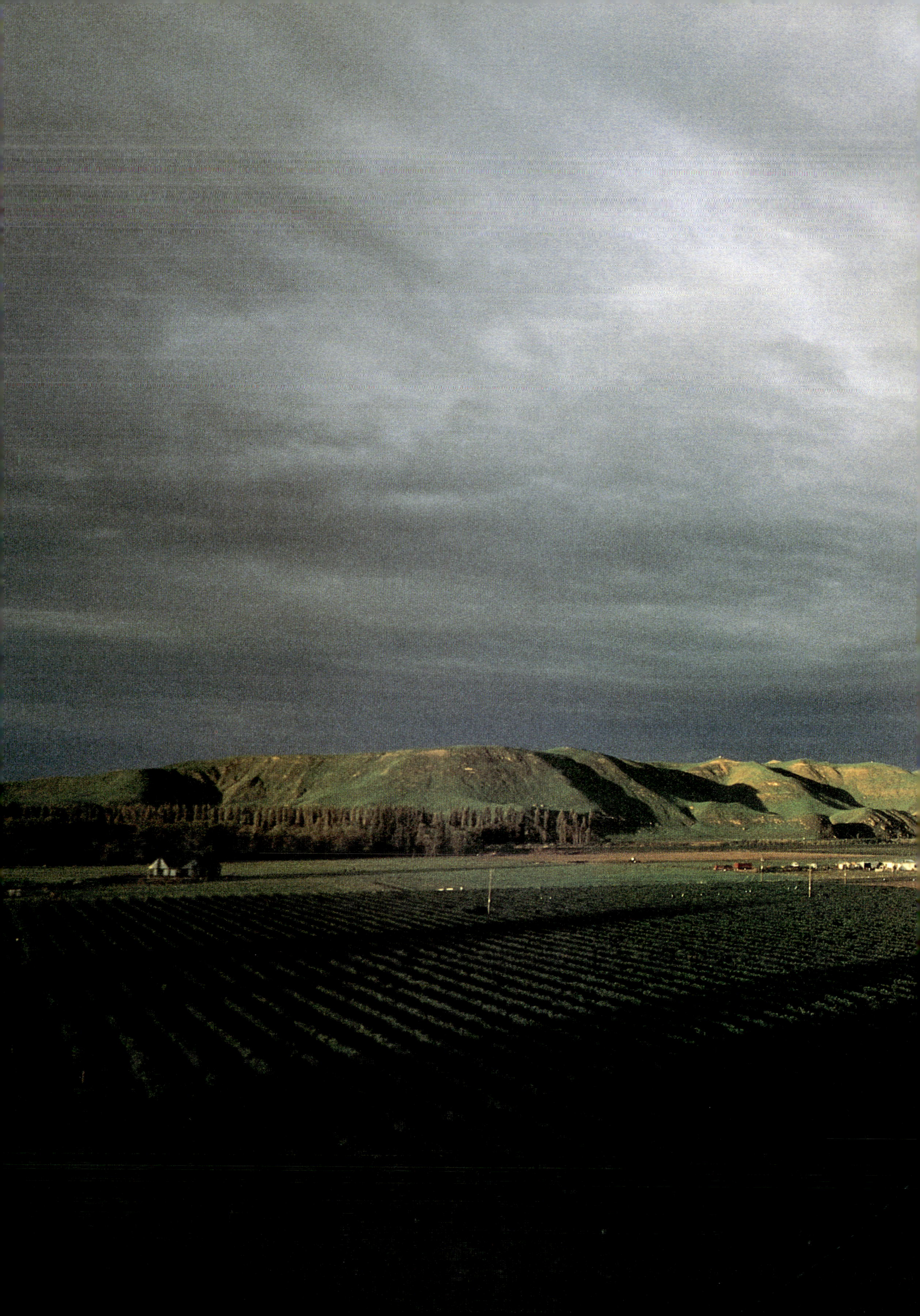

HAWKE'S BAY

PRODUCERS

Akarangi Wines
Bradshaw Estate
Brookfields Vineyards
Brownlie Brothers
C.J. Pask Winery
Clifton Road
Clearview Estate Winery
Crab Farm Winery
Cross Roads Wine Company
Esk Valley Estate
Eskdale Winegrowers
Gunn Estate
Hawkhurst Estate
Huthlee Estate Vineyard
Kemblefield Estate Winery
Linden Estate
Lombardi Wines
Mission Vineyards
Ngatarawa Wines
Park Estate
Red Metal Vineyard
Richard Harrison
Riverside Wines
Rockwood Cellars
Sacred Hill Winery
St George Estate
Stonecroft Wines
Te Awa Farm
Te Mata Estate Winery
The McDonald Winery
Tui Vale
Vidal Estate
Waimarama Estate

Hawke's Bay

'On performance in the shows and in the marketplace, Hawke's Bay has earned its claim to be New Zealand's leading wine-producing region.' That proud 1996 assertion by Alwyn Corban, chairman of Hawke's Bay Vintners, would win no support among the Marlborough wine fraternity. Yet Hawke's Bay, one of the country's pioneer winemaking regions, has preserved its traditional importance, and with such noble varieties as Chardonnay, Cabernet Sauvignon and Merlot, its regional reputation is the highest in the country.

The oldest winemaking concern in New Zealand still under the same management is here – Mission Vineyards, established by the Catholic Society of Mary in 1851. The oldest winery still operating, erected in stages from the 1870s, can be found at the Te Mata Estate. In 1995, with 2276 hectares, Hawke's Bay ranked second to Marlborough, and far ahead of Gisborne, in the extent of its vineyards. Between 1992 and 1995, the region's vineyards expanded by over 40 per cent, carrying its share of the national vineyard from 22 to 27 per cent. After a lull in the mid 1980s, when few new wineries emerged, the Hawke's Bay wine scene is abuzz with the excitement of new companies, new faces, new labels.

The terrain of Hawke's Bay varies from the rugged inland ranges, the Ruahine and Kaweka, climbing to over 1600 metres, to the coastal Heretaunga Plains. Protected by the high country from the prevailing westerly winds, agriculture thrives: pastoralism, process cropping, orcharding and market gardening. The favourably dry and sunny climate supports an easy growth of the vine.

Hawke's Bay is one of the sunniest areas of the country; the city of Napier, for instance, enjoys similar sunshine hours and temperatures to Bordeaux. In summer, anti-cyclonic conditions sometimes lead to droughts (as in 1994); such weather can produce grapes with high sugar contents and forms a key advantage for Hawke's Bay viticulture.

Hawke's Bay is, however, vulnerable to easterly cyclonic depressions and their accompanying rain, including some of the heaviest rainfalls ever recorded in New Zealand. In bad years, such as 1988 and 1995, the autumn rainfall can be a deluge; usually, though, it is markedly less than at Gisborne.

One of Hawke's Bay's prime viticultural assets is its wide range of soil types: the Heretaunga Plains consist mainly of fertile alluvial soils over gravelly subsoils deposited by the rivers and creeks draining the surrounding uplands. 'There are 22 categories of soil types on the Heretaunga Plains', explains Dr Alan Limmer of the Stonecroft winery. 'They range from stones to hard pans to heavy silts. Each has a profound effect on the wine.'

The majority of Hawke's Bay's vineyards are, in quality terms, on the wrong sites, according to Steve Smith, group viticulturist for Villa Maria. 'Between Hastings and the coast – the most fertile area – grapes are too often grown just as cash crops.' Limmer agrees: 'In Hawke's Bay we can grow the best Cabernet Sauvignon in New Zealand, but less than 10 miles [16.9km] away, we can also produce the worst.'

A comprehensive regional study published in 1985 by the Hawke's Bay Vintners stated frankly that 'many soils on the Heretaunga Plains are quite wet and vines grow too vigorously, giving large yields of grapes with poor balance and insufficient ripeness [notably the areas of fertile silty loams having a high water table]. Other more freely draining shingle soils . . . may be too dry in the growing season which would limit proper canopy development for ideal fruit maturation. This is overcome with trickle irrigation.'

Districts warmly recommended for viticulture by the regional study included the Taradale hills, river terraces along the Tukituki and Ngaruroro rivers, Havelock North and Ngatarawa (warm, dry and promising to produce grapes 'of the highest quality').

Most of the expansion in the past five years has been on low-vigour sites. The shingly Gimblett Road area west of Hastings – site of the Babich Irongate, C.J. Pask and other vineyards – has recently excited much interest. Steve Smith – most impressed with the inland parts of the Heretaunga Plains – has pointed out that, during vintage, rainfall figures drop steeply from the coast to the Ngatarawa/Gimblett Road area.

Alan Limmer, whose Stonecroft winery lies in Mere Road, just north of Gimblett Road, likens the area 'more to Australia than New Zealand. The climate is much hotter than the rest of Hawke's Bay, because the only cooling factor, the sea breeze, doesn't have the same influence here as it does on the coast. And the temperature warms up much more quickly: we can get temperatures up to 40 degrees C.' The wines grown in these top sites vary much less in quality from one vintage to the next than those from lesser vineyards.

Steve Smith points out that few Hawke's Bay vineyards are grown in the hills. 'One of the problems has been the old New Zealand agriculture attitude "you have to have a big tractor", which means that people have not planted these hill sites. It will make a huge difference to the wines.' Morton Estate's relatively cool Riverview vineyard, inland and at a slightly higher elevation at Mangatahi, has yielded a stream of outstanding Chardonnays and Pinot Noirs.

Only in the past 30 years has viticulture reached significant proportions in Hawke's Bay: in the late 1930s, for instance, only 25 hectares of vines were grown in the province. Then in 1967 contract growing extended to Hawke's Bay. For decades the dominant force in the Bay was McWilliam's, with its dry white Cresta Doré, sparkling Marque Vue and red Bakano virtually household names. Founded in 1944, the New Zealand company was wholly Australian-owned until 1962, and grew rapidly until 1961 when it merged with McDonald's Wines to become the largest winery in the country. Following a series of mergers and takeovers, the former McWilliam's crushing and fermenting complex at Pandora has become Corbans' major facility in Hawke's Bay.

Yet, although McWilliam's, headed by the legendary winemaker, Tom McDonald, with a famous string of Cabernet Sauvignons from 1965 and several fine Chardonnays, early proved the province's ability to produce some superb table wines, vine plantings to 1980 almost eschewed these grapes. However, since then the composition of the vineyards has been revolutionised, with swift expansion of classic *vinifera* grapes. The 1995 vineyard survey revealed that the six most important varieties planted here are (in order): Chardonnay, Cabernet Sauvignon, Müller-Thurgau, Sauvignon Blanc, Merlot and Pinot Noir.

The annual Harvest Hawke's Bay celebration is the highlight of the Hawke's Bay wine calendar, with the Hawke's Bay Vintners Charity Wine Auction the focal point of the four-day festival staged in February at a score of wineries.

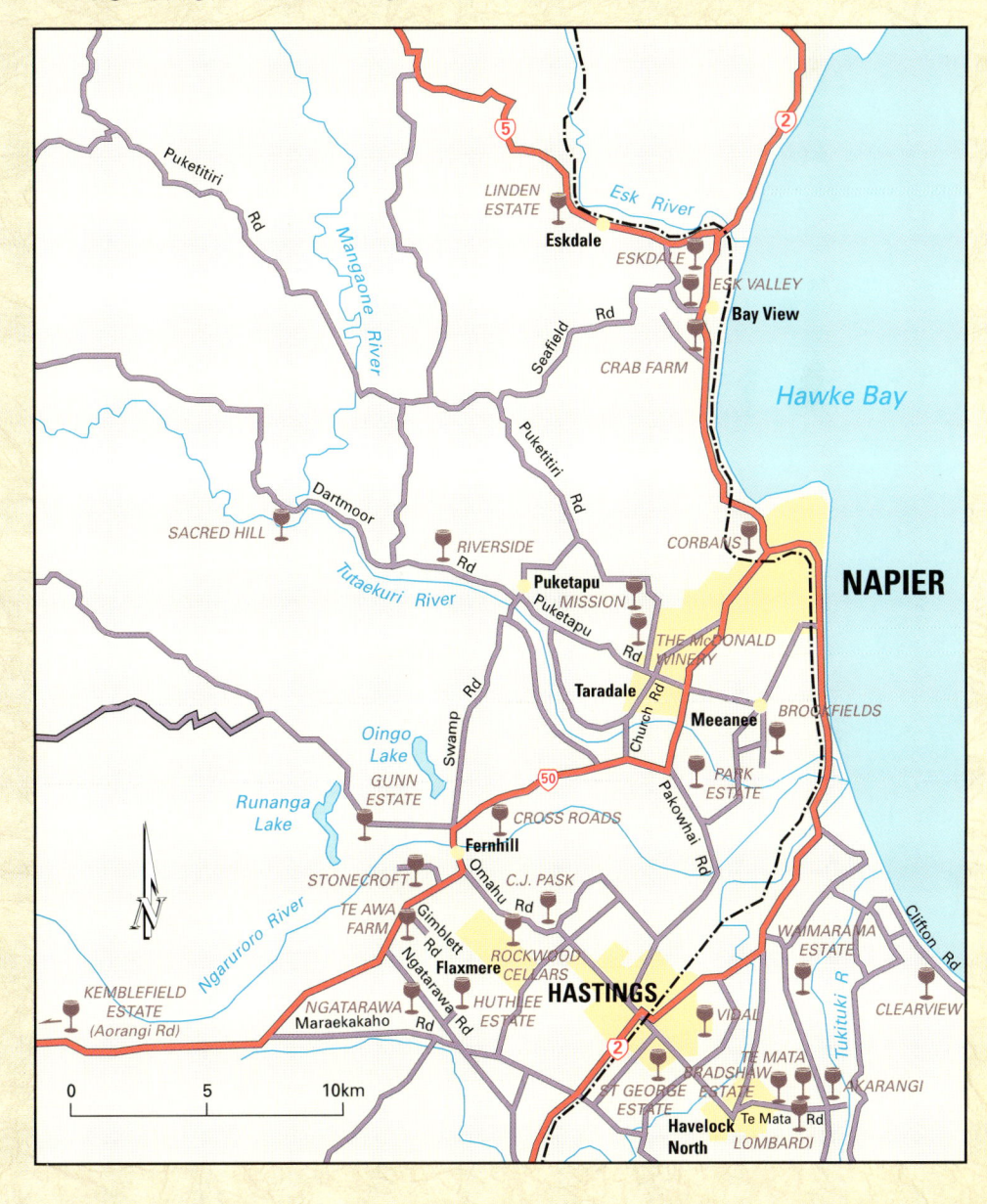

The Akarangi ('heavenly vines') winery lies in River Road, on the banks of the Tukituki River. With its annual output of less than 1000 cases, Akarangi is one of the country's smallest wineries.

Morton Osborne, raised in Ngaruawahia, graduated with an MA and Diploma in Clinical Psychology from Waikato University. A clinical psychologist, he is moving towards a full-time career in wine. For several years he and his wife, Vivien, sold the crop from their three-hectare vineyard to local wineries. After making small amounts of fruit wines since 1973, in 1987 Osborne produced the first wine under the Akarangi label.

The vineyard (originally established by Warwick Orchiston, until recently manager at the Mission) is planted in a broad array of grapes: principally Chenin Blanc, Sauvignon Blanc, Chardonnay, Riesling, Cabernet Sauvignon, Merlot and Cabernet Franc. A five-hectare apple and pear orchard currently provides the majority of Osborne's income, but over the next few years he plans to lift his wine production to 3000 cases.

Akarangi's modest corrugated-iron winery started life as a boat-building shed. The wine is stored and sold in a century-old Presbyterian church, which the Osbornes bought for $600 and shifted from Clive to River Road.

A decade ago, Osborne set out to make wine with minimal intervention, and keep it bone-dry. 'I've never done a formal winemaking course – there's a lot of enjoyment in finding things out, rather than following set recipes. My idea was to get the fruit off the vine and run it through quite minimally, in the belief that the less you do to the juice, the more you preserve in the final product. I've achieved that with some of my wines. But slightly sweet wines moved a tremendous amount faster, so now the white wines all have a hint of sweetness.'

Akarangi's partly barrel-fermented Chenin Blanc is an austere style with green-apple flavours and biting acidity; Osborne finds it 'honies up at about three years'. The limey, tangy Sauvignon Blanc and crisp, lemony, partly barrel-fermented Chardonnay are both light in flavour. The Cabernet/Merlot is typically a soft, light red with moderate depth of herbal and red berry-fruit flavours.

Akarangi Wines

River Road, Havelock North

Owners:
Morton and Vivien Osborne

Key Wines:
Chenin Blanc, Sauvignon Blanc, Chardonnay, Dry Red, Cabernet/Merlot

Despite his high academic qualifications, Morton Osborne sees himself as 'more of a practical, outdoorsy sort of person than a behind-the-desk type'.

Peter Robertson, the quiet owner of the Brookfields winery, only a kilometre from the sea at Meeanee, is rarely in the publicity spotlight. 'I just putt along, concentrating on making the wines,' he says. 'The wines can talk for themselves' – which they manage to do most eloquently.

Brookfields' flagship, the 'gold label' Cabernet/Merlot, from one vintage to the next, is one of the darkest, most powerful and rich-flavoured reds found in Hawke's Bay. The robust, savoury Reserve Chardonnay can also reach great heights. These are strapping, generously flavoured wines; richness of body and flavour are hallmarks of the Brookfields' style.

Robertson, raised in Otago, had his interest in wine sparked as a student in the early 1970s, when he took a holiday job at Barker's fruit winery at Geraldine. After graduating with a BSc in biochemistry, he joined McWilliam's in Hawke's Bay, working under the legendary winemaker Tom McDonald, initially as a cellarhand, then as a laboratory chemist. 'After a couple of years I had itchy feet,' he recalls. 'I was working in a winery, but couldn't prune a vine. When I left, the first thing I did was go pruning.'

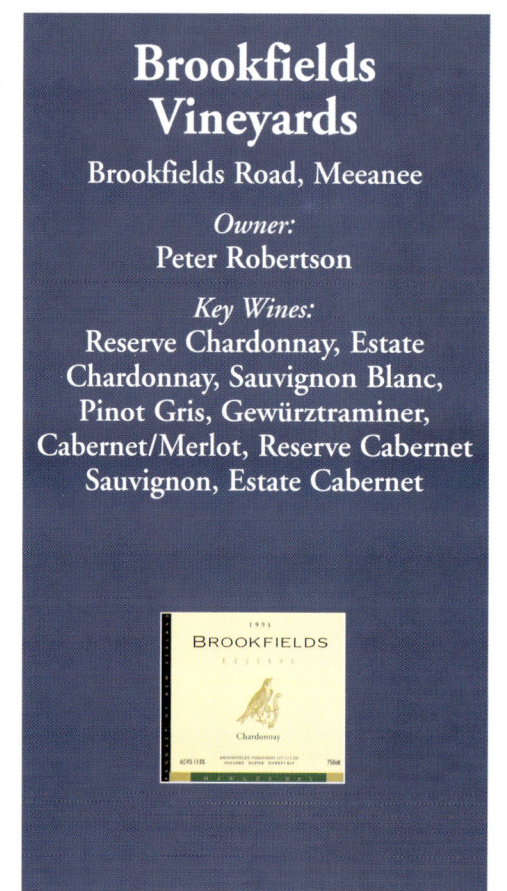

Brookfields Vineyards

Brookfields Road, Meeanee

Owner:
Peter Robertson

Key Wines:
Reserve Chardonnay, Estate Chardonnay, Sauvignon Blanc, Pinot Gris, Gewürztraminer, Cabernet/Merlot, Reserve Cabernet Sauvignon, Estate Cabernet

In 1977 Peter Robertson purchased the old Brookfields winery, traditionally a sherry specialist. 'Dick Ellis, the founder, had died and his son, Jack, wasn't interested in carrying on.'

Today, Brookfields has a fairly low output: about 9000 cases per year. Only a small proportion of grapes are drawn from the silty, 2.5-hectare estate vineyard, planted in Sauvignon Blanc and Chardonnay.

Cabernet Sauvignon and Merlot are purchased from a grower at Tukituki, and Chardonnay from Fernhill. Pinot Gris, Gewürztraminer and Sauvignon Blanc have been coming on stream since 1991 from a shingly vineyard in Ohiti Road, behind Roy's Hill.

The winery is a delight to visit. To enhance the atmosphere of the original building, erected in 1937 from concrete blocks handmade on the property, in 1989 Robertson added a brick entrance-way, a new gable and colonial windows. In the cellar, full of rustic, heavy, black wooden tables and benches, the original concrete barrel racks are still nursing casks.

Brookfields' winery restaurant opens for lunch on Friday, Saturday and Sunday, all year round. 'My wines are made to be drunk with food,' says Robertson. 'They're mouth-filling, with firm alcohol. Food wines also need a bit of acidity. And because of the wines' chemical balance, they live and develop.'

Brookfields' lower-priced range includes a stylish, lightly wooded Sauvignon Blanc with a touch of complexity and rich gooseberry/passionfruit flavours; a bone-dry, impressively weighty and spicy Gewürztraminer; a perfumed, peachy and peppery Pinot Gris; a fresh, soft, flavourful, American oak-aged Estate Chardonnay; and a gutsy, characterful Estate Cabernet. The jewels in Brookfields' crown, however, are the more expensive Reserve Chardonnay, Reserve Cabernet Sauvignon and 'gold label' Cabernet/Merlot.

Peter Robertson avoids the show circuit, but has quietly built Brookfields into one of Hawke's Bay's most respected producers.

Based on the 'pick' of the Chardonnay crop, the Reserve Chardonnay is a bold, robust wine with rich, grapefruit-like, mealy, buttery flavours and barrel-ferment complexity. The Reserve Cabernet Sauvignon is a strapping, dark-hued wine with a rush of spice and blackcurrant flavours and taut tannins; proof of the variety's ability to produce superb unblended reds.

'The Cabernet/Merlot is the one I really go for in the winery,' says Robertson. Grown on a warm, north-facing slope across the Tukituki River from the Akarangi winery, and matured for a year in new French oak barriques, this is a voluptuous red, dark, perfumed and very substantial, with the intense, spicy, plummy, almost sweet flavours of well-ripened fruit and the weight and structure to flourish for a decade.

Red wines oozing the taste delights of very ripe fruit first swung the spotlight on this small-to-medium-sized Hastings winery. Now its mouth-filling, intensely flavoured Reserve Chardonnays are coming to the fore.

C.J. Pask winery is operated by Chris Pask, with a minority stake taken in 1993 by winemaker, Kate Radburnd, and her Australian family, the Berrimans. Pask, a burly former top-dressing pilot, was for many years a contract grapegrower. Having each year turned out a couple of barrels of wine for his friends and relatives and, he says, being 'interested in adding value', in 1985 he moved into commercial wine production under his own label.

The original C.J. Pask winery – a converted tractor shed – and vineyard in Korokipo Road, Fernhill, were in 1989 sold to Montana. A new Mediterranean-style winery, featuring stained glass and prominent columns, soon afterwards rose on the north side of Hastings.

The 1985 to 1990 vintages of C.J. Pask wines were made by Chris Pask himself, but his white wines lacked the consistently high quality of his reds. 'The company had grown enormously and needed a professional wine-maker,' says Kate Radburnd (formerly Marris) who joined C.J. Pask in late 1990. Adelaide-born, Radburnd is a Roseworthy College graduate who worked as an assistant winemaker at Vidal and Villa Maria during the mid 1980s and then built a glowing reputation during her 1987–90 spell as winemaker at Vidal.

Chris Pask has a stake in 53 hectares of vineyards in Gimblett Road, planted

C.J. Pask Winery

Omahu Road, Hastings

Owners:
Chris Pask and the Berriman family

Key Wines:
Chardonnay, Reserve Chardonnay, Sauvignon Blanc, Roy's Hill White, Cabernet Sauvignon, Cabernet/Merlot, Reserve Cabernet/Merlot/ Malbec, Reserve Merlot, Pinot Noir, Roy's Hill Red

Kate Radburnd joined C.J. Pask in 1990 because she 'wanted to see how a smaller winery works, especially one where you grow your own grapes'.

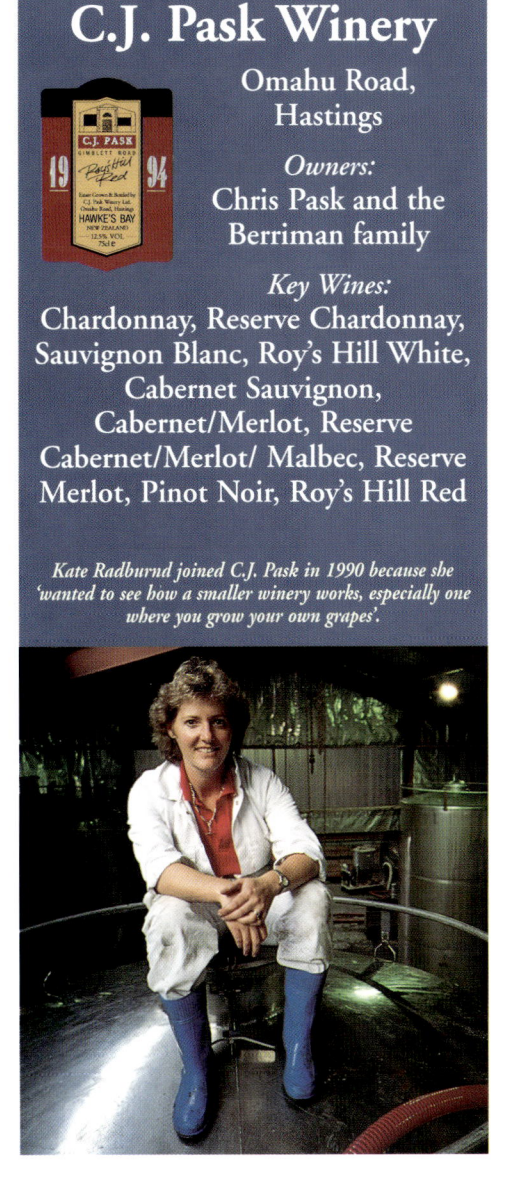

principally in Chardonnay, Sauvignon Blanc, Cabernet Sauvignon, Cabernet Franc and Merlot, with small plots of Pinot Noir and Malbec. First planted in 1982, these dry, stony vineyards excite Radburnd: 'They're very free-draining and shingly, but with enough fertile soil on top to establish young vines without irrigation. There's no doubt the area is best for Chardonnay and Cabernet-based reds, although you can also grow a good tropical-style Sauvignon Blanc there.'

At their best, the Cabernet Sauvignon and Cabernet/Merlot are delicious drinking – muscular, supple and bursting with sweet-tasting fruit – but recent vintages have tended to lack the power and lushness of the past, veering towards a lighter, more herbal style.

Roy's Hill Red – a blend of Cabernet Sauvignon, Cabernet Franc and 20 per cent Merlot, softened by brief oak-aging – is a fresh, berryish, minty, smooth red designed for early consumption. The Pinot Noir is typically fragrant, soft and raspberryish. Pask's finest red to date, however, is the Reserve Merlot, a perfumed red with a surge of complex, plummy, spicy flavours.

Roy's Hill White is a low-priced, non-wooded dry Chenin Blanc for no-fuss drinking. Fresh, vigorous, ripe and and lushly fruity, with a sliver of sweetness, the Sauvignon Blanc is very appealing. The briefly barrique-aged Chardonnay is vigorous, citrusy, crisp, slightly nutty and buttery. C.J. Pask's outstanding white wine is the Reserve Chardonnay – crisp and tautly structured in cooler years; mouth-filling, mealy, rich-flavoured and soft in top vintages.

'I'm a bit of a gold-digger,' grins Tim Turvey, co-owner of the tiny but spectacularly successful Clearview Estate winery. Last year, Clearview Reserve Chardonnay 1994 won a gold medal at the Liquorland Royal Easter Wine Show; the Reserve Old Olive Block 1994 won the trophy for champion red at the inaugural Bragato Wine Competition in Blenheim; and the Reserve Merlot 1994 scooped the trophy for top Merlot at the Air New Zealand Wine Awards.

Turvey, tall, tanned and confident, made his first wines while still a schoolboy. After graduating with a BA from Massey University, he 'always worked on the land, from contract grapegrowing to growing pineapples in Australia'. His Te Awanga land, right on the coast with a glorious view of Cape Kidnappers, was bought in 1985. The first vines were planted in 1988 and a year later the first wine flowed, based on bought-in grapes.

Helma van den Berg, Turvey's partner, is a viticulturist who also runs Clearview's popular vineyard restaurant.

The shingly estate vineyard, an old Vidal block first planted in 1916, today covers five hectares of Chardonnay, Cabernet Sauvignon, Merlot and Cabernet Franc vines, pruned for low yields and not irrigated. 'It's a frost-free, amazingly well-drained site,' says Turvey. The proximity to the sea keeps temperatures up at night, which helps ripen the grapes early. Turvey and van den Berg also manage a further six hectares of vines at Te Awanga.

Clearview's Reserve Chardonnay is exceptionally powerful *(see panel)*. Another top wine is the weighty Reserve Fumé Blanc, a barrel-fermented style with strong ripe, non-herbaceous fruit, powerful toasty oak influence and a crisp, long finish.

Clearview's three top reds are powerful, exuberantly fruity wines, crammed with flavour. The Reserve Merlot is dark, with a seductive intensity of spicy, vibrant, almost sweet-tasting fruit flavour. The Reserve Cabernet Franc is a serious yet sensuous red, chock-full of colour, body and flavour.

Even better is the Reserve Old Olive Block, a blend of Cabernet Sauvignon, Cabernet Franc and Merlot. This is an arrestingly bold and voluptuous red, richly perfumed and bursting with blackcurrant, spice, plum and sweet-oak flavours. This is a great new red-wine label on the rise.

'We've put tremendous work into Clearview,' says Helma van den Berg. 'Tim and I have rammed every post, grafted and planted every vine.'

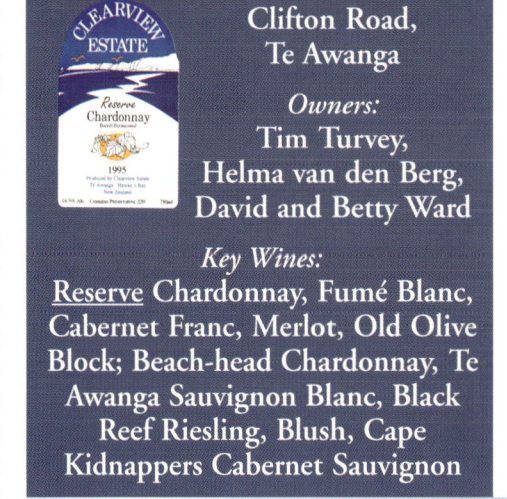

Clearview Estate Winery

Clifton Road, Te Awanga

Owners:
Tim Turvey, Helma van den Berg, David and Betty Ward

Key Wines:
Reserve Chardonnay, Fumé Blanc, Cabernet Franc, Merlot, Old Olive Block; Beach-head Chardonnay, Te Awanga Sauvignon Blanc, Black Reef Riesling, Blush, Cape Kidnappers Cabernet Sauvignon

---

CLEARVIEW ESTATE RESERVE CHARDONNAY

Clearview's most celebrated wine is its strapping, explosively flavoured, barrel-fermented Reserve Chardonnay.

Ultra-ripe fruit is the key to the wine's style. 'The grapes are golden, honeyish, with an amazingly luscious fruit character,' says Turvey. 'We never harvest them below 25 brix [sugar], which gives around 14 per cent alcohol, even in cooler years like '92 and '93.' The 1994 vintage was 14.4 per cent, the 1995 vintage 14.8 per cent alcohol.

The super-ripe, hand-picked grapes are fermented in all-new French oak barriques and then the wine is wood-matured for up to a year, with regular lees-stirring. About 25 per cent of the final blend undergoes a softening malolactic fermentation.

'The Reserve Chardonnay reflects Tim's personality – complex and upfront,' laughs Helma van den Berg. It's a hedonist's delight: a bold, succulent wine overflowing with peachy, oaky, mealy flavour, with the power and structure to flourish in the cellar for several years.

Crab Farm Winery

125 Main Road North, Bay View, Napier

Owner: James Jardine

Key Wines: Chardonnay, Sauvignon Blanc, Gewürztraminer Dry, Gewürztraminer Late Harvest, Jardine Cabernet, Cabernet/Merlot, Pinot Noir

When Hamish Jardine's great-grandfather first acquired land at Petane, it was a mud-flat covered with rushes and crawling with crabs.

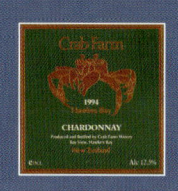

Hamish Jardine, winemaker at the little Crab Farm winery at Bay View, has no desire to expand his current output of 3000 cases. 'I like to be hands-on, right through the grapegrowing and winemaking processes.'

James Jardine, Hamish's father, who planted his first vines just south of Esk Valley in 1980, for several years sold the grapes to local wineries. In 1987 an implements shed was converted into a small, vertical-timbered winery. Hamish Jardine, who gained his early winemaking experience at Matawhero in Gisborne and Château Reynella in Australia, was appointed winemaker.

The 10-hectare vineyard adjoining the winery, which contains pockets of shingly and silty soils, is planted principally in Chardonnay and Gewürztraminer, with smaller plots of Cabernet Sauvignon, Merlot and Pinot Noir. Grapes are also purchased from the nearby Brownlie vineyard.

Crab Farm's white wines were plain in the past, but an increasing reliance on estate-grown fruit has brought a marked upswing in the wines' quality. The Chardonnay is full-bodied, ripely fruity and crisp. The Sauvignon Blanc is a fresh, non-wooded style with ripe, passionfruit and capsicum-evoking flavours. Two styles of Gewürztraminer are produced: a crisp, spicy, lemony Gewürztraminer Dry, and a slightly sweet Late Harvest Gewürztraminer packed with fresh, well-spiced, delicious flavour.

The Pinot Noir is a chunky, savoury wine, always full of character. The Cabernet/Merlot has supple red berry/plum flavours in a full, smooth style. In superior vintages a richer-flavoured model appears, labelled Jardine Cabernet.

Cross Roads Wine Company

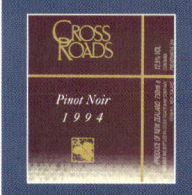

Korokipo Road, Fernhill

Owners: Lester O'Brien and Malcolm Reeves

Key Wines: Chardonnay, Reserve Chardonnay, Riesling Dry, Gewürztraminer, Sauvignon, Sauvignon Oak Aged, Cabernet/Merlot, Barrel Selection Cabernet Sauvignon; Pinot Noir; Springwood Chardonnay, Merlot/Cabernet

Cross Roads is one of the most characterful wineries to emerge in the Bay in recent years, with gold medals for Cabernet Sauvignon, Riesling and Chardonnay already under its belt.

Malcolm Reeves, wine columnist for *The Evening Standard* for 16 years, is a former senior lecturer in food technology, specialising in sensory evaluation and fermentation technology. When Reeves launched his own 1990 vintage wines under the Cross Roads label, it was therefore no surprise that their quality instantly won respect.

Reeves has set up his Fernhill winery in partnership with Lester O'Brien, a Victoria University chemistry graduate he met in the early 1970s. Why was the winery named Cross Roads? Reeves suggested forming the company to O'Brien when the two met again in Paris, long after their paths had first crossed at university.

Cross Roads' 1990 to 1993 vintages were produced at a variety of premises. A new winery rose on State Highway 50, one kilometre on the Taradale side of Fernhill, in time for the 1993 vintage. In the company's adjacent five-hectare vineyard, which has blocks of shingly loams and sandy loams, Müller-Thurgau has been replaced with Riesling and red-wine varieties. Hawke's Bay growers supply most of the grapes.

The top wines carry the Cross Roads label, with a range of lower-priced, drink-young wines sold as Springwood.

Cross Roads combines the management experience of Lester O'Brien (left) and the in-depth winemaking knowledge of Malcolm Reeves.

The white wines are uniformly impressive with their clear, deep varietal flavours.

With his research background, Reeves is naturally eager to pursue red wines. 'The potential for reds in Hawke's Bay hasn't been fully explored yet,' he believes. The flagship Barrel Selection Cabernet Sauvignon is very weighty, smooth and rich-flavoured. The Pinot Noir is one of the best in Hawke's Bay, with a beguiling perfume, richness and velvety mouthfeel. It is also bargain-priced. 'We aim to offer good value,' says Reeves.

Voluptuous, silky, Merlot-based reds are the principal glory of this Bay View winery. Under its latest name, Esk Valley, the old Glenvale winery on the coast just north of Napier has been transformed into a tourist drawcard. A Mediterranean theme is reflected in the fresh-painted concrete building and vine-draped terraces. The wines are among the best in the Bay.

Villa Maria acquired the winery in 1987 from Robbie and Don Bird, grandsons of Glenvale's founder, Englishman Robert Bird.

In 1933 Bird bought five hectares of land at Bay View, planning to establish a market garden and orchard. But during the Depression the return for grapes of under twopence per pound soon encouraged Bird to enter the wine industry. In the original cellar, a tunnel scooped out of the hillside, early Glenvale wines were vinted using the humble Albany Surprise variety.

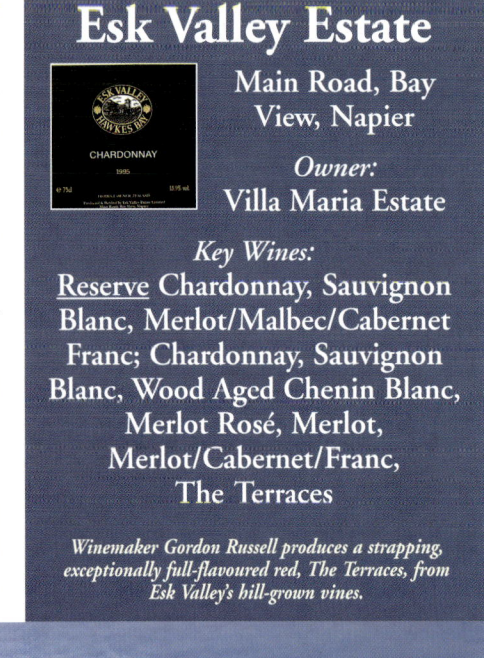

By the time of his death in 1961, Robert Bird owned a 28-hectare vineyard and a large winery. His son (the second Robert) extended the vineyards to over 100 hectares of principally hybrid varieties. He retired in 1979, opening the way to the top for Robbie and Don while they were still in their mid-twenties.

Under three generations of Bird family management, Glenvale grew steadily into one of New Zealand's largest family-run wineries. Its production traditionally emphasised fortified wines, but by the mid 1980s the table wines were reliable and competitively priced. The Bird brothers' undoing, however, was to over-expand in the highly price-sensitive cask-wine market. The ferocious wine-price war of 1985–86 brought the company to its knees, leading to Villa Maria's takeover a year later.

Villa Maria immediately set about repositioning Glenvale – swiftly renamed Esk Valley – as a top-end-of-the-market, 'boutique' producer.

On terraces carved 40 years ago out of the north-facing slope alongside the winery, Merlot, Malbec, Cabernet Sauvignon and Cabernet Franc vines have been planted for a premium estate red. The founder, Robert Bird, originally planted these terraces with Albany Surprise; the vines flourished and produced very early-ripening grapes but, owing to high labour costs, in the late 1950s they were replaced by pines.

Esk Valley Estate

Main Road, Bay View, Napier

Owner: Villa Maria Estate

Key Wines:
Reserve Chardonnay, Sauvignon Blanc, Merlot/Malbec/Cabernet Franc; Chardonnay, Sauvignon Blanc, Wood Aged Chenin Blanc, Merlot Rosé, Merlot, Merlot/Cabernet/Franc, The Terraces

Winemaker Gordon Russell produces a strapping, exceptionally full-flavoured red, The Terraces, from Esk Valley's hill-grown vines.

The new hillside vineyard, densely planted and irrigated to ensure adequate vine growth on this very drought-prone site, yields only about 250 cases of wine, labelled The Terraces, each year. 'I'm the custodian of what is potentially one of New Zealand's greatest vineyards,' says winemaker Gordon Russell. 'What a responsibility and what an honour.' A further half-hectare of Chardonnay is grown at the winery. The vast majority of Esk Valley's grapes, however, are drawn from contract growers scattered throughout Hawke's Bay.

Esk Valley sits on one of the most stunning vineyard sites in the country, with magnificent views of the Hawke's Bay coastline and the Pacific Ocean. George Fistonich of Villa Maria, who from the start saw the potential, has greatly enhanced the old winery's efficiency and visual appeal.

The heart of the Glenvale winery, a strong concrete structure over 50 years old, has been preserved. But the changes have been radical: the former bottling-line was scrapped; outside tanks were enclosed; a new press was installed; refrigeration capacity was increased five-fold; a new, half-underground, temperature-controlled barrel fermentation room was added; hundreds of casks were purchased; and a side was carved out of old concrete storage tanks to transform them into storage bins for bottled wines. The entire complex has been modernised.

Winemaker Gordon Russell arrived at Esk Valley in 1990. After a childhood in the Manawatu, he studied town planning, then fell in love with wine. 'At first I worked in various pubs and licensed establishments in England. When I came back to New Zealand, I worked at Bellamour, and then in 1988 joined Villa Maria.' After rising to chief cellarhand, in 1990 he was appointed assistant winemaker at Esk Valley. In 1993 – when Grant Edmonds shifted to Auckland as chief winemaker of the Villa Maria/Esk Valley/Vidal group – Russell stepped into the top job at Esk Valley.

Esk Valley is 'Merlot country', according to the winery newsletter. 'Merlot prospers more consistently here than other red-wine varieties,' says Russell. In their pursuit of a 'mouth-watering, not mouth-puckering' style of Merlot, Esk Valley's winemakers ferment the wine in open vats, every few hours hand-plunging the grapes' skins into the juice, and mature the Reserve wine for up to two years in French oak barriques.

Esk Valley's straight varietal Merlot is a hard-to-resist wine with rich colour, good depth of raspberry, plum and spice flavours and a seductively smooth finish. The Reserve Merlot-based red (the exact blend varies slightly from vintage to vintage) is a dark, vibrantly fruity wine bursting with ripe, almost sweet-tasting, blackcurrant, plum and French oak flavours. This is one of New Zealand's champion Merlots, with a distinguished record in show judgings. Esk Valley also produces a top-flight, dryish Merlot Rosé with strong, fresh, crisp, strawberryish flavours, full of drink-young charm.

The Terraces – the estate-grown red – is one of New Zealand's most striking and distinctive wines. Merlot and Malbec are typically the major ingredients, supplemented by the two Cabernets: Sauvignon and Franc. Muscular, with a warmth and concentration rare in New Zealand reds, it is dark, spicy, meaty, complex and tannic, with an intriguing extra dimension that reflects its high Malbec content (30 per cent in 1991, 25 per cent in 1994). The monumental 1991 vintage is staggeringly good.

The non-wooded Sauvignon Blanc, a mouth-filling style with ripely herbal, melon and capsicum-like flavours in warmer vintages, in cooler years is lighter, brisker and more green-edged. The rarer Reserve Sauvignon Blanc is a gorgeous wine: deeply scented, with a basket of fresh, pure, crisp, tropical-fruit flavours and exceptional length.

The Wood Aged Chenin Blanc, briefly aged in French and American oak casks, used to lack charm in its youth, but of late has become a lot riper and more attractive. 'The one thing we're looking for is pineapple flavours, and the riper the fruit the stronger the flavour,' says Russell. With bottle-aging, rich, slightly honeyish flavours unfold.

Esk Valley Chardonnay, half barrel-fermented but entirely oak-aged, is an elegant, citrusy, slightly buttery and mealy wine with a lot of character in its mid-price range. The Reserve Chardonnay, a stylish rather than sledgehammer style, is made from hand-picked fruit which is whole bunch-pressed, barrel-fermented and lees-matured. This is an intense, citric-flavoured wine, subtle and sustained, with the 1994 vintage the richest, creamiest, most concentrated yet.

'Nothing's changed,' says Kim Salonius, the owner of one of Hawke's Bay's smallest vineyards. Eskdale lies unobtrusively alongside the highway through the Esk Valley, its presence marked only by a carved wooden sign at the gate. A strong individualist, Salonius makes characterful, robust, very rich-flavoured wines, typically matured in the cask and bottle for several years prior to their release.

Kim Salonius came to Auckland from his native Canada in 1964 to read for a degree in history. As a child he watched while his father made wine for home consumption from grapes brought north from California. Later, while advancing his medieval studies in Germany, his interest in winemaking was rekindled. By 1973 his first vines were in the ground. From 1973 to 1977, when he made his first commercial release of wine, Salonius and his wife, Trish, survived on her teaching salary and lived for part of that period in the local school house. His first wines were produced out in the open on a concrete pad. The award of silver medals to two early vintages, Cabernet Sauvignon 1977 and Chardonnay 1978, was an auspicious debut.

Salonius prefers a low profile, and not to advertise his wine or participate in industry affairs. 'I try to avoid all the argo-bargo of promotion, and ego confused with marketing. My ego's under control.'

Eskdale's sole source of fruit is the silty, four-hectare home vineyard between the winery and the road. Established in Cabernet Sauvignon, Chardonnay and Gewürztraminer, viruses have forced its gradual replanting. 'These days I'm one of

Eskdale Winegrowers

State Highway 5, Eskdale

Owners:
Kim and Trish Salonius

Key Wines:
Chardonnay, Gewürztraminer, Cabernet Sauvignon

Without any fanfare, Kim and Trish Salonius produce a trio of wines whose quality and individuality can be quite absorbing.

the few winery owners who spends most of his time in the vineyard,' says Salonius. 'I keep tearing out older material and replanting, and there are a couple of new varieties I plan to pursue.'

His tiny winery, with wooden trusses, white plastered walls and stained-glass windows, looks every inch like a shrine to Bacchus. Salonius built it himself, using bricks and Douglas fir, placing his storage tanks underground to preserve the winery's beauty. A second building is used for the storage of casks and bottled wines. Everything is planned to last: 'This is home, I'll die here,' he says contentedly.

Salonius favours robust, strong-flavoured wine: 'As big as I can get it.' His grapes are held on the vines to ripen to very advanced levels before the hand-pickers move in. The juice is held on its skins as long as possible after crushing to get maximum flavour. The wines are barrel-aged longer than at any other winery in the country – two years for Chardonnay, three for Cabernet Sauvignon – and then bottle-matured. 'I like to present wine to people that they know they can drink fairly soon,' says Salonius. 'I don't like saying the wine will be terrific in seven years.'

The arched brick storage bins near the winery door hold an absorbing trio of wines for sale. Eskdale wines are scarce; Salonius' annual output is only about 1500 cases. In 1993, he produced nothing. 'Hail on New Year's Eve took out about 40 per cent of the crop. Then the season stayed wet and cold. It was such a terrible year I thought: "I'm not going to defend what's left".'

Eskdale Cabernet Sauvignon is a powerful red with rich cassis, dark chocolate, herbal and spicy flavours, complex and lingering. The Chardonnay is mouth-filling, with concentrated, ripe fruit flavours and barrel-ferment complexity. The style of the Gewürztraminer varies from dry to medium-sweet, depending on the vintage, but is always full-flavoured and peppery, and sometimes (as in 1994) brilliant.

Huthlee Estate Vineyard

Montana Road, Bridge Pa

Owners:
Devon and Estelle Lee

Key Wines:
Cabernet Sauvignon, Merlot, Kaweka Red, Rosé

What do you call a new winery? Devon and Estelle Lee weighed up local place names. 'We live in Montana Road – so that was out!' recalls Devon. 'In the end we chose Huthlee, a combination of Estelle's maiden name, Huthnance, and our married name, Lee.'

Huthlee Estate, to date a red-wine specialist, lies in Bridge Pa, only a couple of kilometres as the crow flies from the Ngatarawa winery. Raised in Hamilton, Devon Lee came to Hawke's Bay as a builder, then worked as a building inspector for the Hastings City Council until 1990.

In 1984, Devon and Estelle bought their 'lifestyle block', planted in peaches and two hectares of Merlot and Cabernet Franc vines. 'The vineyard was my hobby,' says Estelle. 'We phased out the peaches and sold the grapes. We got a half-tonne in 1984 and a year later, 25 tonnes.' Why did the Lees plunge into winemaking? 'We toured France in 1990 with David Jackson [a pioneer of Canterbury viticulture] and developed an extreme interest in wine. And we had premium, sought-after grapes.'

Huthlee Estate's first vintage, made at the Esk Valley winery, flowed in 1991. Show success followed swiftly; the 1992 Cabernet Franc, 1992 Merlot and 1993 Cabernet Sauvignon all won silver medals.

The eight-hectare, irrigated vineyard of Cabernet Franc, Merlot and smaller plots of Cabernet Sauvignon, Pinot Gris and Sauvignon Blanc is planted in free-draining sandy loams overlying river shingles. 'It's only good for grazing sheep or growing grapes,' says Devon. The majority of the fruit is still sold to other wine companies; Huthlee Estate's annual production still totals less than 1000 cases.

The wines, since 1994 made on-site by Devon Lee, have so far all been red or rosé, although a Pinot Gris and Sauvignon Blanc are planned from 1997. Kaweka Red, blended from Merlot and Cabernet Franc, is a decent oak-aged quaffer made in a fresh, supple, easy to drink style. The Merlot-based reds are perfumed, plummy and spicy in a ripe, smooth, very approachable style, and the Cabernet Sauvignon exhibits plenty of colour, body and flavour. These are consistently attractive wines.

Devon and Estelle Lee produce attractively ripe and supple reds, with the first white wines due shortly.

Kemblefield Estate Winery

Aorangi Road, Mangatahi

Owners:
John Kemble and Kaar Field

Key Wines:
Chardonnay, Sauvignon Blanc, Reserve Sauvignon Blanc, Gewürztraminer, Merlot, Cabernet Sauvignon/Merlot

For John Kemble, the US market beckons: 'There's very little New Zealand wine sold in the States,' he notes, 'but we've got the distribution contacts.'

In the past, American investment in the New Zealand wine industry proved transitory. Seagram, the giant distilling and winemaking multinational, in 1973 bought a 40 per cent stake in Montana but bailed out during the glut-induced wine-price war of 1985/86. Randy Weaver, the Oregonian co-founder of Coopers Creek at Huapai in 1981, returned to the United States in 1988, leaving only Pennsylvania-born David Hoskins to keep the stars and stripes flying at the small Heron's Flight vineyard at Matakana.

Now, Californians John Kemble and Kaar Field are pouring several million dollars into developing the Kemblefield Estate vineyard and winery at Mangatahi, 25 kilometres inland from Hastings. The stocky, curly-haired Kemble graduated in viticulture from the University of California, Davis in 1983 and for the next nine years was assistant winemaker at Ravenswood, a Sonoma winery renowned for its muscular Zinfandels.

While visiting New Zealand in early 1992, Kemble 'picked a couple of dozen wines off the shelves and found vegetative [unripe] qualities in some of the South Island reds. But I was impressed with Morton Estate's Riverview vineyard at Mangatahi and very impressed with the black label reds from that vineyard. Then I heard there was a 200-hectare property down the road that was potentially available for purchase.'

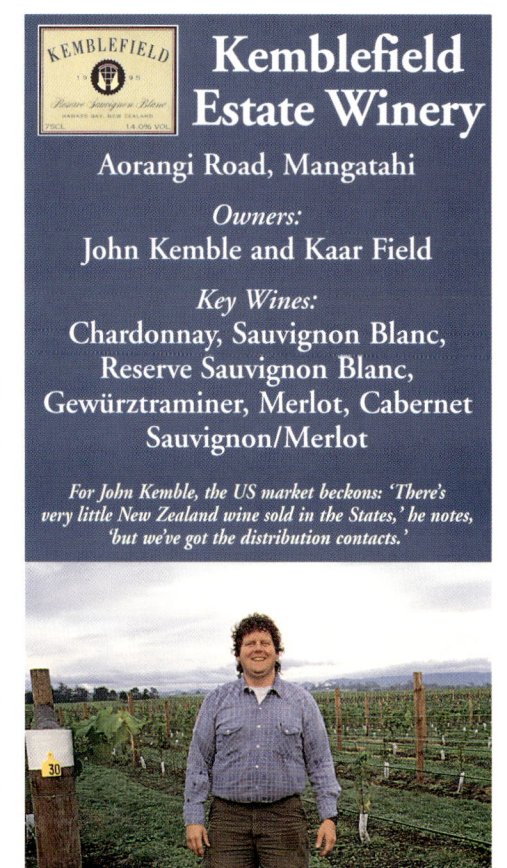

With his California-based partner, tax attorney and Ravenswood accountant Kaar Field (the 'field' in Kemblefield), Kemble has established a winery and 44 hectares of Chardonnay, Sauvignon Blanc, Merlot and Cabernet Sauvignon vines on the banks of the Ngaruroro River. Kemblefield is no 'boutique'. If all goes according to plan, by the year 2000 its output will reach 25,000 cases and Kemblefield will rank among this country's few middle-sized producers.

The Gewürztraminer is deep-flavoured, with rich, ripe gingerbread and cinnamon characters. Two Sauvignon Blancs are made: a non-wooded style that is appealingly fresh, ripe-flavoured and crisp, and the more complex, weighty, creamy, rich-flavoured Reserve label, fermented and lees-aged in French oak casks. The barrel-fermented Chardonnay is mouth-filling, ripe, fleshy and buttery, with loads of flavour.

The early reds – Merlot and Cabernet/Merlot – have been light and slightly green-edged, but can be expected to improve as the estate-grown grapes come on stream.

The first Linden Estate wine flowed in 1991, 20 years after Wim van der Linden planted his first vines. 'Tom McDonald of McWilliam's said he wanted 100 acres [40.5ha] of contract-grown grapes and we had 48 hours to make our minds up. We had 30 acres [12.1ha] of suitable land, and during 1971 and 1972 planted it all in Palomino and Müller-Thurgau.'

After Wim's son, John, started planting classic *vinifera* vines, in 1991 the van der Lindens plunged into winemaking.

Wim van der Linden came to New Zealand from the Netherlands in 1951 to work as an engineer. 'He's the boss,' says John, a tutor in viticulture at the local polytechnic. John's brother, Stephen, runs the vineyards and in 1995 Nick Chan, formerly of Lincoln, was appointed winemaker.

The Linden Estate vineyard and winery are in the heart of the Esk Valley. Twenty-two hectares of Sauvignon Blanc, Chardonnay, Cabernet Sauvignon and Merlot are cultivated. The majority of the vineyard is planted on the sandy, silty Esk Valley floor. A three-hectare site called the Dam Block has been carved out of the surrounding hills to create a sheltered, north-facing vineyard with hard limestone soils; this favoured site is the foundation of Linden Estate's flagship red wines.

Nick Chan's arrival prior to the 1995 vintage produced an immediate surge in the quality of the Chardonnays. Both wines are toasty, buttery, ripe, full-flavoured and forward, with the fully barrel-fermented, strongly malo-influenced Reserve wine slightly fatter, softer and more complex than its stablemate.

The fragrant, soft, tropical-fruit-flavoured Sauvignon Blanc is partnered by a partly barrel-fermented, red currant-flavoured, crisp, tight-structured Reserve Sauvignon Blanc. The Reserve Gewürztraminer is weighty and rounded, with plenty of ripe, gingery, peppery flavour.

Linden Estate's Merlot and Cabernet/Merlot are middle-weight reds with pleasant, berryish, moderately ripe flavours. The Reserve Cabernet/Merlot, partly grown in the Dam Block, is darker and more concentrated, illustrating the crucial importance of site selection.

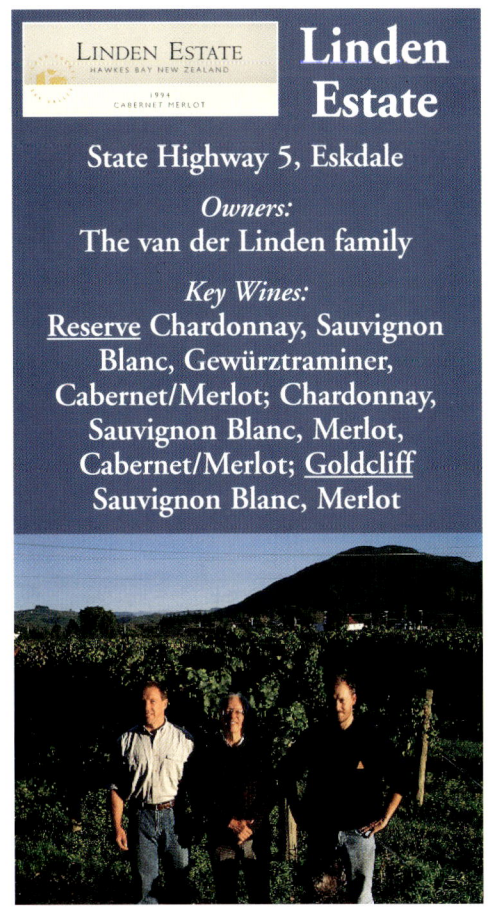

Linden Estate

State Highway 5, Eskdale

Owners:
The van der Linden family

Key Wines:
Reserve Chardonnay, Sauvignon Blanc, Gewürztraminer, Cabernet/Merlot; Chardonnay, Sauvignon Blanc, Merlot, Cabernet/Merlot; Goldcliff Sauvignon Blanc, Merlot

Esk Valley grapegrowers-turned-winemakers, Wim van der Linden (centre) with his sons, John (left) and Stephen.

For many years Lombardi was the oddity of the Hawke's Bay wine trail, preserving the fortified-wine traditions of an almost-vanished era. Now, with new owners at the helm, change is underway.

In 1948 English-born W.H. Green and his wife Tina planted a 1.2-hectare vineyard on a soldier's rehabilitation block in Te Mata Road, near Havelock North. Green, who until his death in 1992 still carried out all the spraying and pruning, learned about wine when he joined the Vidal brothers' staff in 1937. After Mrs Green, born in the Bay of Naples, turned to her grandparents in Italy for additional winemaking advice, 1959 brought the first Lombardi vintage.

The founders' son, Tony, made the wines until recently, focusing on Italian-style liqueurs and vermouths, supplemented by a range of sherries, ports and quaffing table wines. However, in 1994 the Greens sold the business – but not the land or winery – to their neighbour, Andy Coltart (who describes himself as a 'property developer and farmer'), and his partner Kim Thorp, a creative director for a Wellington advertising agency.

Coltart immediately set about 'redeveloping' Lombardi. The three-hectare vineyard is being completely replanted in Sangiovese and Montepulciano ('to keep the Italian theme'), Cabernet Franc, Riesling, Sauvignon Blanc and Chardonnay. A range of more upmarket varietal table wines was bought in (replacing the old Riesling-Sylvaner and Pinotage), and the popular liqueurs were relabelled and repackaged in attractive 500-ml. bottles. 'We aim to hold on to Lombardi's traditional clientele, while developing a new following for the table wines,' says Coltart.

Lombardi's output is low, about 1500 cases per year. The range of liqueurs – packing only a soft punch at just below 23 per cent alcohol, the legal maximum – features Anisette ('Sambucca style'), Astrega ('Drambuie style'), Caffé Roma (coffee) and Triple Sec (orange). The Marsala is a deep amber-green, full-flavoured, mellow drink flavoured with herb essence imported from Italy. The vermouths range from Dry (white) to Vermouth Di Torino (medium red) and Vermouth Bianco (sweet white).

The new breed of table wines features a robust, ripely herbal, non-wooded Sauvignon Blanc, a citrusy, buttery, straightforward Chardonnay and a plummy, slightly herbal, oak-aged Cabernet Sauvignon. These are decent, everyday-drinking wines, priced right.

Lombardi Wines

Te Mata Road, Havelock North

Owners:
Andy Coltart and Kim Thorp

Key Wines:
Sauvignon Blanc, Chardonnay, Cabernet Sauvignon, sherries, ports, vermouths, liqueurs

Tina Green and Andy Coltart – preserving a touch of Italy in the hills of Havelock North.

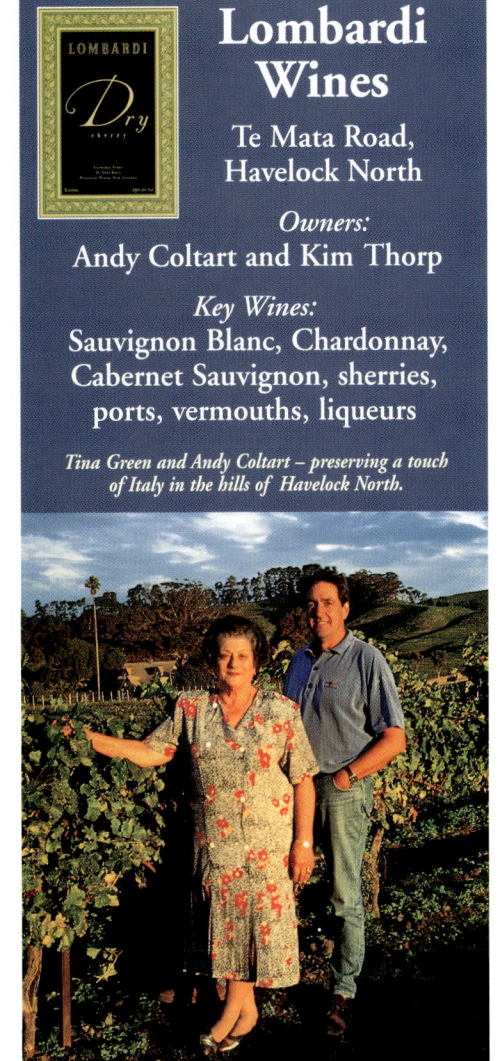

The old Mission winery, nestled at Greenmeadows against the flanks of the Taradale hills, is currently on a high. Outdoor vineyard concerts by Kiri Te Kanawa (20,000 flocked to the Mission to bask in the evening sun, sip 'Kiri in Concert' Chardonnay and Cabernet Franc, and listen to that famous, creamy-rich voice), Ray Charles, Dionne Warwick and Shirley Bassey have greatly boosted the winery's profile, while its flow of top awards in competitions has never been better.

The present site is the last of several occupied by the Marist mission during its long history in Hawke's Bay. Father Lampila and two lay brothers, Florentin and Basil, after mistaking the Poverty Bay coast for their real destination, Hawke's Bay, planted vines near Gisborne in 1850. A year later they moved south and planted more vines at Pakowhai, near Napier.

A Maori chief, Puhara, took the French missionaries under his protection at Pakowhai. The brothers taught and nursed the local Maori, and gardens and vineyards were laid out. After Puhara was killed, however, in an inter-tribal clash in 1857, the brothers were forced to move again, this time to Meeanee.

For several decades wine production at Meeanee was very limited, sufficient only to supply the brothers' needs for sacramental and table wines. A son of a French peasant winemaker, Brother Cyprian, arrived in 1871 to take charge of winemaking – but not until around 1895 were the first recorded sales made, mainly of red wine.

Two years later, local rivers burst their banks, flooding the Meeanee plains and inundating the Mission cellars. After deciding to shift to higher ground, the Society of Mary bought 240 hectares of Henry Tiffen's estate at Greenmeadows – including 0.2 hectares of Pinot Noir – and established a four-hectare vineyard there. Only in 1910, after further disastrous floods, was the seminary itself moved to Greenmeadows; the wooden building was cut into sections and hauled there by steam engine. Fire almost destroyed the wine vaults in 1929, and thousands of gallons of wine were lost in the Napier earthquake of 1931, but of late nature appears

Mission Vineyards
Church Road, Taradale

Owner:
Greenmeadows Mission Trust Board

Key Wines:
Jewelstone Chardonnay, Cabernet Sauvignon/Merlot, Noble Nectar Rhine Riesling; Chardonnay, St Peter Chanel Vineyard Chardonnay, Sauvignon Blanc, Reserve Sauvignon Blanc, Rhine Riesling, Gewürztraminer, Pinot Gris, Müller-Thurgau, St Mary, White Mirage, Mirage, Cabernet Sauvignon, Cabernet/Merlot, Cabernet Franc

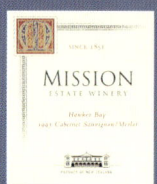

Winemaker Paul Mooney (right, pictured with vineyard manager, Dave London), produces deliciously fat, rich-flavoured Chardonnays under Mission's Jewelstone label.

to have made its peace with the Mission.

Brother Martin, the Mission's affable resident historian, each year guides thousands of visitors around the venerable, barrel-lined cellars. With its lovely setting, hosted winery tours and extensive array of wines for tasting, a visit to the historic Mission winery is one of the highlights of the Hawke's Bay wine trail.

The church retains its commitment to the winery; Mission is New Zealand's only 19th-century wine producer still under the same management. 'For decades, the vineyard and winery were an integral part of the seminary,' recalls winemaker Paul Mooney, who arrived in 1979. 'A lot of the brothers worked in the winery, and the students used to pick grapes by hand.' A few years ago, the Society of Mary's seminary shifted to Auckland, but the vineyard and winery are still viewed as important assets contributing to the financial support of the seminary. The graceful, cream and green hillside building remains, transformed from a seminary into a hostel for polytechnic students and a popular luncheon restaurant with a sweeping view over the vineyards.

Much of the Mission's grapes are drawn from its own vine plantings at Meeanee and Greenmeadows. The fertile, 16-hectare Meeanee vineyard is viewed as a 'bulk' site, but the lower-vigour soils of the 16-hectare Greenmeadows vineyard (including the 'Chanel block') produce riper fruit that forms the basis of some of the Mission's finest wines, notably the mouth-filling, splendidly full-flavoured Jewelstone Chardonnay. A new, 10-hectare vineyard of Cabernet Sauvignon, Syrah, Merlot and Petit Verdot is being planted in what Mooney describes as 'the worst block in the whole Gimblett Road area. It's pure shingle – doesn't even grow grass.'

Hawke's Bay growers supply about half of the Mission's fruit intake, supplemented by a small amount from Gisborne. A crucial factor in the recent surge in the Mission's wine quality has been the coming on stream of fruit from two vineyards in Ohiti Road, near Roy's Hill. 'They're sheltered from the sea breezes, and so a little bit warmer,' says Mooney, 'and the shingle in the soil aids ripening. The Cabernet Sauvignon grapes possess very pure, blackcurrant-like flavours and the Cabernet Franc is wonderful – plummy, with fine tannins.'

A medium-sized winery by New Zealand standards, in the past decade the Mission has doubled its annual output from 30,000 to 60,000 cases and penetrated the German, Dutch, Swiss, Canadian, Hong Kong, Thai and Fijian markets.

The Mission markets a diverse array of wines, typically bargain-priced. As an ideal introduction, try the Pinot Gris – a tangy, full-bodied wine with hints of apricots and earth, a sliver of sweetness, and loads of flavour for its modest price tag.

Mission Sauvignon Blanc is a fresh, crisp wine with pleasant but not concentrated melon/capsicum flavours and a distinct touch of sweetness. The partly barrel-fermented Reserve Sauvignon Blanc is usually full of character, its crisp, lively herbal flavours overlaid with nutty oak.

Three Gewürztraminers are produced: an aromatic, full-flavoured, spicy, semi-dry wine labelled simply Gewürztraminer; the powerful, weighty, rich-flavoured Jewelstone Gewürztraminer Dry; and the freeze-concentrated, sweet and lemony, forthrightly spicy Jewelstone Ice Wine Gewürztraminer. Riesling also appears in three guises: the consistently delicious, perfumed, incisively flavoured, medium Rhine Riesling; the oak-aged, honeyish Jewelstone Botrytis Late Harvest Rhine Riesling; and the mouth-filling, stunningly rich and treacly Jewelstone Noble Nectar Rhine Riesling.

'Chardonnay is our greatest strength,' says Mooney – and he's right. The bottom-tier wine, labelled Chardonnay, is surprisingly good. Fresh, fruity and flavoursome, it also shows a touch of complexity derived from partial barrel-fermentation, lees-aging and malolactic fermentation. The middle-tier St Peter Chanel Vineyard Chardonnay is grown in the same block as its Jewelstone big brother *(see panel)*, and is barrel-fermented, but shows less new-oak influence and is barrel-matured for a shorter time.

The quaffing white-wine range includes White Mirage, a blend of Chardonnay and Pinot Gris, fractionally sweet and very smooth-flowing; the distinctly medium Müller-Thurgau; and the crisp, slightly drier St Mary.

Mission's lower-tier reds, the Cabernet Sauvignon and Cabernet/Merlot, are sound, honest wines, matured in seasoned oak casks. They lack flavour generosity in cooler years, but in warmer vintages like 1991 and 1994 display medium-full body, strong, attractive, spicy, blackcurrant-like flavours and soft, easy tannins. The Cabernet-based, briefly oak-aged Mirage is a light, rustic quaffer, priced right.

Mission Cabernet Franc (also marketed as 'Macabre') is a delightful wine that places its accent on vibrant, plummy fruit flavours, with an almost imperceptible sliver of sweetness to heighten its supple, drink-young charm. Mission's flagship red, however, is clearly the highly fragrant, rich, concentrated Jewelstone Cabernet Sauvignon/Merlot, a plummy, spicy, tannic red that bursts with sweet, ripe-fruit flavours.

MISSION JEWELSTONE CHARDONNAY

The label is punchy, rich and full of character – and so is the wine. Mission's star Jewelstone Chardonnay is 'given the whole works', says Paul Mooney.

Jewelstone is based on the cream of the crop from the Chanel block at Greenmeadows, which 'ripens a week ahead of most other Hawke's Bay vineyards, so it's less likely to be hit by rain during the harvest. The vineyard has been there since the early part of this century, so the soil is not very fertile. The foliage-to-crop ratio is good and the vines crop lightly: below three tonnes per acre [7.2 tonnes per hectare].'

The grapes are hand-picked, whole bunch-pressed and fully barrel-fermented. The young wine is then matured on its yeast lees in French (predominantly) and American oak casks (25 per cent new), with regular lees-stirring. The majority of the final blend undergoes a softening malolactic fermentation.

The result is a high impact, unforgettable wine, excitingly weighty and concentrated, with a powerful surge of grapefruit-and-peach, mealy, oaky flavour, a deliciously creamy texture and rich, sustained finish. Jewelstone Chardonnay is the Mission's flagship, and a Hawke's Bay classic.

Ngatarawa is a small but growing winery and a force to be reckoned with in the quality stakes. Alwyn Corban produces a tight range of robust, deep-flavoured dry wines, supplemented by gorgeous honey-sweet Rieslings.

Ngatarawa (meaning 'between the ridges') winery, ten minutes' drive west of Hastings near Bridge Pa, is a partnership formed in 1981 between Corban and the Glazebrook family, of the 2400-hectare Washpool sheep station, who have owned the site of the present vineyard for over half a century. Ngatarawa's initial vintage, 1982, was based on Te Kauwhata fruit; the first Hawke's Bay wines flowed in 1983.

Alwyn Corban, a reserved and gentle personality, is the son of Alex Corban, the

Ngatarawa Wines

Ngatarawa Road, Bridge Pa, Hastings

Owners:
Alwyn Corban and Garry Glazebrook

Key Wines:
Glazebrook Chardonnay, Cabernet/Merlot, Noble Harvest; Stables Chardonnay, Sauvignon Blanc, Classic White, Late Harvest, Cabernet/Merlot; Old Saddlers Sherry, Port

Alwyn Corban's latest Chardonnays and Cabernet/Merlots under the top Glazebrook label are the finest yet.

Wine Institute's first chairman. After capping his impressive academic record with a master's degree in oenology at the University of California, Davis, Corban spent a year at the Stanley Wine Company in South Australia, followed by four years at McWilliam's in Napier, before founding Ngatarawa with Garry Glazebrook.

The Ngatarawa winery is based on a converted stables built of heart rimu and totara in the 1890s. While the building's soft exterior lines have been preserved – creating 'a winery that doesn't look like a winery' says Corban contentedly – the internal walls have been gutted to free up space for wine storage and a new concrete floor laid.

Barely visible at the rear of the old stables winery, a newer building accommodates most of the winemaking equipment.

Ngatarawa's 18 hectares of vineyards are in the 'Hastings dry belt', a recognised low-rainfall district. The irrigated estate vineyard, on sandy loam soils overlying alluvial gravels, which dry out swiftly in summer, is where Riesling, Sauvignon Blanc and Cabernet Sauvignon vines are planted. A second vineyard to the west is established in Chardonnay, Cabernet Sauvignon, Merlot and Cabernet Franc. About half of each year's fruit intake is purchased from other Hawke's Bay growers.

Ngatarawa's current annual output of about 15,000 cases is divided between the mid-priced Stables range and a trio of premium wines under the Glazebrook label.

Alwyn Corban's devotion to Riesling has few parallels in the region. To encourage the onslaught of 'noble rot' on his Riesling grapes, Corban doesn't use anti *Botrytis* sprays – thus risking ignoble rot – and hangs the ripening bunches late on the vines. Stables Late Harvest displays a pure, delicate, intensely floral bouquet and a medium-sweet, appealingly concentrated lemony/honeyish palate. Corban sees it as his 'fruit style' – meaning it doesn't have the qualities of a heavily botrytised wine.

The gorgeously botrytised, honey-sweet Glazebrook Noble Harvest is made from a high percentage of shrivelled, nobly-rotten Riesling fruit, for which the hand-pickers make several separate sweeps through the vineyard. This gloriously perfumed and nectareous beauty is one of New Zealand's most exceptional 'stickies'.

Stables Cabernet/Merlot has long enjoyed a strong following. With its typical excellent fruit ripeness and soft tannins, this is an ideal red for drinking in its youth.

Stables Sauvignon Blanc is a limey, non-wooded, bone-dry style with ripe, persistent flavours. Its Chardonnay stablemate is a robust, partly barrel-fermented wine with strong citrusy fruit, restrained oak flavours and a well-rounded finish; a drink-young style with a touch of complexity.

Glazebrook Chardonnay is a very stylish wine with intense, citrusy, mealy flavours interwoven with steely acidity. The wine has always been based on estate-grown, Mendoza Chardonnay, but over the years Corban has changed from using a mix of new and older puncheons to predominantly new French oak barriques; cut back on the degree of malolactic fermentation, employing it not to lower acidity but to add complexity; and switched from maturing the wine on its heavy lees to aging on light lees. Corban sees the latest vintages as 'tighter – more like a racehorse than a draughthorse'; I consider them the most expressive, high-flavoured, downright delicious Glazebrook Chardonnays yet.

Glazebrook Cabernet/Merlot is the winery's flagship red: a deep-hued wine with concentrated cassis, plum and spice flavours and powerful but not austere tannins. The latest vintages are more complex, accessible and attractive in their youth than previously, reflecting a rising presence of Merlot in the blend (and a small percentage of Malbec, but not Cabernet Franc). More intensive vineyard management, more rigorous fruit selection, stronger new-oak influence, and longer cask-aging have all helped to lift the label to new heights in recent vintages.

Riverside Wines

Dartmoor Road, Puketapu

Owners:
Ian and Rachel Cadwallader

Key Wines:
Chardonnay, Barrel Fermented Sauvignon Blanc, Sauvignon Blanc, Boathouse White, Rosé, Cabernet/Merlot, Merlot/Cabernet

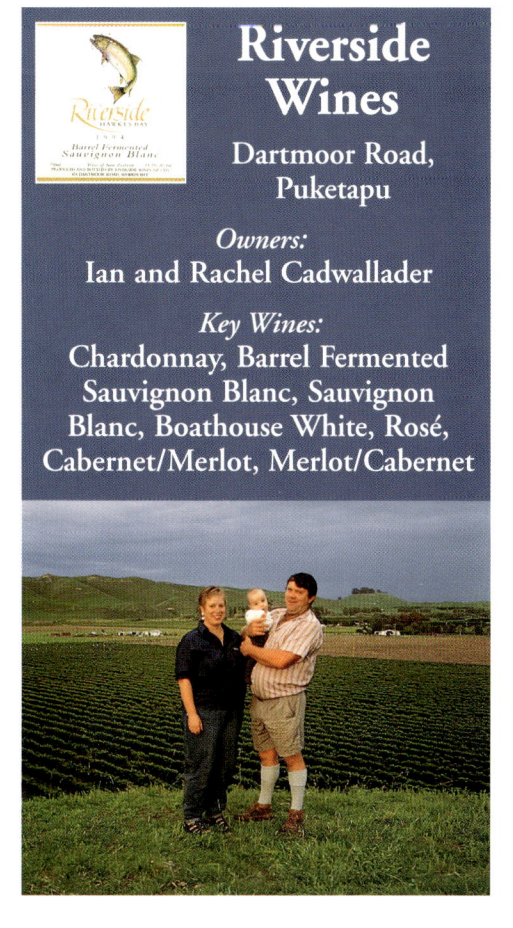

The rainbow trout that dominate Riverside's labels abound in the Tutaekuri River. The winery sits on a slightly elevated plateau in a peaceful pastoral setting, with sweeping views across the original vineyard and the flat green paddocks of the Dartmoor Valley to the river.

Ian and Rachel Cadwallader planted the first vines at Rosemount, the family farm, in 1981, but sold all the grapes to established wineries until their own first vintage in 1989. Ian Cadwallader, whose great-great-grandparents settled in the Dartmoor Valley in 1851, runs a sheep, beef and cropping farm as well as the 18-hectare vineyard. Rachel, a registered nurse, has studied winemaking at the local polytechnic.

On the alluvial river flats in front of the winery, Cabernet Sauvignon, Merlot, Sauvignon Blanc and Chardonnay are cultivated. On a river terrace with lighter, red metal soils behind the winery, Cabernet Sauvignon, Pinotage and Sémillon have recently been added. With their annual output of around 3000 cases, the Cadwalladers are still able to sell the majority of their crop to other winemakers.

The wines have been made on-site since 1991, originally in a tiny converted boatshed, but since 1993 in a new, purpose-built winery. Aran Knight, a Roseworthy College graduate, has made the 1994 and subsequent vintages, with assistance from the Cadwalladers and consultant Nick Sage.

'We're heading into red blends,' says Ian Cadwallader. 'This is a very good area for reds, and wines based on our grapes have scored well in competitions for other companies.' Riverside Cabernet/Merlot is a flavoursome but green-edged wine, slightly less attractive than the riper-tasting, medium-bodied, plummy, spicy, French oak-aged Merlot/Cabernet.

Riverside Chardonnay, a barrel-fermented style, is full, ripe and forward, with pleasing depth of peachy, savoury, buttery-soft flavours. The Cabernet Sauvignon-based Rosé is strawberryish, grassy, slightly sweet and soft.

Rachel Cadwallader has no regrets about getting into the wine industry. 'You can battle away as a farmer, but who knows about it? As a winemaker, you can make a mark and help bring more tourists to the Bay.'

Ian Cadwallader – whose family has farmed in the Dartmoor Valley for 145 years – and his wife, Rachel, view the valley as red-wine country.

Sacred Hill Winery

Dartmoor Road, Puketapu

Owners:
The Mason family

Key Wines:
Reserve Barrique Fermented Chardonnay, Sauvage Sauvignon Blanc, Barrel Fermented Sauvignon Blanc; Cabernet Sauvignon/Merlot, Pinot Noir; Late Harvest Sauvignon Blanc, Late Harvest Gewürztraminer, Whitecliff Sauvignon Blanc, Chardonnay, Gewürztraminer, Cabernet Rosé

The Sauvignon Blancs in several styles – non-wooded, oak-fermented, honey-sweet – are the most distinctive wines flowing from this small winery in the back-country hills of the Dartmoor Valley.

David and Mark Mason produced Sacred Hill's first wines in 1986. David oversees the company's administration and Mark, who holds a wine marketing diploma from Roseworthy College, is immersed in viticulture and winemaking. Their father planted the family's first vines near Puketapu ('sacred hill') in 1982.

The brothers enjoy first choice of the grapes cultivated in the family's vineyards. The fertile, silty 12-hectare Dartmoor vineyard, just down the road from the winery, is established in Sauvignon Blanc, Chardonnay, Gewürztraminer, Pinot Noir, Cabernet Sauvignon, Cabernet Franc and Syrah.

A couple of kilometres further up the valley, on a spectacular site overlooking white limestone cliffs carved by the Tutaekuri River, the 7.5-hectare Whitecliff vineyard is planted in a wide array of varieties. Here the soils – red volcanic ash overlying limestone – are of very low fertility ('We can't grow anything except vines there,' says Mark Mason) and the lighter crops better suited to premium wines. Only a small portion of the crop from the two vineyards is sold to local wineries.

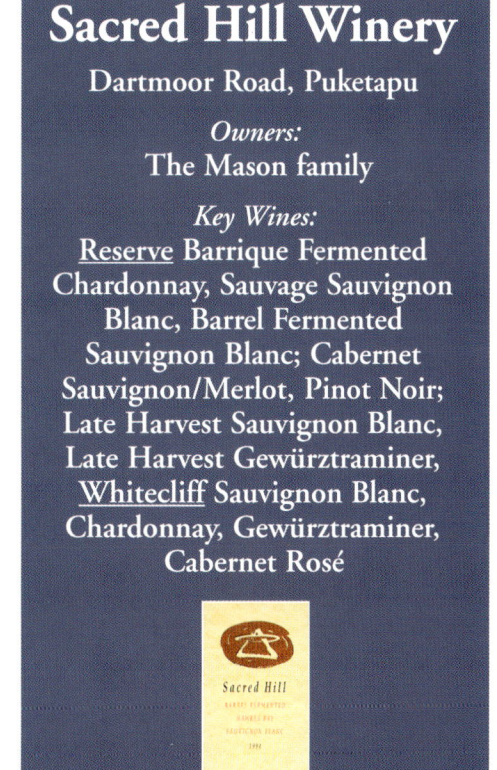

'We're so sheltered here,' says Mark Mason. 'We don't get the coastal breezes; our soils are warmer than on the plains and the fruit ripens earlier.'

Surrounded by trees alongside the main road through the Dartmoor Valley, the rustic Sacred Hill winery was originally a farm building, extended in 1991 by excavating into the hillside and adding a gravity-fed pressing area and refrigerated cellar for barrel maturation. Production has soared during the last five years from 5000 to 13,000 cases, but is expected to plateau soon at about 15,000 cases.

The top wines are sold as Sacred Hill Reserve, and the everyday-drinking wines are labelled Whitecliff. Since 1994, the Mason brothers have also produced wine at Hastings under the Rockwood Cellars label (see page 113).

Sauvignon Blanc is Sacred Hill's speciality. 'At the start, that's what we had most planted,' says Mark Mason. 'Whitecliff is oriented towards tropical-fruit flavours and great

David Mason (pictured) and his brother, Mark, produce some highly distinctive wines in their charmingly rustic Dartmoor Valley winery.

drinkability; the Barrel Fermented Sauvignon Blanc is also ripe and soft. But our flag-bearer, the Sauvage Sauvignon Blanc, is designed as a tightly structured, long-lived Graves style.'

Whitecliff Sauvignon Blanc is a non-wooded style with fresh, delicate, melon and capsicum-evoking flavours. The Barrel Fermented Sauvignon Blanc displays lush, figgy flavours with a touch of oak/lees complexity. Sauvage – based on hand-picked fruit, fermented with wild yeasts in brand-new French oak casks, and not given any softening malolactic fermentation – is a powerful, ripe, woody, strong-flavoured wine that demands cellaring. There is also a full, rich-flavoured, barrel-fermented and lees-aged Late Harvest Sauvignon Blanc, brimming with floral, fruity, honeyish scents.

Whitecliff Chardonnay is a fresh, crisp, drink-young style with delicate lemon and melon-like flavours. The Barrique Fermented Chardonnay is a powerfully oaked, strongly citrusy wine of high quality, rich, savoury and tight.

The Cabernet Rosé is pink, fresh and aromatic, with lively, crisp, strawberryish flavours. The reds include a berryish, plummy, but slightly leafy Cabernet Sauvignon/Merlot and a fragrant, cherryish, supple Pinot Noir with mellow oak influence and attractive sweet-fruit flavours.

Sacred Hill's outdoor vineyard restaurant serves lunches during summer, with bookings essential. 'In the future, our output will stay the same,' says Mark Mason, 'but we'll make more of the Reserve wines and more reds, especially Merlots. And we'll have a bit of fun with late-picked Sauvignon Blancs and Gewürztraminers.'

St George Estate, on the Havelock North-Hastings highway, is truly a boutique-scale operation – diners in the humming vineyard restaurant consume much of the output.

The company began in 1985 as a partnership between Martin Elliott, formerly proprietor of the Havelock North wineshop, and Michael Bennett, who gained his early winemaking experience making 'vinho verde' in Portugal, before joining Villa Maria/Vidal for three years and Te Mata between 1979 and 1984. 'The winery was built on my land and I was always the majority shareholder,' says Elliott. 'I leased the business to Michael in 1990, but we ended that by mutual agreement in late 1993.' Following Michael Bennett's departure, St George Estate is wholly owned by Martin Elliott and his wife, Gillian.

On flat, silty soils in front of the winery, the two-hectare home vineyard is planted in Muscat, Merlot and Cabernet Franc. Sauvignon Blanc and Chardonnay grapes are bought from local growers.

The elegant Cape Dutch-style winery was built out of concrete blocks and timber by Bennett and Elliott themselves. The annual output is very low at around 1250 cases, made by Martin Elliott with the assistance of a winemaking consultant.

St George Estate wine is all sold directly from the winery: in the restaurant, over the counter or by mail-order. Perfumed, slightly sweet and fruity, the totally undemanding July Muscat is the most popular wine. 'When people try it, they're hooked!' says Elliott. His selection also includes a Cabernet Franc-based Rosé, Chardonnay, Sauvignon Blanc and Merlot.

St George Estate
St George's Road South, Hastings

Owners:
Martin and Gillian Elliott

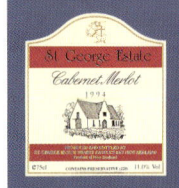

Key Wines:
July Muscat, Chardonnay, Sauvignon Blanc, Rosé, Merlot

Martin Elliott produces wine principally for the pleasure of diners in his cosy vineyard restaurant.

If you ask Dr Alan Limmer, of the small Stonecroft winery, to name his favourite wines, he doesn't hesitate: 'Rhône reds. Syrah is very seductive wine. I'm seduced.'

Stonecroft (the name means 'stony small farm') lies in Mere Road, on part of the same shingle block as Gimblett Road in the Roy's Hill area west of Hastings. Limmer studied earth sciences and chemistry at Waikato University, where he earned his doctorate, and then in 1981 moved to Hawke's Bay to manage a laboratory servicing agricultural needs. He planted the first vines in his stony, extremely free-draining gravels in 1983 and made his first wines in 1987.

Stonecroft's four-hectare estate vineyard is planted in Chardonnay, Gewürztraminer, Sauvignon Blanc, Cabernet Sauvignon, Merlot and Syrah. These silty, sandy gravels running 10 metres deep can change from a state of water saturation to vine-stressing aridity in only four or five days. 'This gives consistent vintages,' says Limmer. 'The weather changes from one year to another but my fruit is much the same.' The vineyard yields low crops – around six tonnes per hectare – and the fruit is left on the vines as long as possible, ripening to very high sugar levels and sometimes shrivelling.

A second vineyard, Tokarahi ('many stones') has recently been planted in a warm, sheltered, north-facing bowl at the foot of Roy's Hill. In this exclusively red-wine vineyard, three hectares of Syrah and Merlot have been established, together with New Zealand's first trial plantings of Zinfandel (California's equivalent of Syrah), Cinsaut and Mourvedre (both traditional varieties of the Mediterranean south of France).

Limmer, with his arresting series of dense-

Stonecroft Wines

Mere Road, Hastings

Owner:
Dr Alan Limmer

Key Wines:
Chardonnay, Gewürztraminer, Gewürztraminer Late Harvest, Sauvignon Blanc, Cabernet/Merlot, Ruhanui, Syrah

Alan Limmer is renowned for his strapping, peppery Syrah, but his white wines and Cabernet-based reds are also rewarding.

coloured, robust, rich-flavoured reds, is New Zealand's first winemaker to consistently produce a satisfying Syrah *(see panel)*. Syrah thrives in a warm environment and past growers struggled to ripen their fruit. So what spurred Limmer to plant an experimental row of Syrah vines in his arid, stony Mere Road soils in 1984?

'Two things. Of the world's top reds, to me Hermitage is the best. The reds of the northern Rhône have everything – fragrance, structure, aging ability. And last century, Syrah looked promising here. So everything pointed to the fact we'd overlooked a good red-wine variety.'

Limmer is not a great fan of Australia's Shiraz-based reds. 'The Australian wines are big, upfront, with jammy fruit and American oak, but they tend to be one-dimensional. Rhône reds have better structure and length. Our wines are heading in that direction; they're New Zealand wines, but more in the mould of the French. For instance, we don't use American oak.'

Stonecroft's two other reds – the Cabernet/Merlot and the blended Ruhanui – share the sturdiness and flavour generosity of their Syrah stablemate. Dark, intense and tannic, the Cabernet/Merlot achieves a high standard even in very cool vintages and matures well over the long haul. Ruhanui – a densely coloured blend of Cabernet Sauvignon (principally), Syrah and Merlot – is a softly mouth-filling wine with an enticing fragrance and notably rich, supple, spicy flavour.

Stonecroft's white wines are also classy. The Chardonnay is a bold style with searching grapefruit-like flavours, oak and lees-aging complexity and a long, steely finish. The Sauvignon Blanc, not wood-aged, is typically weighty and ripe-flavoured.

The Gewürztraminer is a powerful, slightly sweet wine with a lovely spread of lychees and pepper flavours; at its best the Late Harvest Gewürztraminer overflows with luscious, spicy, honeyish flavour. These wines are full of character.

STONECROFT SYRAH

Stonecroft Syrah is a muscular red with flashing purple-black hues and concentrated red-berry, plum and black pepper flavours, rich, tannic and long. Tasting the 1991 last year, I was vividly reminded of a good Crozes-Hermitage.

'It's a hot vineyard site and the soils are low-vigour,' says Alan Limmer, analysing the reasons for his Syrah's consistently top-flight quality. 'The vines crop lightly at around two tonnes per acre [4.8 tonnes per hectare]. We hang the grapes out as long as we can, until we think they are in danger of collapsing from *Botrytis* or the leaves are falling off. That's when you get the big flavour changes, from herbaceousness through black-pepper characters to violets.'

In the winery, Limmer handles the Syrah simply. 'We open-ferment on the skins, hand-plunge, and macerate the skins in the wine for a week after the fermentation.' The wine is matured for 18 months in French oak (50–60 per cent new), then egg-white fined but not filtered prior to bottling.

Limmer predicts a big future for Syrah in New Zealand. 'We won't make large volumes of well-fruited $15 reds; our climate is too marginal. But in this country's hottest, driest areas, we could perhaps rival the top Hermitages.'

Fine red wines are the target of the Lawson family, founders of Te Awa Farm. 'I believe New Zealand can do it; my ambition is to do it consistently,' says Gus Lawson. 'Premium red-wine production in this country is very young – there's plenty of room for improvement.'

The Lawsons, contract grapegrowers since 1980, searched for five years for a new site to grow top red wines and Chardonnay before purchasing Te Awa Farm, on the corner of Ngatarawa Road and State Highway 50, in 1992. Subdivided in 1906 from the original Longlands Station, the name of the 173-hectare property is an abbreviation of Te Awa-O-Te-Atua, which means 'river of God', a reference to the subterranean streams which flow through the district.

Gus Lawson, the manager of Te Awa Farm's wine venture, also acts as a viticultural consultant to several other grapegrowers and wine companies in the region.

In Te Awa Farm's free-draining, shallow alluvial soils, 32 hectares of close-planted Cabernet Sauvignon, Merlot, Syrah, Cabernet Franc, Malbec, Pinot Noir, Chardonnay and Sauvignon Blanc vines have been planted. 'It's a very, very hot area,' says Gus Lawson. 'I've registered temperatures up to 45°C in the sun.'

Te Awa Farm's first vintage flowed in 1994. So far the wines have been made at another local winery, but in the near future the Lawsons plan to build their own winery and employ a specialist winemaker. The annual production is expected to grow to around 20,000 cases.

The top selection is labelled Boundary and the more widely available wines as Longlands. The initial releases have included a lean, citrusy, delicate, flinty Longlands Chardonnay and a flavour-packed 1995 Longlands Cabernet/Merlot.

Te Awa Farm
State Highway 50, Roy's Hill

Owner:
The Lawson family

Key Wines:
Boundary Chardonnay, Merlot;
Longlands Chardonnay, Cabernet/Merlot

Ian Lawson and his son, Angus ('Gus'), plan to produce premium Cabernet-based reds and Chardonnay in the warm, sheltered Roy's Hill area.

Three of New Zealand's most striking wines – Coleraine and Awatea Cabernet/Merlots and Elston Chardonnay – flow from this illustrious Hawke's Bay winery. Te Mata Estate, which in 1996 proudly claimed to be 'the first New Zealand winery to make a century', is one of New Zealand's foremost wineries, with consistently outstanding wines and a rich winemaking heritage.

'The fine vineyard of 35 acres [14.2ha] situated at Te Mata, Havelock North, owned by Mr Bernard Chambers, is now the leading one in the Dominion,' wrote S.F. Anderson, the Government vine and wine instructor, in the *New Zealand Journal of Agriculture* in May 1914. 'Mr Chambers's wines are principally hocks, claret and sweet, and are commanding a large sale.'

Chambers, a wealthy grazier and prominent local body politician, had his interest in winemaking kindled by a French guest at the Te Mata homestead, who pointed out the viticultural potential of the surrounding slopes. In 1892, the first vines – cuttings of Pinot Noir obtained from the Society of Mary's Mission Vineyards at Taradale – struck root at Te Mata Vineyard.

The vineyard flourished. Chambers converted a brick stable erected in 1872 into his cellar (still used today for cask storage), and by March 1895 the first wine was flowing. 'My wine is turning out very well,' he wrote in 1898. 'I made claret and chablis and have given a lot away. I won't begin selling for another year, until the wine is more matured.'

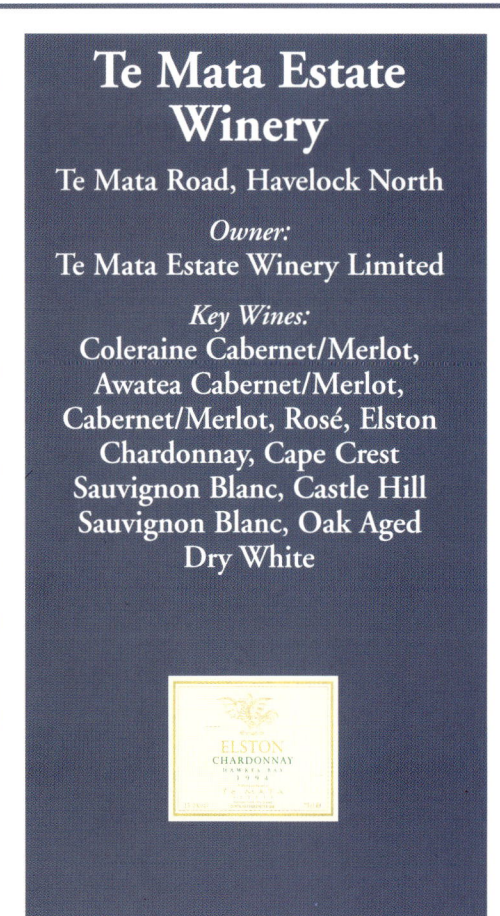

With Australian winemaker J.O. Craike (who won gold medals for Te Mata at the Franco-British and Japanese-British Exhibitions) at the production helm, by 1909 Chambers' vineyard was the largest in the country, with an annual output of 12,000 gallons (54,551L) of wine from Meunier, Syrah, Cabernet Sauvignon, Riesling and Verdelho vines. Among the stream of eminent visitors to Te Mata Vineyard were Prime Minister Richard Seddon and the Governor, Lord Ranfurly.

But, from this early peak, production declined as the influence of the prohibition movement intensified and Chambers ran into problems with birds, mildew, frost and labour. A series of new owners failed to restore the vineyard's fortunes.

The revival of Te Mata's reputation began in 1974, when Michael Morris and John Buck, both then active as wine judges,

Te Mata Estate Winery
Te Mata Road, Havelock North

Owner:
Te Mata Estate Winery Limited

Key Wines:
Coleraine Cabernet/Merlot, Awatea Cabernet/Merlot, Cabernet/Merlot, Rosé, Elston Chardonnay, Cape Crest Sauvignon Blanc, Castle Hill Sauvignon Blanc, Oak Aged Dry White

acquired the run-down company. Morris, a Wellington accountant, is a non-working partner. Buck, the managing director, has enjoyed a high profile on his career path leading finally and triumphantly to the hills of Havelock North.

The cellars, built of brick and native timbers, were restored to their original condition and equipped with stainless steel tanks and new oak casks. The new owners' first vintage, 1979, was an unusually wet one. 'I soon discovered how many friends I had,' recalls Buck. 'I'd been a merchant, judge and critic, but many people were dismissive of the whole idea of me going into production.'

1980 brought a rapid change of fortune. 'We were fortunate to acquire the Awatea vineyard and it had a small block of old Cabernet on it. I guess we picked three or four tonnes off it and the moment we crushed those grapes we knew that our assertion as to the right variety to grow on these hills was correct.' Te Mata 1980 Cabernet Sauvignon then carried off the trophy for the best red at the 1981 National Wine Competition (a feat repeated by the 1981 vintage in 1982) and Te Mata was on its way.

The winery until 1989 marketed all its top wines with a vineyard site designation. Coleraine Cabernet/Merlot, for instance, was sourced from John and Wendy Buck's own two-hectare vineyard called Coleraine, planted with Cabernet Sauvignon, Merlot and Cabernet Franc. Since the 1989 vintage, however, Te Mata's red wines have been produced in a tiered group, with Coleraine at the top, closely followed by Awatea, and then a third wine called Te Mata Cabernet/Merlot. All three are a blend of wines from Te Mata's spectrum of vineyards. 'This development gives us access to a far greater range of flavours when assembling the wines, providing more flexibility . . . to craft even finer wines,' said Buck.

Te Mata Estate owns no vineyards, although individuals within the company do, and some other vineyards are leased or managed by Te Mata. Buck, Morris, winemaker Peter Cowley and their families own the eight-hectare 'red metal' Bullnose vineyard, planted in Cabernet Sauvignon, Merlot, Cabernet Franc and Syrah, midway between Ngatarawa and Maraekakaho.

At Woodthorpe Terraces, on the south side of the Dartmoor Valley, over several years a 120-hectare vineyard and fully self-contained winery are being established in a major joint venture between Te Mata Estate and Ghuznee Buildings Limited, a family investment company in which John Buck's wife, Wendy, has holdings. Planting – principally of Cabernet Sauvignon, Merlot and Chardonnay – started in 1994 on free-draining, north-facing terraces 30 metres above the Tutaekuri River.

Buck and Cowley's determination to produce long-lived wine styles is a central strand in Te Mata's approach to winemaking. 'To gain true international recognition, an industry has to be capable of making wines that improve with age – that's the ultimate quality factor,' says Buck. '[People need to be able to] put wine into their cellars with confidence and know that when they pull them out they will be a damn sight better than when they put them in.'

Awatea – blended in 1994 from 45 per cent Cabernet Sauvignon, 36 per cent Merlot and 19 per cent Cabernet Franc – is voluptuously fragrant, rich and supple, and invariably more approachable in its youth than the Coleraine of the same vintage. Both Coleraine *(see panel)* and Awatea are great wines, firmly in the vanguard of New Zealand's reds.

Te Mata's third-tier claret-style red, labelled Cabernet/Merlot, is a simpler but still highly enjoyable wine, forward and full-flavoured in its appeal.

Elston Chardonnay is a very mouth-filling, citric-flavoured, mealy, firm-structured wine, wholly barrel-fermented and matured on its yeast lees for 'ages', according to Peter Cowley. At about four years old it is a notably 'complete' wine, powerful, very rich-flavoured and complex. Elston, too, is consistently one of the greatest New Zealand examples of its style.

Of Te Mata's Cape Crest and Castle Hill Sauvignon Blancs, more often than not the Cape Crest has the edge in weight and flavour depth. Since the 1991 vintage, Cape Crest has been partly barrel-fermented, in a bid to more clearly differentiate its style from that of Castle Hill. Both wines are classic examples of the Hawke's Bay Sauvignon Blanc style: robust, ripely herbal and sustained. Castle Hill in its youth is the more obviously 'varietal' of the two; Cape Crest potentially the more complex.

Easily overlooked in the Te Mata range is the Oak Aged Dry White, typically an American oak-aged blend of Sauvignon Blanc and Chardonnay. This is a full, fresh and unexpectedly flavour-packed wine, bargain priced. The Rosé, recently blended from Cabernet Sauvignon and Merlot, is bright pink, strawberryish, dry and refreshingly crisp.

'People haven't seen the finished Te Mata yet, the completion of our 20-year plan,' says John Buck.

Te Mata Coleraine Cabernet/Merlot

With a series of extraordinarily elegant wines since the memorable 1982 debut, climaxing in the latest – and greatest – 1991 and 1994 vintages, Coleraine has carved out a reputation second to none among New Zealand reds.

Compared to its Awatea stablemate, Coleraine is more new oak-influenced and more slowly evolving. The 1994 vintage is dominated by Cabernet Sauvignon (74 per cent), blended with 17 per cent Cabernet Franc and 9 per cent Merlot.

The standard of most of the Coleraines from the mid-late 1980s has been surpassed by the 1989–91 and 1994 vintages (there was no 1992 or 1993). These are magical reds: the 1989 dark, concentrated, spicy and still youthful; the 1990 deliciously perfumed, ripe and supple; the 1991 and 1994 both magnificently fragrant and complex, with a tight-knit array of cassis, plum, spice and new-oak flavours, braced by firm tannins.

What is the key to Coleraine's ascending quality? 'Prior to 1989, it was a single-vineyard wine,' says John Buck. 'Since then, it's been no longer a site-specific wine, but a blend of the fruit we want to put into it.' Te Mata's upgrading of its winemaking equipment has also been critical.

About 2000 cases of Coleraine Cabernet/Merlot are produced each year, and some is exported to Europe, principally the UK, Switzerland and Germany. How do the French respond to the most Bordeaux-like of all New Zealand's reds? 'They pick up quickly on the shortcomings,' says Buck. 'The key factor is the lack of vine age, which will give the wine greater concentration, length and nuances of aroma. But their remarks are fairly flattering.'

Intense interest has surrounded the 1991 and subsequent releases of Church Road Cabernet Sauvignon/Merlot. The most prestigious red wines in the world are French, so when the largest New Zealand winery called in a major Bordeaux house to upgrade its red wine production, everyone wanted to taste the result.

With much fanfare, in 1988 and 1989 Montana thrust into Hawke's Bay, snapping up $6 million worth of existing vineyards and the old McDonald winery at Taradale. Its goal: to elevate the standard of the giant company's previously unspectacular red wines and – to a lesser extent – Chardonnays.

Although deeply rooted in the Gisborne and Marlborough regions, Montana had previously been absent in Hawke's Bay. Montana's purchase of Penfold's (NZ) in late 1986 first triggered its involvement in Hawke's Bay, by linking it with Penfold's contract growers. By also purchasing 238 hectares of vines, Montana swiftly staked out a significant share of the region's vineyards. Its acquisition of the McDonald winery – which it swiftly rejuvenated and named The McDonald Winery – also gave it a small-scale production facility ideal for making limited volumes of top-flight wines.

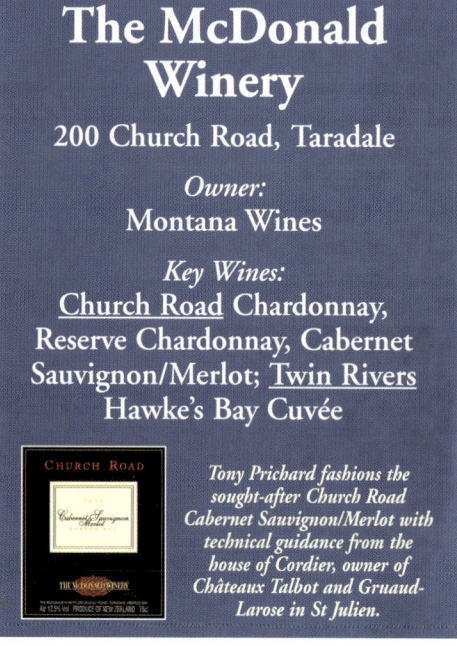

'Red wines will be the focus here,' says winemaker Tony Prichard, a Massey University food technology graduate who joined Montana at its Gisborne winery 13 years ago. To boost its red-wine chances, Montana formed a close relationship with Cordier, one of Bordeaux's major wine firms.

Cordier gave Montana clear guidelines on how to boost the standard of its Hawke's Bay reds. 'Prior to their involvement, we were trying lots of techniques, but didn't have a

The McDonald Winery

200 Church Road, Taradale

Owner:
Montana Wines

Key Wines:
Church Road Chardonnay, Reserve Chardonnay, Cabernet Sauvignon/Merlot; Twin Rivers Hawke's Bay Cuvée

Tony Prichard fashions the sought-after Church Road Cabernet Sauvignon/Merlot with technical guidance from the house of Cordier, owner of Châteaux Talbot and Gruaud-Larose in St Julien.

clear direction,' says Prichard. 'Cordier have focused us on a narrower range of concerns: the quality and amount of tannins, barrel handling [no American oak], blending and – the key thing – eliminating herbaceousness.'

The extended roots of The McDonald Winery run back to the closing years of the 19th century. In 1896 Bartholomew Steinmetz, a native of Luxembourg, resigned his position as a lay brother at the Society of Mary's Marist Mission to settle in Taradale and marry. Steinmetz purchased two hectares from the estate of pioneer winemaker Henry Tiffen, planted vine cuttings supplied by the adjoining Mission, and by 1901 the first vintage of Taradale Vineyards' wines was in the barrel.

For the next 25 years Steinmetz made his living selling table grapes and wine. In 1926, Steinmetz leased his winery to 19-year-old Tom McDonald, whose later exploits with the Cabernet Sauvignon variety were to indivisibly link the name McDonald with fine quality reds (see page 93).

Montana's refurbishment of the winery shop in the art deco style popular in Hawke's Bay, opening of a luncheon restaurant, and creation of the country's first wine museum, with strikingly lifelike models toiling with pioneer winemaking equipment, have transformed The McDonald Winery into one of the highlights of the Hawke's Bay wine trail.

The popular Church Road Chardonnay places its accent on rich, ripe, citrusy fruit flavours, with barrel-fermentation and lees-aging adding toasty, biscuity characters and partial malolactic fermentation giving a touch of butteriness. This is a deliciously full, flavour-packed and skilfully balanced wine. The Reserve model, fermented in two-thirds new French oak barriques, is more powerful, with intense, grapefruit-like fruit flavours and a savoury, mealy, oaky complexity.

Twin Rivers Hawke's Bay Cuvée is a full, moderately yeasty wine of good but not outstanding quality, priced in the middle of the market.

Church Road Cabernet Sauvignon/ Merlot stands out, not as a blockbuster, but for its elegance and finesse. In top vintages like 1991 and 1994, it displays a rich, dark hue and a deep-scented bouquet of cassis and oak. Fleshy and supple, with a surge of blackcurrant and spice flavours, smooth and sustained, this is a stylish, superbly well-balanced red – an auspicious start to Montana's and Cordier's journey into New Zealand's red-wine future.

Vidal Estate
913 St Aubyns Street East, Hastings

Owner:
Villa Maria Estate

Key Wines:
Reserve Chardonnay, Fumé Blanc, Gewürztraminer, Cabernet Sauvignon, Cabernet Sauvignon/Merlot; Methôde Traditionnelle Brut, Chardonnay, Fumé Blanc, Sauvignon Blanc, Gewürztraminer, Müller-Thurgau, Chenin Blanc/Chardonnay, Merlot Rosé, Cabernet Sauvignon/Merlot, Pinot Noir

The prestigious trophy for champion wine of the show at the Air New Zealand Wine Awards in 1992 and 1993 went to Vidal Reserve Cabernet Sauvignon/Merlot 1990, one of the most glorious reds ever produced in this country. The old Hastings winery is now a key part of the Villa Maria empire.

Anthony Vidal, the founder, came to New Zealand from Spain at the age of 22 in 1888. After eleven years working with his uncle, Wanganui winemaker Joseph Soler, Vidal experimented with viticulture at Palmerston North before shifting to Hawke's Bay. In 1905 he bought a half-hectare property at Hastings, converted the existing stables into a cellar and planted grapevines.

The winery flourished; a new, three-hectare vineyard was established at Te Awanga in 1916 and, a few years later, another three hectares was acquired from Chambers' Te Mata vineyard. After Anthony Vidal's death, control of the company passed to his three sons: Frank, the winemaker; Cecil, who concentrated on sales; and Leslie, who supervised the vines. For decades the winery enjoyed a solid reputation. John Buck, now of Te Mata Estate, in 1969 stated in his book *Take a Little Wine*, that Vidal's Claret and Burgundy were 'the two finest, freely available dry reds on the New Zealand market'. Using Cabernet Sauvignon, Meunier and hybrid fruit, the brothers produced a Burgundy of 'style, good colour, body and balance' and a Claret 'lighter in body and more austere to taste'.

After 1972, when Seppelt's of Australia acquired a 60 per cent share of Vidal, standard lines were dropped, labels changed and the quality of the wine began to fall away. The slide continued under another owner, Ross MacLennan, from 1974 to 1976.

The restoration of Vidal's reputation began in 1976, after Villa Maria bought the company. In 1979 the first vineyard restaurant in New Zealand (today a brassiere serving brunch, lunch and dinner) opened at Vidal. The grapes, almost all contract grown, are drawn largely but not entirely from the Hawke's Bay region – a reality reflected in the company's 1994 name change from Vidal of Hawke's Bay to Vidal Estate.

Elise Montgomery, Vidal's winemaker since 1990, graduated in 1985 as a Bachelor of Horticultural Science from Massey University, and in 1986 from Roseworthy College with a Graduate Diploma in Wine (Oenology). After working successive vintages in Victoria, California and France,

Elise Montgomery's Reserve Chardonnays and Cabernet-based reds rank among the classiest in the Bay, with a proud record in show judgings.

Montgomery joined Villa Maria as an assistant winemaker in early 1990. 'The big joke at Villa Maria was that for the first time I'd have to work two vintages at the same place. It didn't happen – in late 1990 I was appointed winemaker at Vidal.'

Vidal is a medium-sized winery, with an annual output of about 45,000 cases. Under its commercial label, Vidal markets a range of well-priced, often impressive varietals, including a top-flight Müller-Thurgau and Merlot Rosé; a full, soft, briefly barrel-aged Chenin Blanc/Chardonnay; a spicy, citrusy, slightly sweet Gewürztraminer; a vibrantly fruity, limey, lemony Sauvignon Blanc; a Fumé Blanc which is a tasty amalgam of ripe tropical-fruit flavours and subtle toasty oak; a fresh, lightly wooded Chardonnay with ripe citrus and melon-like flavours; a floral, supple, middle-weight Pinot Noir; and a sturdy, ripe, easy-drinking Cabernet Sauvignon/Merlot.

The Methôde Traditionnelle Brut, a blend of Chardonnay and Pinot Noir, matured on its yeast lees for several years, is a soft, very fruity and creamy style. The rarer Blanc de Blancs and Blanc de Noirs versions are both classy.

The jewels in the Vidal crown are its formidable line-up of Reserve wines. Bursting with powerful, ripe, intense Hawke's Bay fruit flavours, they are also stylish, extremely well-balanced wines.

Vidal Reserve Chardonnay, barrel-fermented and lees-aged in French oak barriques, is mouth-filling with an explosion of ripe, figgy, citrusy flavours; the latest vintages, with a more reined-in oak influence, are the most stylish. The Reserve Gewürztraminer is restrained in its youth but blossoms with age. The Reserve Fumé Blanc, both tank and cask-fermented, bursts with seductively ripe, passionfruit and melon-like fruit flavours, with richness and complexity added by the subtle oak/lees characters.

VIDAL RESERVE CABERNET SAUVIGNON AND RESERVE CABERNET SAUVIGNON/MERLOT

Vidal's superb Reserve Cabernet Sauvignon serves as a reminder that New Zealand's top Cabernet-based reds don't always have to be blended to achieve distinction. This is a power-packed, spicy, cedary, tannic red of great richness and length. Its stablemate, the marvellously fragrant Reserve Cabernet Sauvignon/Merlot, is a more voluptuous style, its delicious surge of plummy, minty fruit and strong oak flavours underpinned by firm tannin. These are great reds.

'Obviously, the fruit is the key,' says winemaker Elise Montgomery, 'although we've sourced it from different vineyards.' The Merlot component of the great 1990 Reserve Cabernet Sauvignon/Merlot was grown in Peter Lyons' vineyard in Mere Road; the Cabernet Sauvignon in Ash Henderson's block at Clive. The 1992 and 1994 reds were drawn from Greg Duley's vineyard near Fernhill. In the future, Villa Maria's new red-wine vineyard on State Highway 50, near Gimblett Road, will be a major source of grapes.

The wines are not produced every vintage: both were made in 1990 and 1991; only the Reserve Cabernet Sauvignon/Merlot in 1992; neither in 1993; only the Reserve Cabernet Sauvignon in 1994.

Vinification is 'pretty standard', says Montgomery. 'We try to get as much flavour as we can from the grapes via cap management [pumping the fermenting juice over the skins] and macerate the skins in the wine for a couple of weeks after the fermentation to extract more fruit tannin. Then we get the wines to barrel early, so that the oak tannins can integrate with the wine at an early stage.' The wine is matured in French oak barriques (typically 50 per cent new) for 18 months in a good vintage; 15 months for a lighter year.

Montgomery experiments constantly. 'We're not static with the style. For instance, we're playing around with proportions of hand-plunged material to get more "lifted" aromas. The '94 Reserve Cabernet Sauvignon is basically off one vineyard, but the grapes were handled in three different batches. Individually they look quite good – together they look even better.'

For most of his adult life, John Loughlin dreamed of producing 'the finest possible Bordeaux-style red wines'. He purchased his ideal site, a sheltered, north-facing slope at the foot of Te Mata Peak, in 1972, but not until 1991 did the busy eye surgeon produce the first vintage at Waimarama Estate.

The dream started to become reality in 1988, when the first vines were planted on the slope running from Loughlin's house down to River Road. 'I planted Cabernet Sauvignon and Merlot because my mentor up the road, John Buck, had obviously got it right.'

Overlooking the Tukituki River (Waimarama means 'moonlight on water'), the estate vineyard is planted in surface loams of moderate fertility over volcanic ash, with a hard pan beneath. Four hectares are established in Cabernet Sauvignon, Merlot, Cabernet Franc and Malbec.

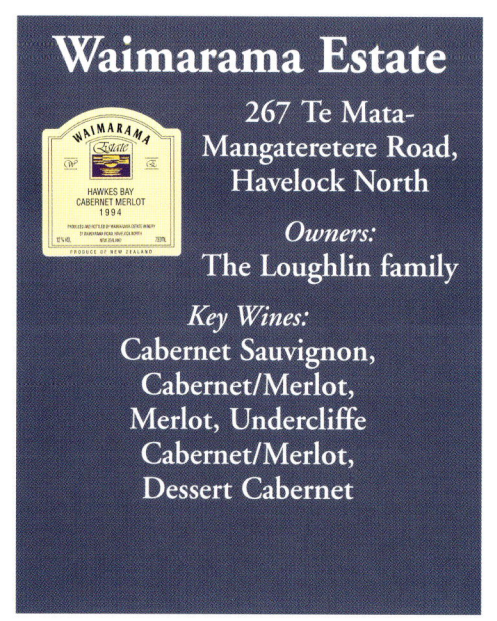

John Loughlin's neighbour, Terry Coxon, also has a two-hectare vineyard, entirely devoted to Syrah, which Waimarama Estate is managing. Loughlin's son – also called John – and his wife, Kathryn, also own the four-hectare Askern Vineyard a few kilometres away in Te Mata-Mangateretere Road, planted in white-wine varieties: Sémillon, Sauvignon Blanc, Riesling, Gewürztraminer and Chardonnay. Waimarama Estate's retail outlet can also be found here.

The reds, French oak-matured, clearly reflect Loughlin's dedicated, fastidious approach. The Cabernet/Merlot, Cabernet Sauvignon and Merlot are all bold, dark-hued, intensely fruity wines with rich

Waimarama Estate

267 Te Mata-Mangateretere Road, Havelock North

Owners:
The Loughlin family

Key Wines:
Cabernet Sauvignon, Cabernet/Merlot, Merlot, Undercliffe Cabernet/Merlot, Dessert Cabernet

blackcurrant, herbal, spicy, plummy flavours, quality oak handling and supple tannins.

Undercliffe Cabernet/Merlot, the second-tier label, is a lighter, earlier-drinking style. Waimarama also makes a sweet, fortified, oak-aged Dessert Cabernet, sold as a 'stunning companion to chocolate desserts'. The first white wines, from the Askern Vineyard, flowed from the 1996 vintage.

Waimarama Estate is set to grow fast: from 2000 cases in 1995 to 7000 cases in the year 2000. 'One of these days I'll have to give up my medical practice,' says Loughlin. 'But I'm a firm believer that you shouldn't retire at 65.'

John Loughlin and his son, John, produce robust, rich-flavoured Cabernet Sauvignon and Merlot-based reds, and are now starting to diversify into white wines.

Other Producers

Bradshaw Estate
Owned by accountant Wayne Bradshaw, the winery and four hectares of Sauvignon Blanc and Merlot are just over the road from Lombardi in Te Mata Road, Havelock North, on the site of the original Vidal 'No 1' vineyard. The first vintage was 1994. The early releases, made by Dutch winemaker Hans Peet, formerly assistant winemaker at Vidal, have been based on bought-in fruit, because the grapes from the estate vineyard were contracted to another winery until after the 1996 vintage. The Merlot is light, but the non-oaked Chardonnay is attractively full, fresh and soft.

Brownlie Brothers
On the main highway at Bay View, this is a partnership between brothers Roger, Chris and Stephen Brownlie. Much of the crop from their vineyard is sold to other wineries, but in 1990 the brothers started producing a trickle of their own wine. I have tasted a solid, slightly sweet Gewürztraminer and a full, soft, ripe Sauvignon Blanc.

Clifton Road
Close to the coast at Te Awanga, Wayne Harrison and Terri Coats own a 2.5-hectare vineyard that since 1992 has yielded a chunky, spicy, green-edged Cabernet Sauvignon and a Sauvignon Blanc that — at its best — is very aromatic, rich and flavourful. Some of the grapes are sold to other producers, who in turn make the Clifton Road wines. No tasting facilities.

Gunn Estate
The Gunn brothers – Alan, a contract grapegrower since 1982 and Denis, a Roseworthy College graduate and former assistant winemaker at Villa Maria – have produced consistently impressive Chardonnays since their first 1994 vintage. The brothers get the first 'pick' of the fruit off Alan's 14 hectares of vines at Fernhill and Ohiti Road, across the Ngaruroro River from Gimblett Road. The range, made at the Kemblefield winery, also includes an attractive Merlot/Cabernet.

Hawkhurst Estate
Owned by father and son team John and Jon Smith, this is a Cabernet Sauvignon and Merlot vineyard in Napier Road, Havelock North. The vineyard, first planted in 1978 to supply grapes to other wine companies, is named after the family's ancestral village, Hawkhurst, in Kent. The wines produced on the Smiths' behalf at local Hawke's Bay wineries have been solid but typically lack depth. No on-site sales.

Park Estate
The Bay Classic winery in Pakowhai Road is best known for fruit wines but also produces a few grape wines under the Park Estate label. I have tasted a solid, semi-dry Gewürztraminer and a slightly herbaceous, quaffing Cabernet Sauvignon.

Red Metal Vineyard
Grant Edmonds (formerly chief winemaker for the Villa Maria group) and his wife, Sue, are partners with Auckland-based Gary and Diane Simpson in this red-wine vineyard in Maraekakaho Road, near Bridge Pa. The three-hectare vineyard (to be expanded to eight hectares) of Cabernet Sauvignon, Cabernet Franc and Merlot yielded its first wine in 1996.

Richard Harrison
Three hundred metres above sea level in Central Hawke's Bay, Sir Richard Harrison, former Speaker of the House of Representatives, has a half-hectare experimental vineyard planted in nine grape varieties. The wines, made by Malcolm Reeves of the Cross Roads winery, and sold by appointment on-site in Paget Road, Takapau, include an appley, steely, Chablis-like Chardonnay; vigorous, penetratingly flavoured Chenin Blanc; and fragrant, supple, raspberry/plum-flavoured Pinot Noir.

Rockwood Cellars
The Mason brothers of Sacred Hill, winemaker Tony Bish, and other shareholders own this contract crushing facility in Omahu Road, Hastings. The wines produced under the Rockwood Cellars label since 1994 have included a buoyant, smooth, drink-young style of Merlot/Cabernet and a muscular, mealy, rich-flavoured Reserve Selection Chardonnay. Visits by appointment only.

Tui Vale
Keith Crone, in the past a viticulturist for Cooks, markets a range of Hawke's Bay wines made at local wineries. His Cabernet-based reds have been sturdy and flavoursome in a spicy, slightly leafy style.

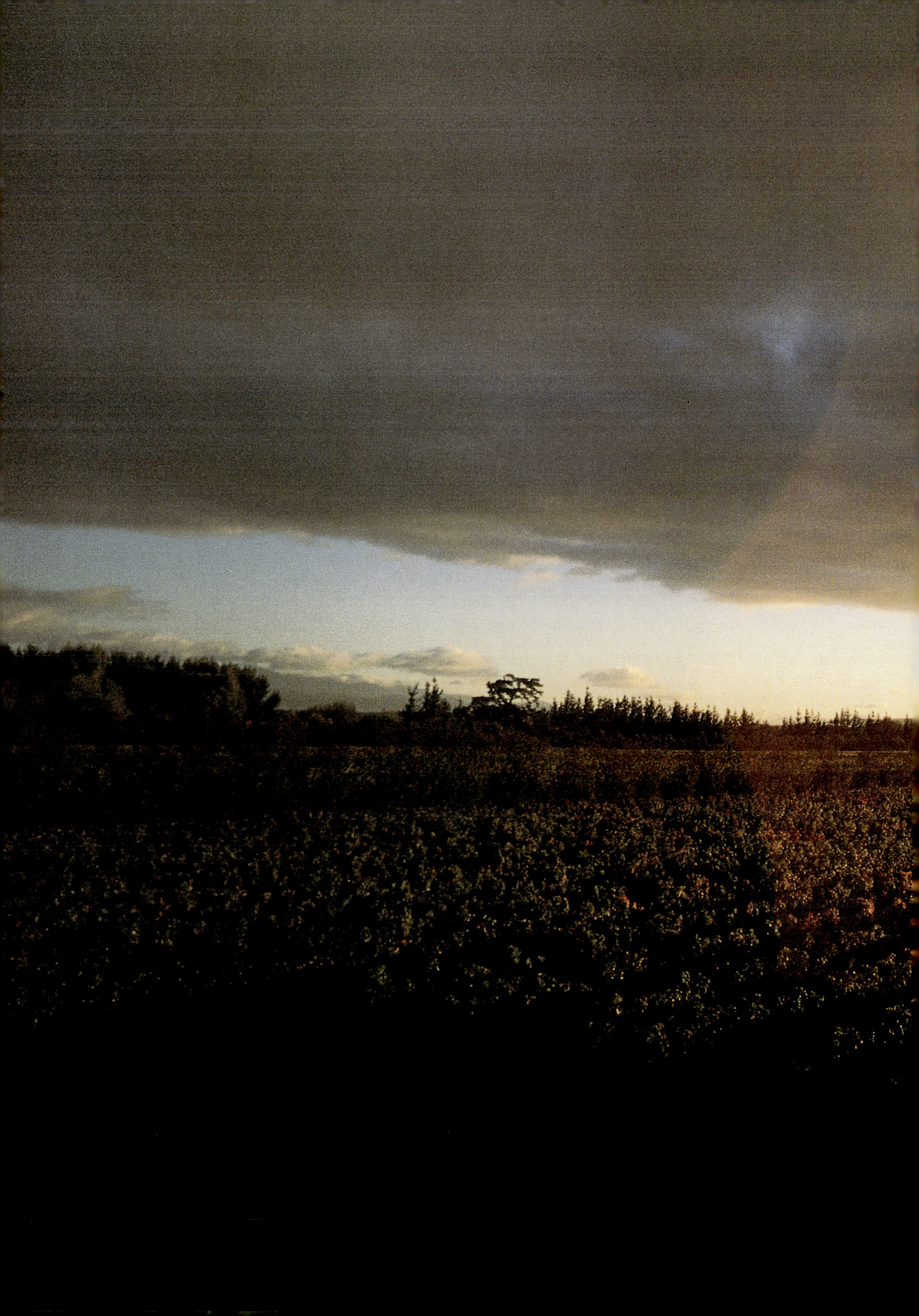

WAIRARAPA

PRODUCERS

Alexander Vineyard
Ata Rangi Vineyard
Benfield & Delamare Vineyards
Bloomfield Vineyards
Blue Rock Vineyard
Canadoro Wines
Chifney Wines
Dry River Wines
Gladstone Vineyard
Hau Ariki
Lintz Estate
Margrain Vineyard
Martinborough Vineyard
Muirlea Rise
Murdoch James
Nga Waka Vineyard
Palliser Estate Wines
Te Horo Estate
Te Kairanga Wines
Voss Estate
Walker Estate
Walnut Ridge Estate
Winslow Wines

WAIRARAPA

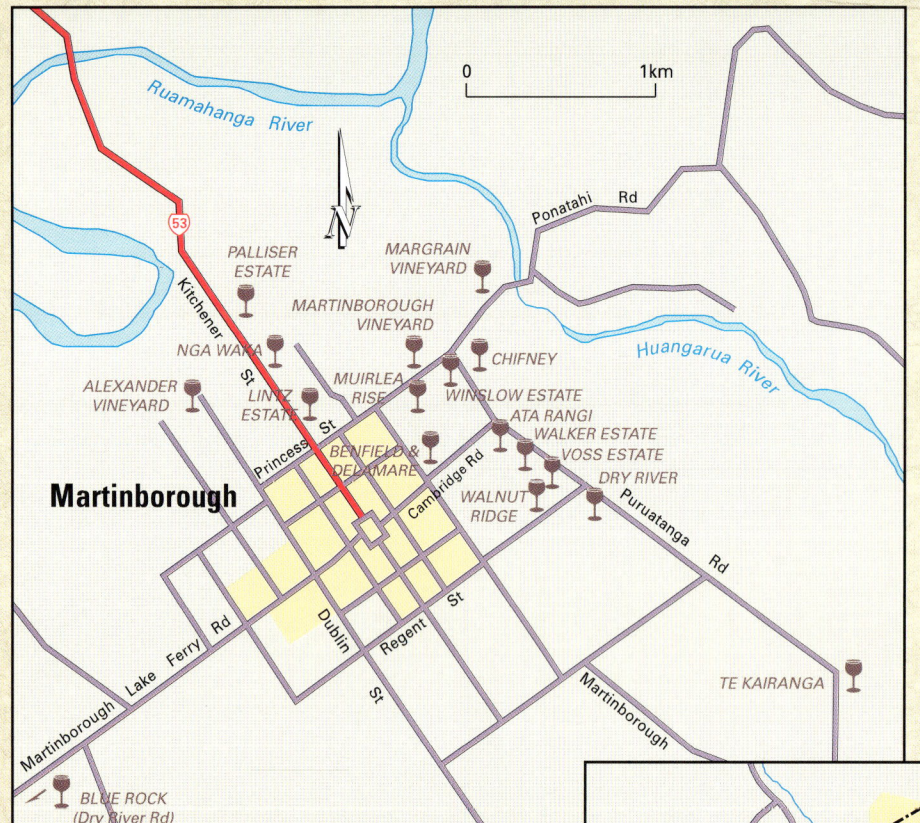

The Wairarapa – in particular its most famous wine district, Martinborough – has in the past decade emerged as one of New Zealand's most prestigious winegrowing regions. The first modern-era Wairarapa wines were bottled in 1984, and since then the flow has been of exciting quality. New arrivals are mushrooming: the Wairarapa wine trail now boasts over 20 wineries.

The major impetus for the resurgence of interest in Wairarapa winemaking came from Dr Derek Milne's 1979 report, pinpointing similarities between Martinborough's climate and soils and those of premium French wine regions. Following a 1977 visit to Germany and Alsace, Milne looked closely at New Zealand's climate regions. 'Climatic comparisons with Europe indicated that there were many areas well suited to vinifera grape production as yet unexploited, most being in areas which traditionally have been regarded as too cold to ripen grapes. Martinborough was one of those areas and it was developed because it was closest to Wellington, where the original pioneers [of Martinborough wine] were based.'

A 'gang of four' pioneered the planting of commercial vineyards in Martinborough: Dr Neil McCallum of Dry River in 1979, followed in 1980 by Clive Paton of Ata Rangi, Stan Chifney and Derek Milne himself – who was a founding partner in Martinborough Vineyard.

Several, though not all, of the early winemakers in Martinborough shared a conviction that their district is a sort of 'southern Burgundy' in terms of climate, and accordingly planted the Burgundian grapes Pinot Noir and Chardonnay. Others rejected the parallel, pinning their hopes on the Bordeaux varieties Cabernet Sauvignon and Merlot. The 1995 vineyard survey revealed that Wairarapa growers have commonly planted both Burgundy and Bordeaux grapes: Pinot Noir, Chardonnay, Cabernet Sauvignon, Sauvignon Blanc and Merlot are (in that order) the most heavily planted varieties.

Pinot Noir has been the greatest success story in the Wairarapa, with Ata Rangi and Martinborough Vineyard enjoying especially illustrious reputations. Yet in three out of four years (1992 to 1995) the trophy for the champion Sauvignon Blanc at the Air New Zealand Wine Awards was awarded to a Wairarapa wine.

With 271 hectares in 1995, the Wairarapa is now New Zealand's fifth largest wine region, with a greater area devoted to vineyards than Auckland. (New regional boundaries officially describe the region as Wellington, which includes Wellington city and Te Horo to the west, with the Wairarapa as a district within the Wellington region.)

Martinborough is the driest area in the North Island. In March and April, the vital months leading into the harvest, Martinborough's average daily temperature of 14.7°C is more akin to Marlborough's 14.3°C than Hawke's Bay's 15.8°C. The cooler autumns enable the development of intense flavour in the berries without any pronounced loss of acidity.

The chief weather drawback here is the wind: the shape of the trees tells the story. Martinborough is pummelled by strong southerlies from Cook Strait and exposed to regular northwesterly gales. The Merlot variety is especially vulnerable to the winds' onslaught, suffering severe shoot damage and loss. Shelter belts are a necessity.

Martinborough's three basic soil types are not all equally well suited to quality viticulture. Neither the areas of poorly drained clay loam overlying silt pans, nor the fertile silt loams well supplied with water, are regarded as ideal for grapes. Most highly sought-after are the pockets of friable, gravelly silt loams overlying free-draining alluvial gravels.

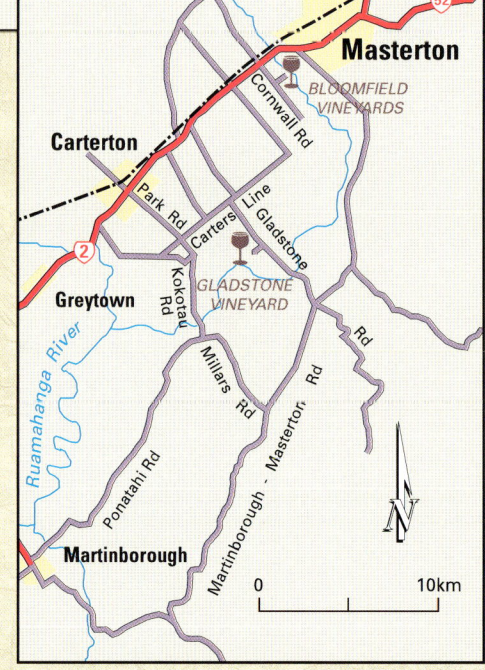

Clive Paton, the founder of Ata Rangi, and his wife, Phyll Pattie, in mid 1995 formed a partnership with Clive's sister, Alison, and her husband, Oliver Masters. A few days later, the partners learned that Ata Rangi Pinot Noir 1993 had scooped the trophy for champion Pinot Noir at the International Wine and Spirit Competition in London.

Paton, a quiet winemaker, set up his Ata Rangi ('new beginning') winery to specialise in red wines. His deliciously perfumed and supple Pinot Noir now ranks among the finest in the country, with a glowing record in show judgings.

After taking a diploma in dairying from Massey University, Paton went sharemilking before buying his Puruatanga Road property in Martinborough in 1980. He worked the 1981 vintage with Malcolm Abel and the 1982 vintage at Delegat's before erecting his own small wooden winery in 1987. Phyllis Pattie, formerly a Montana winemaker at Blenheim, then moved north to join him.

The restructuring of Ata Rangi's ownership in 1995 has given this small company the luxury of three winemakers. 'We are all working partners, fully involved in the day-to-day stuff,' says Pattie. The four are equal shareholders in the winery, while retaining their own vineyards. Alison, Clive's sister, has long grown grapes for Ata Rangi on an adjoining property. Oliver Masters graduated with a Bachelor of Technology degree from Massey University before studying for a postgraduate diploma in viticulture and oenology from Lincoln Univeristy.

Ata Rangi's three-hectare vineyard – principally Pinot Noir, Cabernet Sauvignon and Merlot, with smaller amounts of Syrah and Chardonnay – is planted in free-draining gravelly soils beneath a shallow layer of top soil. Sangiovese and Nebbiolo, the great Italian red-wine varieties, are being trialled. Alison's two-hectare vineyard, planted in Pinot Noir, Cabernet Sauvignon and Cabernet Franc, is a key source of fruit, and Ata Rangi manages two other vineyards in Martinborough. Chardonnay and Merlot grapes are bought from the Craighall vineyard, across the road, and Chardonnay is also drawn from Dalnagairn Vineyard in Hawke's Bay.

Ata Rangi's annual production is set to climb from 3500 to 6000 cases. The first stage of a new winery complex (a fermentation hall and insulated barrel room) was operational for the 1996 vintage, and will be followed by a new shop and offices.

Ata Rangi's second specialty is Célèbre, a Cabernet Sauvignon, Merlot and Syrah blend in which the typical 15 per cent Syrah makes its presence well felt. 'I wanted to create a wine distinctively mine,' says Paton. 'Cabernet is a bit boring on its own and I enjoy Rhône reds' weight and power. Syrah fills the palate up, taking the flavour to all corners of the mouth.' With its brilliant, deep red hue, smoky, spicy bouquet and rich, firm, distinctly minty flavour, this is a sturdy, complex red.

Two barrel-fermented Chardonnays are produced. Mouth-filling, mealy, concentrated and taut, Craighall Chardonnay is grown in Martinborough and designed for long-term cellaring. Dalnagairn Chardonnay, from Hawke's Bay, is a rich, citrusy, slightly buttery style, irresistible in its youth. Both are consistently top-flight. There is also a vivacious, pink-hued, dryish, richly flavoured Summer Rosé based on Cabernet Sauvignon, Merlot and Syrah.

Ata Rangi Vineyard

Puruatanga Road, Martinborough

Owners:
Clive Paton, Phyllis Pattie, Oliver Masters and Alison Paton

Key Wines:
Pinot Noir, Célèbre, Craighall Chardonnay, Dalnagairn Chardonnay, Summer Rosé

Clive Paton and Phyll Pattie (left), recently joined in the Ata Rangi partnership by Clive's sister, Alison, and her husband, Oliver Masters, produce one of New Zealand's most celebrated Pinot Noirs.

ATA RANGI PINOT NOIR

This multiple gold medal and trophy-winning Pinot Noir is a winning marriage of perfumed, cherryish, seductively sweet-tasting fruit with astute oak handling.

'The style I'm after has Pinot Noir's lovely sweetness and velvety character,' says Clive Paton, 'but also a bit of muscle.' The 1994 vintage, which cropped at below five tonnes per hectare, was soaked on its skins prior to the fermentation, fermented in small batches with regular hand-plunging of the cap, and given some whole-bunch fermentation.

'A great site, good clones and low yields' are the key factors in the wine's quality, according to Paton, 'and a passion to learn, I guess'. The soils are low-vigour, and in Martinborough's cool grape-growing climate the fruit 'doesn't get overblown, even in warm years like '89'.

Paton believes the quality of his Pinot Noir will rise as his vines mature. His original vines came from Malcolm Abel, founder of the now-defunct Abel & Co winery at Kumeu. 'When Malcolm was still a customs officer, a vine was confiscated from a guy who'd hopped over the fence at Romanée-Conti (the fabled grand cru of Vosne-Romanée), taken a cutting and hidden it in his gumboot. Malcolm got the first vines out of quarantine.'

Paton's goal for the future is to get more stuffing into the wine, while retaining its sweet, supple fruit characters. 'It'll come as the vines age,' he says with a gleam in his eye.

In a region of microscopic wineries, of late Benfield & Delamare has been almost invisible, making this an extremely collectible red-wine label. The first 'commercial' release from the 1990 vintage amounted to 42 cases, followed by 150 cases in 1991. A devastating November frost slashed the 1992 output (which was declassified) to 25 cases, and 1993 only produced 50 cases, again sold as 'Regional Red'. After heavy rain during flowering, the 1994 season yielded only 120 cases, making the 1995 vintage production of 375 cases look gigantic.

Bill Benfield was born in Christchurch and for many years practised architecture in Wellington. After shifting to Martinborough in 1992, Benfield is now a full-time winemaker. His partner, English-born Sue Delamare, is a former librarian who also works full-time in the vineyard and winery.

Benfield and Delamare began planting in 1987. Their close-spaced, 2.5-hectare vineyard in shallow, gravelly soils is established principally in Cabernet Sauvignon and Merlot, with smaller plots of Cabernet Franc and Malbec.

Benfield sees viticulture as 'very important. We only lay down one cane per vine, trained low to the soil to get below the wind and allow the fruit to ripen in the heat reflected from the ground. We ripen our Cabernet Sauvignon a month ahead of the other Cabernet in the district; even ahead of 90 per cent of the Pinot Noir.'

Why the emphasis on Cabernet Sauvignon and Merlot, in a district better known for its Pinot Noirs? Benfield has written that Martinborough's 'rainfall distribution, length of season, heat summation and frost incidence are all positive pointers towards Cabernet and Merlot grape varieties'. He initially set out to produce a Cabernet Sauvignon-based red, but now Merlot is 'figuring larger. We're moving towards a Merlot-predominant blend'.

In Benfield's small winery he produces a single claret-style red.

Slightly leaner than the foremost claret-style reds of Hawke's Bay, Benfield & Delamare displays impressive depth of colour, strong, vibrant, spicy, concentrated fruit flavours and a taut tannin grip. Its eye-catching quality and New Zealand and North American gold medals have helped elevate the reputation of the Wairarapa's Cabernet Sauvignon-based reds. We need more of it.

Benfield & Delamare Vineyards

Cambridge Road, Martinborough

Owners:
Bill Benfield and Sue Delamare

Key Wine:
Benfield and Delamare

Bill Benfield and Sue Delamare are exploring Martinborough's ability to produce distinguished claret-style reds.

No road sign beckons visitors to the Bloomfield winery in Solway Crescent, just off the highway south of Masterton. 'People have a real sense of achievement when they *do* find us,' notes winemaker David Bloomfield. 'We really value our privacy and we're not geared up for cellar-door sales. But if people come in, we're happy to serve them.'

Bloomfield Vineyards is a partnership involving David Bloomfield, his wife, Janet Saunders, a local GP, and his parents Eric and Pamela. After planting their first vines in 1981, the family processed their first commercial vintage in 1986.

Masterton-born David Bloomfield worked as an architectural draughtsman in Wellington until in 1986 he launched into his full-time career in wine. Bloomfield is an engaging personality, affable, lively and intelligent: books crowd his office and opera fills the air in his small concrete winery.

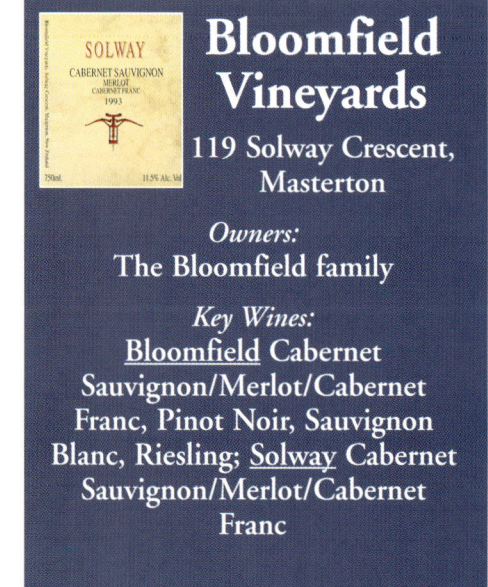

Bloomfield's eight-hectare estate vineyard, called Solway, is planted in deep river shingles, making cultivation extremely difficult. Cabernet Sauvignon (which David Bloomfield finds 'a bit of a difficult customer in terms of ripening'), Merlot and Cabernet Franc are the principal varieties, with smaller plots of Pinot Noir and Sauvignon Blanc.

The cooler Lyndor Vineyard is cultivated on a north-facing clay and limestone slope in the hills to the east of the town. Owned by Janet Saunders' parents, this 1.5-hectare vineyard is planted in Merlot, Cabernet Sauvignon and Cabernet Franc. A further vineyard with one hectare of Cabernet Sauvignon lies at Te Ore Ore. Fruit is also purchased from local growers.

Bloomfield Vineyards

119 Solway Crescent, Masterton

Owners:
The Bloomfield family

Key Wines:
Bloomfield Cabernet Sauvignon/Merlot/Cabernet Franc, Pinot Noir, Sauvignon Blanc, Riesling; Solway Cabernet Sauvignon/Merlot/Cabernet Franc

David Bloomfield (pictured with vineyard manager Tina Theedom) is carrying on Masterton's winemaking tradition established by William Beetham over a century ago.

The winery's output is low – about 3000 cases per year. However, David Bloomfield is keen to see production grow to around 10,000 cases. 'That way, I can still be hands-on, but we'll be economic and I'll get an export trip to London each year.' The top wines are labelled Bloomfield, with the second-tier red branded as Solway.

The flagship Bloomfield Cabernet Sauvignon/ Merlot/Cabernet Franc is held on its skins for up to 25 days after the fermentation, to maximise colour and flavour extraction, and barrel-matured for up to 20 months. This is a full-bodied, dark, spicy, herbaceous, chocolatey wine with plenty of flavour and a firm tannin grip. Solway, the second-tier red, is a lighter style, but still flavoursome and satisfying.

Blue Rock Vineyard

Dry River Road, Martinborough

Owners:
The Clark family

Key Wines:
Chardonnay, Sauvignon Blanc, Riesling, Méthode Traditionnelle, Pinot Noir, Cabernet Sauvignon, Cabernet Franc, Magenta

Eight kilometres south-west of the wineries huddled in and around Martinborough township, Blue Rock sits on an elevated, wind-buffeted site commanding lovely views over the southern Wairarapa. The vineyard's name is derived from 'the area called Blue Rock up the road, where the stones in the river are blue', says founder Nelson Clark.

The Clarks planted their first vines in late 1986 and made their first commercial wines in 1991. This is a family affair: Nelson Clark is involved in all aspects of the venture; his wife, Beverley, focuses on grapegrowing and sales; their daughter, Jenny, is the winemaker.

Nelson Clark has farmed in the Wairarapa for most of his life, and still has a 150-hectare sheep and cattle farm, but the winery is already a bigger income earner. 'Farming was shot, so we chose to diversify. With other types of horticulture we're defeated by the [westerly] wind but with grapes it's not such a problem.'

In their north-facing vineyard, principally clay with a band of shingle running through the centre, the Clarks have planted six hectares of Chardonnay, Sauvignon Blanc, Riesling, Pinot Noir, Cabernet Sauvignon, Cabernet Franc, Meunier and Syrah.

Blue Rock's 1990–91 vintages were produced by Phyll Pattie and Clive Paton of Ata Rangi. Jenny Clark, who has worked in Oregon, and in 1990 gained a post-graduate Diploma in Horticultural Science from Lincoln University, made the 1992 vintage 'under the stars'. Blue Rock's winery, built from steel and macrocarpa and pine grown on the farm, rose in time for the 1993 vintage.

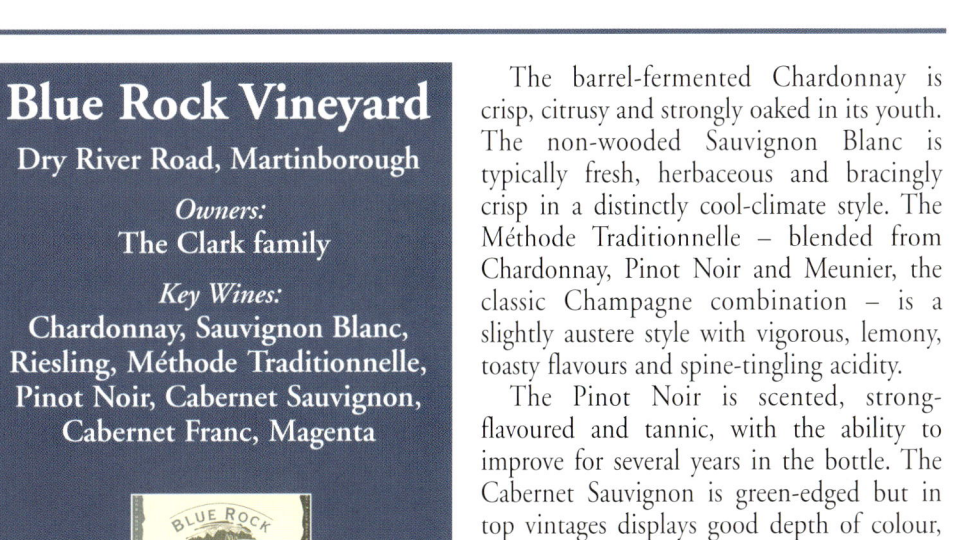

The barrel-fermented Chardonnay is crisp, citrusy and strongly oaked in its youth. The non-wooded Sauvignon Blanc is typically fresh, herbaceous and bracingly crisp in a distinctly cool-climate style. The Méthode Traditionnelle – blended from Chardonnay, Pinot Noir and Meunier, the classic Champagne combination – is a slightly austere style with vigorous, lemony, toasty flavours and spine-tingling acidity.

The Pinot Noir is scented, strong-flavoured and tannic, with the ability to improve for several years in the bottle. The Cabernet Sauvignon is green-edged but in top vintages displays good depth of colour, body and minty, blackcurrant-like flavour.

Nelson Clark and his winemaker daughter, Jenny. Strong winds, which allow trees to grow limbs only on one side, also keep the vineyard's crops light and the grapes largely free of Botrytis rot problems.

In a region where Pinot Noir rules, Stan Chifney has hung his hat on Cabernet Sauvignon. His 1986 Cabernet Sauvignon won a gold medal – Martinborough's first for a Cabernet-based red – and the 1994 vintage repeated the triumph at the 1996 Liquorland Royal Easter Wine Show.

The snowy-bearded, gentlemanly, London-born owner of Chifney Wines in Huangarua Road arrived in this country in 1972 after a career spent in vaccine manufacture in Africa and the Middle East. He and his wife, Rosemary, having made their own fruit wines, thought winemaking would be an ideal retirement hobby. They haven't stopped working since.

'I decided I'd retire to Hawke's Bay and have a little vineyard for myself and friends,' recalls Chifney. 'Then I discovered I could

Chifney Wines

Huangarua Road, Martinborough

Owners:
Stan and Rosemary Chifney

Key Wines:
Chenin Blanc, Gewürztraminer, Chardonnay, Chiffonnay, Rosé, Cabernet Sauvignon, Enigma, Old Stan's Tawny

Stan and Rosemary Chifney, their daughter Sue, and her husband, Steve Marsden, have consistently coaxed good wine from two varieties unfashionable in Martinborough – Cabernet Sauvignon and Chenin Blanc.

get 10 acres [4ha] of Martinborough dirt for the cost of one acre [0.4ha] in Hawke's Bay.' When in 1983 the Chifneys erected their concrete-based winery with its partly subterranean cellar, it was the first one in the town. Their four-hectare vineyard of Cabernet Sauvignon, Merlot, Cabernet Franc, Chardonnay, Chenin Blanc and Gewürztraminer, planted in loamy surface soils overlying stony subsoils, yielded its first commercial crop in 1984.

Chifney's output has only totalled about 1000 cases in recent vintages, but he is planning to double that by 1997. Grapes are purchased from the Garden of Eden vineyard in Martinborough and from other regions. Stan and Rosemary's daughter, Sue, and her husband, Steve Marsden, work in the vineyard and winery.

The Cabernet Sauvignon is the highlight of the range. This is a scented, generous red, with sweet American oak fleshing out the strong, blackcurrant-like flavours.

Garden of Eden Red, a single-vineyard wine, has been a drink-young style blended from such varieties as Pinot Noir, Cabernet Sauvignon, Meunier, Cabernet Franc and Syrah. From the 1995 vintage, this fresh, fruity, raspberryish red has been replaced with a similar wine labelled Enigma.

The standard of Chifney's white wines has soared in the past few vintages. The most distinctive is the partly oak-fermented Chenin Blanc with its fresh, dry, tart, lemony, appley flavours. The barrel-fermented, briefly lees-aged Chardonnay displays grapefruit-like, slightly buttery flavours and a long, flinty finish.

Only a trickle flows from Dry River – rare wines with a sky-high reputation. Dr Neil McCallum produces half a dozen varietal wines, ranging in style from dry to super-sweet, and almost all of them rank among the finest in the country.

McCallum's immaculate, slowly evolving Martinborough wines fascinate wine buffs for several reasons. Most of the wines are cultivated on the estate vineyard in Puruatanga Road or at the nearby Craighall vineyard, giving them precise 'single vineyard' origins. He produces a splendid Pinot Noir and Chardonnay, but has also demonstrated the outstanding quality of currently less fashionable grape varieties like Gewürztraminer, Riesling and Pinot Gris. In their infancy, the wines are tight and cry out for a lengthy spell in the cellar. These are

Dry River Wines

Puruatanga Road, Martinborough

Owners:
Dr Neil and Dawn McCallum

Key Wines:
Pinot Gris, Gewürztraminer, Riesling, Chardonnay, Sauvignon Blanc, Selection and Botrytis Selection sweet whites, Pinot Noir

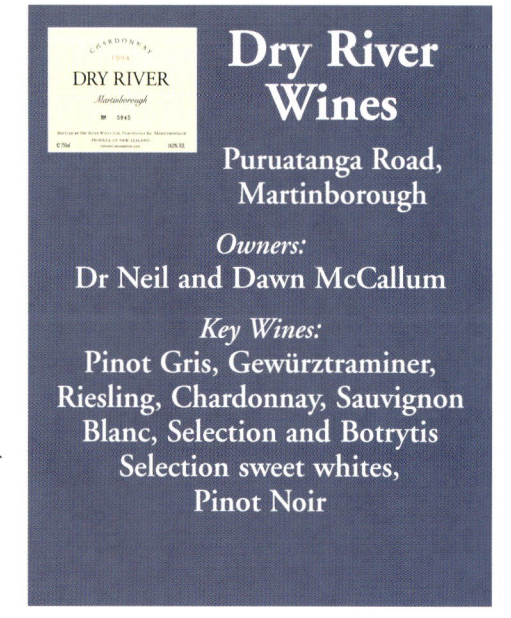

classic wine styles for the 'serious' collector.

The emergence of Neil McCallum as a gifted, individualistic winemaker has been greatly assisted by his previous career as a DSIR scientist. Born in Auckland, he capped his high-flying academic record with an Oxford doctorate, awarded for his dissertation on penicillin substitutes. At one memorable Oxford dinner he was 'bowled over' by a Hochheimer Riesling – and launched on his love affair with wine.

McCallum and his wife, Dawn, planted the first vines on their shingly, free-draining block at Martinborough in 1979. Today the four-hectare vineyard is close-planted in Gewürztraminer, Sauvignon Blanc (to be partly replaced with Viognier, a traditional grape of the northern Rhone), Pinot Gris, Chardonnay and Pinot Noir vines, trained

Neil McCallum's learned, deeply thoughtful and meticulous approach to winemaking has yielded exceptional results with Pinot Gris, Gewürztraminer, Riesling, Chardonnay and Pinot Noir.

on the Scott-Henry system and not irrigated. Riesling, Chardonnay and Pinot Noir are also bought from the more sheltered, slightly earlier-ripening Craighall vineyard 200 metres down the road, and botrytised grapes are sometimes purchased from Marlborough.

McCallum describes his approach to winemaking as 'low-tech, involving minimum processing and placing an emphasis on cellaring qualities rather than short-term attractiveness for early drinking'.

'Cellaring' is a popular word in the McCallum vocabulary. His ability as an organic chemist to precisely control each stage of the winemaking process lies at the heart of the slow-maturing style he has evolved. The 'oxidative' approach to winemaking, which involves deliberately exposing grapejuice or wine to oxygen in a bid to enhance its early drinking appeal, finds no favour with him. McCallum wants to produce wines capable of maturing over the long haul and unfolding the subtleties of old age. One-year-old Dry River Pinot Gris only hints at the wealth of savoury, earthy, stone-fruit flavours it will later unfold.

Dry River wines are stylish, with lots of extract (stuffing). The Gewürztraminer has precise peppery/spicy varietal characteristics, without the pungent seasoning of the more ebullient Gisborne-grown examples of this variety. This is a 'fine-grained' (to borrow McCallum's adjective) dry wine of excellent weight and unusual flavour depth.

The Dry River label is inextricably linked in most wine lovers' eyes with the Pinot Gris variety; McCallum's is the finest in the country. His Pinot Gris vines, sourced from Mission Vineyards, are probably an old Alsace clone called Tokay à petit grain (small berry Pinot Gris) known for its low yields. Dry River Pinot Gris is strapping and savoury with a subtle bouquet (which McCallum describes as having a hint of roasted chestnuts) and concentrated, slow-building peachy/earthy varietal flavours.

Dry River Chardonnay is a bold wine with concentrated grapefruit-like flavours, rich, biscuity characters from barrel fermentation and lees-aging, and fresh, steely acidity. The Riesling, also a classic, features a lovely outpouring of *Botrytis*-enriched scents, concentrated lime/lemon fruit flavours, a hint of sweetness (except in very ripe vintages, when the sugar level soars) and tense acidity.

Dessert wines are also a feature of the Dry River range; McCallum has produced sweet whites from five different varieties: Riesling, Gewürztraminer, Sauvignon Blanc, Pinot Gris and Chardonnay. The style varies from light, exquisitely fragrant and delicate sweet whites to strapping, excitingly powerful wines, their sweetness unobtrusive amid great richness of flavour and body.

'People love pigeon-holes,' says McCallum, 'and it seems that the media has created one called "Alsace specialist", then hung our name on it. In fact we are equally pleased with our other wine styles.' Dry River first found fame with its aromatic white wines – Pinot Gris, Gewürztraminer and Riesling – but now also produces a magnificent Pinot Noir.

Dry River Pinot Noir

Since the breakthrough 1993 vintage, this wine has shown startling body and flavour density – a grandness of scale that places it right in the vanguard of New Zealand's Pinot Noirs.

'In the past, I made the wine more conservatively,' recalls Neil McCallum, 'knowing there was a fragility there in its lack of tannin structure.' In 1993, the Pinot Noir crop was a miserly 1.5 tonnes per acre [3.6t/ha]. 'We made a concerted effort in the vineyard, with leaf-plucking and bunch-thinning, to build the structure of the wine and fill out its mid-palate with fine tannins.'

Eighty per cent of the grapes are of the superior 'Pommard' (no. 5) clone; the rest are 10/5. The juice is soaked on its skins prior to the fermentation (which McCallum finds 'extracts more attractive tannins than post-fermentation skin contact'). About 50 per cent whole-bunch fermentation, and a lot of whole-berry fermentation of the destemmed fruit, contribute 'intense fruit characters'. The wine is matured for a year in French oak barriques (25 to 30 per cent new) and not filtered prior to bottling.

McCallum doesn't believe Martinborough has any natural advantages over Marlborough or Canterbury in the production of fine Pinot Noir. 'In Martinborough, the individuals who are focusing on Pinot Noir are running low crop levels, putting profitability second to quality.'

The 1989 to 1992 vintages of Dry River Pinot Noir are impressively fragrant, fleshy and supple. The 1993 and subsequent vintages, however, are darker, richer, spicier and more tautly structured than before. How they mature will be intriguing to trace.

Wineries are only occasionally sold in New Zealand; most remain in the same family's hands for generations. Dennis Roberts created a showplace vineyard and winery, won the trophy for champion Sauvignon Blanc at the 1993 Air New Zealand Wine Awards – but then in late 1995 sold Gladstone Vineyard to David and Christine Kernohan.

The winery lies midway between Masterton and Martinborough. The local climate, says Roberts, is 'a bit harsh, with cold, cold winters and hot summers. We've struggled with dryness and heat from January to March. Those huge mountains [the Tararuas] keep the clouds away.'

On old alluvial terraces which once formed the bed of the nearby Ruamahanga River – where in the past oats and pines grew

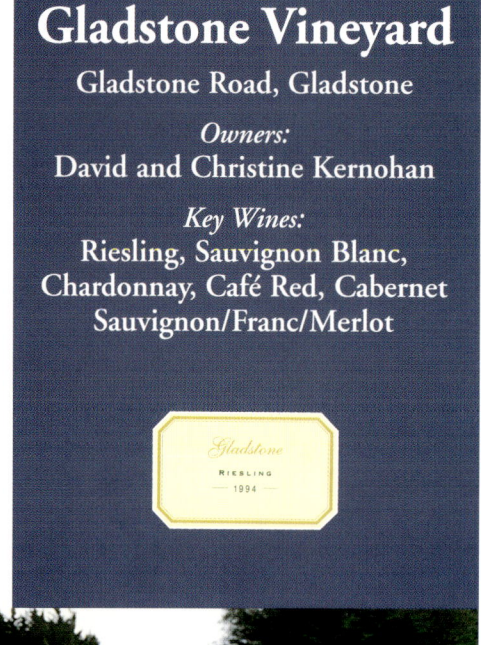

Gladstone Vineyard

Gladstone Road, Gladstone

Owners:
David and Christine Kernohan

Key Wines:
Riesling, Sauvignon Blanc, Chardonnay, Café Red, Cabernet Sauvignon/Franc/Merlot

and sheep grazed – Roberts and his partner, Richard Stone, planted three hectares of Sauvignon Blanc, Riesling, Cabernet Sauvignon, Merlot, Cabernet Franc and (latterly) Pinot Gris. Chardonnay was also purchased from Hawke's Bay.

The handsome, verandahed, two-storeyed winery, set amid landscaped grounds and thousands of trees, was erected in time for the second 1991 vintage. A late 19th-century house was also trucked to the site from Masterton.

Gladstone Vineyard's output has been small – about 2000 cases. The Riesling is a classy, floral wine with intense lemon/lime flavours, a whisker of sweetness and tense acidity. The Sauvignon Blanc is very pure and delicate with ripely herbacous flavours, lively and incisive. Packed with sweet-tasting, supple fruit, the Cabernet Sauvignon/ Merlot/Franc is lush, silky and very easy-drinking in style. In lesser vintages, a lighter, less ripe-tasting Café Red appears.

The new proprietors of Gladstone are David and Christine Kernohan. Christine – an MBA who came to New Zealand in 1977 from Scotland – manages the vineyard and winery; David is dean of the School of Architecture at Victoria University. 'It was the right place at the right time,' says Christine Kernohan. 'I've always enjoyed wine and fell in love with the vineyard.' To smooth the transition, Roberts worked with the Kernohans during the 1996 vintage.

Dennis Roberts founded a model boutique vineyard and winery, but recently sold Gladstone to David and Christine Kernohan.

Chris Lintz loves 'to do something different'. Like everyone else, he makes a Chardonnay, Sauvignon Blanc and Pinot Noir or Cabernet-based red (both, in his case). Far less predictably, he also produces a Rosé based on Meunier, a sweet wine made from the rare Optima variety, and a sparkling Riesling.

The Lintz Estate winery, with its conspicuous tower and New Zealand flag, lies on the main road into Martinborough, not far from Palliser. The tower conceals an elevated, gravity-fed crushing and destemming system. During vintage the grapes are sucked up by a pneumatic system and then fed down through the crusher into joint drainer and fermenter tanks. 1991 was the winery's first vintage.

Lintz Estate

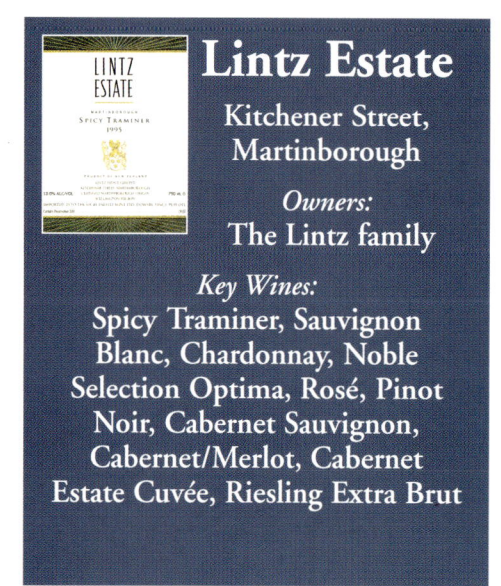

Kitchener Street, Martinborough

Owners:
The Lintz family

Key Wines:
Spicy Traminer, Sauvignon Blanc, Chardonnay, Noble Selection Optima, Rosé, Pinot Noir, Cabernet Sauvignon, Cabernet/Merlot, Cabernet Estate Cuvée, Riesling Extra Brut

Chris Lintz's parents, Harold and Uni, came to New Zealand from Germany after the Second World War. Lintz, a zoology graduate from Victoria University, has worked on a wine estate in the Saar once owned by the Lintz family, and in 1988 gained a diploma in viticulture and oenology from the famous Geisenheim Institute. After returning to New Zealand, he worked at Montana and Brookfields, and then in 1989 planted his first vines in Martinborough.

The 0.5-hectare plot of Riesling vines adjacent to the winery has been planted for 'image' reasons. The two-hectare Vertesse vineyard, across the road from Ata Rangi, planted in Cabernet Sauvignon and Gewürztraminer, has recently been sold, but

Chris Lintz (pictured with his wife, Doris), produces highly distinctive wines, including strapping Cabernet-based reds, a Riesling-based bubbly and an opulent, rampantly botrytised, ultra-sweet Noble Selection Optima.

Lintz Estate still buys the fruit. The eight-hectare Moy Hall vineyard, between Dry River and Te Kairanga, is planted in Merlot, Cabernet Franc, Cabernet Sauvignon, Pinot Noir, Meunier, Gewürztraminer, Sauvignon Blanc, Riesling, Chardonnay and Optima.

Lintz Estate's output is currently 4500 cases, but is planned to grow to around 7500 cases by 1998. The white wine range includes a mouth-filling, partly barrique-fermented, ripely herbal and complex Sauvignon Blanc of high quality, and a very perfumed, musky Spicy Traminer with strong orange-and-spice flavours.

With his distinctive bottle-fermented Riesling Extra Brut, Chris Lintz is aiming for 'a more exciting, appetising start to a meal, rather than the more mealy, fatter Champagne styles'. Matured on its yeast lees for up to two years, this is a floral, vigorous sparkling with plenty of lemony, limey, tangy flavour. The dryish Rosé, based on Meunier (a key grape of Champagne) is deep-coloured, with strong, sappy, raspberryish flavours.

Both the Cabernet Sauvignon (promoted as 'Martinborough's biggest red') and Cabernet/Merlot (made principally from the two Cabernets – Sauvignon and Franc) are sturdy, tannic, flavour-packed reds that in top vintages display a lot of power and class. The Pinot Noir also has the Lintz stamp of muscular body and a taut tannin structure.

The amber-hued, super-sweet Noble Selection Optima – made from an early-ripening cross of Müller-Thurgau with another crossing of Riesling and Sylvaner, picked at extraordinarily high (up to 49 brix) sugar levels – is a rampantly botrytised style, oily and treacly. The *Botrytis*-affected berries are individually selected in the vineyard. 'A picker working in this way will pick around five kilograms a day,' says Lintz, 'enough to make around half a bottle of finished wine.'

With 11 vintages of Pinot Noir under his belt and a distinguished collection of gold medals and trophies from both sides of the Tasman, Larry McKenna is still learning how to make fine Pinot Noir. 'It's an on-going challenge,' he admits. 'The learning curve hasn't got any flatter. You open one door and you open another 20.'

McKenna, as Martinborough Vineyard's winemaker and general manager, is often in the limelight. The company's success also reflects the talents of its founding partners: Dr Derek Milne, formerly a soil scientist with the DSIR and now a consultant; his brother Duncan and his wife Claire Campbell; and pharmacist Russell Schultz and his wife Sue.

The company first planted vines in Martinborough's gravels in 1980. After the first 1984 vintage yielded a tiny amount of outstanding Pinot Noir and Sauvignon Blanc, the challenge was to reproduce these standards in larger-volume wines. For the first commercial vintage in 1985, the winery's roof was erected only days before the harvest. McKenna arrived in early 1986, the first experienced winemaker in the district.

McKenna, an Australian, graduated with a diploma in agriculture from Roseworthy College, and then crossed the Tasman in 1980 to work under John Hancock, an old friend from his boarding-school days in Adelaide, at Delegat's. Following Hancock's departure for Morton Estate, McKenna headed Delegat's winemaking team for three years, until in early 1986 he was lured south by Martinborough Vineyard.

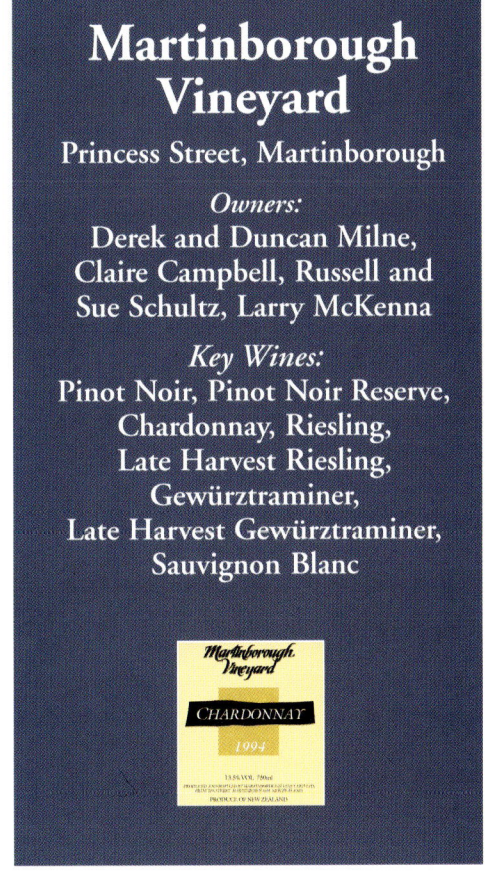

Burly and soft-spoken, McKenna loves outdoor pursuits: climbing, tramping, trout fishing. But he came to Martinborough for other reasons. 'I thought the district had a lot of potential, which was confirmed after I had a look at all the wines . . . I wanted to be fully involved in a winery in all aspects from viticulture to marketing. I also had the possibility to have a share in a vineyard and winery.' Of Martinborough Vineyard's annual output of around 10,000 cases, two-thirds is Pinot Noir and Chardonnay.

Much of the annual grape intake is grown in the company's 10 hectares of vineyards adjacent to the winery, planted principally in Pinot Noir and Chardonnay, with some Sauvignon Blanc; Riesling and Gewürztraminer have recently been phased out in favour of Pinot Noir. The nearby

---

Martinborough Vineyard

Princess Street, Martinborough

Owners:
Derek and Duncan Milne, Claire Campbell, Russell and Sue Schultz, Larry McKenna

Key Wines:
Pinot Noir, Pinot Noir Reserve, Chardonnay, Riesling, Late Harvest Riesling, Gewürztraminer, Late Harvest Gewürztraminer, Sauvignon Blanc

A turning point in Martinborough's wine history was the 1986 arrival of the first experienced winemaker, Larry McKenna.

Smith vineyard, a two-hectare block of Pinot Noir, Riesling and (to be uprooted) Cabernet Sauvignon, was purchased in 1996. A further four hectares of Pinot Noir, Chardonnay and Pinot Gris is bought from the Cleland and McCreanor vineyards, managed on a day-to-day basis by Martinborough Vineyard. Other growers in the district supply about 20 per cent of the fruit, but no grapes are drawn from outside Martinborough.

Martinborough Vineyard Chardonnay is almost as widely acclaimed as the Pinot Noir *(see panel).* Bold, ripe, stone-fruit flavours and strong, biscuity oak are hallmarks of the winery's Chardonnay style. Powerful and chewy, with long, complex flavours from its barrel fermentation, partial malolactic fermentation and lengthy lees-aging, this is a firm, mealy, buttery, very stylish wine.

The Riesling is a distinctly cool-climate style, with a lovely outpouring of citric/lime aromas and strong, slightly sweet, lingering flavours. The Gewürztraminer is a strapping, medium-dry wine with very rich, gingerbread and lychee-like flavours. The Sauvignon Blanc is a fresh, non-wooded style with ripe, passionfruit-like, gently herbaceous flavours.

About a third of Martinborough Vineyard's wine is exported, mainly to the UK but also to Australia, Hong Kong and Germany. The winery no longer enters competitions in New Zealand, but its Pinot Noir still regularly wins gold medals and trophies in Australia.

Looking back over his decade in the district, Larry McKenna says his 'biggest thrill' came at the 1989 Air New Zealand Wine Awards, when the trophies for champion Chardonnay, Riesling, Müller-Thurgau and Pinot Noir, and top wine of the show, were all scooped by Martinborough Vineyard: 'That really put us on the map.'

MARTINBOROUGH VINEYARD PINOT NOIR

This was the first distinguished Pinot Noir made in New Zealand, and it is still in the front rank. The stunning 1986 vintage, the first to transcend the light, simple, shallow style of Pinot Noir that was previously the norm in this country, set the stage for the string of unprecedently robust, rich-flavoured and multi-faceted wines that followed.

What characters is Larry McKenna pursuing in his Pinot Noir? 'Berry fruit flavours, with something more than strawberry ripeness, underpinned by quality oak and complexity – that earthy, mushroomy character that is almost indefinable.'

When he first set out to produce a top Pinot Noir, McKenna focused on fruit ripeness. 'Most winemakers in the mid 80s saw Pinot Noir as a thin, light-coloured red of no interest. I wanted colour and depth and knew the easiest way to get those is fruit ripeness. So we made a big effort with trellising to get good fruit exposure. 1988 and '89 turned out to be back-to-back hot beauties of vintages, so we hit the market with two very ripe wines.'

The next stage was sorting out the oak handling. 'We embarked on a lot of barrel experiments and, contrary to my initial belief, found Pinot Noir needs less wood than Chardonnay, so we've settled on about 30 per cent new oak.' Next came an investigation into fermentation techniques. 'We looked at whole-bunch and whole-berry fermentations and extended skin maceration, before and after the fermentation.'

The current focus is back on the vineyard in a search for smaller, more concentrated berries. This involves a fresh look at trellis design, rootstocks, clones and pruning techniques.

Martinborough Vineyard Pinot Noir is an enticingly scented, savoury and supple red. Cherry-hued, it is very fine and complex on the palate, with the delectable, rich, smoky, mushroomy characters of fine Pinot Noir and a long, velvety finish. In top vintages like 1991 and 1994, a more substantial, meatier Pinot Noir Reserve appears, firm-structured, very deep-flavoured and highly concentrated.

Willie Brown arrived in Martinborough nine years ago, a 50-year-old wine merchant turning winemaker. 'I thought I had a great empathy with Pinot Noir. Years ago someone gave me a bottle of Chambolle-Musigny; it was pure sunshine and buttercups. I keep looking for that experience again.'

Brown and his wife, Lea, planted the first vines on their Princess Street site, just across the road from Martinborough Vineyard, in 1988. Brown first became absorbed in wine while working in Wellington's retail liquor trade. After spending 10 years at the giant distribution company, New Zealand Wines and Spirits, and three years at Brown and Garvey, a small Auckland wine distribution company he co-founded, Brown headed for Martinborough.

Soon after the Browns arrived, their 120-year-old cob cottage was torched. 1991 brought further tragedy, when a November frost turned the vineyard black. 'A whole year's work disappeared before my eyes,' recalls Willie.

Brown's 1.5-hectare vineyard is planted in a mix of clay and gravel soils. Close-planted Pinot Noir vines take up two-thirds of the space, with smaller plots of Syrah and Cabernet Sauvignon. The Browns' son, Shaun, has also purchased a 0.8-hectare block next door, being planted in Syrah and Cabernet Sauvignon.

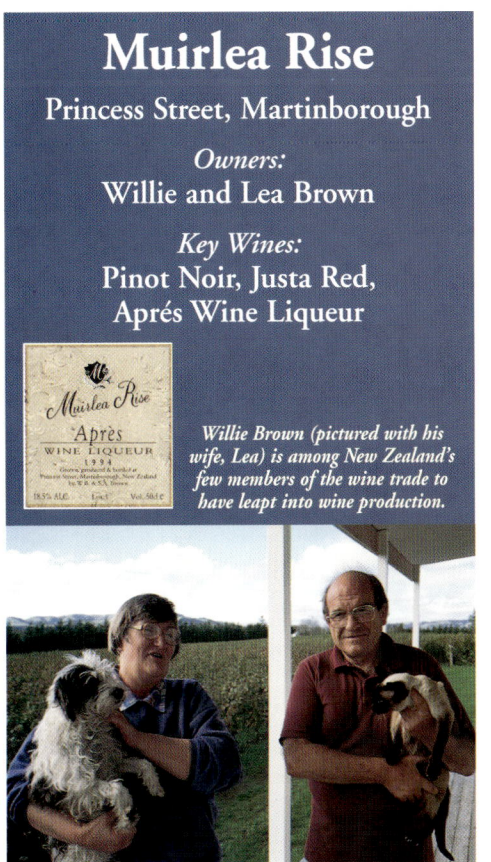

Muirlea Rise will always be a tiny company, producing less than 1000 cases each year even when at full throttle. The vineyard café, serving soups and ploughman's lunches, opens year-round on Fridays and at weekends. 'We want Muirlea Rise to be known as an interesting place to visit, making wines of consistent quality without pretensions or hype,' says Brown.

'Feminine' is the style of Pinot Noir Brown is pursuing. 'That means soft and subtle, with fruit-persistent flavour.' His wine exudes floral fruit aromas and strong, vibrant, cherry/plum flavours, with a rich, silky finish.

'Justa Red' is an easy-drinking wine based on casks of Pinot Noir not selected for the top label, blended with Cabernet Sauvignon or Syrah. Aprés Wine Liqueur, a briefly oak-matured fortified wine, based on Syrah (predominantly) and Cabernet Sauvignon, is a dark, decadent mouthful, deliciously rich and creamy-smooth.

Muirlea Rise
Princess Street, Martinborough

Owners:
Willie and Lea Brown

Key Wines:
Pinot Noir, Justa Red, Aprés Wine Liqueur

Willie Brown (pictured with his wife, Lea) is among New Zealand's few members of the wine trade to have leapt into wine production.

Nga Waka is one of the fast-rising stars of the Martinborough wine scene. Nga Waka's deep-scented, vibrantly fruity Sauvignon Blanc 1995 stood in solitary splendour at the end of the 1995 Air New Zealand Wine Awards – the only wine out of several hundred from the exceptionally wet 1995 vintage to score a gold medal.

Nga Waka is a white-wine specialist. Why no Pinot Noir? 'It partly reflects where my own interest lies,' says winemaker Roger Parkinson. 'I like Pinot Noir, but I don't have a passion for it. We want to be the best we can, and New Zealand's greatest strength is its outstanding white wines with their penetrating, vibrant flavours.'

The four-hectare vineyard and winery lies between Palliser and Lintz in Kitchener Street. The entire vineyard was planted in 1988; the first vintage flowed in 1993. The name Nga Waka is derived from the three hills, Nga Waka A Kupe ('The Canoes of Kupe'), which lie like upturned canoes as a backdrop to Martinborough.

Nga Waka is family-owned. Parkinson oversees the production and marketing, while his wife, Carol, an accountant, controls the finances 'and helps with pruning'. Roger's parents, Gordon (a retired diplomat) and Margaret, are also involved financially.

After graduating with a BA in history and French, and working for several years as a training manager, in 1986 Parkinson and his family bought land in Martinborough. He graduated from Roseworthy College in Australia in 1988 with a graduate diploma in wine, and then worked the 1989 vintage in Bordeaux.

The estate vineyard, planted in 'excessively' drained, stony, silty soils, is established principally in Sauvignon Blanc and Chardonnay, with 20 per cent Riesling. In future Nga Waka will also draw grapes from two other Martinborough vineyards it does not own but is 'setting up from scratch'.

Parkinson's wines are immaculate, with a voluminous fragrance and fresh, deep, bone-dry, lingering flavours. The non-wooded Sauvignon Blanc is a classic cool-climate style, aromatic, ripely herbaceous and zingy. The Riesling is unflinchingly dry, with strong lemon/lime flavours and good aging potential. The robust, barrel-fermented, mealy and steely Chardonnay is also designed for the long haul. These are consistently concentrated classy wines.

Nga Waka Vineyard
Kitchener Street, Martinborough

Owners:
Roger and Carol Parkinson, Gordon and Margaret Parkinson

Key Wines:
Sauvignon Blanc, Riesling, Chardonnay

Roger Parkinson (pictured with his wife, Carol), makes penetratingly flavoured, steely, bone-dry whites designed for long-term cellaring.

It's taken only eight vintages for this smallish Wairarapa producer to establish itself as one of New Zealand's premier wineries. Its handsome cream and green-coloured colonial-style winery looks the part, and its Sauvignon Blanc, Riesling and Chardonnay are consistently outstanding.

'Wyatt Creech [now an MP and Minister of Education] was the driving-force in the early days,' says managing director Richard Riddiford. 'He established the vineyards and is still a shareholder.' Creech planted the first vines in his Om Santi vineyard in 1984 and four years later formed an unlisted public company to take over his vineyard and build a winery. Om Santi, the name first proposed for the winery, was dropped in favour of Palliser Estate – derived from Cape Palliser, the southern-most tip of the North Island.

Palliser Estate is owned by about 135 shareholders: 'None of them is large,' says Riddiford. A scion of a wealthy Wairarapa farming family, Riddiford graduated from Victoria University with a BCA degree, spent 10 years at Borthwicks as a marketing manager for such by-products as sheep-skins, and was one of the original investors in Palliser Estate. 'I'm not a wine person,' he says. 'My background is in marketing.' In December 1994, Palliser Estate became the first New Zealand winery to achieve ISO 9002 accreditation (based on an internationally recognised audit of the company's management systems).

Palliser's extensive vineyards, totalling 30 hectares, are all within 300 metres of the winery. The block adjacent to the winery is planted in Riesling and Sauvignon Blanc. Two further vineyards have been established in Chardonnay, Riesling, Sauvignon Blanc and Pinot Noir. Grapes are also purchased from growers in the Wairarapa and other regions.

Palliser's first 1989 vintage was produced by Larry McKenna at Martinborough Vineyard, and the 1990 by Australian winemaker Rob Bowen. Allan Johnson took over the winemaking reins in late 1990. While growing up in Hawke's Bay, Johnson worked in vineyards during the school holidays, and in 1980 joined McWilliam's as a cellarhand.

After graduating from Roseworthy College in 1984, Johnson was winemaker at Capel Vale in Western Australia for the 1985 to 1989 vintages, but says he 'yearned to get back to New Zealand. Our fruit has more concentration of flavour, more power in the middle and end palate.'

Palliser Estate's annual production is 20,000 cases, of which a third is exported, principally to the UK, but also to Switzerland, the USA and several niche markets.

The wines are marketed under two labels: Palliser Estate (reserved for wines grown predominantly in Martinborough) and Palliser Bay (for wines grown in other regions, or lower-tier Martinborough wines). 'There's a finite number of people who drink high-priced wine,' says Riddiford. 'And we need flexibility. If you are dependent on one region, you are constrained by grape prices and the weather.'

The six wines forming the Palliser Estate range are consistently top-flight. The Chardonnay is very stylish, with intense citrusy flavours and a buttery, mealy richness. Barrique-fermented and lees-aged, it is a delicious wine with early-drinking appeal yet plenty of cellaring potential.

The non-wooded Sauvignon Blanc overflows with lush, ripe tropical-fruit aromas and flavours in a mouth-wateringly fresh and vibrant style. This is one of Martinborough's – and New Zealand's – greatest Sauvignon Blancs. (The Oak-Aged Sauvignon Blanc under the Palliser Bay label can also be stunning.)

The Riesling, typically a blend of Martinborough and Marlborough fruit, is a fractionally off-dry style with great fragrance, searching, lemon/lime fruit flavours and zingy acidity. The Late Harvest Riesling – sometimes grown in Martinborough, sometimes in Marlborough; sometimes botrytised, sometimes not – is always perfumed, delicate and classy.

The style of Palliser Estate's Pinot Noir reflects Allan Johnson's fondness for 'rich Pinot Noir with the roast coffee aromas of ripe fruit and good structure'. With its bold cherryish fruit flavours underlaid by charry, smoky wood, this is an impressively complex, savoury and supple red. Also Pinot Noir-based, the bright pink Rosé of Pinot is full of fresh, buoyant cherry/plum flavour, with an appetisingly crisp, dry finish.

Palliser Estate Wines

Kitchener Street, Martinborough

Owner:
Palliser Estate Wines of Martinborough Limited

Key Wines:
Palliser Estate Chardonnay, Sauvignon Blanc, Riesling, Late Harvest Riesling, Rosé of Pinot, Pinot Noir; Palliser Bay Oak Aged Sauvignon Blanc, Chardonnay, Admiral's Dry Red

---

Managing director Richard Riddiford (left) and winemaker Allan Johnson head one of Martinborough's largest and most prestigious wineries.

Te Kairanga ('the land where the soil is rich and the food plentiful') winery rests on a stunning site above the Huangarua River, against a backdrop of sunlit green hills. After a hesitant start a decade ago, its Chardonnays and Pinot Noirs are now consistently impressive and sometimes exceptional.

Tom Draper is a former building contractor and co-founder of one of Wellington's winetasting groups, the Magnum Society. Tom and his wife, Robin, in 1983 bought the first modern-era Martinborough vineyard, planted in 1978 by Alister Taylor, but then in a run-down state. After the Drapers brought in partners, the Te Kairanga and – across the road – East Plain vineyards spread out.

Tom Draper retired in 1993, but the Drapers still have the largest holding in Te Kairanga Wines, an unlisted public company with about 160 shareholders. The key staff members – general manager Andrew Shackleton, viticulturist Glenys Hansen and winemaker Chris Buring – also have a stake.

Twenty-six hectares of free-draining, stony river terraces are planted in irrigated Chardonnay, Sauvignon Blanc, Riesling, Pinot Gris, Pinot Noir, Cabernet Sauvignon and Merlot vines. 'The two vineyards yield differently flavoured grapes,' says Buring. 'The East Plain vineyard, more exposed to wind chill, gives tighter, finer Pinot Noir. The grapes in the Te Kairanga vineyard ripen earlier, giving a broader, softer, more floral style of Pinot Noir.' Grapes are also purchased from growers in Gisborne and Hawke's Bay.

After the first 1986 vintage, the wines released during the mid-late 1980s proved disappointing. A winery was erected for the 1988 vintage, and a 128-year-old, pit-sawn timber cottage removed from Martinborough township to the vineyard site. Originally built by the founder of Martinborough, John Martin, for a farm worker and his family, it now enjoys a new lease of life as Te Kairanga's sales and administration facility.

The appointment of Chris Buring as Te Kairanga's first full-time winemaker in late 1989 has been followed by a marked upswing in wine quality, assisted, Buring says, by 'a major upgrading of equipment'. Buring, a scion of the famous Australian winemaking family, holds a bachelor's degree in fermentation science from the University of California, Davis. After 23 years at Lindemans, where he rose to the post of production manager, in 1986 Buring left to pursue a career as a wine consultant, columnist and vineyard tour operator. He came to New Zealand because he 'wanted to get back into production and it was an opportunity to build something almost from the ground to a reasonable size'. Soon after, Buring set the seal on his involvement at Te Kairanga by marrying one of the partners.

With its current annual output of about 16,000 cases, Te Kairanga is one of the district's most widely seen labels, and production is planned to grow to over 20,000 cases. The wines, exported to the UK and USA, form a three-tier range, with Reserve wines at the top, the key varietal selection in the middle, and Castlepoint wines at the bottom.

Does Te Kairanga have specialties? 'Without question,' says Andrew Shackleton. 'Chardonnay and Pinot Noir are the two varieties we're absolutely committed to. They're the best for this area, with the greatest future in terms of quality and demand. We're also keen to introduce Riesling and Pinot Gris.' Te Kairanga's first Riesling and Pinot Gris are due in 1999.

Of the two Sauvignon Blancs – one grown in Martinborough, the other a Gisborne/Martinborough blend – the verdant, zesty, locally grown wine is clearly superior. The Chardonnay, partly barrel-fermented, can be highly impressive, with a rich, creamy palate and long, flinty finish. The fully barrel-fermented and lees-aged Reserve Chardonnay, based on the ripest fruit, is a powerful, explosively flavoured, vigorous, complex wine with great richness and a taut acid spine.

The Cabernet Sauvignon-based reds are of varying quality. In cooler years they tend to be light in body, with unripe, leafy-green characters. In warmer vintages, however, they can be enjoyably fresh, crisp and berryish, with lots of drink-young charm.

The Pinot Noir, matured in seasoned oak barrels, places its accent on strong, almost sweet-tasting berry/plum fruit flavours, fresh and supple. The Reserve Pinot Noir is more powerful, complex and lush, with stronger oak influence and the ability to flourish in the bottle for several years, developing great fragrance and subtlety.

Te Kairanga Wines

Martins Road, Martinborough

Owner:
Te Kairanga Wines Limited

Key Wines:
Reserve Chardonnay, Pinot Noir; Martinborough Sauvignon Blanc, Gisborne/Martinborough Sauvignon Blanc, Chardonnay, Rosé Dry, Pinot Noir, Cabernet Sauvignon; Castlepoint Dry White, Cabernet Sauvignon

---

Winemaker Chris Buring and viticulturist Glenys Hansen have lifted the standard of Te Kairanga's Chardonnays and Pinot Noirs to new heights in recent vintages.

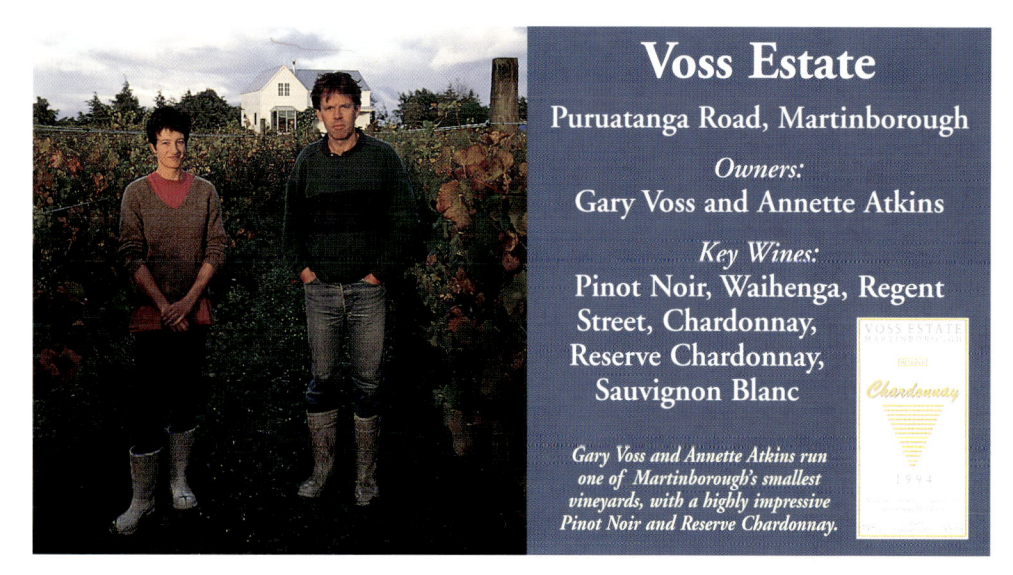

Voss Estate

Puruatanga Road, Martinborough

Owners:
Gary Voss and Annette Atkins

Key Wines:
Pinot Noir, Waihenga, Regent Street, Chardonnay, Reserve Chardonnay, Sauvignon Blanc

Gary Voss and Annette Atkins run one of Martinborough's smallest vineyards, with a highly impressive Pinot Noir and Reserve Chardonnay.

The initial 1991–93 vintages of Voss Estate's wines were promising, but not memorable. 'Our early releases coincided with El Nino and Pinatubo,' Gary Voss points out. The exciting quality of his 1994 Pinot Noir and Reserve Chardonnay, however, suggests this tiny winery has a big future.

Voss and his partner, Annette Atkins, bought land next to Ata Rangi in 1987. 'When I tasted Clive's [Paton of Ata Rangi] '86 Pinot Noir I was excited; I thought it was the best Pinot Noir made in New Zealand or Australia,' recalls Voss. 'Then I tasted his Cabernet Sauvignon-based Célèbre and liked that too.' So in 1988 Voss and Atkins planted both red-wine varieties.

Voss, who has a BSc in zoology, is a former Fisheries Research diver. After studying oenology for a year in Australia, he worked vintages at De Redcliffe and Ata Rangi before moving full-time into wine under his own label. Annette Atkins is a former Fisheries Research kahawai specialist. 'I do more of the work in the vineyard,' she says. 'Gary calls the shots in the winery, whereas I'm just the "cellar-rat".'

The two-hectare estate vineyard was originally planted in equal areas of Pinot Noir, Chardonnay, and red Bordeaux varieties: Cabernet Sauvignon, Merlot and Cabernet Franc. Having concluded that 'you only get really good red wine from Cabernet Sauvignon here about two years out of five', Voss and Atkins have since top-grafted some of their Cabernet Sauvignon vines over to Sauvignon Blanc. About two-thirds of the annual fruit intake is purchased from the nearby Craighall vineyard and other growers in Martinborough and Hawke's Bay.

The low-cropping estate vineyard yields only five tonnes of grapes per hectare. 'We're grassing down to reduce vigour, leaf-plucking to maximise the exposure of the fruit to the sun, and reducing the crop loads per vine as low as possible,' says Voss.

For the 1991 and 1992 vintages, Hawke's Bay grapes were used; the first Martinborough wine flowed in 1993. The winery's annual output is less than 2000 cases: 'That's where we want to stay,' says Voss. 'We can handle that ourselves, even though we're absolutely knackered at vintage.' The only staff employed are grape-pickers.

The Sauvignon Blanc exhibits pure, crisp, passionfruit and lime-like flavours. Two Chardonnays are produced: a partly barrel-fermented Hawke's Bay wine designed for early drinking, and the opulent, estate-grown Reserve Chardonnay, which is fully barrel-fermented and given extensive lees-aging. Fat, savoury, oaky, mealy and buttery, this is a high-flavoured wine of arresting quality.

Two claret-style reds are made, notably Waihenga (the Maori name for Martinborough) Cabernet/Merlot/Franc, a berryish, minty, firm-structured wine, predominantly estate-grown. The second-tier red, Regent Street, is usually blended from Hawke's Bay and local grapes.

For Annette Atkins, Pinot Noir is 'a dream variety. It's not hard work in the vineyard, and it crops consistently'. Dark, perfumed, very rich-flavoured and supple, with an underlay of fine, silky tannins, this may well emerge as one of the district's Rolls-Royce Pinot Noirs.

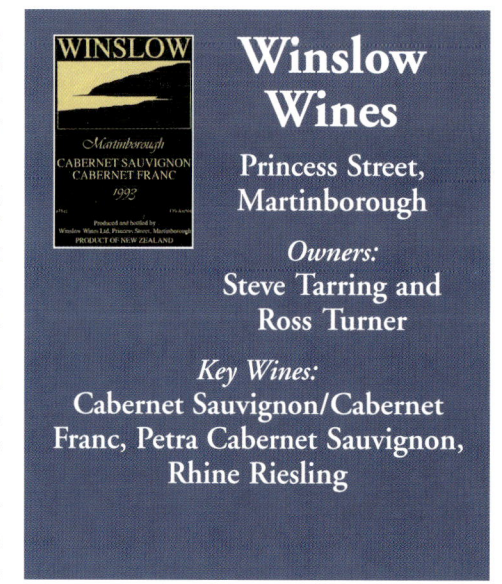

Winslow Wines

Princess Street, Martinborough

Owners:
Steve Tarring and Ross Turner

Key Wines:
Cabernet Sauvignon/Cabernet Franc, Petra Cabernet Sauvignon, Rhine Riesling

Winslow had humble beginnings. 'We began by selling our wine from a caravan,' recalls co-founder Ross Turner. 'I'd park an Austin Seven in the road with a sign in the window saying "Open". It didn't say *what* was open.'

Today Winslow has a smart-looking winery in Princess Street and a reputation for producing some of the Wairarapa's finest claret-style reds. 'I think we get enough sun and heat in Martinborough to ripen Cabernet Sauvignon,' says Steve Tarring, Turner's son-in-law. 'By New Zealand standards, even in poorer years we make an average Cabernet, and in good vintages we produce a very good wine.'

Turner and Tarring bought their property in 1985. Turner, a former national operations manager for New Zealand Rail, organised the planting of the vineyard while Tarring, a former marine biologist for Fisheries Research, worked overseas as an executive of a filtration equipment manufacturer.

Strat Canning, the winemaker, is a half-brother of Chris Canning, the founder of De Redcliffe. Canning has a degree in oenology from Charles Sturt University in New South Wales and worked the 1987 to 1990 vintages at De Redcliffe as an assistant winemaker. He owns a four-hectare vineyard in Martinborough, is currently vineyard manager for Palliser Estate, and joined Winslow on a part-time basis in 1994.

The two-hectare, shingly estate vineyard is planted in 90 per cent Cabernet Sauvignon, 10 per cent Cabernet Franc. Grapes are also drawn from Hawke's Bay. Only about 1000 cases of wine are produced each year, but the partners plan to double this.

Winslow is a red-wine specialist, but it also produces a slightly sweet, deliciously perfumed and zingy, incisively flavoured Rhine Riesling.

In favourable vintages like 1991 and 1994, the two Cabernet-based reds are of eye-catching quality. The Cabernet Sauvignon/Cabernet Franc (especially) and Petra Cabernet Sauvignon are dark, lush, vibrant, concentrated reds with supple tannins and a delicious burst of almost sweet blackcurrant and plum flavour. These are distinguished wines.

Ross Turner (left), Strat Canning and Steve Tarring have staked their future on Cabernet Sauvignon, and in warmer vintages produce a deliciously lush, vibrantly fruity and flavour-packed red of high quality.

Other Producers

Alexander Vineyard

A single, claret-style red of high promise has started to flow from Kingsley and Deborah Alexander's 1.5-hectare Martinborough vineyard in the Dublin Street extension, across the highway from Princess Street. The high density, low-trellised, severely pruned Cabernet Sauvignon, Cabernet Franc and Merlot vines yielded their first, deliciously rich-flavoured and supple wine in 1994.

Canadoro

Wellingtonians Greg and Lesley Robins own this 1.2-hectare vineyard in New York Street, Martinborough. 1993 yielded the first Cabernet Sauvignon, followed by a full, creamy-soft, barrel-fermented Chardonnay in 1995.

Hau Ariki

The Hau Ariki marae in Regent Street, Martinborough, is the first marae in New Zealand to make wine on a commercial footing. The three-hectare vineyard, planted in the late 1980s, is tended by voluntary workers from the marae. Since the first 1994 vintage, three oak-matured wines – Pinot Noir, Cabernet Sauvignon and Sauvignon Blanc – have been released, and a slightly sweet, Meunier-based Rosé.

Margrain Vineyard

Graham and Daryl Margrain own several luxury accommodation villas and a conference facility in Ponatai Road, Martinborough. The 4.5-hectare vineyard, planted in Chardonnay, Pinot Gris, Merlot and Pinot Noir, yielded its first wine in 1994.

Murdoch James

A rare, highly perfumed, rich-flavoured, double gold medal-winning Pinot Noir flows from this Martinborough vineyard, whose owner, Roger Fraser, lives in Australia. About 200 cases are made each year by Clive Paton at the Ata Rangi winery.

Te Horo Estate

Not in the Wairarapa at all, but in the Horowhenua, Te Horo Estate lies on the main highway south of Otaki. Owned by Alistair Pain and David Holland, the company also produces fruit wines under the Parsonage Hill brand. Pinot Noir, Chardonnay, Cabernet Sauvignon and Merlot are the key varieties in the three-hectare vineyard, planted in deep alluvial soils. Fruit is also drawn from growers in Te Horo, Hawke's Bay and Marlborough. Locally grown white wines are labelled Waterfall Bay, local reds Druid Hill, and all other wines Aurora. The grape wines, launched from the 1990 vintage, have included an occasional success, but their quality has been inconsistent.

Walker Estate

Next to Ata Rangi in Puruatanga Road, Brendan and Elizabeth Walker have a one-hectare vineyard planted in Riesling, Chardonnay and a red-wine variety, initially believed to be Syrah, for which the Walkers are seeking positive identification. The wines, launched from the 1993 vintage, are produced at a local winery by the Walkers' son, James.

Walnut Ridge

Bill Brink, from Iowa, and his wife, Sally, a New Zealander, own a 2.5-hectare vineyard and winery in Regent Street, Martinborough. The Brinks have planted Sauvignon Blanc, Cabernet Sauvignon and Pinot Noir, but for their initial releases (first vintage 1994) have concentrated on red wines. The Cabernet Sauvignon is solid but green-edged; the Pinot Noir riper and classier in a chewy and tannic style. There are no gate sales.

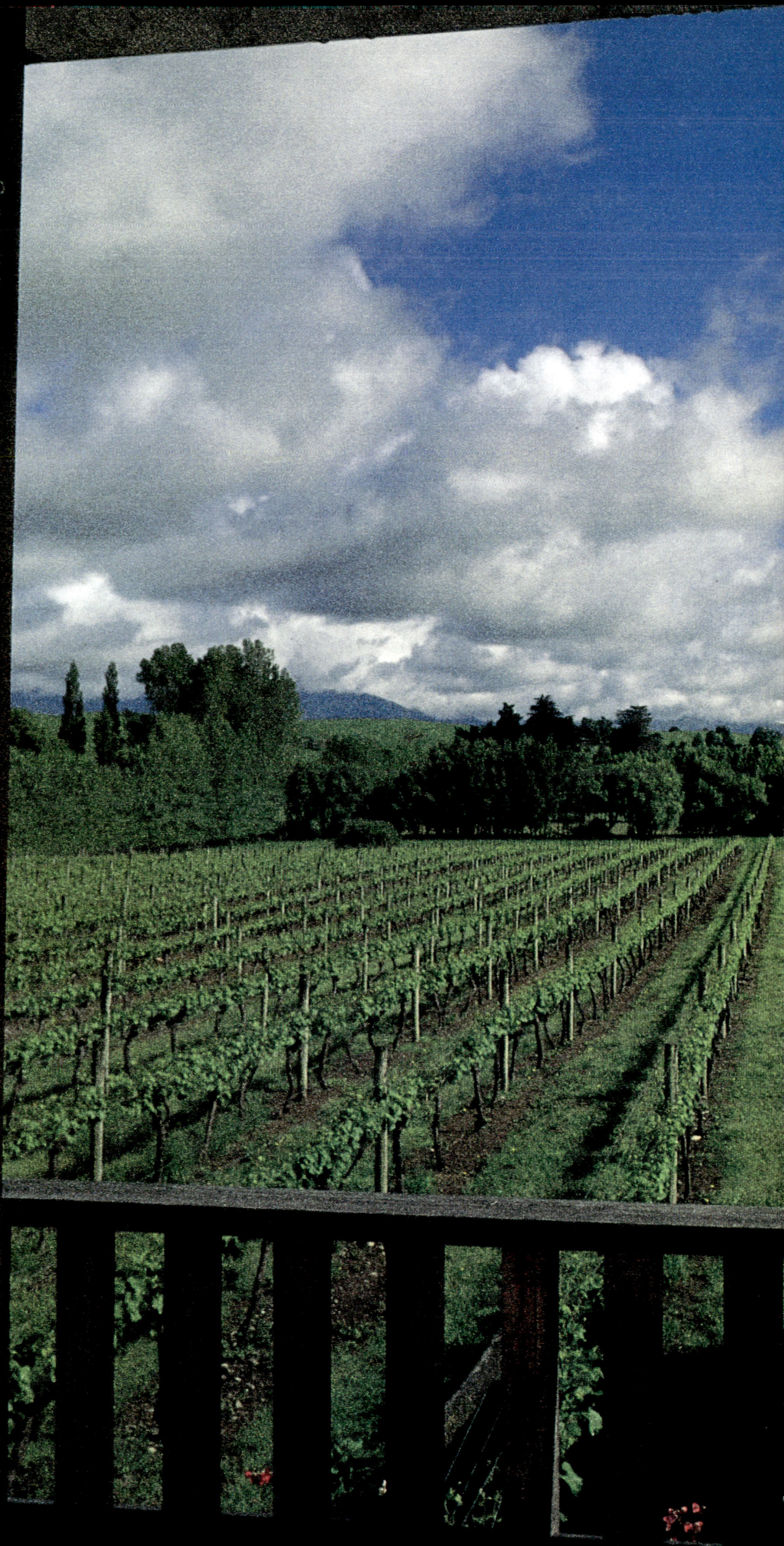

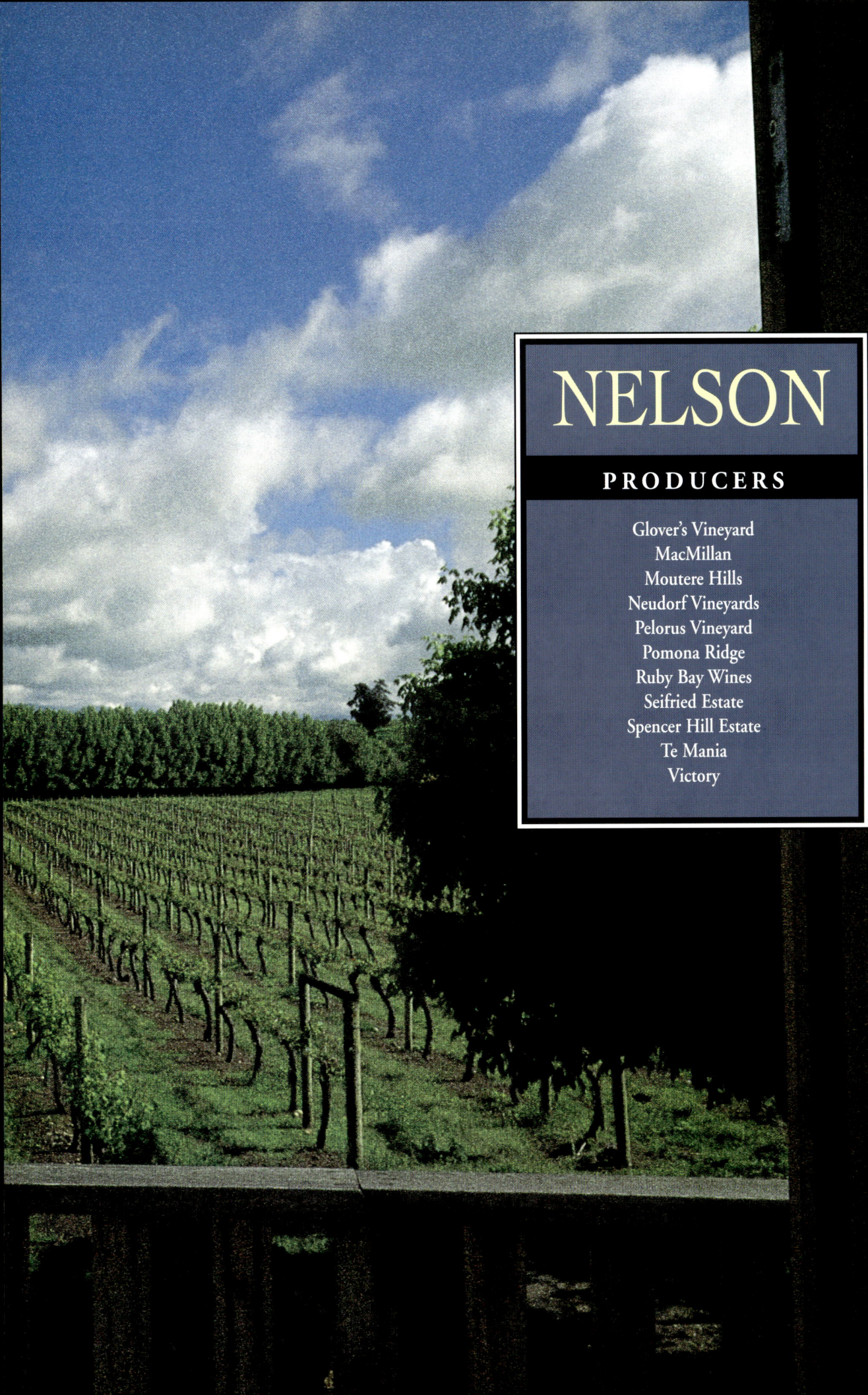

NELSON

PRODUCERS

Glover's Vineyard
MacMillan
Moutere Hills
Neudorf Vineyards
Pelorus Vineyard
Pomona Ridge
Ruby Bay Wines
Seifried Estate
Spencer Hill Estate
Te Mania
Victory

NELSON

Overshadowed by Marlborough's glamorous, bustling industry over the hills to the east, Nelson wine was for many years dominated by two Upper Moutere producers: the industrious, middle-sized Seifried Estate (now based at Rabbit Island) and the tiny but brilliant Neudorf Vineyards. With such a small industry and few memorable labels, Nelson has never enjoyed a high wine profile. Yet, today, with about 40 registered grapegrowers and a flurry of recent vine plantings, Nelson is one of New Zealand's fastest growing wine regions.

Why the sudden interest? 'People read in the paper about grape shortages and high grape prices,' says the indefatigable Hermann Seifried, who 22 years ago pioneered commercial winemaking in Nelson. 'Others are attracted to the area as a nice place to live,' says Tim Finn of Neudorf. 'But at last there's also a general acceptance that Nelson can make good wine.'

Early German winemakers who landed at Nelson in 1843 and 1844 looked askance at the steep, bush-clothed hills and departed for South Australia. Other problems have included a shortage of large holdings suitable for viticulture and the region's distance from principal transport routes.

The undoubted climatic advantages for viticulture – warm summers and high sunshine – are reduced by the risk of damaging autumn rains as harvest approaches. In this respect Nelson parallels most North Island wine districts more closely than other South Island regions. Nelson winemakers thus sometimes struggle to match the sugar levels achieved over the hills in the relatively dry Marlborough climate. 'Nelson's typically higher rainfall in March, compared to Marlborough's, puts more pressure on to achieve quality,' says Craig Gass, former owner of the Korepo (now Ruby Bay) winery, who now produces a range of Marlborough wines under the Conders Bend label.

Austrian-born Seifried, who established his vineyard in the hills at Upper Moutere in 1974, has so far produced the most wines. But others preceded him. In the 1890s, F.H.M. Ellis and Sons were 'substantial' winemakers at Motupipi, near Takaka, according to historian Dick Scott. Established in 1868, making wine from cherries and wild blackberries as well as grapes, the Ellis winery stayed in production for over 70 years, until it was converted into a woolshed in 1939.

Later, Viggo du Fresne, of French Huguenot descent, from 1967 to 1976 made dry red wine at a tiny, half-hectare vineyard planted in deep gravel on the coast at Ruby Bay. The vineyard, dating back to 1918, was originally established with Black Hamburgh table grapes; du Fresne took over in 1948 and waged a long, unsuccessful struggle to establish classical vines. After his Chardonnay, Sémillon and Meunier vines all failed – probably due to viruses – he produced dark and gutsy reds from the hybrid Seibel 5437 and 5455 varieties.

Today, across the pancake-flat Waimea Plains and in the soft, blue-green folds of the Upper Moutere hills, grapevines are sprouting. Most of the recent plantings are small, two to four-hectare blocks on the silty, sometimes stony, Waimea Plains. Many of the growers are part-timers who plan to sell their grapes to existing wineries, rather than make wine under their own label. 'I see the plains as quite like the Wairau Valley in viticultural terms,' says Finn. 'You've got similar alluvial flats with stony bands; it's windy; and the heat over the season is similar. The Waimea Plains are ideal for Marlborough-style wines.'

Nelson is largely white-wine country. Sauvignon Blanc, Riesling and Chardonnay, the three most common varieties, account for nearly two-thirds of all plantings, although Pinot Noir and Cabernet Sauvignon are also established. With 137 hectares under vine in 1995 (1.7 per cent of the national total), Nelson ranks with the Waikato as New Zealand's eighth most heavily planted wine region.

In the past 20 years, the efforts of a small knot of enthusiasts – most prominently Hermann and Agnes Seifried and Tim and Judy Finn – have put Nelson on the New Zealand wine map. Tourists responding with ever-increasing enthusiasm to promotion of the Nelson wine trail are able to explore wines varying in quality from plain to world class in some of the most stunning vineyard settings in the country.

TANNIN reads the number-plate on Dr David Glover's car. He also wears a T-shirt vowing that his wine is Merlot-free. Taut, grippy tannins are the hallmark of Glover's style, reflecting his firm opinions on the vital role of tannins during the aging of red wines.

'It's not tannin I'm promoting – it's longevity,' he says. 'I'm not after a "big Ocker" image; the tannins are there as a preservative.'

Glover's Vineyard lies in pretty, undulating countryside at Upper Moutere, between the inland and coastal Nelson-Motueka highways. Glover and his wife, Penny, planted their first vines in Gardner Valley Road in 1984.

David Glover, a former Wellingtonian, spent 16 years in Australia, where he gained a

Glover's Vineyard

Gardner Valley Road, Upper Moutere

Owners:
Dr David and Penny Glover

Key Wines:
Front Block Pinot Noir, Back Block Pinot Noir, Cabernet Sauvignon, Mt Lodestone Cabernet, Riesling, Late Harvest Riesling, Sauvignon Blanc

PhD in algebra and worked in the Defence Department. The Glovers came to Nelson for two key reasons: 'I'd always thought the Upper Moutere climate was ideal for winemaking, and after tasting Tim Finn's '82 Cabernet Sauvignon, I knew the potential was there,' recalls David. And Nelson's a hell of a good place to live.'

The three-hectare estate vineyard lies on a gentle, north-facing slope. In low-fertility clay threaded with decomposing rock, the Glovers have planted Pinot Noir, Cabernet Sauvignon and Sauvignon Blanc. At five tonnes per hectare, this is a low-cropping vineyard. Grapes are also bought from growers in Nelson and (sometimes) Hawke's Bay.

Glover's annual output is very small – around 1000 cases. Since the first 1989 vintage, the bold, beefy, tannic, estate-grown Pinot Noirs have attracted the most attention. Grapes from the hotter slope behind the winery yield a bold, strong-flavoured Back Block Pinot Noir with new-oak influence and furry tannins that demands cellaring. By contrast, the Front Block Pinot Noir, aged in seasoned oak casks, is a fragrant, more supple and forward style.

'You can always ripen Pinot Noir here,' says Glover, 'but you have to be a gambler with Cabernet Sauvignon. When you do get it ripe, you get something exceptional.' His unblended Moutere Cabernet Sauvignon ('Merlot can dissipate Cabernet's structure') is a dark-hued, muscular red with concentrated, brambly flavours and a tight tannin grip. Mt Lodestone Cabernet, launched from the 1995 vintage, is a second-tier label for lighter wine.

Glover's Sauvignon Blanc is pale, nettley and very zesty in cooler vintages, lusher and rounder in top years. The Riesling, grown at Richmond, bursts with lemony, appley flavours in a dryish, freshly acidic style. The medium-sweet Late Harvest Riesling is perfumed, citrusy, tangy and slightly honeyish.

Visitors to the Glovers' combination house and winery sample wine in the family's lounge, surrounded by books and classical CDs. Tasting his flavour-packed reds with Glover while swirling, dramatic Wagnerian opera fills the room is one of the great experiences of the New Zealand wine trail.

Dr David Glover produces sturdy, rich-flavoured Upper Moutere reds, cloaked with tannin.

Neudorf is a model vineyard and winery that inspires its visitors to rush off and plant grapes. The setting is idyllic and the powerful, opulent Chardonnay is one of New Zealand's most magnificent white wines.

Neudorf derives its name (pronounced Noy-dorf) from the surrounding district, settled by Germans last century. The winery lies not far from the village of Upper Moutere, just off the Nelson-Motueka inland highway.

Tim Finn, the founder, born in India and raised in Wellington, is an MSc graduate and a former dairying advisory officer with the Ministry of Agriculture and Fisheries. His wife, Judy, a former rural reporter for radio, is deeply involved in the company's sales and administration.

Neudorf Vineyards

Neudorf Road, Upper Moutere

Owners:
Tim and Judy Finn

Key Wines:
Chardonnay, Riesling, Sémillon, Sauvignon Blanc, Pinot Noir

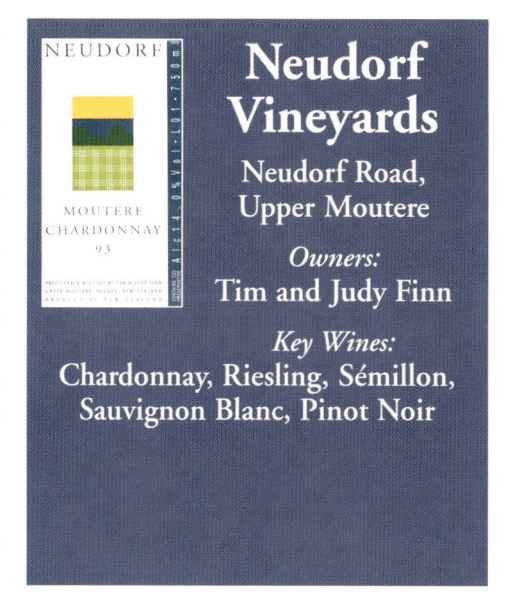

For their first vintage in 1981, the Finns used an old stables on the property as a temporary winery. For 1982, Tim Finn built a handsome macrocarpa winery, pitching its roof high to accommodate his fermentation and storage tanks inside. 'In the beginning, people thought we weren't so serious, planting in Nelson rather than Marlborough,' recalls Finn. 'Then, after we got 18 tonnes of grapes in our first year, the third year we got 12 tonnes. Our budget didn't go that way at all. We had to buy in grapes and borrow off Judy's mum.'

Today, Neudorf ranks among New Zealand's leading small wineries.

Asked for the key reasons behind the consistently outstanding quality of his wines, the soil is the first thing Finn points to. 'I like heavier soils. Light soils give lightness and clays give depth of flavour; I don't know why it is. I base that observation on Chardonnay; mine has more depth than Marlborough's, yet the two regions' climates are pretty similar.'

The six-hectare, non-irrigated vineyard is planted on Moutere clays, threaded with layers of gravel. Having experimented with numerous varieties, the Finns are now concentrating on Chardonnay and Pinot Noir (especially), Sauvignon Blanc and Riesling, although they still grow Sémillon and Cabernet Sauvignon. The estate-grown crop is sometimes supplemented by a relatively small amount of fruit from Marlborough.

To devigorate Neudorf's vines, Finn is gradually uprooting every second row and replacing it with two new rows – thereby reducing the spacing between the rows of vines from three to two metres. 'With 50 per cent more rows,' says Finn, 'we can reduce each vine's vigour yet still increase the total grape crop.'

Neudorf wines are rare; each year the Finns produce only about 4000 cases. The Chardonnay *(see panel)* is the Nelson region's greatest wine.

Neudorf's distinguished white-wine range also features a floral, vibrantly fruity, flavour-packed Riesling with racy acidity; a zingy, non-wooded, ripely herbal Sémillon; and a Sauvignon Blanc as fresh, aromatic and penetrating as Marlborough's.

Neudorf used to produce a popular, floral, supple, luncheon-style red from Pinot Noir. Its success encouraged Tim Finn to attempt a 'serious' Pinot Noir – with impressive results. Neudorf Pinot Noir is deep-coloured and perfumed, with good weight and intense, cherryish, spicy, complex flavours, buttressed by a firm tannin structure. Knowing Finn, it probably won't be long before the quality of his Pinot Noir matches that of his spellbinding Chardonnay.

Tim and Judy Finn own a small Nelson winery with a big reputation, especially for its glorious Chardonnay, a powerful wine with bottomless flavour.

Neudorf Moutere Chardonnay

Some Chardonnays knock your socks off with their sheer power and concentration, others with their subtlety and finesse. Neudorf Chardonnay combines all these qualities: a magnificently rich, mouth-filling wine with a creamy texture and stylish, savoury, searching flavours.

'Fruit ripeness is the key ingredient,' says Tim Finn. 'To build up fruit intensity and get fullness of flavour through the mid and back-palate, you must be willing to walk a knife-edge towards the end of harvest, even if there's a bit of *Botrytis* around. The length of flavour is also enhanced by a lower crop level.'

Once the grapes are in the winery, it's a matter of style. 'I like to layer the fruit with sophisticated oak and lees characters, but they don't swamp the wine,' says Finn. 'I also go for a very hot ferment, which gives vinous [winey] characters and helps to integrate the flavours, and put about a third of the final blend through a malolactic fermentation.'

Australian judges have compared Neudorf Chardonnay to 'Bâtard-Montrachet or Meursault'. Does Finn see parallels between his wine and white Burgundy? 'Our barrel-ferment and lees-aging characters are similar, but white Burgundy goes through a total malolactic fermentation so it has far less acid – it's less spiky – than ours.'

Neudorf Chardonnay has won major trophies in England and on both sides of the Tasman. It matures superbly – the 1989 vintage is currently in devastating form.

One of the fast-rising stars of Nelson wine is the Pelorus winery at Hope, south of Richmond. Ravishingly scented, with piercing, zingy flavour, the Riesling is one of the classiest in the country, with gold medals to prove it.

Andrew Greenhough and his partner, Jenny Wheeler, bought Pelorus Vineyard, then called Ranzau Wines, from its founder, Trevor Lewis, in early 1991. Lewis, a medical technologist who tended his vines and wines in spare hours in the evenings and at weekends, planted the vineyard in 1980. In his tiny, concrete-block winery, from 1983 Lewis produced a rivulet of wine rarely seen beyond Nelson.

Greenhough, a former Aucklander, holds an MA in art history. 'Dad's always drunk wine, which encouraged us to buy and cellar it. Wine's always been a hobby.' After working at Villa Maria as a cellarhand in 1990, Greenhough produced his first wine at Pelorus in 1991. Jenny Wheeler, who also runs a company supplying children's books to libraries and schools throughout the South Island, 'does the books and looks after the sales over summer'.

Pelorus Vineyard takes its name from the Pelorus River, which rises in the Richmond hills. Chardonnay, Riesling, Sauvignon Blanc and Pinot Noir are the four varieties Greenhough is concentrating on: 'There's plenty of heat for early-ripening red varieties like Pinot Noir and Merlot, but not enough for Cabernet.'

The three-hectare estate vineyard, planted in river pebbles and silt overlying clay loams with good moisture-retaining capacity, is devoted principally to Pinot Noir and Chardonnay, with smaller plots of Riesling and Merlot. During summer the vineyard is covered with netting: 'Otherwise the birds are devastating.' Chardonnay and Sauvignon Blanc are also purchased from Nelson growers.

In 1995, Greenhough and Wheeler converted the original winery into a tasting complex and the winemaking operation was shifted into an adjacent building that formerly served as a kiwifruit packhouse. Pelorus' annual output is around 2500 cases and climbing, but is not expected to exceed 5000 cases. Most of the wine is sold at the winery during summer and in shops and restaurants around Nelson.

Uniformly immaculate wines are flowing from Pelorus. The Sauvignon Blanc is flavour-packed and zippy with green-edged, capsicum-like characters. The barrique-fermented Chardonnay is citrusy, mealy and crisp, and the Riesling is awash with lemon/lime aromas and flavours in an appetisingly tangy style. The Pinot Noir, matured in seasoned French oak barriques, showcases ripe, sweet-fruit flavours in a buoyant and supple style.

'When we came here, I'd hardly ever set foot in a vineyard,' recalls Greenhough. 'And I'd never made wine before, except as a cellarhand at Villa Maria, just taking orders. But we felt we could do it, and we've produced something people want. Now we know we can go on.'

Pelorus Vineyard

Patons Road, Hope, Richmond

Owners:
Andrew Greenhough and Jenny Wheeler

Key Wines:
Chardonnay, Riesling, Sauvignon Blanc, Pinot Noir

Andrew Greenhough and Jenny Wheeler – crafting immaculate Nelson wines with impressive fragrance and finesse.

Ruby Bay's north-facing coastal vineyard site is one of the most stunning in the country. Here winemaker David Moore produces a deliciously powerful, flavour-packed and buttery Reserve Chardonnay.

Ruby Bay started life as the Korepo winery, founded by Craig Gass (now proprietor of Conders Bend), who planted his first vines in 1976. David and Christine Moore bought the property in 1989: 'I wanted to make wine more than anything else,' says David, 'and Nelson appealed for the lifestyle.'

David Moore has an MSc from Lincoln University, and for 16 years lectured in biochemistry at Christchurch Polytechnic, where he also taught courses in wine appreciation. After gaining a Graduate Diploma in Wine from Roseworthy College in South Australia, Moore made the 1989 vintage at Torlesse Wines in Canterbury, before heading north to Ruby Bay.

The three-hectare vineyard on a clay and gravel slope, terraced for ease of cultivation, is planted principally in Pinot Noir, Sauvignon Blanc, Riesling and Chardonnay, with a 'bit' of Sémillon. The site is warm and sunny, says Moore, with little wind. 'Our fruit is picked a good two or three weeks ahead of the other vineyards in the area. One result of this is the decreased likelihood of rain at harvest.' Fruit is also purchased from growers in Nelson, Marlborough and the North Island.

Ruby Bay's annual output is low at around 2000 cases of wine, but Moore plans to double his production by 1998. 'I'm especially interested in Chardonnay and

Ruby Bay Wines

Korepo Road, Ruby Bay

Owners:
David and Christine Moore

Key Wines:
Reserve Chardonnay, Sauvignon Blanc, Riesling Medium, Late Harvest Riesling, Pinot Noir, Cabernet/Merlot

Pinot Noir,' he says, 'because they have the greatest input from the winemaker. With Riesling and Sauvignon Blanc, once the fruit is ripe and balanced, it just goes straight through into the bottle with minimal intervention. Chardonnay and Pinot Noir, I can play around with.'

The Reserve Chardonnay, fermented in a mix of French and American oak barriques, is a robust, high-flavoured style, peachy, toasty and soft. The Riesling Medium, a full, strongly citrusy, tangy wine, is partnered by a lemony, medium-sweet, slightly honeyish Late Harvest Riesling, held on the vines for several weeks after the main harvest. The Pinot Noir offers a very appealing array of cherry, raspberry and oak flavours in a rich, ripe and supple style.

During summer visitors throng into Ruby Bay's Mediterranean-inspired vineyard restaurant, built in 1993, to devour 'simple' foods like homemade breads and preserves, terrines, cheeses and pickles, washed down – of course – with the Moores' rock-solid Nelson wines.

On the coast at Ruby Bay, David and Christine Moore (pictured with their sons, Stephen, right and Andrew) produce rich, supple, ripe-flavoured Chardonnays and reds.

Seifried Estate, by far the largest Nelson winery, for many years had a reputation for sound, sharply priced, but rarely exciting wines. During the 1990s, however, their quality has soared – the 1993 Sauvignon Blanc won the Silverado Trophy for champion Sauvignon Blanc at the 1994 International Wine and Spirit Competition in London.

The Seifried label, proudly adorned with the Austrian eagle, early won respect when, from the first vintage, the Sylvaner 1976 won a silver medal. Hermann Seifried graduated in wine technology in Germany, and made wine in Europe and South Africa before arriving in New Zealand in 1971, as winemaker for the ill-fated venture by the Apple and Pear Board into apple-wine production. In spring 1974 Seifried planted his own vineyard in the clay soils of the Upper Moutere. A year later his wife Agnes, a Southlander, resigned her teaching job to join him in the winery. Today she oversees the company's administration, exports and public relations.

'It's satisfying to be employing 60-odd people today,' says Agnes, 'when in the early days the experts said you couldn't grow grapes in Nelson. We were discouraged by the Department of Agriculture and Fisheries. Instead of being able to borrow money from the Rural Bank at 3.5 to 5 per cent, we had to go elsewhere and pay 14 per cent.'

The original Seifried winery (for many years called Weingut Seifried), lies on the outskirts of the tranquil village of Upper Moutere. The 12-hectare Moutere Valley vineyard is planted in Chardonnay, Riesling, Sylvaner and Pinot Noir. The Seifrieds also own a 22-hectare, earlier-ripening vineyard in the Redwood Valley, where the principal varieties are Sauvignon Blanc, Riesling and Gewürztraminer. On sandy loams overlying gravels on the coast at Rabbit Island, 34 hectares are planted in Chardonnay, Sauvignon Blanc, Pinot Noir and Cabernet Sauvignon. A third of the annual crush is bought from growers in Nelson and over the hills in Marlborough.

Seifried's handsome vineyard restaurant, on the corner of State Highway 60 and Redwood Road, Appleby, opened in 1993. A new winery was built here, prior to the 1996 vintage, followed by the closure of the original winery at Upper Moutere.

Since 1988, Seifried's annual output has more than doubled, from 20,000 to 45,000 cases. 'We'll stay around that level,' says Hermann. Andrew Blake, a Cantabrian with degrees from Lincoln University and

---

Seifried Estate

Redwood Road, Appleby

Owners:
Hermann and Agnes Seifried

Key Wines:
Seifried Estate Riesling, Riesling Dry, Gewürztraminer, Ice Wine, Chardonnay, Barrel Fermented Chardonnay, Sauvignon Blanc, Müller-Thurgau, Sekt, Pinot Noir, Cabernet Sauvignon; Old Coach Road Sauvignon Blanc, Chardonnay

Hermann Seifried's formidable energy, for many years focused largely on Riesling and Gewürztraminer, is now also yielding impressive, sharply priced Chardonnays and Sauvignon Blancs.

Roseworthy College, and winemaking experience in Australia, Chile, Spain and France, was appointed winemaker in 1996.

Seifried built its early reputation on a selection of Rieslings and Gewürztraminers in varying styles, but lately Sauvignon Blanc and Chardonnay have also come to the fore. Does the winery specialise in any particular grapes? 'We follow everybody with Chardonnay and Sauvignon Blanc,' says Hermann Seifried, 'but in the 1980s we were very strong with Riesling. Many others pulled out their Riesling during the vinepull scheme of 1985/86; we kept ours. Today we're facing stiffer competition with Riesling, especially from Marlborough; most of our recent expansion has been in Sauvignon Blanc and Chardonnay.'

The prices for Seifried wines are modest. 'Our philosophy has been to be affordable – within the average person's reach,' says Agnes. 'As Hermann has put it: with our volumes, regardless of winning the Silverado Trophy, we don't want to be selling at $22 for Sauvignon Blanc.' Most of the wines are labelled as Seifried Estate, with an even lower-priced range (sometimes unexpectedly good) sold under the Old Coach Road brand.

One of my favourite Seifried wines is the Riesling Dry, a steely, austere style with strong lemon and lime-evoking flavours and spine-tingling acidity. The wine simply labelled as Riesling is a full-bodied, citrusy, slightly sweet style, fresh-scented and zesty.

The medium-dry Gewürztraminer is perfumed, well-spiced and crisp in a very easy-drinking style. The rich, honey-sweet Ice Wine, a freeze-concentrated blend of Gewürztraminer and Riesling, at its best is ravishingly full-flavoured and spicy, with a super-charged bouquet: 'Every second person who calls at the cellar requests a taste,' says Agnes Seifried.

The Chardonnay – both stainless steel and oak-fermented, but fully barrel-aged – is citrusy, nutty and crisp, with impressive depth and vigour. The weighty, lemony, tangy Barrel Fermented Chardonnay is a more wood-influenced style, designed for cellaring. The non-wooded Sauvignon Blanc, a weighty, ripe style with intense, lush, gooseberry and melon-like flavours and a zingy finish, achieves real distinction in favourable vintages.

The Cabernet Sauvignon is fresh, berryish and plummy, with a touch of oak complexity. The Pinot Noir is typically a light, supple, raspberryish style with lots of drink-young appeal.

Seifried Estate wines are currently exported to the United Kingdom and Canada, and in small volumes to Germany, Singapore and Japan. Chris Seifried, Hermann and Agnes' son, is studying winemaking in Australia. In the future, says Hermann, 'we'll have a few more acres, our family will enter the business – and we'll keep giving the public good wines.'

When American Philip Jones came to New Zealand to make wine, he hit the ground running. His first 1994 Chardonnays under the Tasman Bay label instantly attracted attention with their eye-catching packaging and gold medal success followed swiftly.

Jones came to the Upper Moutere hills to make great wine. 'The Moutere is a difficult place to grow grapes, especially on the hillsides,' he says. 'The clay is tough and so are the hills. The slowness of the vines' growth is tough. It's tough seeing the guys on the plains getting crops after two years, when it's taking us five years to get a decent crop. But all over the world, many of the greatest vineyards are on the hills.'

Spencer Hill lies in Best Road, off Gardner Valley Road, between Neudorf and Glover's. Jones and his wife, Sheryl, planted their first

Spencer Hill Estate

Best Road, Upper Moutere

Owners:
Philip and Sheryl Jones

Key Wines:
Spencer Hill
Merlot/Franc/Cabernet;
Tasman Bay Chardonnay, Reserve
Chardonnay, Pinot Noir,
Merlot/Cabernet/Franc

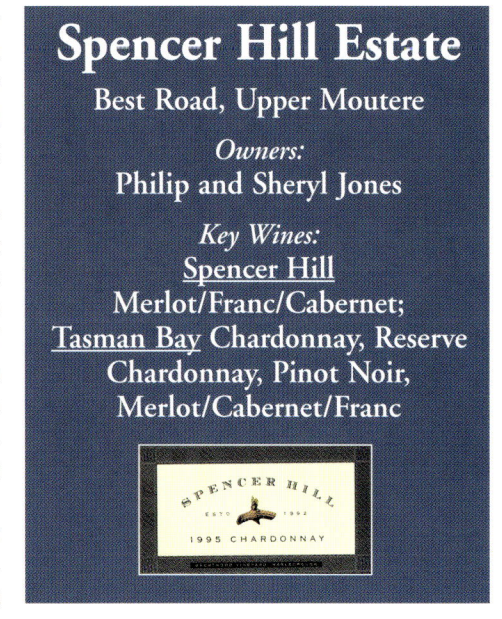

vines there in 1990, naming the winery after their son, Spencer.

Philip Jones studied winemaking at university but then got 'side-tracked' for 18 years before he fulfilled his dream of establishing a winery. Born in London, and raised in Canada and the United States, he took degrees in viticulture and pest management in California 'and did all the winemaking courses at Fresno State University.' The sidetrack came after he started an agricultural consultancy business that grew to employ 90 people. 'I started coming to New Zealand in 1985 to get away,' he recalls, 'and really liked it. So I decided I'd come to live here and plant a vineyard.'

The sloping, 12.5-hectare estate vineyard is planted in heavy, low-fertility clays. Chardonnay, Sauvignon Blanc and Pinot

Noir occupy two-thirds of the partly terraced vineyard, with smaller plots of Sémillon, Pinot Gris, Merlot, Cabernet Franc, Pinotage and Cabernet Sauvignon.

Jones also draws fruit from growers as far afield as Marlborough, Hawke's Bay and Gisborne. 'I'm a real blender,' he says. 'This country, with its cool climate, is marginal for grapegrowing, so we've got to blend regions and varieties to achieve consistency of quality.' Regional blending to give the wines drink-young appeal is a feature especially of the Tasman Bay range.

The premium Spencer Hill selection ('The wines *I* truly like,' says Jones) is intended to be a more vineyard-designated, oak-influenced range for longer aging. 'I like Sauvignon Blancs that are barrel and lees-aged with full malolactic fermentation; that's what I'm going to make. Your fruit characters here are fabulous, so the grapes can stand up to lots of oak and "malo" influence; it's not like that in California.'

Spencer Hill's output is climbing swiftly, from 2500 cases in 1994 to 8000 cases in 1996. Tasman Bay Chardonnay, fermented in French and American oak casks and given a full, softening malolactic fermentation, is a fragrant, forward wine with a delicious surge of grapefruit-like flavour and a touch of mealy complexity. The bold Reserve model is a very similar style with greater richness.

The Tasman Bay reds include a chunky, flavoursome Merlot/Cabernet/Franc. Spencer Hill Merlot/Franc/Cabernet is a more complex style, fragrant, robust, full-flavoured and supple.

Philip Jones, a Californian, has set out to make world class wines in the hills of the Upper Moutere.

Other Producers

MacMillan

Saralinda MacMillan, an Australian graduate of Roseworthy College, and winemaker at Seifried Estate between 1988 and 1992, produces a trickle of barrel-fermented Nelson Chardonnay under her own label. First produced in 1993, the wine is mostly sold in the Nelson region.

Moutere Hills

The 1.7-hectare Moutere Hills vineyard is near the old Seifried winery in Sunrise Valley, Upper Moutere. Ex-teachers Simon and Alison Thomas have converted an old shearing shed into a winery and plan a maximum annual output of only 1000 cases. The initial releases, a Chardonnay, Riesling and Cabernet/Merlot, will be joined by a Sauvignon Blanc and Pinot Noir.

Pomona Ridge

Pinot Noir is the specialty at this 1.2-hectare vineyard and winery in Pomona Road, Ruby Bay. The vineyard was planted in 1979 on a north-facing Moutere clay slope by Andy du Fresne, son of Viggo du Fresne, a pioneer of Nelson wine. The current owners – Peter and Jeanette Hancock, and John and Jenny Marchbanks – produced 140 cases of their first Pinot Noir in 1994. A café is planned for the future.

Te Mania

Waimea Plains grapegrowers Jon and Cheryl Harrey produced the first Sauvignon Blanc and Riesling under their Te Mania ('The Plains') label in 1995. The range, made at a local winery, will include a Chardonnay and reds.

Victory

Victory Grape Wines is a pocket-size vineyard on the main road south at Stoke, near Nelson city. Rod Neill made his first trial plantings in 1967 and began hobbyist winemaking in 1972. The red wines, rarely seen beyond Nelson, can be attractive.

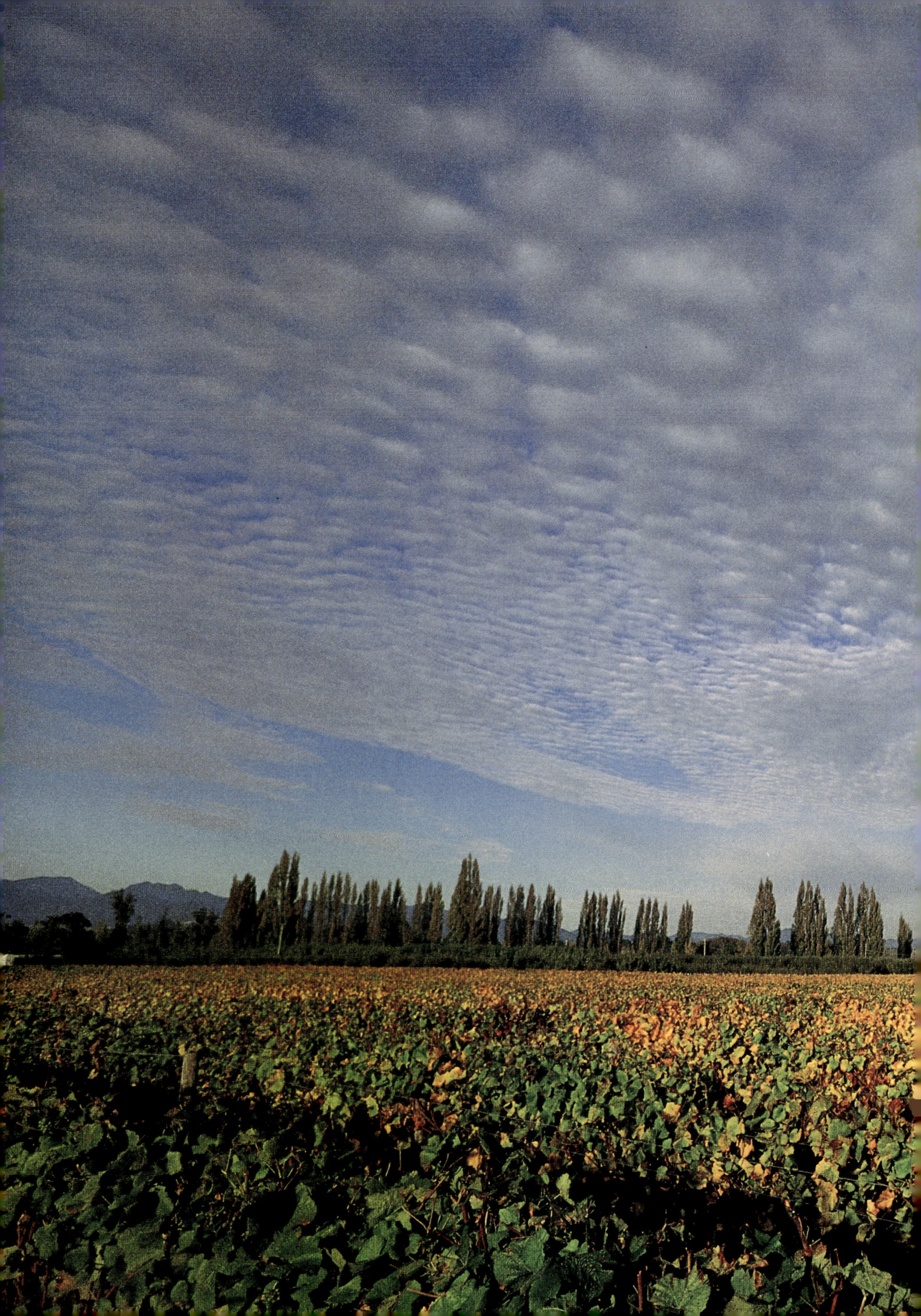

MARLBOROUGH

PRODUCERS

Allan Scott
Cairnbrae
Cellier Le Brun
Cloudy Bay
Conders Bend
Domaine Chandon (NZ)
Forrest
Foxes Island
Framingham
Fromm
Gillan
Grove Mill
HawkesBridge
Highfield
Hunters
Isabel Estate Vineyards
Jackson
Johanneshof
Kindale
Lake Chalice
Lawson's Dry Hills
Mount Linton
Merlen
Nautilus
Omaka Springs
Ponder
Rothbury Estate
Saint Clair
Te Whare Ra
The Brothers Vineyards
Vavasour
Wairau River
Whitehaven
Wither Hills

Marlborough

It's August 1973. You are touring the vineyards of New Zealand, and have just spent several days visiting the wineries of West Auckland and Hawke's Bay. From the 2000 hectares of vines in the North Island, you have tasted an occasional Cabernet Sauvignon, Pinotage or 'Pinot Chardonnay' (Chardonnay), a stream of 'Riesling-Sylvaners' (Müller-Thurgaus) and hybrid-based whites and reds, and a multitude of 'sherries' and 'ports'.

Crossing Cook Strait, you land on the South Island – and there's hardly a grapevine to be seen. Several North Island winemakers have told you that the South Island is too cold to support commercial viticulture. You drive from the ferry landing at Picton up to Blenheim, the main town in Marlborough – and witness a pivotal event in New Zealand wine history.

The first vine in the modern era of Marlborough wine was planted by Montana on 24 August 1973. Watched by a sceptical group of industry leaders flown south for the occasion, Frank Yukich, the driving force behind Montana's relentless rise, and company chairman Sir David Beattie dropped a silver coin – the traditional token of good fortune – into the hole, and with a sprinkling of sparkling wine dedicated the historic vine. Three years later, the first crops of Marlborough Müller-Thurgau and Cabernet Sauvignon were shipped across Cook Strait and trucked through the night by Mate Yukich – Frank's brother – to Montana's winery at Gisborne.

Today, with 3233 hectares of vines recorded in 1995, Marlborough has emerged as the country's most heavily planted wine region, far ahead of Hawke's Bay and Gisborne. The Marlborough wine trail features some of the great names of New Zealand wine: Montana, Corbans, Cloudy Bay, Hunter's. Marlborough also enjoys a higher international profile than any other New Zealand wine region: according to British wine writer Hugh Johnson, 'No region on earth can match the pungency of its best Sauvignon Blanc.'

Marlborough, the north-eastern edge of the South Island, contains the inland Kaikoura Ranges (3000m approx.) and snow-fed rivers, with farms and pine forests extending far up the valleys, deep into the high country.

The Wairau River, draining the ranges of silt and gravel, descends from the back country to the Wairau Plains; it is on the plains, formed by massive alluvial deposits from the river, that Montana, Corbans and others have planted their vines. From 14 kilometres wide at its eastern end, where it meets the coast at Cloudy Bay, the Wairau Valley tapers to its inland extremity, 26 kilometres from the sea. To the north rear the Richmond Ranges, whose dusky silhouette is seen around the world on the Cloudy Bay label. The southern boundary is marked by a series of ranges which give rise to three side valleys, now recognised as sub-regions within the Wairau: the Brancott, Hawkesbury and Waihopai Valleys.

Marlborough is one of the few South Island regions that is sufficiently warm for viticulture on a commercial scale. The heat summation figure, 1150–1250 degree days Celsius, is higher than at Geisenheim on the Rhine, in Germany, which has 1050–1250 degree days Celsius. Blenheim frequently records the highest total sunshine hours in the country, and this plentiful, although not intense, sunshine affords the grapes a long, slow period of ripening. The combination of clear, sunny days and cold nights keeps acid levels high in the grapes, even when sugars are rising swiftly. According to Montana, Marlborough's heat and sunshine are usually sufficient for 'good sugar levels to be attained in white grapes and adequate to good levels in red grapes'.

The risk posed by heavy autumn rains is lower than across the hills in Nelson. March is usually the driest month of the year; April rainfall, averaging 61mm, compares favourably with the average 72mm in Bordeaux during the harvest month. However, according to Cloudy Bay, 'while on average rainfall is spread evenly over the year, it is in practice notoriously unpredictable.' The unrelenting rains of April 1995 are still fresh in every grower's mind.

The warm, dry north-westerly winds that 'come out of the Kaituna Valley like a freight-train', according to viticulturist Richard Bowling, can pose drought problems, dehydrating the vines and severely reducing crop sizes. Most vineyards have installed a trickle-irrigation system, feeding water to the vines and greatly enhancing grape yields. An extensive aquifer within the valley's deep alluvial gravels provides a critical source of irrigation water.

'Spring frosts are rare,' reports Cloudy Bay, 'but frosts are a potential hazard during the latter stages of harvest.' A heavy frost in the autumn of 1990 killed the vines' leaves, preventing the full ripening of Riesling, Sauvignon Blanc and Cabernet Sauvignon: 'The whole valley turned black overnight,' recalls Jane Hunter.

The maritime influence ensures relatively high humidity during the vines' growing season. During the critical harvest month of April, however, the average temperature is quite low, which by slowing the spread of disease allows the grapes to be left late on the vines to ripen fully.

Not all the various soil types found on the plains adapt well to viticulture. Large areas of deep silt loams are very fertile, with a high water storage capacity. The preferred sites are of lower fertility, with a noticeably stony, sandy loam topsoil overlying deep layers of free-draining shingle with sand infilling. These shallow, stony soils promote a moderately vigorous growth of the vine. 'The key benefit of the stones is that they reduce the soil's fertility,' says John Belsham of Foxes Island.

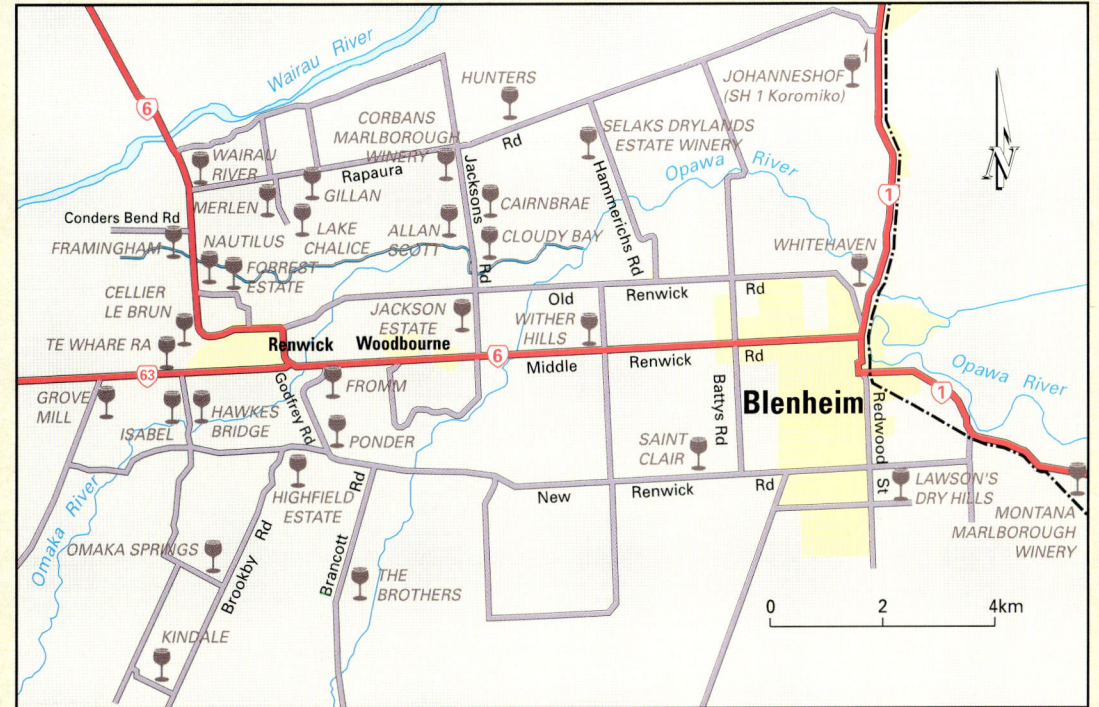

In the decade to 1995, Marlborough's share of the national area in vines soared from 24 to 39 per cent. Sauvignon Blanc and Chardonnay account for 54 per cent of all plantings, followed by Müller-Thurgau (down 12 per cent since 1992), Riesling, Cabernet Sauvignon, Pinot Noir, Sémillon and Merlot.

Since 1985, when Australian capital financed the erection of Cloudy Bay's handsome concrete winery in the heart of the Wairau Valley, overseas investment has streamed into the Marlborough wine scene. Corbans Marlborough Winery, now wholly Corbans-owned, was initially funded by Corbans and the Australian company, Wolf Blass (now Mildara Blass).

The Fromm winery has been set up by Swiss immigrants, Georg and Ruth Fromm. Almuth Lorenz, winemaker at Merlen, who was raised in the Rheinhessen, and Edel Everling, co-founder of Johanneshof Cellars, who was born at Rudesheim on the Rhine, enhance the region's slightly European flavour.

Links between Marlborough and the great houses of Champagne are also mounting. Deutz has lent technical assistance and its own name to Montana's bottle-fermented sparkling, Deutz Marlborough Cuvée. Veuve Clicquot Ponsardin is now the majority shareholder in Cloudy Bay.

Two of the three shareholders in the Highfield winery are Asians, also involved in the Champagne house of Drappier. Möet & Chandon's Australian subsidiary, Domaine Chandon, produces its Marlborough bottle-fermented sparkling at Hunter's winery.

That Sauvignon Blanc and Riesling thrive in Marlborough's cool ripening conditions has been demonstrated by Montana for many years. A decade ago, the region's Chardonnays often lacked the weight and flavour richness of those from the North Island, but lately their standard has soared. The power and subtlety of Vavasour Reserve, Corbans Cottage Block and Private Bin Marlborough, Montana Renwick Estate, Cloudy Bay, Villa Maria Reserve Marlborough, Hunter's and others is proof that Marlborough has now emerged as a formidable rival to Hawke's Bay and Gisborne in the Chardonnay quality stakes.

Pinot Noir early proved to be an ideal base for bottle-fermented sparkling wines, and now, with superior clones becoming available, is also starting to shine as a red-wine variety. Marlborough's Cabernet Sauvignons, however, often display strong leafy-green flavours; the variety has traditionally flourished in a warmer climate. 'With careful site selection you can produce good Cabernet-based reds,' says John Belsham, 'but you don't get enough warm years to consistently produce good wines.'

Marlborough's Merlots are another story. Merlot ripens two to three weeks earlier than Cabernet Sauvignon in Marlborough, giving the grapes a much higher chance of achieving optimal ripeness. Merlot and Pinot Noir, rather than Cabernet Sauvignon, hold the keys to the region's red-wine future.

GROWER LABELS

Once upon a time, if you wanted to be a winemaker you planted a vineyard, built a winery, bought a crusher, press, tanks and barrels – and set to work. Then, 30 years ago, wineries eager to expand their output but avoid the capital costs of establishing major new vineyards encouraged farmers to diversify into grapegrowing on a contract basis. Now, many of those growers are developing their own wine labels, depriving the established companies of some of their best grapes and hotting up the competition on retailers' shelves.

A string of 'grower labels' has recently emerged from Marlborough, including Saint Clair, HawkesBridge, Ponder Estate and Framingham. The term 'grower label' is usually applied when a former specialist grape-grower keeps part or all of his/her crop back, pays for the wine to be made by someone else at a local winery and then controls the marketing of the wine under a separate brand.

Jackson Estate, the acclaimed Sauvignon Blanc producer, is a classic case. Warwick and John Stichbury own an extensive vineyard in Jacksons Road, but no winery. Martin Shaw, an Australian consultant, makes the wine at Rapaura Vintners, the local contract winemaking facility.

Rapaura Vintners is a strictly utilitarian-looking cluster of buildings and over 100 stainless-steel tanks on the corner of Rapaura Road and the Blenheim-Nelson highway. In the past called Vintech, until recently it crushed about a third of Marlborough's total grape harvest for 30 clients.

After Vintech's facilities failed to cope with the demands of the exceptionally wet and compressed 1995 vintage, the company was purchased by four wine producers – Shingle Peak (Matua Valley), Negociants New Zealand (owners of the Nautilus brand), Foxes Island (owned by John Belsham, general manager of Rapaura Vintners), and Wairau River. The new owners of Rapaura Vintners retained about half of Vintech's 30 clients – principally those for whom the company was not only de-juicing grapes, but also fermenting, processing and bottling.

'We don't actually make the wine for our clients,' says Belsham, stressing that wines processed at Rapaura Vintners don't all taste the same. 'Making wine is not about transferring it from one tank to another. It's choosing a style, having the right vineyard, choosing the right picking dates and so on. Our clients do all that.'

Why do specialist grapegrowers plunge into the highly competitive winemaking arena? 'It completes the circle,' says Mike Ponder, who sells the majority of the grapes from his 20-hectare vineyard in Old Renwick Road, but in 1994 produced about 1000 cases of his first Ponder Estate Sauvignon Blanc. 'When you've planted a vineyard, it's natural to want to see your own wine in the bottle.'

Neal Ibbotson of Saint Clair, a grapegrower since 1978, is enticed by the prospect of greater control: 'We came to the conclusion we should control not only the fruit, but also the final product.'

Not all the growers' labels will succeed in an already crowded market. For wine lovers, however, there is a flood of new labels to explore.

Allan Scott Wines and Estates

Jacksons Road, Blenheim

Owners:
Allan and Catherine Scott

Key Wines:
Allan Scott Sauvignon, Riesling, Chardonnay, Autumn Riesling, Merlot; Mount Riley Chardonnay, Classic Red

Allan and Catherine Scott produce a small range of wines packed with the pure, deep flavours of Marlborough fruit.

One of Marlborough's top Rieslings flows from this small, family-owned winery, which is equally renowned for the rustic, rammed-earth charm of its Twelve Trees Restaurant.

Allan Scott, formerly Corbans' national vineyards manager, launched his own label with a 1990 Sauvignon Blanc. After years of 'wheeling and dealing in land and having faith in the district's wine future,' Scott and his wife, Cathy, now own 'about as much of the stony Jacksons Road area as anyone.' Their atmospheric winery was built in early 1992, just across Jacksons Road from Cloudy Bay. Chardonnay, Riesling and – inevitably – Sauvignon Blanc are the mainstays of the Scotts' range.

Allan Scott has long been a key figure in the development of Marlborough's vineyards. He was born on a North Canterbury farm; Cathy is from Blenheim. When Montana arrived in Marlborough in 1973, Scott got a job as a vineyard labourer, tearing down fences and planting vines. Within a month he was appointed vineyard foreman, and later supervisor of Montana's Fairhall vineyard.

Scott switched horses in 1980, joining Corbans to oversee the establishment of their Marlborough vineyards – notably Stoneleigh. By 1982 he was Corbans' national vineyards manager. After resigning from Corbans in 1989 Scott set up as a viticultural consultant, but has recently been absorbed in developing the Allan Scott range of wines.

In mid 1993, the Scotts sold their vineyards, cellar and restaurant to Appellation Vineyards, in return for a share of Appellation. A year later, they withdrew from Appellation and returned to direct ownership of the business they had created.

Since regaining control of the company, the Scotts have also taken a half share in a new North Canterbury producer, Waipara Estates, which markets its wines under the Chancellor brand (see page 181).

The Scotts' vineyards encircle the winery, spreading over 22 hectares on both sides of Jacksons Road. Sauvignon Blanc, Riesling and Chardonnay are the chosen grapes, with red-wine varieties to be added. Fruit is also purchased from other growers in the district.

The early releases were crushed and fermented at Vintech. Prior to the 1996 vintage, fermentation tanks, a barrel hall, bottling hall and warehouse were erected, allowing most of the production to occur on-site. The Scotts' output is growing swiftly, from 10,000 cases in 1993 to around 20,000 cases in 1996. The UK is the major export market: 'It's good for our egos and overseas trips,' grins Scott.

Visitors to the Allan Scott winery enjoy a tight range of well-crafted wines. The top wines carry the Allan Scott brand, and a selection of 'low-key, good-value' wines are labelled as Mount Riley.

Allan Scott Sauvignon is a non-wooded style, brimming with pure, melon-like, moderately herbal, appetisingly crisp flavours. Allan Scott Chardonnay is weighty, citrusy and slightly buttery.

At its best, Allan Scott Riesling is full-bloomed, intense and lively, with rich lemon/lime flavours, a light touch of sweetness and zingy acidity. Autumn Riesling is a late-harvested style, perfumed and sweet; in top vintages it is rampantly botrytised, oily and treacly.

There is nothing flash about Cairnbrae. Visitors step into a cottage-like winery: 'We like traditional buildings,' says Daphne Brown, 'and we're homely sort of people.' The wines, principally white, are pure Marlborough – fresh, mouthwateringly crisp and awash with flavour.

Murray and Daphne Brown produced the first Cairnbrae wines in 1992, 12 years after they began planting vines in Jacksons Road. 'After farming in Southland, we came to Marlborough in 1979, looking for a stock property,' says Daphne. 'After working for a friend who was developing a vineyard, we decided grapes were a better idea. When Corbans came to Marlborough in 1980, we were the first growers to sign up.' The Browns still sell part of their crop to other wineries.

Cairnbrae (meaning 'pile of stones on a hillside') was chosen as the winery name because of the stony ridges that run through the vines. Today the 18-hectare vineyard surrounding the winery (with Cloudy Bay just over the fence) is divided evenly between Sauvignon Blanc, Sémillon, Riesling and Chardonnay, with Cabernet Franc to be added. About 10,000 cases of wine are made each year at another local winery, since Cairnbrae itself has no on-site winemaking facilities.

The consistently fresh, flavoursome and frisky Sauvignon Blanc is partnered by a crisp, vigorous Sémillon, bursting with nettley flavour. The Chardonnay, a lightly oaked style, is designed for early consumption. My favourite is the invigoratingly crisp Riesling, with its strong, slightly sweet lemon/lime flavours.

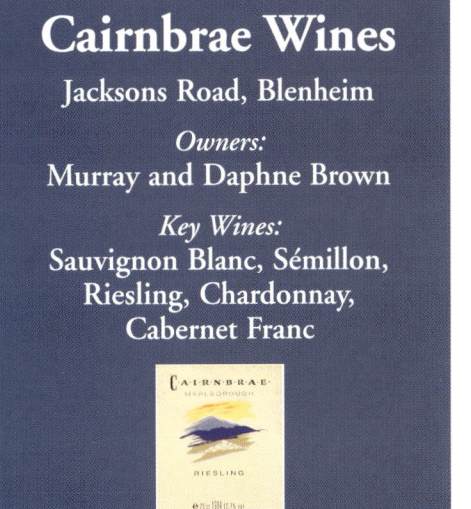

Diners in Cairnbrae's vineyard restaurant enjoy fresh Marlborough produce seated indoors, outdoors in a sheltered courtyard, or on an upstairs balcony that offers a panoramic view of vineyards carpeting the plains as far as the eye can see.

Cairnbrae Wines

Jacksons Road, Blenheim

Owners:
Murray and Daphne Brown

Key Wines:
Sauvignon Blanc, Sémillon, Riesling, Chardonnay, Cabernet Franc

Over the fence from Cloudy Bay, Murray and Daphne Brown offer consistently attractive wines and one of the Wairau Valley's most memorable views.

In a blind tasting of New Zealand's sparkling wines, it's usually easy to pick the Le Brun. These are characterful, high impact wines that fill your mouth with rich, toasty, yeasty, nutty flavour.

Daniel Le Brun (who withdrew from the company in mid 1996) is a Champenois, the scion of a family of French Champagne makers stretching back over 12 generations to 1648. In search of new horizons, Le Brun came to New Zealand and at Renwick, near Blenheim, he discovered the combination of soil and climate he wanted. His ambition: to fashion a bottle-fermented sparkling wine in the antipodes able to challenge the quality of Champagne itself.

Le Brun, an intense, passionate personality, speaks with a thick French accent. He was born at Monthelon, only a few kilometres south of Épernay, and recalls, 'the only thing for me to do was to carry on the family tradition'. However, after graduating from the École de Viticulture et Oenologie at Avize, he grew more and more frustrated by the very tight restrictions placed on the size of individual landholdings in Champagne.

After visiting New Zealand in 1975, he emigrated here, and three years later met his future wife, Adele, in Rotorua. By 1980 they had purchased land just outside Renwick and had begun establishing their vineyard.

Le Brun set out to duplicate the cool subterranean storage conditions of Champagne by burrowing 12 metres into his Renwick hillside, to form steel-lined caves under four metres of earth. In these cool caves, varying only a couple of degrees in temperature between summer and winter, the Le Brun bottle-fermented sparklings age after bottling.

The classic varieties of Champagne – Chardonnay, Pinot Noir and Meunier – are naturally featured in Cellier Le Brun's 16 hectares of vineyards. The vines, planted in river gravels, are densely spaced as in Champagne. Some fruit is also purchased from local growers for Le Brun's table wines under the Terrace Road label.

Daniel Le Brun was intent on 'carrying on the old techniques – everything is handled according to Champagne tradition'. To make his beloved Méthode Champenoise Brut, he blended the base wine from the three varieties and across vintages. After adding yeasts and sugar for the second fermentation, the wine is then bottled and rests on its lees for two years.

Daniel Le Brun Méthode Champenoise Brut – which constitutes a large slice of the winery's output – is a distinctively bold, full-flavoured style, reflecting Le Brun's liking for 'gutsy' sparkling wines: 'I'm a fan of Bollinger rather than Taittinger,' he says. Blended from 60 per cent Pinot Noir, 30 per cent Chardonnay and 10 percent Meunier, this is a mouth-filling wine with plenty of yeast-derived complexity and impressive flavour richness.

Cellier Le Brun's purely Chardonnay-based Blanc de Blancs is stunningly bold for a style often cast in the 'light and fresh' mould. Le Brun himself views New Zealand's bottle-fermented sparklings as 'bigger and fruitier' than their Champagne counterparts, principally due to their more advanced fruit ripeness.

The Le Brun range also includes an onion-skin-coloured Méthode Champenoise Rosé, a rich-flavoured, strawberryish and slightly earthy blend of 80 per cent Pinot Noir and 20 per cent Meunier; and a light-pink, Pinot Noir-based, raspberryish and yeasty Blanc de Noirs. As a tribute to his wife, Daniel Le Brun also produced the classy, tight-structured, delicately flavoured, slowly evolving Cuvée Adele.

Regal Salmon Limited gained a controlling interest in Cellier Le Brun in 1987, but Daniel Le Brun stayed on as the winemaker and a director, Adele Le Brun continued to oversee sales, and the Le Bruns and other original investors retained a minority shareholding. The owners of Cellier Le Brun then agreed in mid 1993 to sell their shares to Appellation Vineyards Limited (a holding company for the Morton Estate, Allan Scott and Cellier Le Brun wineries) for shares in Appellation, in which Regal Salmon was the largest shareholder. After Appellation's plans for a public share float collapsed, Wellington-based Resene Paints Limited purchased a majority shareholding in Cellier Le Brun in late 1994, with the Le Bruns retaining their substantial minority stake.

In mid 1996 the Le Bruns' financial and working involvement in the company was abruptly terminated.

Cellier Le Brun

Terrace Road, Renwick

Owner:
Resene Paints Limited

Key Wines:
Daniel Le Brun Méthode Champenoise Brut, Vintage Méthode Champenoise Brut, Blanc de Blancs, Blanc de Noirs, Méthode Champenoise Rosé, Cuvée Adele; Terrace Road Sauvignon Blanc, Pinot Noir

Sixteen years after founding one of Marlborough's best-known wineries, in mid 1996 Daniel Le Brun departed from the company.

Daniel Le Brun Vintage Méthode Champenoise

Of Daniel Le Brun's range of bottle-fermented sparklings, his vintage wine was his favourite. 'It's not a drink-young style like the non-vintage,' he says. 'The vintage is bigger in structure and higher in acidity, for longer life.'

The Vintage Méthode Champenoise is typically a 50/50 blend of Pinot Noir and Chardonnay. Unlike the non-vintage, it includes no Meunier: 'Meunier makes the wine age faster,' says Le Brun. 'The vintage wine is for keeping up to five years.'

The Le Brun vintage sparkling is based on riper grapes than those employed in the non-vintage. 'We pick the fruit for the vintage wine last, to give the wine bolder structure. Lower acids aren't a problem; Marlborough grapes keep their acidity.' The vintage wine is then matured on its yeast lees for two and a half years – six months longer than the non-vintage.

The bouquet is enticingly rich and yeasty. A flavour-packed style, it is toasty and mouth-filling, with lots of yeast-derived complexity and a rich, trailing finish. From one vintage to the next, this is a five-star wine.

Cloudy Bay Vineyards

Jacksons Road, Blenheim

Owner: Cape Mentelle (NZ)

Key Wines: Sauvignon Blanc, Chardonnay, Pelorus, Late Harvest Riesling, Cabernet/Merlot, Pinot Noir

Part-owner David Hohnen (right) and winemaker Kevin Judd are the key figures behind New Zealand's most internationally acclaimed wine – Cloudy Bay Sauvignon Blanc.

No other New Zealand wine has generated as much fervour around the world as Cloudy Bay Sauvignon Blanc. It's been lauded as 'New Zealand's finest export since Sir Richard Hadlee' (David Thomas, *Punch*); as 'the best example of this varietal I have ever tasted from New Zealand' (Robert Parker, *The Wine Advocate*); and as 'like hearing Glenn Gould playing the Goldberg variations, or seeing Niki Lauda at full tilt' (Mark Shields, *Sun Herald*, Melbourne).

When Kevin Judd arrived in Marlborough in 1985 to take up his new job as Cloudy Bay's winemaker, no fanfare greeted him. 'We had no vineyards, no winery, no equipment, nothing,' recalls Judd. 'Things could only get better.' Explosively flavoured and stunningly packaged, Cloudy Bay's 1985 Sauvignon Blanc swiftly sent a ripple through the international wine world.

In the conviction that the quality of New Zealand-grown Sauvignon Blancs could not be equalled in Australia, David Hohnen, part-owner of Cape Mentelle, a prestige Western Australian winery, had crossed the Tasman to set up a second winery in Marlborough. Cape Mentelle's reputation was based on having captured the Jimmy Watson Trophy – awarded to the top one-year-old Australian red – in successive years, with its 1982 and 1983 Cabernet Sauvignons.

Hohnen had first tasted New Zealand wine when a party of four Kiwi winemakers visited his winery in 1983. 'I had my '82 Sémillon/Sauvignon Blanc in barrels and said: "Get a load of this." They said: "If you think that's herbaceous, see what we've got in the car." Penfolds 1983 Sauvignon Blanc from Marlborough just blew me away. It was a bit sweet, but it had fruit characters that we would never get in Australia.'

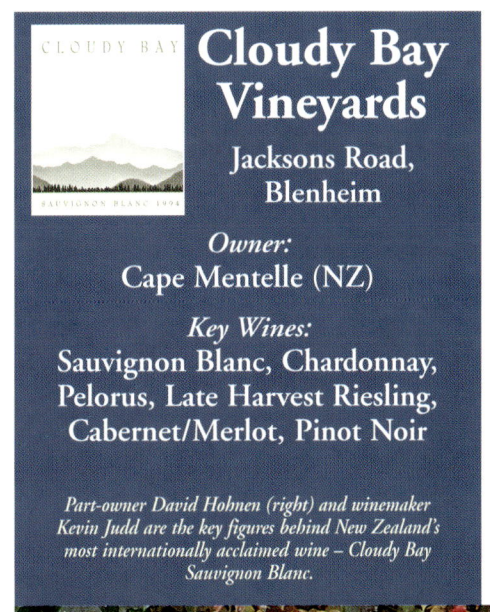

When Hohnen plotted to establish a new winery in Marlborough, his accountants advised him to stay out of the New Zealand wine industry, then on the verge of the cut-throat price war of 1985–86. 'It was a terrific gamble. I just had this gut feeling that told me it was the right thing to do. New Zealand Sauvignon Blanc simply hadn't been discovered and seemed to me to have a great future.'

Cloudy Bay, the name of the nearby bay whose waters, when the Wairau River fills them with silt, turn cloudy, was finally chosen as the name of the new venture, but not before the name of a prominent local

cape had been entertained but swifty rejected – Farewell Spit.

Construction of the handsome, concrete-slab winery in Jacksons Road, Rapaura, began in August 1985 under the direction of Australian-born Judd, a Roseworthy College graduate who elevated the standard of Selaks' wines between 1983 and 1985.

Judd, a lean, greying, quiet figure, today has responsibility for the day-to-day running of Cloudy Bay. Hohnen crosses the Tasman several times each year for crucial blending decisions, but 'the final decisions are Kevin's,' says Hohnen.

In 1990 Veuve Clicquot Ponsardin, the illustrious Champagne house, purchased a majority interest in Cape Mentelle – and thus Cloudy Bay. David Hohnen has retained a 20 per cent shareholding. In Judd's eyes, the link with Veuve Clicquot has brought two key benefits: 'Financial stability and greater access to overseas markets.' Cloudy Bay wines are now exported to about 25 countries, principally Australia and the UK.

On flat, stony, well-drained land (once described as a place 'where a rabbit wouldn't survive without a cut lunch') surrounding the winery, the 60-hectare Cloudy Bay vineyard is planted in Sauvignon Blanc, Chardonnay and Sémillon, with small plots of Pinot Blanc, Merlot and Malbec. Six growers on long-term contracts, supported by Cloudy Bay's full-time viticulturist, Ivan Sutherland – himself a grower – supply much of the winery's annual grape intake. Two 50-hectare blocks in the Brancott Valley and at Renwick, purchased by Veuve Clicquot prior to its acquisition of Cloudy Bay, will also be planted over the next decade.

Why was the first 1985 Sauvignon Blanc (based on grapes bought from Corbans and made by Judd at Corbans' Gisborne winery) such a roaring worldwide success? 'It all came together,' says Judd. 'We had a simple name, attractive label and a distribution system in place in Australia. The flavour obviously had wide appeal. When I was at Selaks I used to say: "I shouldn't be here making this. I should be in Australia selling it – they'll freak when they see it".'

How does Cloudy Bay Sauvignon Blanc – so arresting in its youth – perform in the cellar?

A vertical tasting two years ago of every vintage from 1985 to 1994 proved beyond all doubt that the wine doesn't go from strength to strength in the bottle. But nor does it run out of steam. It lives for at least 10 years, softening, but staying lively and a joy to drink. Served blind, I'd have guessed the light yellow hued, attractively soft and rich-flavoured 1985 vintage was half its age.

Cloudy Bay's output of over 50,000 cases per year (planned to reach 100,000 cases by 2000) makes it a medium-sized winery by New Zealand standards. Chardonnay, Pinot Noir, Cabernet/Merlot and Pelorus, the bottle-fermented sparkling, are the four other key wines in the Cloudy Bay line-up.

A strapping, citrusy, mealy, taut wine, the Chardonnay is barrel-fermented and held on its yeast lees for a full year. A powerful style with great concentration and complexity, it ranks among New Zealand's foremost Chardonnays, with a proven ability to cellar well for up to a decade.

The Cabernet/Merlot is robust, spicy, complex and firm, but reveals a distinct touch of the leafy greenness characteristic of very cool-climate Cabernet-based reds. Its production level is not rising and the wine is sold largely in New Zealand.

Pinot Noir is a fast-rising star of the Cloudy Bay range. First released on a nationwide basis from the 1994 vintage, this is a weighty, rich-flavoured and complex wine, smoky, savoury and supple. Judd is confident Pinot Noir has a strong future in Marlborough, where it ripens the best part of a month before Cabernet Sauvignon.

Pelorus, a bottle-fermented sparkling of rare class, is produced under the guidance of Harold Osborne, a Californian sparkling wine specialist who is anxious to avoid 'undue fruitiness'. Blended from Pinot Noir and Chardonnay, the wine is made with minimal sulphur-dioxide, fermented at warm temperatures in a mix of stainless steel tanks and oak barrels, allowed to undergo a full malolactic fermentation, and matured on its yeast lees for three years. The outcome is an exceptionally power-packed wine with lush, intricate, toasty flavours, strong yeast autolysis and a rich, trailing finish.

The Cloudy Bay range also includes a trickle of oak-aged, steely, succulent, ravishingly perfumed and nectareous Late Harvest Riesling. In the future, a Gewürztraminer is a strong possibility, and Hohnen and Judd are already working on a barrel-fermented Sauvignon Blanc.

CLOUDY BAY SAUVIGNON BLANC

This is a striking wine overflowing with fresh, ripely herbaceous aromas and zingy, downright delicious flavour; one you can devour six months after it was a bunch of grapes on the vine.

Kevin Judd seeks to produce Sauvignon Blanc having 'a lively gooseberries and lychees – rather than green peas – fruit character and a touch of oak complexity.' Little has changed over the years in the way the grapes are handled in the winery. As David Hohnen puts it: 'Our Sauvignon Blanc winemaking is modern babysitting. It's very different to making a Chardonnay, where you're *inducing* things like malolactic fermentation and yeast autolysis. By contrast, Sauvignon Blanc is early release; it's very straightforward, do-it-by-numbers winemaking to retain fruit characters.'

Does the presence of Sémillon in the blend, and a touch of barrel fermentation, explain the Cloudy Bay style? Not according to Judd. 'The Sémillon has very little impact,' he stresses. 'It was as high as 15 per cent in the 1985, but zero in the 1990. The Sémillon content of the wine averages 5 to 10 per cent, but it has very similar aromas to Sauvignon.' About 10 per cent barrel fermentation gives the wine 'a subliminal dimension, something extra, but it's hard to taste oak in the wine'.

The irresistibly aromatic and zesty style of Cloudy Bay Sauvignon Blanc and its rapier-like flavours stem, Judd is convinced, from 'the fruit characters that are in the grapes when they arrive at the winery. It's our viticulture, rather than our vinification, that's evolved over the years. Scott-Henry trellising, leaf-plucking and irrigation management are now giving us much riper flavours in the cooler years.'

Judd drinks his exceptional Sauvignon Blanc as an aperitif or with salads or seafood. And when is the best time to pull the cork? 'I like it when it's brand new – around Christmas when it opens up with all its exuberance and fruitiness. You get it at the maximum at that age. But at about six years old, when the lifted fruit has gone, it's easier to match with food.'

Craig Gass has a plan and he's sticking to it. 'I know the styles I want to make – white wines from fully ripe Marlborough grapes. I won't compromise. If the grape quality isn't good enough, I don't make the wine.'

Gass is a disarmingly ebullient personality who describes himself as 'looking like a cross between Fred Dagg and a front-row forward for the Auckland Blues.'

After owning the Korepo (now Ruby Bay) winery in Nelson from 1976 to 1989, he worked for a year at James Halliday's Coldstream Hills winery in the Yarra Valley, Victoria.

'That's where I gained a liking for *ripe* fruit characters, which enable you to do all sorts of extra things to the wine without destroying its fruit flavours. I saw all the grand Aussie reds, decided to focus on white wines, and came back to Marlborough to do it.'

Craig and his wife, Jane, still live in Nelson, but that region's typically wetter autumn persuaded the Gasses to base their new winemaking venture over the hills in Marlborough.

Conders Bend owns no vineyards and no winery. When Gass worked at Vintech (now Rapaura Vintners) from 1991 to 1993, he 'saw all the fruit coming in from different vineyards. I consciously went out and pursued the top growers.' Today he buys grapes from five vineyards spread around the Wairau Valley.

Since the first 1991 vintage, the stream of Conders Bend wines has risen to 4500 cases and is expected to reach over 8000 cases by 1999.

The Sauvignon Blanc is consistently mouth-filling and lush, with rich (and yes, well-ripened) tropical-fruit flavours.

The Riesling is fresh, vigorous and flavour-packed. The barrel-fermented, strongly 'malo'-influenced Chardonnay is a robust, deep-flavoured, citrusy, buttery-soft, forward style.

These are delicious wines, and a 1995 vintage Blanc de Blancs bottle-fermented sparkling, based on hand-picked Chardonnay, is also in the pipeline.

Conders Bend Wines and Estates

Owners: Craig and Jane Gass

Key Wines: Sauvignon Blanc, Chardonnay, Riesling, Blanc de Blancs

Craig Gass gathered his initial winemaking experience in Nelson, but is now producing a stream of high class Marlborough white wines.

Dr John Forrest makes highly scented, lush, pure and penetrating white wines with racy acidity. 'Ripe fruit and big acid defines my style,' says Forrest. 'They're full-on wines – reflecting my personality.'

The Forrest family has deep roots in Marlborough; John Forrest's great-great-grandfather arrived during the first wave of European settlement in the 1840s. Born in Marlborough, Forrest gained his doctorate from Otago University. After resigning from his job as a DSIR biochemist, he gained his early winemaking experience by working as a cellarhand at Corbans Marlborough Winery in 1989 and Grove Mill in 1990. His first wine, a 1990 Cabernet Rosé, enjoyed instant success when it won the trophy for the champion rosé at that year's Air New Zealand Wine Awards.

Forrest is revelling in his new career. 'It's much better than being an under-funded, frustrated Government scientist. Winemaking suits my personality because it combines science and art. My scientific training tempers me a bit, but I can express my affable, arty side much better now than when I was a scientist.'

From the Forrest winery, visitors enjoy a stunning view over vine-swept plains to the Richmond Range on the valley's northern flanks. Sémillon, Sauvignon Blanc, Chardonnay, Merlot, Cabernet Franc and Cabernet Sauvignon are the principal varieties in the 16-hectare estate vineyard, where the first vines were planted in 1989. From a half-hectare of vines planted in 1995, Forrest plans to produce an off-dry Chenin Blanc with 'very high acid and a bit of *Botrytis* that will be a very long-keeper; and maybe a "sticky".' About 20 per cent of his annual fruit intake is purchased from local growers.

In a rare reversal of the usual trend of northern investment in the south, John Forrest is also part-owner of the Cornerstone Vineyard in Hawke's Bay. Bob Newton, an Australian viticulturist, and Forrest have planted 16 hectares of Cabernet Sauvignon, Merlot, Malbec, Cabernet Franc and Pinot Noir on the corner of Gimblett Road and State Highway 50. Some of the grapes are sold, and the early Cornerstone Vineyard wines have been produced at local Hawke's Bay wineries. The first 1994 Cornerstone Vineyard Cabernet/Merlot is a very attractive red, spicy, plummy and enticingly fragrant.

Forrest Estate's initial vintages were made elsewhere, while the Forrests expanded the original garage on their property into a house, wine store and little wine bar with armchairs 'where people sit for hours and become friends'. However, Forrest's own, full-processing winery was erected prior to the 1996 vintage. About 4000 cases of Marlborough wines are produced each year.

The Chardonnay is a non-oaked, crisp style with fresh, delicious fruit flavours – green-appley in a cool year, more tropical in

Forrest Estate

Blicks Road, Renwick

Owners: Dr John and Brigid Forrest

Key Wines: Forrest Estate Chardonnay, Sauvignon Blanc, Reserve Fumé Blanc, Riesling, Cabernet Rosé, Gibson's Creek; Cornerstone Vineyard Cabernet/Merlot

warmer vintages. Forrest doesn't use wood because he wants 'to step away from what every other winery in New Zealand and Australia does. I first got interested in wine while working as a molecular biologist in California. There were a lot of unoaked Chardonnays there, made with extended lees [yeast] contact, and I really liked the style. I give my Chardonnay extended lees contact – up to six months – but you must have very ripe fruit for it to stand alone without oak.'

Forrest's early Sémillons were grassy and bracingly crisp, but the Sémillon-predominant, French and American oak-fermented Reserve Fumé Blanc is a more subtle and complex style. A 'less overtly fruity' Australian clone, wood handling and a full, softening malolactic fermentation have all toned down the herbaceousness of this weighty, rich-flavoured wine.

The Sauvignon Blanc is emerging as one of Marlborough's finest, with a lovely outpouring of fresh, ripe fruit aromas and lush, mouth-wateringly crisp, lemon/capsicum flavours. The Riesling is equally distinguished – a lovely harmony of searching, citrusy flavours, crisp, engaging acidity and a distinct touch of sweetness.

Gibson's Creek, the American oak-aged, medium-priced label blended from Cabernet Sauvignon, Merlot and Cabernet Franc, is unexpectedly dark, rich and minty. The Cabernet Rosé is charmingly fragrant and lively; a salmon-pink, cherryish, raspberryish, garden-fresh delight.

Dr John Forrest produces one of Marlborough's finest Sauvignon Blancs and Rieslings and a delicious non-oaked Chardonnay.

Georg and Ruth Fromm didn't migrate from Switzerland to Marlborough to produce yet another herbaceous, zingy Sauvignon Blanc. 'Our winery is specialising in reds,' says Georg. 'Everybody makes white wines here. We thought: if Chardonnay and Sauvignon Blanc thrive in Marlborough, so should reds.'

The Fromm winery lies on the corner of Godfrey and Middle Renwick Roads, between Woodbourne and Renwick. The Fromms planted their first vines here in 1992, in the same year they produced their first wines from bought-in grapes. Hatsch Kalberer, a tall, gentle Swiss winemaker who previously worked nine vintages at Matawhero, has also been deeply involved from the start.

Georg (commonly called 'George' in New Zealand), whose family has made wine in Switzerland for four generations, still owns a 3.5-hectare vineyard in Switzerland, planted predominantly in Pinot Noir. 'After my grand-uncle emigrated to New Zealand, we visited in 1991, met Hatsch at Matawhero, and joked that we couldn't go back to Switzerland because of the Gulf War. When we went home, we felt homesick for New Zealand.'

The 4.5-hectare estate vineyard is planted on slightly richer land than at Rapaura, with layers of top soil over clay and free-draining shingle. Only red-wine grapes are planted – Pinot Noir, Merlot, Syrah, Malbec, Cabernet Franc, Cabernet Sauvignon and Sangiovese. The vineyard has been close-planted, with more than double the average vine density in New Zealand. Fruit is also drawn from local growers.

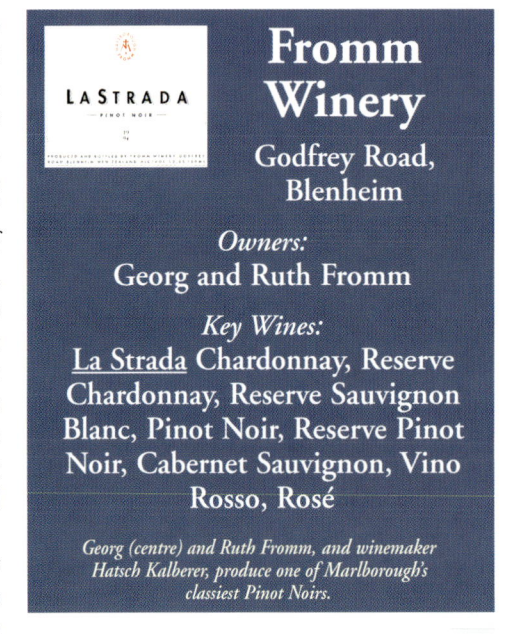

Fromm Winery

Godfrey Road, Blenheim

Owners:
Georg and Ruth Fromm

Key Wines:
La Strada Chardonnay, Reserve Chardonnay, Reserve Sauvignon Blanc, Pinot Noir, Reserve Pinot Noir, Cabernet Sauvignon, Vino Rosso, Rosé

Georg (centre) and Ruth Fromm, and winemaker Hatsch Kalberer, produce one of Marlborough's classiest Pinot Noirs.

'Holistic' is a common word in the Fromms' vocabulary. What does it mean? For the vine, says Ruth, 'it's the difference between machines coming through and knocking you around, and people handling you with care.' Manual shoot-thinning, leaf-plucking, bunch-thinning and harvesting are all standard practice.

Fromm's annual output of around 4000 cases is expected to double by 1998. A third to a half of the production is earmarked for export to Switzerland, where Georg believes his Pinot Noir 'will compete well with Burgundy'.

The majority of the wines are blended from different vineyards and sold under the brand name La Strada ('The Road'). Single-vineyard wines are also marketed under a designated vineyard label.

Georg Fromm expects Pinot Noir and a Merlot-based blend to be among the winery's specialties. 'Pinot Noir was my favourite grape in Switzerland, but it has much higher potential here.' The La Strada Pinot Noir is very generous, warm and supple, and the La Strada Reserve Pinot Noir is notably dark, mouth-filling, richly fruity and spicy – full of character and sweet-fruit delights.

La Strada Cabernet Sauvignon offers plenty of crisp, berryish flavour. The lower-priced La Strada Vino Rosso is fragrant, fresh, fruity and flavourful, offering greater satisfaction than most Marlborough reds.

The non-wooded Fromm La Strada Chardonnay is weighty, ripe-tasting and well-rounded. Barrel-fermented, La Strada Reserve Chardonnay is a savoury, nutty, complex style with a creamy texture and notable depth.

In the small town of Blenheim, Terry and Toni Gillan at first made their mark with extensive property investments and Toni's columns in the *Marlborough Express*. Their splash-making prowess was well demonstrated again in 1994, when their first release under the Gillan Estate label won the trophy for champion Sauvignon Blanc at that year's Air New Zealand Wine Awards.

A West Coaster, at the age of 23 Toni went on a working holiday to England, renting a bedsitter in north London. Her landlord was Terry. Raised in London, Terry at first pursued a career in the film industry, then spent many years buying, renovating and selling London houses and flats, until in 1987 the Gillans' desire for an improved lifestyle attracted them to Marlborough.

The Gillans entered the wine industry as the largest (but not majority) shareholders in Grove Mill. When their bid to buy a controlling stake was rebuffed by the other partners, the Gillans withdrew from Grove Mill and eventually set up their new company with Hamish and Anne Young.

'It's a pooling of talents,' says Toni. 'Hamish is the grapegrower, Terry is the manager and I'm the marketer.' Hamish Young, a former president of the Marlborough Grape Growers' Association, and his wife, Anne, are equal shareholders with the Gillans in a company, Gillan and Young, which purchases the Youngs' grapes and owns the Gillan Estate wines.

The Youngs' Eastfields vineyard was planted in 1980. Today, nine hectares of Sauvignon Blanc and Chardonnay are established in relatively fertile silt loams.

The new Gillan Estate winery lies in Rapaura Road, between Corbans and Merlen. The Mediterranean-styled winery is used primarily for storage of the sparkling wine during its lengthy maturation on yeast lees; most of the processing is done away from the site. Winemaker Sam Weaver, a former English wine merchant who came to New Zealand in 1990, spent three years as assistant winemaker at Hunter's.

The Sauvignon Blanc is full and forthcoming in a delightfully fragrant, lingering style. The Chardonnay, a fruit-uppermost style with restrained oak handling, is citrusy and slightly buttery. The plummy, slightly leafy Merlot is less impressive, but the Brut Reserve is appealingly vigorous, delicately flavoured and creamy.

Gillan Estate Wines

Rapaura Road, Renwick

Owner:
Gillan and Young Company Limited

Key Wines:
Eastfields Sauvignon Blanc, Eastfields Chardonnay, Merlot, Brut Reserve

The entrepreneurial Terry and Toni Gillan (left), and grapegrowers Hamish and Anne Young, enjoyed instant show success with their debut Sauvignon Blanc.

Grove Mill's first decade hasn't been easy, with key shareholders coming and going, a winery transplant and constant expansion. A crucial force from the start, however, has been winemaker David Pearce, who has crafted an array of immaculate Sauvignon Blancs, Rieslings, Gewürztraminers and Chardonnays.

Pearce oozes confidence. Christchurch-born, as a child he helped his father make cider for home consumption, and by the time he left school he had decided to be a winemaker. Corbans hired him in 1978 at Henderson as a cellarhand and laboratory technician; then he did a food technology degree at Massey University. After graduating, he returned to the Corbans fold, working his way up at the giant Gisborne winery from trainee to assistant winemaker to the top post – winemaker. In 1988, excited by the potential of Marlborough and the opportunity to 'build everything from scratch', he came south to join the fledgling Grove Mill.

Grove Mill was originally funded by 23 shareholders, including Terry and Toni Gillan, who have since withdrawn. Today the over 30 shareholders – almost all local – include Pearce and the majority of the company's grapegrowers.

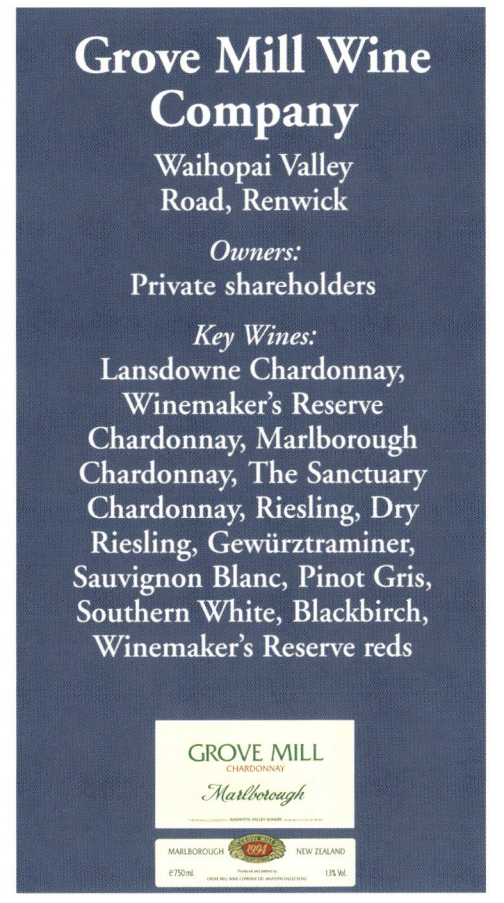

The winery was at first sited in Blenheim in a brick-walled remnant of the 138-year-old, former Wairau Brewery. This small, richly atmospheric building, however, could only accommodate a production of about 10,000 cases. Rising output forced a shift in 1994 to a new, larger winery at the Waihopai Valley turnoff from State Highway 63, near the township of Renwick.

Grove Mill's own vineyards, surrounding the winery, are planted in wind-blown loess and stones deposited by the Waihopai River. The first 17 hectares of Chardonnay and Sauvignon Blanc are to be supplemented by other varieties, including Gewürztraminer, Pinot Gris and Pinot Noir. Growers scattered around the Wairau Valley ('for the very good reason of risk management against frost,' says Pearce) supply the majority of the fruit intake.

The two-storeyed, cream and red winery produces 30,000 cases of wine each year, which is planned to peak at 45,000 cases. Grove Mill wines are currently exported to the UK and USA, Australia, Hong Kong and the Netherlands.

Chardonnay, Sauvignon Blanc and

Grove Mill Wine Company

Waihopai Valley Road, Renwick

Owners:
Private shareholders

Key Wines:
Lansdowne Chardonnay, Winemaker's Reserve Chardonnay, Marlborough Chardonnay, The Sanctuary Chardonnay, Riesling, Dry Riesling, Gewürztraminer, Sauvignon Blanc, Pinot Gris, Southern White, Blackbirch, Winemaker's Reserve reds

Riesling are the three principal strings to Grove Mill's bow. Lansdowne Chardonnay, the company's white wine flagship – named after Blenheim's main rugby ground – is a fatter, richer wine than its lower-priced Marlborough Chardonnay stablemate, with greater barrel-ferment complexity. Yet the Marlborough Chardonnay is a fine wine in its own right – savoury and lemony, with a deft touch of oak and invigorating acidity. The Winemaker's Reserve Chardonnay, based partly or wholly on Gisborne fruit, is a deliciously bold, savoury, rich, mealy style. The Sanctuary Chardonnay, by contrast, places its accent squarely on fresh, uncluttered, crisp, appley fruit flavours.

Grove Mill Sauvignon Blanc is a classic Marlborough style, fresh and frisky with incisive gooseberry/capsicum aromas and flavours. Two Rieslings are produced – a crisp, appley Dry Riesling and a perfumed, rich-flavoured medium style, labelled simply as Riesling. David Pearce's Rieslings are consistently delightful – tangy and light, with a ravishing fragrance and delicacy.

The line-up of Grove Mill wines also includes a satisfyingly well-spiced Gewürztraminer; a soft, peachy, slightly sweet Pinot Gris; a dark, chunky, Cabernet-based Blackbirch red notable more for weight than fragrance or finesse; and Southern White, a light, fresh, medium, middle-of-the-road marriage of Riesling and Müller-Thurgau.

David Pearce fashions impressive Sauvignon Blancs, Rieslings and Chardonnays, but is also exploring Marlborough's potential for less fashionable varieties like Gewürztraminer and Pinot Gris.

When the fledgling Highfield winery changed hands in 1991, its new owners wanted to mark 'the birth of a new tradition'. They did it in style. Highfield's dramatic, 14-metre high observation tower, modelled on a 16th-century Tuscan tower, is visible from all over the plains.

The concrete winery sits on a knoll overlooking the Omaka Valley, on the south side of the Wairau. It was founded in 1989 by Bill Walsh – a grapegrower since the mid 1970s – and his sons Philip and Gerald. The early wines were not well-respected and in 1991 Highfield slid into receivership.

The major shareholder in the new company is Shin Yokoi, the Osaka-based managing director of Yokoi Manufacturing, which makes fire-fighting apparatus. Shin Yokoi also holds the Japanese agency for Drappier Champagne.

Tony Hooper, a lanky South Australian who is a graduate of Roseworthy College, and was previously winemaker at Yarra Burn in Victoria and Esk Valley in Hawke's Bay, processed his first Highfield vintage in 1991.

The 1.5-hectare estate vineyard is planted in Chardonnay, Sauvignon Blanc and Merlot. Highfield also owns a 10-hectare vineyard in the middle of the Wairau Valley, recently re-planted in Sauvignon Blanc and Chardonnay, and purchases fruit from local growers.

The Sauvignon Blanc exhibits the incisive melon/capsicum flavours typical of Marlborough in a very fresh, aromatic and springy style. The off-dry Riesling is equally buoyant and zingy, with strong lemon/lime flavours. The French oak-fermented Chardonnay is robust, with good depth of citrusy, mealy, nutty, buttery-soft flavour.

Highfield's first bottle-fermented sparkling, from the 1993 vintage, is a 50/50 blend of Chardonnay and Pinot Noir. Partly barrel-fermented, and lees-aged for three years, it is being released in late 1996 as part of a new, premium range featuring a wood-aged Sauvignon Blanc, Chardonnay and Merlot/Cabernet Sauvignon.

A delectably perfumed and honeyish Müller-Thurgau, labelled Noble Late Harvest 1990, earned Highfield's first gold medal at the 1991 Air New Zealand Wine Awards, and has been followed by an equally gorgeous, golden, headily perfumed and treacly 1994 vintage, based on Riesling.

Highfield Estate
Brookby Road, Blenheim

Owners:
Shin Yokoi, Tom Tenuwera and Neil Buchanan

Key Wines:
Limited Edition Chardonnay, Sauvignon Blanc, Merlot/Cabernet Sauvignon, Méthode Traditionnelle; Chardonnay, Sauvignon Blanc, Riesling, Estate White, Noble Late Harvest, Merlot

'By 1998,' says winemaker Tony Hooper, 'we hope to be selling more wine offshore than in New Zealand.'

What thoughts does the name 'Hunter's' conjure up in your mind? I think instantly of Jane Hunter, the famous owner – and a Sauvignon Blanc as aromatic, explosively flavoured and zesty as you can get.

Ernie Hunter, his spectacular career tragically cut short at the age of only 38, at the time of his June 1987 death in a motor accident had started to savour worldwide applause for the Marlborough wines he toiled so tenaciously to promote.

An ebullient Ulsterman, Hunter joined the retail liquor trade in Christchurch, started a hotel wine club, then bought 25 hectares of land at Blenheim to grow grapes for Penfolds. After meeting Almuth Lorenz – a young German winemaker here on a working holiday – at a New Year's Eve party in 1981, at her suggestion he elected to move into commercial winemaking.

With Lorenz as winemaker the first, 1982 vintage of Hunter's wines was made under primitive conditions using borrowed gear at an old Christchurch cider factory. Observers were soon startled when, after entering six wines in that year's National Wine Competition, the fledgling company emerged with six medals. The promise in that performance was not fulfilled, however, in the 1983 vintage wines.

Suffering severe financial and marketing problems in 1984, Hunter turned his formidable energy to export – and successfully shipped thousands of cases of wine to the UK, USA and Australia. In his widow Jane's words: 'Ernie didn't just sell Hunter's wines. When he was in New Zealand he always talked about Marlborough wines and when he was overseas he talked about New Zealand wines.' His most publicised successes came at the 1986 and 1987 Sunday Times Wine Club Festivals in London when the public voted his 1985 Fumé Blanc and 1986 Chardonnay as the most popular wines of the shows.

After Ernie Hunter's premature death, Jane stepped in as managing director. Born in 1954 into a South Australian grapegrowing family, she graduated in agricultural science from Adelaide University, majoring in viticulture and plant pathology, and came to Marlborough in 1983 to take up the job of Montana's chief viticulturist.

The charismatic Ernie Hunter had established Hunter's as a 'person' winery, a tradition Jane at first had to work hard to uphold. 'I used to find it difficult, being so much quieter than Ernie,' she recalls, 'but

Hunter's Wines

Rapaura Road, Blenheim

Owner:
Jane Hunter

Key Wines:
Sauvignon Blanc, Sauvignon Blanc Oak Aged, Chardonnay, Riesling, Gewürztraminer, Spring Creek Vineyard Sauvignon Blanc/Chardonnay, Pinot Noir, Cabernet/Merlot, Brut

From one vintage to the next, Jane Hunter and winemaker Gary Duke produce one of the most arresting Marlborough Sauvignon Blancs, coupling exceptional intensity of varietal character with a hard-to-resist freshness and vigour.

travelling overseas has helped a lot. If we're involved in a dinner or a talk to a wine club, it has to be done by me, or [winemaker] Gary Duke and me. We've built Hunter's around the name – and I'm the only one with the name.'

'Very organised' is how Duke describes his boss. 'She gets hold of an idea and really goes for it hard, paying very good attention to detail, from A to Z. And she works hard to keep a quality image.'

Gary Duke is a tall, quiet Australian who worked at the Tisdall and Hanging Rock wineries in Victoria before joining Hunter's in 1991. 'It was a chance to do something different,' says Duke. 'New Zealand wines are going places. Australians can only dream of the intensity of fruit and natural acidity in Marlborough.' Dr Tony Jordan, an eminent Australian oenologist, has been a consultant since the 1986 vintage.

Fruit is drawn from the 18-hectare estate vineyard: Chardonnay, Sauvignon Blanc, Gewürztraminer, Pinot Noir and Cabernet Sauvignon in silty loams overlying riverstones; some is supplied from contract vineyards spread around the Wairau and Awatere valleys.

Deep-scented, elegant white wines of sustained flavour are Hunter's strength. The Sauvignon Blanc Oak Aged, of which only a minority of the final blend is handled in casks, abounds with rich, vibrant Sauvignon Blanc fruit, crisp and fresh, barely toned down by the background hints of wood. Duke sees it as 'a winemaker's wine, riper and less herbaceous' than the equally outstanding, non-oaked Sauvignon Blanc, which is awash with lush, ripe gooseberry and herbal flavours and appetising acidity *(see panel)*.

The Chardonnay is extremely classy, displaying great finesse and delicacy. 'We want obvious fruit,' says Duke, who ferments the wine in a mix of new and older oak casks; a small percentage also undergoes a softening malolactic fermentation. Full, with intense, citrusy, slightly mealy flavours braced by fresh, lively acidity, it performs strongly in the cellar, peaking at about five years old.

Hunter's Gewürztraminer is citrusy, spicy, flavoursome and tangy, with a sliver of sweetness. The off-dry Riesling is fragrant, with good depth of fresh, lemon/lime flavours. However, neither wine quite scales the heights of the Sauvignon Blanc and Chardonnay.

Hunter's best-kept secret is its rare but stylish bottle-fermented sparkling, labelled Hunter's Brut. Made from equal proportions of Chardonnay and Pinot Noir, with a small amount of Meunier 'to fill out the middle palate', it emerges from its two and a half years' aging on yeast lees with intense, invigorating, lemony, yeasty flavours.

In 1993, a year after her 1991 Sauvignon Blanc won the Marquis de Goulaine Trophy for the champion Sauvignon Blanc at the International Wine and Spirit Competition in London, Jane Hunter was awarded the OBE. For the best-known woman in the New Zealand wine industry, things are going well.

Hunter's Sauvignon Blanc

The two great classics of Marlborough Sauvignon Blanc – wines which scale the heights in every vintage and have done for over a decade – are Cloudy Bay and Hunter's.

Unlike Cloudy Bay, the Hunter's wine has no Sémillon, no barrel-fermentation, no oak aging. 'We make our wine to drink young,' says Gary Duke. 'We're after lifted fruit characters and a powerful, round, long palate.'

Jane Hunter sees blending as a crucial ingredient in Hunter's' Sauvignon Blanc recipe. 'We blend fruit from vineyards scattered all around the valley. We get a real mix – some of the grapes are grassy, others give ripe tropical-fruit characters. The trick is the final percentage of each.'

Top Sauvignon Blanc needs a lot of effort in the vineyard; the vines grow luxuriantly ('like weeds') and must be tamed. 'Pluck a ripe, golden, speckled Sauvignon Blanc grape from an exposed bunch of grapes and the flavours tend to be tropical-fruit and passionfruit,' says Duke. 'Now turn the bunch over and taste a green grape from the shaded underside of the bunch. The flavours will probably be far more herbaceous and green. We try to maximise the ripe fruit flavours by trimming excess foliage from the vine and by plucking leaves to expose grape bunches and allow better light penetration into the canopy.'

Deciding when to harvest is vital. 'We're out most days during the vintage, Gary and I,' says Jane. 'We eat Sauvignon Blanc grapes, talk about their flavours – and walk miles.'

Hunter's Sauvignon Blanc breaks into its full stride at only a year old. 'The grassier wines of the past took more time, but today's wines, made from riper fruit, mature more quickly,' says Jane. 'Drink it quickly, at 12 to 18 months.'

The word 'edge' crops up repeatedly in winemaker Warwick Stichbury's conversation. 'We're always looking for new ideas. My brother, John, has receiving equipment keyed into American satellites for long-range weather forecasts. That sort of thing gives us an edge.'

Jackson Estate, the Stichburys' label, has carved out an exceptional reputation. With its arresting intensity of ripe, tropical/herbal flavour, the debut Jackson Estate Sauvignon Blanc 1991 won thousands of fans. Jackson Estate now rivals the likes of Hunter's, Vavasour Reserve and Cloudy Bay at the top of the Marlborough Sauvignon Blanc tree.

Soaps and toiletries, cigarettes and sweets were Wellington-based Warwick Stichbury's major business interests before he plunged into wine: 'I sold my tobacco and confectionery interests in 1987 and was looking around for something else to do.' By 1988, Jackson Estate's first vines were planted at the family property in Jacksons Road.

At first, the Stichburys opted to grow grapes and sell them rather than make wine. 'Later, we realised that if there was a grape glut we had no security, so we decided to go the whole way.'

The 40-hectare vineyard is planted in Sauvignon Blanc, Chardonnay, Riesling and Pinot Noir, pruned for low yields and not irrigated. No grapes are purchased from other growers. The Stichburys do not own a winery. Martin Shaw, an Australian consultant, makes the wine at Rapaura Vintners, the local contract winery.

Jackson Estate Sauvignon Blanc is consistently fresh, fragrant and full, with a lovely surge of ripe, melon and capsicum-like flavour and a sustained, frisky finish. The Chardonnay is also impressive: deep-scented and fat, with intense citrusy fruit flavours fleshed out with toasty oak. The Reserve Chardonnay, strongly new oak-influenced and given a full, softening malolactic fermentation, is even finer, with intense grapefruit-like, mealy flavour and power right through the palate.

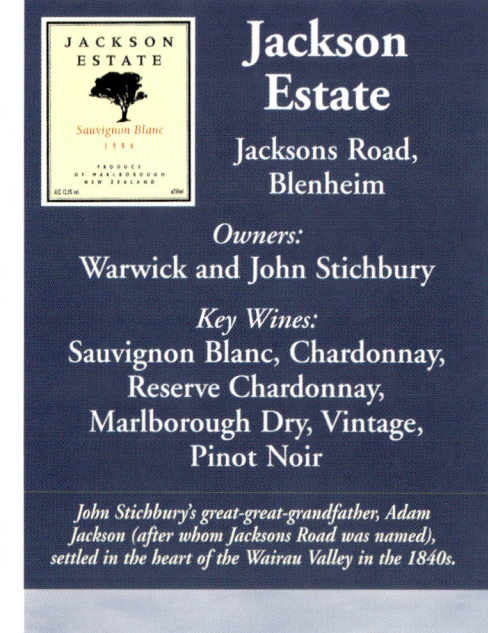

The Marlborough Dry (labelled as such to attract buyers normally reluctant to buy Riesling) is fleshy and firm, with an excellent depth of lush, citrusy, almost passionfruit-like flavour. Jackson Vintage, the bottle-fermented sparkling, blended from Chardonnay and Pinot Noir and lees-aged for three years, is crisp, delicate and vigorous, with intense, 'bready' yeast characters.

Jackson Estate

Jacksons Road, Blenheim

Owners:
Warwick and John Stichbury

Key Wines:
Sauvignon Blanc, Chardonnay, Reserve Chardonnay, Marlborough Dry, Vintage, Pinot Noir

John Stichbury's great-great-grandfather, Adam Jackson (after whom Jacksons Road was named), settled in the heart of the Wairau Valley in the 1840s.

A candle-lit tunnel hewn 45 metres into a Koromiko hillside, full of riddling racks stacked with sparkling wine and mouldy barrels of maturing brandy, makes tiny Johanneshof Cellars a memorable place to visit. 'We want to give people a taste of Europe,' say Warwick Foley and his wife, Edel Everling, who was born at Rudesheim, on the Rhine.

Johanneshof is just south of Koromiko, two-thirds of the way along the road from Blenheim to Picton. The name Johanneshof ('John's courtyard') honours Edel's father, who owned a vineyard in the Rheingau.

Warwick Foley grew up in Marlborough, worked vintages at several wineries, including Montana and the Te Kauwhata Viticultural Research Station, and then spent five years in the Rheingau and Baden, which included study at the famous Geisenheim Institute. Returning to New Zealand in 1990, he joined another Marlborough winery, where he is still on the full-time staff.

Edel, who has a Geisenheim degree in viticulture and oenology, came to New Zealand in 1983 to visit Dr Rainer Eschenbruch, director of the Te Kauwhata station, who had once boarded in Rudesheim with her parents. When she arrived at Te Kauwhata, she met Eschenbruch's own boarder – Warwick.

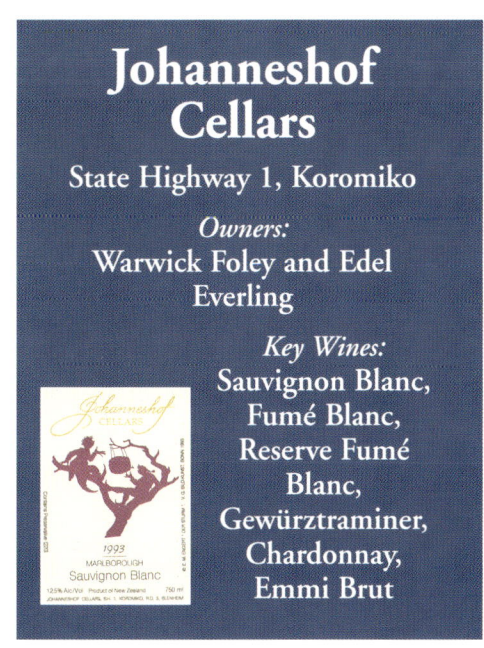

When was Johanneshof founded? 'It's a bit confusing,' says Foley. 'Our winery was built in 1993, but we made our first wine in 1991. We planted our first vines back in 1977, after I saw a photo of a steep German vineyard in one of Andre Simon's books and said to Dad: "Hey, why can't we do something like that?"'

After much trial and replanting, the tiny, sloping estate vineyard is planted in 21 short rows of Pinot Noir. 'We harvest about 10 days after the vineyards on the plains,' says Foley, 'and get a bit more rain, but the high iron content in the sandstone soils should give our wine better alcohol and fragrance.' Grapes are also bought from Marlborough growers.

The stone and concrete winery is intended to be 'typical of the Rheingau'. Johanneshof wines are rare, with an average annual output of only 1000 cases, planned to climb to 3000. Foley likes the German saying 'klein aber fein' ('small but fine').

The wines are sold principally from the cellar door and by mail-order. The Sauvignon Blanc, which displays good weight and strong passionfruit and herbal flavours, is partnered by cask-aged, rich-flavoured Fumé Blancs that mature well for several years.

The barrel-fermented Chardonnay is appley and steely, with a cool-climate feel. Emmi Brut, the bottle-fermented sparkling made from Pinot Noir and Chardonnay, is gutsy, toasty, full-flavoured and vigorous. These are distinctive and characterful wines.

Johanneshof Cellars

State Highway 1, Koromiko

Owners:
Warwick Foley and Edel Everling

Key Wines:
Sauvignon Blanc, Fumé Blanc, Reserve Fumé Blanc, Gewürztraminer, Chardonnay, Emmi Brut

---

Lake Chalice's site, past Merlen at the end of Vintage Lane, near Renwick, is as bony as the next-door quarry. 'You could run the irrigation system here 24 hours a day and it wouldn't flood the vines,' says part-owner Phil Binnie.

Poring over maps in search of a name, the company's owners didn't hesitate when they spied Lake Chalice, 40 kilometres away in the Richmond Range – a chalice is a goblet, or wine cup.

Founding partners, Chris Gambitsis and Ron Wichman, are Lower Hutt restaurateurs. 'Chris does the winemaking,' says Binnie. 'He's worked several vintages at local wineries, where our wines are produced. Ron handles the management side.'

After the vineyard was purchased in 1989 – already planted but badly run-down, having been abandoned several years earlier – the vines were uprooted and replaced with grafted plants. Binnie, who joined his long-time Wellington friends in 1991, is a former policeman who now manages the vineyard.

The nine-hectare home block, called Falcon Vineyard, is established in Sauvignon Blanc, Riesling, Chardonnay, Sémillon, Cabernet Franc, Cabernet Sauvignon and Merlot. 'It's so gravelly, we have problems getting the posts in,' says Binnie. 'But we don't have any vigour problems.' Grapes are also purchased from another Marlborough grower.

Since the first 1992 vintage, which yielded just 60 cases, Lake Chalice's output has climbed to 3000 cases and is heading for twice that. The Riesling and Sauvignon Blanc have oscillated in quality, but at their best are mouth-filling, vigorous and rich-flavoured.

The barrel-fermented Sémillon possesses lemony, moderately grassy flavours, enriched and rounded by the wood. My favourite is the Chardonnay, with its strapping body, lively acidity and spread of rich, ripe, grapefruit and fig-like flavours.

Lake Chalice Wines

Vintage Lane, Renwick

Owners:
Phil Binnie, Chris Gambitsis and Ron Wichman

Key Wines:
Sauvignon Blanc, Sémillon, Riesling, Chardonnay

Phil Binnie switched from the police force to the more peaceful occupation of tending Lake Chalice's vines.

High country musterer, champion shearer (300 sheep a day), trade union organiser, possum hunter, swimming pool builder, contract grapegrower . . . Ross Lawson has been around. With his partners in Lawson's Dry Hills, since 1992 he has produced some of Marlborough's most distinguished white wines.

Lawson's Dry Hills – named after the adjacent Wither Hills, whose low brown folds flank the Wairau Valley to the south – lies in Alabama Road, on the south-eastern outskirts of Blenheim. The winery is a partnership involving Ross Lawson and his wife, Barbara (who runs the cellar door operation), winemakers Mike and Claire Allan, and two grower shareholders.

The Lawsons planted their first vines in 1981. 'We had a few acres of land, which we planted for Penfolds,' recalls Ross. 'Before the vines hit the wire, Frank [Yukich, then owner of Penfolds] was in financial difficulties. We supplied grapes to several wineries; then I met Claire.'

Claire Allan, a Roseworthy College graduate, worked for more than two years at Corbans Marlborough Winery, and for three years 'on-and-off' at Vintech (now Rapaura Vintners). After joining Lawson's Dry Hills as a consultant in 1993, she 'gradually became full-time'. Mike, her husband, also a Roseworthy College graduate, worked for several years at Cloudy Bay, specialising in the production of the sparkling wine, Pelorus, before he also joined Lawson's Dry Hills.

The four-hectare estate vineyard, planted in moderately fertile, clay-based soils, is devoted exclusively to Gewürztraminer. Growers supply the majority of the grapes.

The wines are consistently rewarding, with good weight and rich, concentrated flavours. The bold, intensely varietal Gewürztraminer is one of the country's finest, with mouth-filling body and clear, deep flavours, ripe, citrusy and peppery. The dry Riesling is equally good – highly perfumed and incisively flavoured.

The Sauvignon Blanc is scented, lively and subtle, with a touch of complexity derived from blending with Sémillon and a small amount of barrel fermentation. The French oak-fermented, lees-aged Chardonnay is a powerful style with deliciously rich, savoury, citrusy, tight-structured flavour.

Lawson's Dry Hills
Alabama Road, Blenheim

Owners: Ross and Barbara Lawson, Mike and Claire Allan, and other shareholders

Key Wines: Gewürztraminer, Riesling, Chardonnay, Sauvignon Blanc

In the future, Ross Lawson's winery will add a bottle-fermented sparkling wine and a Pinot Noir to its consistently top-flight whites.

'Merlen Estate Winery Distillery Restaurant', says the sign on Rapaura Road, pointing down no-exit Vintage Lane. Here Almuth Lorenz, one of the great personalities of the Marlborough wine scene, produces fresh, vibrantly fruity white wines and fruit brandies distilled from Marlborough fruits – but no reds.

A tall, extroverted winemaker with a sunny face, Lorenz's conversation is liberally sprinkled with 'Ja's. Raised in the Rheinhessen, as a child she worked in her parents' vineyard and winery, and then studied the production of alcoholic beverages for four years at the Geisenheim Institute. After arriving in New Zealand in 1981, Lorenz built her early reputation as Hunter's winemaker between the 1982 and 1986 vintages.

Lorenz left Hunter's in 1986, and briefly marketed a handful of wines under her own Lorenz label. Jeremy Cooper – who is now her partner, oversees Merlen's marketing and lectures in management at Victoria University – then organised a group of investors to back Lorenz by funding the erection of the Merlen winery. Lorenz says the winery's name is 'derived from the ancient name for Marlborough in England. The area was originally called Merlborough from the legend that Merlin the magician practised his arts there.' After the first wine under the Merlen label, the superb (one is tempted to say spellbinding) 1987 Chardonnay was barrel-fermented in a rented refrigerated container, the small concrete-slab winery near Renwick opened in 1988.

Chardonnay, Gewürztraminer, Sauvignon Blanc, Sémillon and Morio-Muskat are the featured varieties in the sandy, shingly five-hectare estate vineyard. Grapes are also drawn from Marlborough growers.

Chardonnay is 'no headache' in the vineyard, soaring to very high sugar levels – up to 26 brix. This is a bold, fat, ripe-tasting wine, packed with strong stone-fruit flavours and lees-aging complexity.

For her beloved Riesling, Lorenz aims for 'the equivalent of a kabinett halbtrocken: light, with a touch of *Botrytis*, and closer in style to a Rheingau than Mosel.' It's a medium-dry style with lemony, appley flavours and and a freshly acidic finish.

The Sauvignon Blanc is limey and zingy in cooler vintages, and in warmer years impressively weighty, with lush, exotic fruit flavours. At its best, the off-dry Gewürztraminer is mouth-filling and packed with rich, gingery, peppery flavour. A perfumed and fruity, slightly sweet Morio-Muskat (designed, says Almuth, 'for average people looking for a 5 o'clock drink') and light, but flavourful and zesty, Müller-Thurgau flesh out the Merlen selection.

Lorenz has no plans to make reds. 'I tell my customers to go down the road if they want a red,' she says. 'It's not laziness, but wines should make themselves – like

Merlen Wines
Vintage Lane, Renwick

Owner: Merlen Wines Limited

Key Wines: Chardonnay, Riesling, Gewürztraminer, Sauvignon Blanc, Müller-Thurgau, Morio-Muskat

After 15 years in Marlborough, Almuth Lorenz preserves close links with Germany, where her parents still run their eight-hectare vineyard and 7000-case winery.

Riesling, Sauvignon Blanc and Chardonnay do here. In Marlborough, reds need a lot of work. I want to be here in 50 years, and the long-term plan of a region should be for totally appropriate styles.'

Under the Spirit of Marlborough label, Lorenz also distills a range of brandies from apricots, boysenberries, cherries, raspberries, strawberries, pears and other fruits.

Much of Merlen's annual output of about 7000 cases (which should climb to at least 10,000 cases by 2000) is sold by mail-order or at the winery, where light, German-style food is sold in the cosy 'weingarten'. 'Try our magic' invites the sign in the winery shop. Lorenz herself is often behind the vineyard counter: 'Our mail-order customers like to see me and I like talking about what I'm doing.'

Nautilus Estate

Blicks Road, Renwick

Owner: Negociants New Zealand

Key Wines:
<u>Nautilus</u> Marlborough Sauvignon Blanc, Marlborough Chardonnay, Estate Reserve Chardonnay, Marlborough Cabernet Sauvignon/Merlot/Cabernet Franc, Cuvée Marlborough; <u>Twin Islands</u> Sauvignon Blanc, Chardonnay, Merlot/Cabernet Sauvignon, Marlborough Brut; <u>Half Moon Bay</u> Sauvignon Blanc

---

A lot of Nautilus Cuvée Marlborough corks popped last year; even more than usual. Negociants New Zealand was celebrating its tenth birthday.

Since 17 July 1985, when the company was founded, it has grown to the point that it is now one of New Zealand's best-known wine distributors. Negociants New Zealand is a wholly owned subsidiary of the long-established, family-owned company, S. Smith & Son, whose head office is at the Yalumba winery in the Barossa Valley.

'We're in every part of the New Zealand wine industry – except retailing,' says Clive Weston, Negociants' managing director. Apart from distribution of the company's range of New Zealand and imported wines and wine accessories, Negociants are also importers and exporters of wine, vineyard owners – and winemakers of the Nautilus, Twin Island and Half Moon Bay brands.

The company's own New Zealand wines are produced jointly by Alan Hoey, a senior winemaker at Yalumba who visits New Zealand several times each year, and Auckland-based Allan McWilliams, whose winemaking experience includes spells at Château Pétrus in Pomerol, Amity Vineyard in Oregon and Goldwater Estate on Waiheke Island. The Nautilus and Twin Island wines are produced at Rapaura Vintners (formerly Vintech), in which Negociants has a 25 per cent stake.

The Nautilus brand was launched over a decade ago. While in Australia last year, Weston stumbled across a surviving bottle of Nautilus Hawke's Bay Sauvignon Blanc 1985 – a wine he hadn't realised existed. 'It was probably only ever sold in Australia.'

Today, the Nautilus range is sold in New Zealand and exported to the UK, USA, Canada, Australia, Holland, Fiji, Vanuatu and Hong Kong. The first Chardonnay and first Hawke's Bay Sauvignon Blanc sold in New Zealand were produced in 1989, and the first Cabernet Sauvignon/Merlot in 1990. The first sparkling wine base was laid down in 1991, and 1992 brought the first Marlborough Sauvignon Blanc.

Nautilus wines (apart from a small volume of Hawke's Bay Sauvignon Blanc) are entirely of Marlborough origin. Half Moon Bay wines are grown in Hawke's Bay, and the Twin Islands range of 'affordable, fruit-driven wines for everyday drinking' is blended from vineyards around the country. The annual production of the three ranges is currently around 35,000 cases.

The 11-hectare Nautilus Estate vineyard in Blicks Road, Renwick, purchased in 1992, is planted principally in Chardonnay and Pinot Noir, with a small amount of Sauvignon Blanc. Nautilus' sales outlet is sited here.

Competition success for Nautilus Marlborough Sauvignon Blanc has been dramatic. The 1994 vintage won gold at the Australia National Wine Show in Canberra; gold at Hobart; gold and selection in the Top 100 at the Sydney International Wine Competition; gold at the Air New Zealand Wine Awards; gold at the International Wine Challenge, London; gold and the Silverado Trophy for the champion Sauvignon Blanc at the International Wine and Spirit Competition, London – no other New Zealand Sauvignon Blanc has compiled such an illustrious competition record. From one vintage to the next, this is a striking wine with a voluminous fragrance, lush, incisive flavours and zingy acidity – Marlborough Sauvignon Blanc at its irresistible best.

The Nautilus range also includes a stylish Marlborough Chardonnay with strong grapefruit-like flavours and a slightly creamy texture, and a notably robust, concentrated, figgy, mealy, complex Estate Reserve Chardonnay. Nautilus Cuvée Marlborough, a non-vintage style blended from Pinot Noir (predominantly) and Chardonnay, and matured for 15 to 20 months on its yeast lees, is a fragrant, yeasty, delicately flavoured and smooth-flowing wine, hugely drinkable. The Cabernet Sauvignon/Merlot/Cabernet Franc is full, berryish and minty, with sweet-tasting American oak and a firm tannin grip.

The Twin Islands range includes a fresh, full-flavoured, bargain-priced Sauvignon Blanc; a gently oaked, drink young Chardonnay; a light, berryish Merlot/Cabernet Sauvignon; and a flavoursome, straightforward, non-vintage sparkling.

Half Moon Bay Sauvignon Blanc, grown in Hawke's Bay, is a full and lively wine with good depth of tropical-fruit flavours, clearly varietal and zesty.

Nautilus winemakers Allan McWilliams (pictured) and his Australian colleague, Alan Hoey, produce a superbly deep-scented and lush Sauvignon Blanc that is emerging as a Marlborough classic.

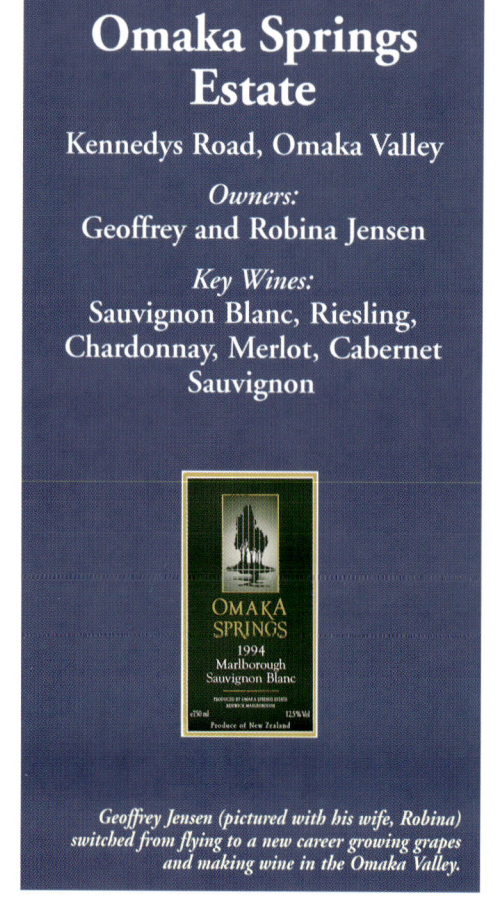

Geoffrey Jensen spent 33 years as a pilot, flying jet fighters off aircraft carriers for the Royal Navy and training other pilots as a senior captain for British Airways. After retiring from flying in 1993 to make wine, his first commercial release, Omaka Springs Sauvignon Blanc 1994, won a gold medal at the 1995 Liquorland Royal Easter Wine Show.

The Omaka Springs winery is in Kennedys Road in the Omaka Valley, south of Renwick. When Jensen, who was raised in Nelson, and his wife, Robina, purchased the property in 1992, they named it after its three spring-fed ponds.

The Jensens own about 40 hectares of vineyards in the heavy clay pans of Kennedys Road ('It's like porridge in winter and concrete in summer', says Jensen) and a kilometre away in lighter, gravelly, free-draining soils in Falveys Road. Some of the grapes are sold to other wine companies. The Jensens plan to sell part or all of their vineyards in Kennedys Road, together with the winery, and build a new winery in Falveys Road.

Omaka Springs is growing fast. The 1994 vintage yielded 600 cases; 1995 some 7000 cases; 1996 over 10,000 cases. 'We'll expand to about 15,000 cases,' predicts Jensen. 'We're already exporting to the UK, but we're not trying to be another Hunter's or Matua.'

Chris Young, a Roseworthy College graduate who has worked at Ata Rangi, Mildara Blass and Yarra Burn Vineyards, is the winemaker, with Tony Bish as a consultant. The top wines carry the Omaka Springs brand, with a second-tier range of wines for everyday-drinking labelled as Mill Creek.

Sauvignon Blanc, harbouring a splash of Sémillon and a sliver of sweetness, is the Omaka Springs flagship. At its best, this is a delightfully fresh and scented wine with ripe, penetrating flavours. The Merlot is chewy, with a touch of complexity and smooth, plummy, spicy flavours.

Omaka Springs Estate

Kennedys Road, Omaka Valley

Owners:
Geoffrey and Robina Jensen

Key Wines:
Sauvignon Blanc, Riesling, Chardonnay, Merlot, Cabernet Sauvignon

Geoffrey Jensen (pictured with his wife, Robina) switched from flying to a new career growing grapes and making wine in the Omaka Valley.

There's a lot going on at Ponder Estate. Michael Ponder's striking oils and watercolours, exhibited internationally, are displayed in a small gallery. From the olive grove, the largest in New Zealand, come olives and olive oil. The extensive vineyard supplies grapes for other companies, and Ponder Estate's own wine is impressive too.

What prompted Michael Ponder, a full-time artist for over 20 years, to make wine? 'As an artist, the only time you're making money is when you're painting,' he says. 'When you're away at exhibitions, you're not earning. Our idea was to have the grapes growing and making money while I'm overseas. And how could anyone live in Marlborough and not be involved in the most exciting thing that's ever hit the area?'

Michael Ponder's forebears settled in Pelorus Sound in the 1850s. Ponder and his wife, Diane, have owned a forestry block in Kenepuru Sound for many years, and in 1987 they purchased a block of bare land on the corner of New Renwick Road and Godfrey Road, at the mouth of the Brancott Valley. Here, six years after planting the first vines in their silty, gravelly soils, in 1994 the Ponders produced their first wine.

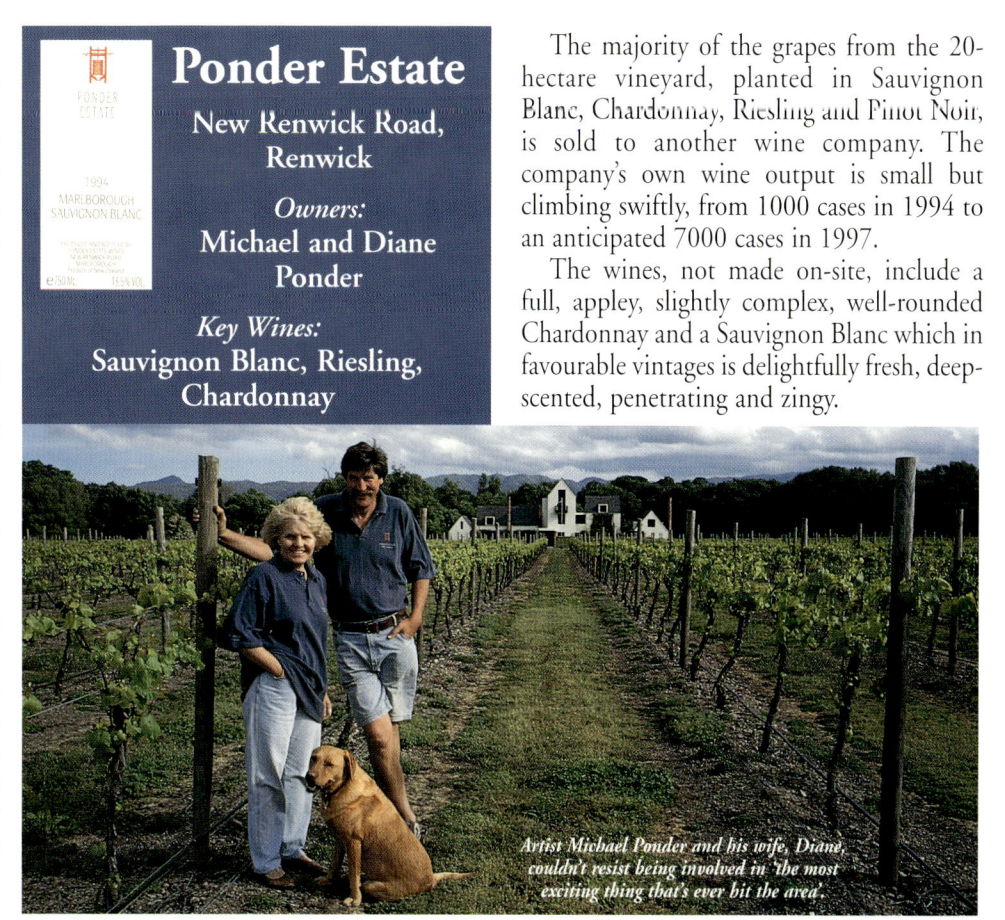

Ponder Estate

New Renwick Road, Renwick

Owners:
Michael and Diane Ponder

Key Wines:
Sauvignon Blanc, Riesling, Chardonnay

Artist Michael Ponder and his wife, Diane, couldn't resist being involved in 'the most exciting thing that's ever hit the area'.

The majority of the grapes from the 20-hectare vineyard, planted in Sauvignon Blanc, Chardonnay, Riesling and Pinot Noir, is sold to another wine company. The company's own wine output is small but climbing swiftly, from 1000 cases in 1994 to an anticipated 7000 cases in 1997.

The wines, not made on-site, include a full, appley, slightly complex, well-rounded Chardonnay and a Sauvignon Blanc which in favourable vintages is delightfully fresh, deep-scented, penetrating and zingy.

Experience counts. Neal Ibbotson, a viticultural consultant and owner of three vineyards, has been growing grapes in Marlborough since 1978. Even in a poor vintage like 1995, Saint Clair makes good wine.

Saint Clair ('not St Clair,' Ibbotson stresses) is on the outskirts of the suburb of Burleigh, at the Blenheim end of New Renwick Road. Last century the family of James Sinclair, the founder of Blenheim, settled here and over time the property's name has evolved from Sinclair to St Clair to Saint Clair.

Neal Ibbotson, born in Dunedin, came to Marlborough as a farm adviser with a Lincoln University diploma. After becoming a private consultant and farm valuer, he began to specialise in viticulture, and for 18 years has grown grapes for other wine companies.

Saint Clair is a partnership between Neal and Judy Ibbotson (the principal shareholders) and Charles and Sandy Wiffen, who have their own vineyard and are actively involved in the marketing of the wine. Their first vintage was 1994.

The Ibbotsons' three vineyards, totalling 38 hectares, are spread over three valleys – the Wairau, Omaka and Awatere – which enhances Saint Clair's blending options. Sauvignon Blanc, Chardonnay, Riesling and Pinot Noir are the key varieties. Ibbotson also share-farms the Wiffens' 13-hectare vineyard.

Saint Clair's output has soared from 4000 cases in 1994 to over 15,000 cases, not produced on-site. The Netherlands emerged as a major export market in 1995.

The Sauvignon Blanc is full, rich-flavoured and lush, with piercing aromas. The Chardonnay is a lively drink-young style with crisp, uncluttered fruit flavours. The Riesling is fragrant, full-flavoured, slightly sweet and zesty.

Saint Clair Estate Wines

New Renwick Road, Blenheim

Owners:
Neal and Judy Ibbotson, Charles and Sandy Wiffen

Key Wines:
Sauvignon Blanc, Riesling, Chardonnay

Neal and Judy Ibbotson's frisky, full-flavoured Sauvignon Blanc is stocked by the 620-store Albert Heijn supermarket chain in the Netherlands.

Don't search for Te Whare Ra wines at your local Liquorland. Allen Hogan only makes 3000 cases of wine each year, sold to his loyal mail-order customers at the tastings he hosts frequently up and down the country. 'I have quite a relationship – not just a customer relationship – with my buyers,' he says.

Bay of Plenty-born Hogan gathered his initial winemaking experience at a small Perth winery, then spent a couple of vintages with Montana at Marlborough and another vintage at the Te Kauwhata research station. He and his wife Joyce, who is also extensively involved in the winery, planted their first vines in Angelsea Street, Renwick in 1979.

Today the Hogans have six hectares of Gewürztraminer, Chardonnay, Riesling, Sémillon (recently replanted in a clone more suitable for botrytised sweet wines), Cabernet Sauvignon, Merlot and Cabernet Franc, planted in variable loam and gravel soils. Local growers supply 'a bit' of the annual fruit intake, including the Sauvignon Blanc.

The cask-matured Chardonnay is a blockbuster wine drunk by heroes: heady, with rich, savoury, peachy-ripe flavours laced with wood. Estate-grown, fully barrel-fermented and matured on its gross lees for a year, the Boots 'N All Chardonnay is chock-full of body and mealy, toasty, complex, slightly buttery flavour, vigorous and long.

Other dry to medium whites include a perfumed, pungently peppery, slightly honeyish Gewürztraminer, a powerful, slightly sweet, ripe-flavoured Riesling, and a robust, grassy, nutty Fumé Blanc, blended from Sauvignon Blanc and Sémillon.

Te Whare Ra Wines

Anglesea Street, Renwick

Owners:
Allen and Joyce Hogan

Key Wines:
Duke of Marlborough Chardonnay, Gewürztraminer, Riesling; Boots 'N All Chardonnay, Fumé Blanc, Botrytis Berry and Bunch Selection sweet whites, Rosé, QDR, Sarah Jennings Cabernet Sauvignon/Merlot/Cabernet Franc

Allen Hogan (rear) describes himself as a 'self-made, bootstraps winemaker' who is 'suspicious of received book wisdom of winemaking techniques'.

Hogan has long crusaded on behalf of Marlborough's Cabernet-based reds, and his Sarah Jennings Cabernet Sauvignon/Merlot/Cabernet Franc (named after the Duke of Marlborough's wife) is more satisfying than most, with berryish/minty aromas and a delicious surge of blackcurrant and red berry-fruit flavours, fresh, vibrant and supple. QDR (Quaffing Dry Red) is a lighter, less-ripe style.

The jewels in the Te Whare Ra crown are the stunning botrytised whites. The Botrytis Bunch Selection Riesling, made from grapes with less than 60 per cent *Botrytis* infection, is 'approximately equal in grape sweetness to a German beerenauslese,' says Hogan. This is a poised, honeyish, delectably botrytised wine, brimming with residual sugar, yet displaying a lovely alcohol/sweetness/acid balance. Even more stunning is the Botrytis Berry Selection Riesling, made not from individual berry pickings, but heavily raisined bunches with 60 to 90 per cent *Botrytis* infection. Harbouring up to 240 grams per litre of residual sugar (equivalent to a German trockenbeerenauslese), intensely botrytised and nectareous, this wine ranks among the most opulent of this country's sweet white wines.

Under Vavasour's Reserve label, Glenn Thomas makes one of Marlborough's most outstanding Sauvignon Blancs and Chardonnays.

Vavasour Wines

Redwood Pass Road, Dashwood

Owner:
Vavasour Wines Limited and Company

Key Wines:
Vavasour Reserve Sauvignon Blanc, Reserve Chardonnay, Reserve Cabernet Sauvignon, Reserve Pinot Noir; Dashwood Sauvignon Blanc, Chardonnay, Cabernet/Merlot, Pinot Noir; Stafford Brook Chardonnay, Cabernet/Merlot

For several years, Vavasour's Sauvignon Blancs and Chardonnays were highly praised but hard to find – the winery was geared to produce only 7000 cases each year. Now, with its annual output planned to rise to 40,000 cases, Vavasour has embarked on a period of dramatic growth.

Vavasour is worth noting for three reasons: its pioneering of winemaking in the Awatere Valley; the outstanding quality of its wines; and finally its glorious site on terraces bordering the Awatere River.

Peter Vavasour is an entrepreneurial Awatere Valley farmer who owns 'The Favourite', part of the Ugbrooke Estate purchased by the Vavasour family in the 1890s. (One of his ancestors served as a cup-bearer for William the Conqueror, thus early setting the family on its wine-tasting path). Until a decade ago his 350-hectare property of stone-and-tussock was devoted exclusively to sheep and beef.

The second prime mover in getting Vavasour off the ground was Richard Bowling, a burly viticultural expert who resigned from the company in mid 1996. Bowling served a seven-year stint with Corbans, at Taupaki and as second-in-charge of their Marlborough vineyards, before branching out as an independent viticultural consultant. Bowling was early convinced of the Awatere Valley's wine potential; in Peter Vavasour he found a natural partner, one equally convinced of the district's viticultural future, but commanding the financial resources and skills to do something about it. To fund the $1.3 million venture, Peter Vavasour formed a special partnership in 1986 with carefully chosen shareholders: wine merchants, advertising executives, merchant bankers and accountants.

Although every winemaker is adamant that their vineyard enjoys a mesoclimate superior to their neighbour's, Vavasour and Bowling researched their project well. The winery site itself is memorable. Mt Tapuaenuku's 2900-metre peak rears to the south; to the north, four kilometres away (and reducing the risk of frosts) lies the sea.

The estate vineyard is planted on the terraced banks of the Awatere River. The river's banks reveal an ideal soil structure for vines: a one-metre-deep surface layer of alluvial silt, over two metres of gravelly, silty substrata, down to a base strata of mudstone (papa), rich in calcium and iron. 'It's a low-vigour site,' says winemaker Glenn Thomas, 'with good drainage and hard, bony soils.' The 12-hectare vineyard, established in 1986, is principally planted in Sauvignon Blanc, Chardonnay, Cabernet Sauvignon and Cabernet Franc, with smaller plots of Pinot Noir, Merlot, Malbec and Syrah.

The handsome concrete and cedar winery was erected in 1988. Thomas, born in England, graduated from Roseworthy College in 1979, and then worked at the Ryecroft, Kaiser Stuhl and Normans wineries in Australia before arriving in New Zealand in 1985.

Appointed winemaker at Corbans' Gisborne winery from 1986 to 1988, from the start Thomas was also involved in handling Marlborough fruit, by making the early vintages of the Stoneleigh Vineyard range. He joined Vavasour 'for the challenge of setting up a small winery in a new area'.

The idea of a *small* winery has been abandoned. As Tony Preston, Vavasour's managing director, puts it: 'In 1990, it was apparent the company was undercapitalised. The Development Finance Corporation, which held debentures over Vavasour, was in receivership, and sent us a bill for $890,000. We had to raise three-quarters of a million dollars from existing shareholders and a few new ones to buy out the DFC.'

After deciding 7000 cases was not a viable size for a non-family-owned winery, Vavasour embarked on a major expansion programme, with the key objective of giving continuity of supply to its Dashwood Sauvignon Blanc. Two new vineyards have been planted, with shareholding links to Vavasour. 'We'll have control over the majority of our grapes,' says Thomas, 'and they'll be Awatere grown.'

The 35-hectare Wakefield Downs vineyard, five kilometres inland, has been planted principally in Sauvignon Blanc. Twenty kilometres up the valley, on a north-facing slope 170 metres above sea level, the nine-hectare Bluffs vineyard has been planted in equal parts of Chardonnay, Sauvignon Blanc and Cabernet Sauvignon.

To handle the surge in production, the original winery is to become a fermentation cellar, a large new barrel hall and tasting room will be built, and a new crusher and two new presses will be installed.

The premium Vavasour label is reserved exclusively for Awatere Valley-grown wines; those carrying the mid-priced Dashwood label may be based on either Awatere Valley or Wairau Valley fruit. In Thomas' eyes Dashwood is 'not a second label, just a different style of wine, with greater complexity in the Vavasour wines, and the Dashwood wines more for early drinking.' Bottom-tier wines are labelled Stafford Brook.

The wines are immaculate. The Sauvignon Blancs are awash with lush, vibrant, penetratingly herbal, mouth-wateringly crisp flavours: the Dashwood a fresh, direct style, the Vavasour Reserve (of which part of the final blend is barrel-fermented) riper and fleshed out by its deft oak handling. The Vavasour Reserve, especially, ranks among Marlborough's greatest Sauvignon Blancs.

The Dashwood Chardonnay is a lightly wooded style placing its accent on fresh, tangy, lemony fruit flavours.

Vavasour Reserve Cabernet Sauvignon is based on hand-picked Awatere Valley fruit, matured for up to 18 months in French oak barriques. This is a lovely, robust wine packed with lush, blackcurrant-like flavours, intense, smooth and very seductive in its youth. It is partnered by the Dashwood Cabernet/Merlot, a fresh, fruity, supple wine, less rich, ripe and complex.

Dashwood Pinot Noir is a stylish, graceful wine with supple, ripe flavours. It is overshadowed, however, by Vavasour Reserve Pinot Noir, a more profound wine with its fragrant, spicy bouquet and rich array of cherry, mushroom and oak flavours, subtle and searching. Like its Reserve Cabernet Sauvignon stablemate, this is one of the few Marlborough reds that can match the quality of top reds of other regions.

Vavasour Reserve Chardonnay

Vavasour's top, cockerel-labelled Chardonnay is impressively taut and complex, with intense, savoury, grapefruit-like flavours and a lingering, steely finish.

'Chardonnay is not a blank canvas; the fruit is very important,' says winemaker Glenn Thomas. The low-vigour, low-cropping, Mendoza clone vines are grown on a stony little ridge in the middle of the estate vineyard. 'Once the grapes are ripe,' says Thomas, 'we do all the hard things that count – hand-pick, whole bunch-press, French oak-ferment, lees-stir.'

Thomas doesn't like big, blowsy wines with no spine. 'Powerful but subtle wines are what I enjoy, with layers of flavour and the structure to last.' Tasted a year ago, the 1991 vintage was at the peak of its powers, still vigorous, with concentrated, citrusy, biscuity flavours and a flinty finish. From one vintage to the next, this is one of Marlborough's greatest Chardonnays.

A powerful Sauvignon Blanc with exceptional depth of lush, nettley flavours and bracing acidity is the finest achievement of Wairau River, whose graceful, low-slung headquarters lies on the corner of Rapaura Road and the main Blenheim–Nelson highway.

Phil and Chris Rose, proprietors of Wairau River, pioneered grapegrowing on the north side of the Wairau Valley. Brought up on a dairying and cropping farm near Spring Creek, Phil initially planted his Giffords Road property in vines as a grower for Montana.

Today, covering over 100 hectares, the Roses' privately owned vineyards are among the most extensive in the valley. In variable silty and stony soils in Giffords Road, right by the river (hence the company name), 60 hectares are planted in a wide range of grapes, principally Sauvignon Blanc, Chardonnay and Pinot Noir. A further 40 hectares of Chardonnay, Sauvignon Blanc, Riesling, Pinot Noir, Pinot Blanc and Meunier is established in bonier soils in Rapaura Road. The three-hectare block at the company headquarters is planted in Sauvignon Blanc. A substantial proportion of the Roses' grapes is still sold to other wine companies.

The wines are made straight over the road at Rapaura Vintners, in which the Roses purchased a 25 per cent stake in 1995. Surrounded by expansive lawns, the company's stylish mud brick and heart rimu headquarters houses a warm, cosy cafe, serving 'simple, fresh Marlborough food'.

The top wines are labelled Wairau River,

Wairau River Wines

Corner Rapaura Road and State Highway 6

Owners:
Phil and Chris Rose

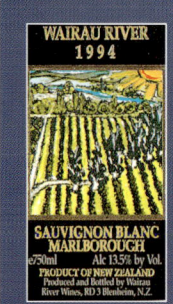

Key Wines:
Wairau River Sauvignon Blanc, Chardonnay; Philip Rose Sauvignon Blanc

with a lower-priced range, notably the crisply herbaceous Sauvignon Blanc, branded as Philip Rose.

Wairau River Chardonnay is a fleshy, succulent wine with lush fruit flavours, toasty oak and a soft, buttery finish. Its Sauvignon Blanc stablemate is an exceptionally full-bodied and ripe style with a tantalising interplay of rich, tropical-fruit flavours and more pungent, zingy, herbaceous characters. Of all Marlborough's Sauvignon Blancs, this is one of the most powerful and richly satisfying.

Phil Rose exports about three times more wine (principally to the UK) than he sells in New Zealand.

The fledgling Whitehaven Wine Company does not own vineyards or a winery – only winemaking equipment. From the start, however, Whitehaven has revealed an ability to make fine wine.

The company is based in the old Grove Mill winery in the heart of Blenheim. The six partners in the venture are Greg and Sue White (the majority shareholders, who also handle Whitehaven's administration and marketing); Auckland-based John Reid and Hugh Molloy; and winemaker Simon Waghorn and his wife, Jane Forrest.

Greg White is a former merchant banker; Sue White was previously involved in marketing at the Bank of New Zealand. 'After several years cruising around the islands, they developed an interest in entering the wine industry and heard the old Grove

Whitehaven Wine Company

1 Dodson Street, Blenheim

Owners:
Greg and Sue White, John Reid, Hugh Molloy, Simon Waghorn and Jane Forrest

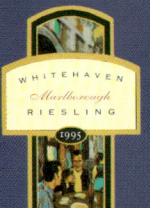

Key Wines:
Riesling, Sauvignon Blanc, Chardonnay, Reserve Chardonnay, Pinot Noir

Mill winery was on the market,' says Waghorn. 'David Pearce [winemaker at Grove Mill] recommended me to the Whites as a winemaker. He was able to offer them the complete package of a winery, equipment and winemaker.'

Waghorn grew up in rural Canterbury. While studying for a BSc in botany at Canterbury University, he worked in a bottlestore, developing a 'consumer interest' in wine. After working as a cellarhand in New Zealand and Australia, and gaining a Roseworthy College post-graduate diploma in viticulture and oenology, from 1988 to early 1995 he held the top job at Corbans' Gisborne winery.

Whitehaven leases the small winery, which is used for making wine not only for Whitehaven, but also for several clients who

Simon Waghorn resigned from the top job at Corbans' Gisborne winery because 'I wanted to be a shareholder, and instead of overseeing the winemaking process, I wanted to get my hands back on the barrels and pumps.'

lack their own production facilities. Whitehaven's grapes are grown on a contract basis at four vineyards – Bladen, deGyffarde, Le Grys and Wairau Peaks – whose owners in some cases also have their own wine made at Whitehaven.

The first vintage was produced in 1994. Sauvignon Blanc (in non-wooded and oak-aged styles), Chardonnay (in lightly oaked and 'Burgundian' styles), Riesling and Pinot Noir will be the mainstays of the range.

The Riesling is full-bloomed, with intense lemon and lime-like flavours and a touch of sweetness balanced by racy acidity. The Sauvignon Blanc is scented, ripe, delicate and lively and the Chardonnay is a very skilfully balanced, easy-drinking style with good flavour depth. For Whitehaven, the early signs are highly auspicious.

Other Producers

Domaine Chandon (NZ)

Wholly owned by Möet et Chandon, Domaine Chandon is the largest and most luxurious winery in Victoria's Yarra Valley. Domaine Chandon Marlborough Brut is produced at Hunter's winery by Dr Tony Jordan, managing director and winemaker of Domaine Chandon, who has been a consultant to Hunter's since 1985. Richard Geoffory, a Champagne-based senior winemaker for Möet et Chandon, is also involved.

The 1992 vintage is arguably the finest sparkling wine ever made in New Zealand – nutty, steely and complex, with extraordinary flavour length and finesse.

Foxes Island

John Belsham, manager and part-owner of Rapaura Vintners, and his wife, Anne Graham, make premium wines under their own Foxes Island label. The wines are based on bought-in fruit and grapes grown in the couple's 4.5-hectare vineyard in Giffords Road, Rapaura. The range includes a very fleshy, rich and savoury Chardonnay and a weighty, smoky, supple Pinot Noir.

Framingham

Exquisitely floral, piercingly flavoured Riesling flows from Rex and Paula Brooke-Taylor's stony, 14-hectare Framingham vineyard in Conders Bend Road, on the outskirts of Blenheim. The Brooke-Taylors, grapegrowers since 1982, produced the first wine under their own label in 1994. Framingham Vineyard Selection Riesling is everything Riesling should be: flowery, delicate, citrusy, honeyish and tangy.

HawkesBridge

Mike Veal and his wife, Judy, own a 13-hectare vineyard alongside the Omaka River in Hawkesbury Road, near Renwick. Some of their grapes are sold to other companies, but in 1994 the Veals released their first Sauvignon Blanc, followed in 1995 by a lightly oaked but full-flavoured Chardonnay.

Isabel Estate Vineyards

A stunningly fragrant, concentrated and velvety 1994 Pinot Noir was the first offering from Michael and Robyn Tiller's vineyard in Hawkesbury Road, just south of Renwick, which has supplied fruit to several wine companies. The close-planted Sauvignon Blanc, Chardonnay and Pinot Noir vines are grown in gravelly soils over a clay sub-soil. The wine is made by Sam Weaver.

Kindale

Errol and Kaye Hadfield, contract grapegrowers since 1978, run a 14-hectare vineyard in Falveys Road, near the Omaka Springs winery. Their own wines, under the Kindale Willowbrook label, include a Medium-Dry White and a crisp, uncomplicated, lightly oaked Chardonnay.

Mount Linton

The MacFarlane family owns a 20-hectare vineyard in the Rapaura district, from which most of the grapes are sold to other wine companies. The family's own wines, named after Mount Linton Station in Southland, include a Sauvignon Blanc launched in 1994 and from the 1995 vintage a deliciously full-flavoured, subtly oaked Chardonnay.

Rothbury (NZ)

Rothbury Estate, the New South Wales wine company, owns a Wairau Valley vineyard managed by Craig Gass of Conders Bend. The range, most of which is exported, includes a consistently rewarding Chardonnay, Sauvignon Blanc and Riesling.

The Brothers Vineyards

This company is operated by Douglas Holmes, a Marlborough grapegrower, his brother Chris, and Chris' wife, Caroline. The company draws its grapes from Douglas' 18-hectare vineyard in Brancott Road and other local growers. The wines, mostly exported, include a soft, citrusy, buttery, lightly oaked Chardonnay and a fresh, direct Sauvignon Blanc/Sémillon.

Wither Hills

Brent Marris, Delegat's winemaker, who was raised in Marlborough, produces a good Sauvignon Blanc and exceptional Chardonnay under his own Wither Hills label. The six-hectare vineyard is planted in Sauvignon Blanc and Chardonnay, with Riesling and Pinot Noir to follow.

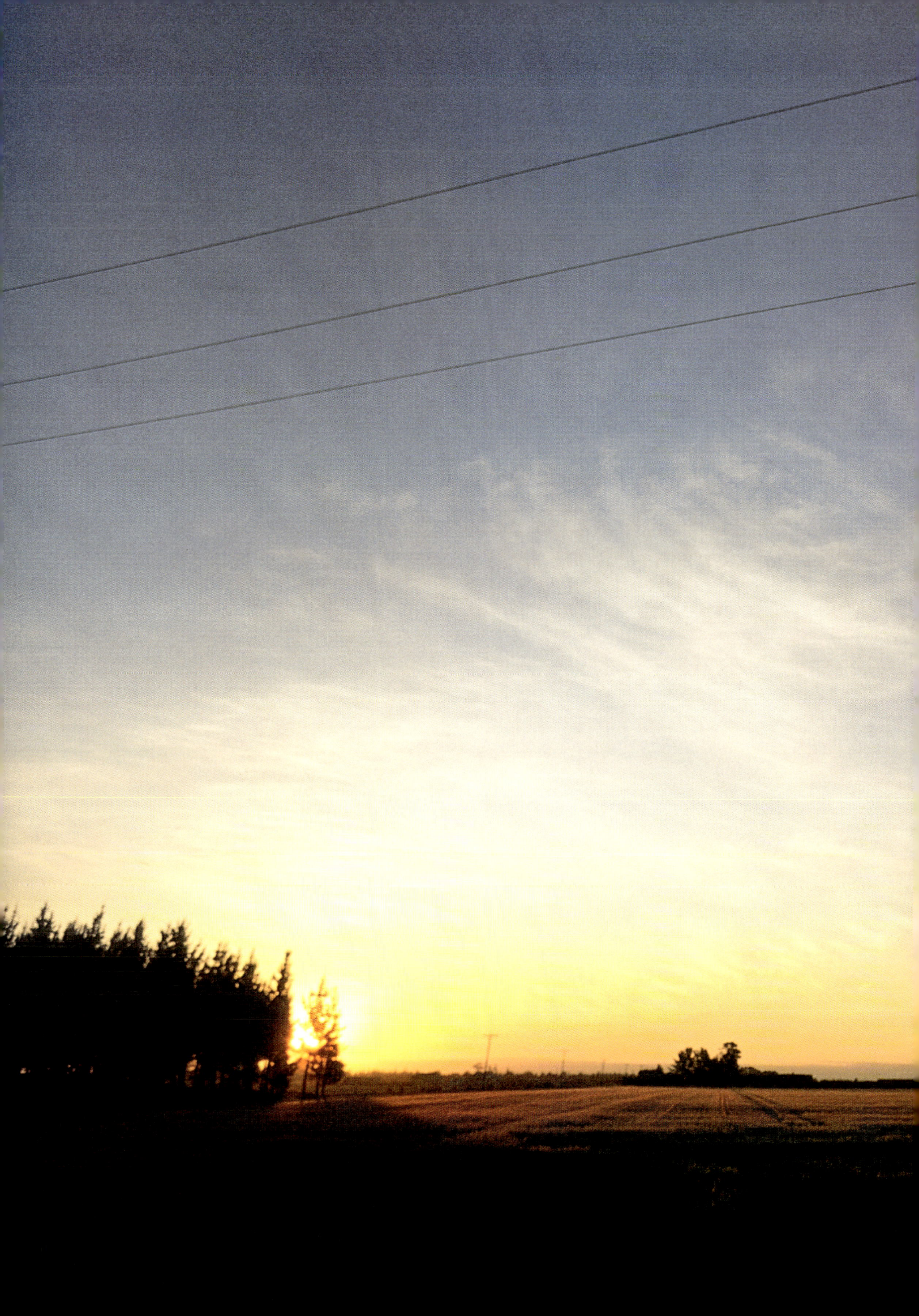

CANTERBURY

PRODUCERS

Darjon Vineyards
French Farm
Gatehouse Wines
Giesen Wine Estate
Glenmark Wines
Kaituna Valley
Langdale Wine Estate
Mark Rattray Vineyards
Omihi Hills Vineyard
Pegasus Bay
Rosebank Estate
Rossendale Wines
St Helena Wine Estate
Sandihurst Wines
Sherwood Estate
Silverstream Vineyard
Torlesse Wines
Waipara Downs
Waipara Estates
Waipara Springs

WAIPARA

Canterbury is New Zealand's fourth largest wine region, behind only Marlborough, Hawke's Bay and Gisborne. The latest 1995 vineyard survey revealed that Auckland, the Wairarapa and Otago all have a smaller area planted in vines than Canterbury. From Waipara in the north to Burnham, south of Christchurch, the Canterbury region now has four per cent of all New Zealand's vines, and 10 per cent of its wine producers. Vineyards are spreading like wild-fire – from 35 hectares in 1986 to 198 hectares in 1992 and 325 hectares in 1995.

Canterbury wines enjoy strong parochial support in local stores and restaurants. But following an unhappy series of cool, ultra low-cropping vintages (in 1994, Canterbury produced less than 0.4 per cent of the national grape crop), Canterbury wine has been in desperately short supply. Even in the 1995 vintage, when the region escaped most of the rain problems further north, Canterbury produced barely one per cent of the national grape harvest. The flurry of recent plantings should do much to alleviate the shortage.

French peasants who landed in 1840 at Akaroa on Banks Peninsula carried vine cuttings, from which wine soon flowed for their domestic consumption. A century after their arrival, W.H. Meyers built a small winery, Villa Nova, in the Heathcote Valley. By 1945 he had a tiny vineyard of about 0.8 hectares planted in Verdelho, Pinot Gris, Muscat and other grapes. Although wine was made, Meyers' vines were uprooted around 1949 after they failed to flourish.

The current resurgence of interest in Canterbury wine stems from research conducted at Lincoln University under the direction of Dr David Jackson. When the first trials commenced in 1973, research focused on identifying the most suitable varieties for Canterbury's cool climate. After losing 70 per cent of his vines to a late frost, Jackson began 'wondering if I really was making a mistake'.

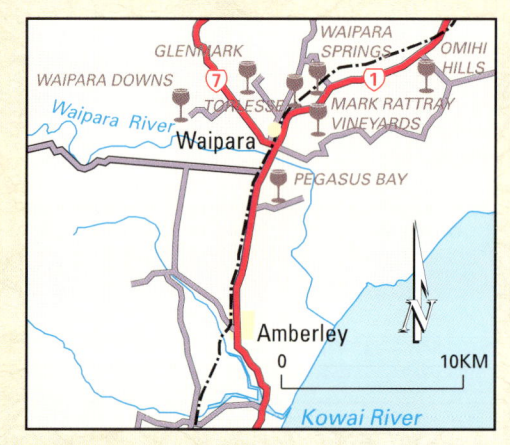

Trial plantings of more than 60 varieties later demonstrated, according to the university, that Canterbury produces grapes of high acidity and high sugar levels. Jackson saw Canterbury as 'borderline' for such mid-to-late season ripeners as Sauvignon Blanc and such late-season ripeners as Cabernet Sauvignon, but Pinot Noir and Chardonnay were 'particularly promising'.

Riesling is also flourishing in Canterbury. The 1995 vineyard survey reveals the four principal varieties planted in Canterbury are (in order): Chardonnay, Pinot Noir, Riesling and Sauvignon Blanc.

Riesling, Chardonnay and Pinot Noir are Canterbury's most rewarding wines. The fleshy, rich, spicy Corbans Private Bin Amberley (in fact, Waipara-grown) Riesling; Giesen's intense, spine-tingling, estate-grown Rieslings; the chunky, flavour-rich Pegasus Bay range and Mark Rattray's consistently stylish and ripe-tasting Pinot Noir and Chardonnay, all prove Canterbury's ability to produce classy wine.

Canterbury's wineries are clustered in two zones: on the pancake-flat plains surrounding Christchurch, and further north in the undulating country around Waipara. Vineyards in both districts are exposed to the assaults of Canterbury's fierce, hot nor'-westers, but at Waipara the Teviotdale Hills shelter the vines from the province's cooling easterly breezes. The best Waipara wines are thus typically more mouth-filling and ripe-flavoured than the leaner, crisper wines from the south.

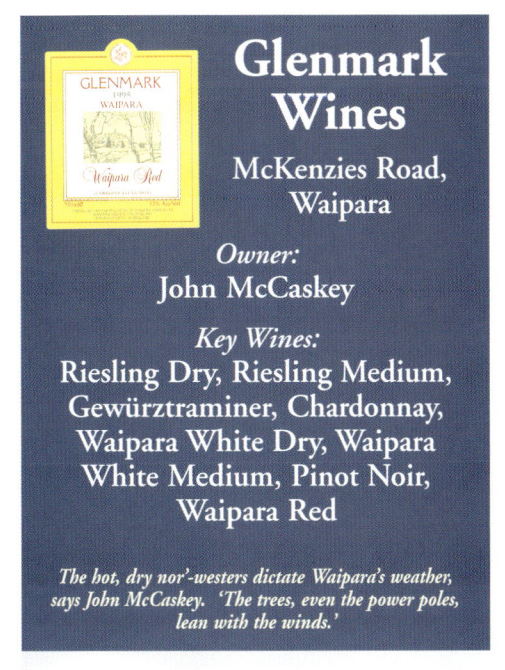

With his weathered face, gravelly voice and laconic manner, John McCaskey is one of the great characters of the Canterbury wine scene. A pioneer of Waipara wine, he produces light, delicate Rieslings that can be quite Germanic in their scentedness and fragility.

McCaskey has spent his life farming his family's property at Weka Pass, and he still grows peas and barley and grazes sheep and cattle. The family property originally formed part of George Henry Moore's 60,000-hectare Glenmark sheep station, and the former Glenmark homestead, 'where peacocks roamed free and swans drifted on the man-made lake', is today the focal point of the winery's labels.

McCaskey's interest in winemaking was first aroused nearly 30 years ago, but, he says, it was not until the Glenmark irrigation scheme was under way that diversification could start. His first vines were planted in 1981 and the first Glenmark wines flowed in 1986.

McCaskey's three-hectare vineyard, planted in light silt loams over a base of clay and gravels, features Riesling as the principal variety with smaller plantings of Müller-Thurgau, Gewürztraminer, Chardonnay, Pinot Noir and Cabernet Sauvignon. Another four-hectare vineyard is being established 'in the grapes we haven't got much of': Chardonnay, Sauvignon Blanc, Cabernet Sauvignon, Merlot and Cabernet Franc.

McCaskey in 1992 sold a half share in his winery building, a converted haybarn on the main highway at Waipara, to Torlesse Wines; Glenmark and Torlesse now share the production facility. They also share a winemaker: Kym Rayner, an Australian who formerly worked for Penfolds at Gisborne and Montana at Blenheim, before becoming a shareholder in Torlesse. Rayner began as McCaskey's winemaker in 1991.

Glenmark's annual output is small: about 2000 cases. Ex-winery sales are now at the 'Weka Plains Winegarden', next to the vineyard in McKenzies Road.

Glenmark's Rieslings (both a Riesling Dry and Riesling Medium are produced) are at their best light, floral and vibrantly fruity, with touches of honey and spine-tingling acidity. McCaskey sees Riesling as a Glenmark specialty: 'It's hardy, fruits regularly and is versatile too.' The wines can take a year or two to open up, but then age gracefully for five years or longer.

Glenmark Waipara White Dry and Waipara White Medium are easy-drinking, blended wines based principally on Müller-Thurgau. The Gewürztraminer is light, fresh and positively spiced. The barrique-fermented, lees-aged Chardonnay is steely, lemony, slightly buttery and complex.

The Pinot Noir is fragrant, with light, strawberryish flavours, but to date the Cabernet Sauvignon-based Waipara Red has been more successful. 'We try to give it a soft finish by blending with Pinot Noir or Merlot,' says McCaskey, 'and avoid giving it extended maceration on skins or new oak.' This is an easy-drinking, green-edged red with fresh, strong, red berry-fruit and minty flavours and a well-rounded finish.

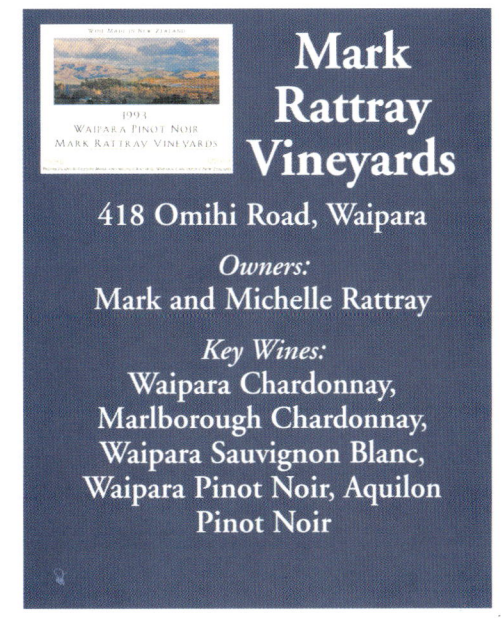

Glenmark Wines

McKenzies Road, Waipara

Owner: John McCaskey

Key Wines: Riesling Dry, Riesling Medium, Gewürztraminer, Chardonnay, Waipara White Dry, Waipara White Medium, Pinot Noir, Waipara Red

The hot, dry nor'-westers dictate Waipara's weather, says John McCaskey. 'The trees, even the power poles, lean with the winds.'

Mark Rattray is a Pinot Noir and Chardonnay specialist. 'I've thought deeply about that,' he says. 'I'm not getting into Rieslings and Cabernets. Pinot Noir and Chardonnay are the grapes we can do extremely well with in Waipara, due to their early ripening ability, and we can sell the wines in the UK and Switzerland.'

Mark Rattray Vineyards is almost straight across the highway from the Waipara Springs winery, of which Rattray and his wife, Michelle, were among the founding partners. Born in Christchurch, Rattray studied at the Geisenheim Institute for two years in the early 1970s and worked at the fabled Schloss Johannisberg in the Rheingau. A long-drained bottle of Lorchhausen Rosenberg Riesling Kabinett 1971, with Rattray's name on the label, is a vivid reminder of the 0.2-hectare vineyard he once owned where the Mittelrhein runs into the Rheingau.

After five years with Montana and six years with Penfolds in Auckland, in 1985 Rattray came south to join St Helena, where he was the winemaker until 1990. After producing the first vintages at Waipara Springs, in early 1993 Rattray withdrew from the company. Since then he has acted as a consultant to several other Canterbury producers, but is now engaged primarily with the development of his own Mark Rattray Vineyards label.

After buying former Cabinet Minister Derek Quigley's house and vineyard, Rattray uprooted the established Gewürztraminer in 1986 and replanted with Pinot Noir, Chardonnay and a small plot of Sauvignon Blanc. Scheurebe is being added for a late

Mark Rattray Vineyards

418 Omihi Road, Waipara

Owners: Mark and Michelle Rattray

Key Wines: Waipara Chardonnay, Marlborough Chardonnay, Waipara Sauvignon Blanc, Waipara Pinot Noir, Aquilon Pinot Noir

harvest style. Sea shells are buried in the chalk-based silty loams, revealing that the vineyard, which now totals four hectares, once formed part of the seabed. Rattray also buys grapes from growers in Waipara and Marlborough, and has leased the French Farm vineyard at Akaroa.

In his winery built prior to the 1994 vintage, Rattray produces around 3000 cases of wine each year, but plans to gradually lift this to 7500 cases. There are no ex-winery sales, except by appointment ('Or if I happen to be there,' says Rattray), but the wines are highly respected in the New Zealand, Swiss, Danish and British markets.

Rattray's Waipara Sauvignon Blanc is less pungently herbaceous than the classic Marlborough style, but attractively full, fresh, limey and zesty. At its best, the barrel-fermented Waipara Chardonnay is fat, full-flavoured, leesy and buttery in a rich and complex style.

The Aquilon ('north wind') Pinot Noir is a delicate, gently oaked style, floral, berryish, soft and supple. Its big brother, the Waipara Pinot Noir, is a consistently stylish wine with intense, ripe, cherryish flavour and a seductive, velvety texture. These are classy, beautifully packaged wines.

After many years working for large wineries, Mark Rattray (pictured with his wife, Michelle) produces a small volume of highly rated Waipara Chardonnay and Pinot Noir.

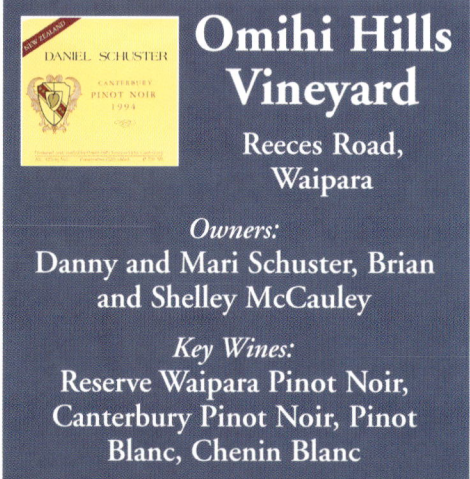

Danny Schuster is an enigma. With his bristling black moustache and all-consuming passion for wine, he has long been a guru of the Canterbury wine scene; his Omihi Hills wines are boldly branded as 'Daniel Schuster'. As co-author of a textbook on viticulture and winemaking, and maker of the gold medal-winning St Helena Pinot Noirs from 1982 and 1984, he inevitably aroused high expectations when he planted his own vineyard in rolling hill country east of the main highway at Waipara. Yet the wines from Omihi Hills have so far been perplexing rather than exciting.

Schuster fields criticism – based principally on his wines' lack of real concentration – with disarming equanimity. 'What am I really doing? Learning about a vineyard – and that takes many years. I have to know how to interpret what it says, how to put the composition together. At some point, my statement will be clear and concentrated and as good as I can make it. That could be 20 years away.'

German-born, Schuster gathered his early winemaking experience in Europe, South Africa and Australia. After arriving in New Zealand in the late 1970s, he helped set up the grape trials and microvinification cellar at Lincoln University. Between 1980 and 1985, Schuster carved out a high profile as the winemaker at St Helena.

The Omihi Hills vineyard, originally called Netherwood Farm, was initially a partnership between Schuster and Christchurch restaurateurs Russell and Kumiko Black. After

> **Omihi Hills Vineyard**
>
> Reeces Road, Waipara
>
> *Owners:*
> Danny and Mari Schuster, Brian and Shelley McCauley
>
> *Key Wines:*
> Reserve Waipara Pinot Noir, Canterbury Pinot Noir, Pinot Blanc, Chenin Blanc
>
> *Apart from his involvement in Omihi Hills, Danny Schuster also acts as a viticultural consultant to Villa Antinori in Tuscany, and such Californian wineries as Stag's Leap and Heitz Cellars.*

the Blacks' withdrawal in late 1989, Schuster and his wife, Mari, formed a new partnership with Brian and Shelley McCauley.

To the north of the elevated, sloping, six-hectare vineyard lie the snow-capped Kaikouras; sheep graze nearby fields; magpies swoop and soar overhead. The vineyard, first planted in 1986, is well protected from cool easterly and southerly winds. The close-planted vines – 85 per cent Pinot Noir, the rest Chardonnay and Pinot Blanc – are planted in heavy clay loams, rich in ironstone. 'The structure and chemical nature of the soils have distinct parallels with Burgundy,' says Schuster.

He doesn't believe in irrigation: 'Some say I'm suicidal, but the vines have roots twenty feet [6.1 metres] deep, and once they're four years old they're safe from water stress. If you want quality, you have to accept you won't get a decent crop until the vines are five years old.'

About 3000 cases of wine flow each year from Schuster's small coolstore winery. The wines are marketed by mail-order and through the retail trade, and exported to the UK and USA, but are not sold directly to the public at the winery. Schuster's approach to winemaking is based on 'minimal intervention', with little use of sulphur dioxide, infrequent racking, and egg-white fining rather than filtering of the reds.

The barrel-fermented, lees-aged Pinot Blanc has been a characterful, savoury, earthy, yeasty dry white. This has recently been supplanted by a rather Chardonnay-like, barrel-fermented and lees-aged Chenin Blanc, grown in Hawke's Bay. 'It's always intrigued me that Hawke's Bay Chenin Blanc has strength and ripeness, but lacks concentration,' says Schuster, 'so we reduce the vines' crop levels to get intensity.' This is a steely, slightly austere wine with a toasty, yeasty complexity.

Two Pinot Noirs are produced: the flagship, estate-grown Reserve Waipara Pinot Noir and the lower-tier Canterbury Pinot Noir, a regional blend. Both are typically light in colour (sometimes deceptively so), with varying levels of extract (stuffing) and moderate depth of savoury, gamey, cherryish flavour. These are mellow, light to middle-weight reds with some appeal, but not yet the great North Canterbury Pinot Noirs Schuster is thirsting to make.

Watch out for the winged horse. With a sextet of excitingly robust and flavourful wines, Pegasus Bay at Waipara has become the first Canterbury winery to produce a comprehensive array of locally grown wines capable of footing it with the rest of the country in quality.

When a wine critic turns winemaker, inevitably his wines attract particularly close scrutiny. Ivan Donaldson, associate-professor of neurology at Christchurch School of Medicine, senior wine judge and weekly wine columnist for the *Press*, can rest easy. The most recent releases of Pegasus Bay's Sauvignon/Sémillon, Chardonnay, Riesling and Pinot Noir are of outstanding quality, and the two Cabernet Sauvignon-based reds are better than any others from Canterbury.

Pegasus Bay is a family affair. 'There are three things in life I'm passionate about,' says Donaldson. 'My family, neurology and wine.' Ivan's wife, Chris, is Pegasus Bay's business manager; their son, Matthew, a graduate of Roseworthy College, holds the winemaking reins; and another son, Edward, is marketing manager.

The Donaldsons planted their first vines in Stockgrove Road, east of State Highway 1 and just south of the Waipara River, in 1986. Now the vineyard covers 23 hectares of Riesling, Chardonnay, Sauvignon Blanc, Sémillon, Pinot Noir, Cabernet Sauvignon, Merlot and Cabernet Franc. 'It's lean country,' says Matthew Donaldson. 'The topsoil is never deeper than a foot [0.3 metres], and below that it's gravel for 100 metres or so.'

The Donaldsons went to Waipara to plant their vineyard for several reasons. The Teviotdale Hills to the east shelter the vines from Canterbury's cooling coastal breezes. In summer, temperatures soar to around 35°C in the shade, and the rainfall, which falls mostly in the spring, is low. In this notably hot, dry climate, the extremely low-cropping vines (below five tonnes per hectare) ripen their fruit fully, yielding powerful wines that fill your mouth with body and flavour.

Ivan Donaldson is clear about the style of wine he wants at Pegasus Bay. 'New Zealand wines typically have no weakness in flavour, but often lack weight, texture, length and longevity. The style we are emphasising depends on more than just upfront fruit; it has weight in the mouth and plenty of length. In addition, we are after a special mid-palate texture; a type of creaminess.'

The wines show the qualities Donaldson is after. The strapping Chardonnay is a classy wine with a delicious surge of citrusy, savoury, slightly buttery flavour and good acid spine. The partly barrel-fermented, lees-aged Sauvignon/Sémillon is a gorgeous wine, mouth-filling and bursting with ripe, exotic fruit flavours. The zingy, off-dry Riesling is shot through with citrusy, limey, honeyish flavour.

The slightly green-leafy Cabernet Sauvignon/Cabernet Franc/Merlot and its riper reserve version, Maestro, are both impressively chewy and flavourful. Pegasus Bay's finest red, however, is the bold Pinot Noir, an enticingly dark and deep-scented blend of Marlborough and estate-grown grapes with layers of cherry, plum and smoky oak flavours and a lingering, velvety finish.

Pegasus Bay
Stockgrove Road,
Waipara

Owners:
Ivan and Christine Donaldson

Key Wines:
Chardonnay, Sauvignon/Sémillon, Riesling, Pinot Noir, Cabernet Sauvignon/Cabernet Franc/Merlot, Maestro

Associate-professor Ivan Donaldson and his wife, Chris, head a family team that is setting new standards in Waipara wine.

The phoenix-like rise of Torlesse after an ill-planned start to its present status as a respected producer of consistently attractive wines is one of the more heartening stories of the Canterbury wine scene.

The early history of the company – named after Mount Torlesse and the Torlesse Range, inland from Christchurch – proved turbulent. Founded at West Melton by 20 shareholders, half of whom were grower-suppliers, Torlesse processed its first vintage in 1987. Three years later, however, the winery slid into receivership. 'It was basically a production rather than market-led company,' says Kym Rayner, the current winemaker.

A new company was formed in 1990 by two of the original shareholders: Andrew Tomlin, an accountant, and Dr David Jackson, a horticultural specialist at Lincoln University. Rayner, who made the 1990 vintage, soon after also became a shareholder. Jackson is no longer involved. Today, the shares are spread evenly between Tomlin (who handles the company's finances); Rayner; Michael and Hazel Blowers of Christchurch; and two Canadian couples, Dick and Vivian Pharis, and Gary and Ann Fabris.

Kym Rayner is a lanky Australian whose parents were grapegrowers in McLaren Vale. After graduating from Roseworthy College in 1975, Rayner spent five vintages at the Southern Vales Co-operative Winery in South Australia, and two vintages at the Stanley Wine Company, before he arrived in New Zealand in 1983 to run Penfolds' new winery in Gisborne. Following Montana's 1986 takeover of Penfolds, Rayner spent the next three years at Montana's Blenheim winery.

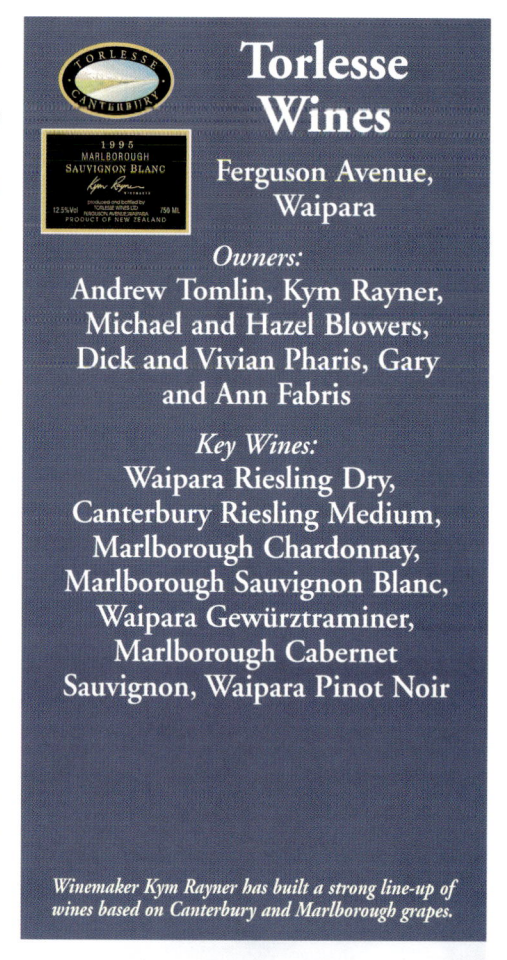

Following the receivership, the original coolstore winery in West Melton was sold to Gatehouse. In 1992 Torlesse purchased a half share in the Glenmark winery building; the two companies now share the production facility at Waipara, plus the services of winemaker Kym Rayner. 'This is not a company merger,' stresses Andrew Tomlin, 'and it doesn't involve any vineyards. We're just sharing ownership of a winery, and the services of a winemaker, with Glenmark.'

Torlesse draws its grapes from Andrew Tomlin's and Kym Rayner's own vineyards at Waipara, and fruit is also purchased from other Canterbury and Marlborough growers. Rayner is excited by his own Waipara grapes: 'Mark Rattray [of Mark Rattray Vineyards] and I are old mates. When I saw the quality of his Pinot Noir and Chardonnay, I thought: That's good enough for me.'

Torlesse's annual production is currently around 8000 cases, but will not exceed 15,000 cases 'in the foreseeable future,' says Rayner. The lack of a retail outlet at the winery is a sales hurdle, but the restructured company has placed its initial emphasis on 'establishing the brand and consolidating the wine styles,' says Rayner. A new winery at Waipara ('at the junction of two major highways which can bring a lot of passing trade') is planned for the future.

Highlights of the Torlesse range have included the fresh-scented, incisively flavoured and zesty Waipara Riesling Dry and – on a slightly lower rung – the lively, lemony Canterbury Riesling Medium. The Canterbury Gewürztraminer (from 1995 of Waipara origin) has offered plenty of crisp, dryish, gingery flavour.

From Marlborough flows a flavour-packed, vibrantly fruity, tangy Sauvignon Blanc of consistently high quality; an equally classy, fragrant and robust, rich-flavoured Chardonnay; and a buoyantly fruity and supple, easy-drinking Marlborough Cabernet Sauvignon. Torlesse's first Pinot Noirs, from Marlborough (1995) and Canterbury (1996) are also starting to flow.

Torlesse Wines

Ferguson Avenue, Waipara

Owners:
Andrew Tomlin, Kym Rayner, Michael and Hazel Blowers, Dick and Vivian Pharis, Gary and Ann Fabris

Key Wines:
Waipara Riesling Dry, Canterbury Riesling Medium, Marlborough Chardonnay, Marlborough Sauvignon Blanc, Waipara Gewürztraminer, Marlborough Cabernet Sauvignon, Waipara Pinot Noir

Winemaker Kym Rayner has built a strong line-up of wines based on Canterbury and Marlborough grapes.

'A farm with a vineyard' is how Keith and Ruth Berry promote their 319-hectare property with its 3000 stock units and four hectares of vines. Waipara Downs, once part of the huge Glenmark Station, lies in Bains Road, off State Highway 7 linking North Canterbury and Nelson.

When the Berrys, both Cantabrians and both former schoolteachers, bought Waipara Downs in 1986, vines were already established, planted a year earlier by the former owner, Jonathan Bain. 'We hummed and hawed for a year,' recalls Keith Berry. 'We wanted to diversify – and into something that wouldn't eat grass. We're prone to droughts, so if we'd gone into deer, for instance, what good would that have been?'

By 1987, the Berrys had started planting their own vines. Today, a four-hectare paddock is covered with irrigated Chardonnay (the principal variety), Riesling, Pinot Noir and Cabernet Sauvignon vines, planted in friable, free-draining clays.

Waipara winemaking consultant Mark Rattray has made the wine since the first 1991 vintage. In the concrete, tilt-slab winery erected for the 1995 vintage, only a few hundred cases of Waipara Downs wine are produced each year, but the Berrys intend to raise this to about 3000 cases.

The Cabernet Sauvignon is green-edged but reasonably full-bodied and flavoursome. The Pinot Noir is still settling down in style. The barrel-fermented Chardonnay is full, fresh, appley and nutty, with flavour complexity and a buttery, rounded finish – this is my pick of the range.

Waipara Downs
Bains Road, Waipara

Owners:
Keith and Ruth Berry

Key Wines:
Chardonnay, Pinot Noir, Cabernet Sauvignon

Ruth Berry (pictured with her daughter, Sarah), and her husband, Keith, are farmers as well as winemakers.

Behind a roadside row of gum trees at Waipara nestles a collection of small grey buildings. Waipara Springs, named after a spring which rises in the nearby hills, has one of the most popular restaurants on the Canterbury wine trail.

The company, which processed its first vintage in 1989, is owned by the Moore and Grant families. Bruce and Jill Moore, who originally owned the property, planted four hectares of Chardonnay in 1982 as contract growers for Corbans. After the Moores formed a partnership in 1987 with Andrew Grant and his mother, Beverley (owners of a local transport company), the vineyard was expanded, and in 1990 a winery was established with a new partner, Mark Rattray, as winemaker. Rattray, however, withdrew from Waipara Springs in 1993.

Consultant winemaker Kym Rayner 'makes all the big decisions,' says Belinda Gould, Waipara Springs' assistant winemaker and marketing manager. 'I do the day-to-day work.' Gould took a Diploma in Horticulture from Lincoln University, spent two years as a guest student at the Geisenheim Institute in Germany, and then worked with viticulturist Dr Richard Smart at Ruakura, before joining Waipara Springs in 1993.

Waipara Springs Wine Company
State Highway 1, Waipara

Owners:
The Moore and Grant families

Key Wines:
Chardonnay, Riesling, Sauvignon Blanc, Pinot Noir, Cabernet Sauvignon, Cabernet Blush

The 20-hectare Hutt Creek vineyard behind the winery is planted in Chardonnay (the principal variety), Riesling, Sauvignon Blanc, Cabernet Sauvignon and a small plot of Pinot Noir. An old woolshed and stable was converted into Waipara Springs' cellar and vineyard restaurant, where during summer thousands of visitors are served.

Waipara Springs' current annual output is about 5000 cases of wine, but the company plans to quadruple this by 1998. About a third of the wine is sold on-site, with the rest consumed principally in Christchurch and the UK.

The Riesling is invigoratingly crisp, with strong, fresh, limey flavour. The estate-grown Sauvignon Blanc is zesty, with rich capsicum and redcurrant-evoking flavours. The French oak-fermented, lees-aged Chardonnay is fleshy, toasty, mealy and buttery.

The berryish, leafy Cabernet Sauvignon and solid Pinot Noir are on a slightly lower plane than the whites, but Waipara Springs also produces a pink, fractionally off-dry, strawberryish, springy Cabernet Blush that is full of youthful charm.

Bruce Moore (right) oversees Waipara Springs' estate vineyard. Andrew Grant looks after the administration and reports he is 'also a good shoveller at harvest'.

CHRISTCHURCH

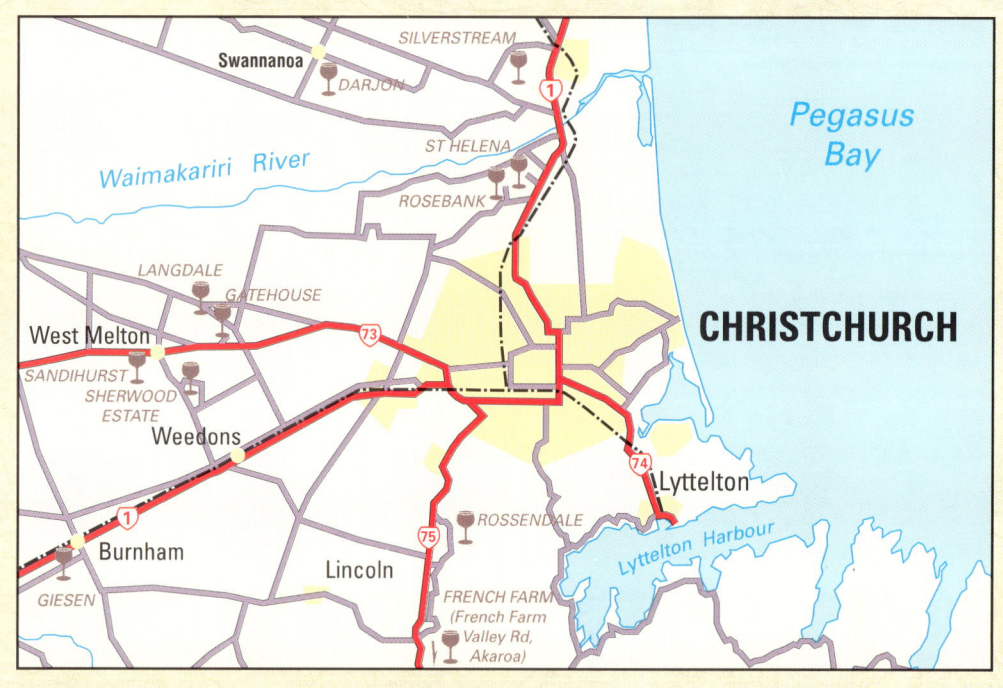

The wine scene around the city of Christchurch was until recently dominated by the two 'giants' of the district, St Helena and Giesen. St Helena's star has faded since the heady days of the early-mid 1980s. The Giesen brothers, more recent arrivals from Germany, have used both Canterbury and Marlborough grapes to build their Burnham winery into the region's largest, winning acclaim for their robust, lush Reserve Chardonnays and steely, honey-sweet Rieslings. A dozen wine producers are now based within a 30-minute drive of Christchurch.

The climatic hazards for viticulture in Canterbury (especially the district around Christchurch) are more severe than for regions further north. Canterbury, although nearer the equator than many European wine regions, in cooler years can fail to accumulate the heat necessary to fully ripen grapes. 'This is a region of very marked vintage swings, from very good to poor,' says St Helena winemaker, Petter Evans.

October spring frosts are a risk (causing problems 'about one year in five', according to Mark Rattray of Mark Rattray Vineyards at Waipara) and April frosts can retard ripening. Canterbury, however, enjoys one vital advantage over most North Island winegrowing regions – low rainfall. During Canterbury's long, dry autumns, the warm days and cool nights enable the fruit to ripen slowly, with high levels of acidity and extract. The fortunate combination of low rainfall and low-to-moderate soil fertility means that excessive vine foliage growth is not a problem here.

You'd never starve on the Canterbury wine trail. Many of the wineries offer fresh, wholesome lunches featuring an array of local specialties, such as eel and salmon, pates and cheeses. Vineyard restaurants are more common here than in any other region in the country. A few 'wineries', which buy most of their grapes from Marlborough, lack their own production facilities and specialise in cafe-style dining, would be more accurately described as vineyard restaurants.

Darjon Vineyards

North Eyre Road, Swannanoa

Owners:
John and Michelle Baker

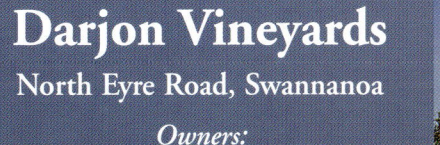

Key Wines:
Swannanoa Riesling, Marlborough Sauvignon Blanc, Marlborough Blush, Swannanoa Pinot Noir, Marlborough Claret

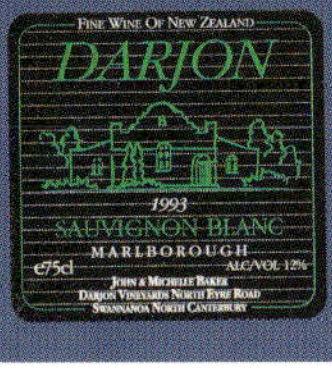

John and Michelle Baker sell most of their tiny output in their vineyard restaurant at Swannanoa.

After planting a vineyard in their stone-strewn block at Swannanoa in 1989, John and Michelle Baker waited six years before picking their first crop. 'The nor'-westers dehydrated the leaves and burned them off,' says John. 'The vines were literally sandblasted by the soil.'

The Bakers run their vineyard and handsome restaurant while still holding down full-time jobs elsewhere. John, a Sheffield engineer who learned fruit winemaking from his mother, came to New Zealand from England in 1967. After spending ten years 'trying to make a Burgundy from plums and other fruits,' John switched to grapes, and in the mid 1980s planted a vineyard (now sold) at Harewood.

In 1986, a nine-hectare block of bare, exposed land was subdivided from Michelle's parents' property at Swannanoa and gradually planted in trees, shrubs and vines. Today, two hectares of Riesling and Pinot Noir vines are established in 'pure old Waimakariri riverbed', and grapes are also purchased from Marlborough growers.

Why the name Darjon? 'I've had a lifelong interest in horses,' says Michelle. 'One of my favourite horses, buried on this property, was called Darjon Dai.'

The first release was a 1992 Claret grown in Marlborough. The wines, not made on-site, are rare – only about 250 cases are produced each year, mostly sold at the property. I have tasted a fresh, crisp Sauvignon Blanc with moderate flavour depth; a raspberryish, Cabernet Sauvignon-based Blush; and a light, pleasant, easy-drinking Claret.

'It really is a labour of love and nobody's going to get rich,' says John. 'It's high risk, low profits and lots of fun.'

Gatehouse Wines

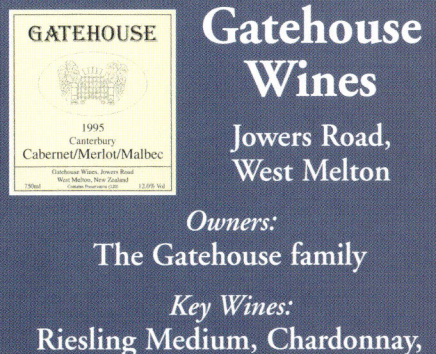

Jowers Road, West Melton

Owners:
The Gatehouse family

Key Wines:
Riesling Medium, Chardonnay, Gewürztraminer, Müller-Thurgau Dry, Estate Wine, Pinot Noir, Cabernet Sauvignon/Merlot/Malbec

Peter Gatehouse and his family produce sound, satisfying West Melton wines, sharply priced.

'True country wines' is how wine writer Peter Saunders describes Gatehouse's West Melton wines – and fair enough. They don't scale any heights, but these are honest, unpretentious, flavoursome wines, priced right.

Peter Gatehouse, the driving force behind the family-owned winery, is a ball of energy. Raised in Christchurch, he graduated with a BSc in geology and now manages an audio-visual unit at Lincoln University. Somehow he also finds time to act as a viticultural consultant, grow grapes and make and market his annual output of less than 1000 cases of wine.

The winery is owned by Peter and his wife, Carol; Peter's parents, Desmond and Esma; and Peter's brothers, Phillip and Stephen. Carol, a part-time teacher, works in the vineyard; Desmond handles the financial administration; Esma helps with the weekend sales.

Peter Gatehouse started experimenting with fruit wines in the late 1960s. 'Some turned out not too jolly bad.' He planted his first vines in Jowers Road, West Melton in the early 1980s. Today the four-hectare vineyard, planted in fine sandy loams overlying shingle and sand, is planted in Riesling, Gewürztraminer, Chardonnay, Pinot Noir, Cabernet Sauvignon, Merlot and Malbec. Grapes are also purchased from another West Melton grower.

'Frosts, especially in late spring, are a big problem,' says Carol. 'But we don't have vigorous canopies to cut back and in our cool climate Riesling develops such good flavour.'

Gatehouse produced his first, experimental grape wines in 1985. In 1987 and 1988 his grapes were sold to the Torlesse winery, in which Gatehouse was a shareholder. The year 1989 brought the first commercial release of wines under Gatehouse's Makariri label – an abbreviation of Waimakariri, the river which flows across the plains to the north.

In his spacious winery (formerly Torlesse's) Gatehouse produces a very solid line-up of wines. The American oak-aged Chardonnay is full and crisp, not highly complex but offering plenty of citrusy, slightly oaky flavour. The steely, appley Riesling unfolds well over three or four years. The blended, wood-matured Estate Wine is a satisfying dry white, mouth-filling and soft. The Pinot Noir is light, berryish and supple; not one of the classics, but very sharply priced.

Riesling, ranging in style from unflinchingly dry to honey-sweet, is the key attraction at the Giesen Wine Estate at Burnham, south of Christchurch. Chardonnay and Pinot Noir are other highlights of the Giesens' comprehensive selection of Canterbury and Marlborough wines.

Winemaker Marcel Giesen was raised at Neustadt in the winegrowing Rheinpfalz region. Granite quarrying, construction and masonry were the family's chief occupation, but the Giesens – like countless other German families – also owned a small plot of grapevines and made wine for their private consumption.

Why did they uproot themselves to start a new life in New Zealand? 'For opportunity, space, clean air and freedom,' says Marcel. Winemaking was not part of their early plans in the new country; Marcel's brothers, Theo and Alexander, were contracted to work for a Canterbury construction company specialising in natural stone.

'One weekend we went to Warners, then *the* bottle-store in Christchurch, and met Ernie Hunter, who founded Hunter's Wines. He loaded our trolley with New Zealand wines. We were confused by the number of Müller-Thurgaus labelled as 'Riesling', and astonished by the lack of dry Rieslings. We thought: 'Why not make some wine in the style we had produced at home?'

The Giesens bought land at Burnham, but not before looking at other potential vineyard sites in Auckland, Hawke's Bay, the Wairarapa and Marlborough. 'We particularly wanted to grow Riesling, which flourishes in a cool climate, so in the end it was obvious we should go south.' The brothers' parents, Kurt and Gudrun, helped to fund the new winery.

The Burham School Road vineyard now covers 20 hectares. Riesling, Chardonnay, Müller-Thurgau, Ehrenfelser (a cross of Riesling and Sylvaner) and Pinot Noir are the major varieties planted in the stony, free-draining soils. Gewürztraminer (which failed to yield satisfactorily), and Sauvignon Blanc and Cabernet Sauvignon (which struggled to ripen) have all been uprooted.

The Giesens have no regrets about coming to Burnham: 'It's as good a vineyard site as any commercial site in the country,' says Alex Giesen. 'The soils are free-draining, and we've had dry *Botrytis* [noble rot] in every year except '92 and '94. We use helicopters, if necessary, to fight frost. The free air flow

Giesen Wine Estate

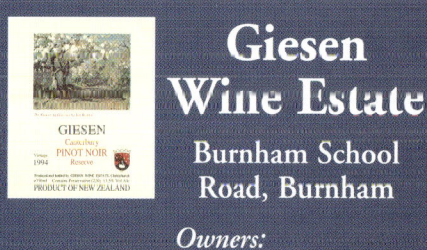

Burnham School Road, Burnham

Owners:
Theo, Alex and Marcel Giesen

Key Wines:
Canterbury Riesling Extra Dry, Riesling Marlborough, Riesling Medium, Reserve Botrytised Riesling, Reserve Chardonnay, Marlborough Chardonnay, Müller-Thurgau, Botrytised Müller-Thurgau, Ehrenfelser, Sauvignon Blanc, Estate Dry White Oak Aged, Pinot Noir, Merlot

Alex Giesen (right, pictured with winemaker Rudi Bauer) regards Riesling, Chardonnay and Pinot Noir as 'the three varieties that are definitely proven as suitable for Canterbury'.

through the vineyard lowers humidity and dries the foliage, so we get little disease.' The six-hectare Two Chain Road vineyard, a couple of kilometres from the winery, is planted in Müller-Thurgau (principally) and Pinot Gris. The Giesens also have a major stake in an eight-hectare, all-Sauvignon Blanc vineyard in Dillon's Point Road, Marlborough, and purchase grapes from Canterbury and Marlborough growers.

To keep this fast-growing, 30,000 cases per year wine company (the largest in Canterbury) on the rails, the Giesen brothers have divided between them the myriad tasks of a modern winery. Theo and Alexander are immersed in administration and marketing. Marcel controls production in the utilitarian, corrugated-iron and timber winery, with the assistance of Rudi Bauer, an Austrian-born winemaker who worked at Rippon Vineyard at Wanaka from 1989 to 1992. For both winemakers German is the first language, but they speak 'mostly English, except quite late at night'.

Marcel Giesen delights in Riesling's mouth-wateringly crisp acidity: 'You need steely acidity for structure, elegance and longevity. With the low yields we get in Canterbury, our grapes have high extract [stuffing] and the wines can carry more acidity. Riesling like this ages longer than Chardonnay or Sauvignon Blanc.'

Giesen's stunning sweet Rieslings are only made in vintages favourable to the spread of 'noble rot'. Based on estate-grown, hand-harvested, rampantly botrytised fruit with soaring sugar levels, Giesen Botrytised Riesling is a ravishingly full-bloomed, golden, honeyish beauty, its sweetness balanced by tense acidity. This is an outstanding wine by any standards, one of New Zealand's most glorious sweet whites.

Giesen's most widely seen Rieslings are the easy-drinking Riesling Medium, grown in Marlborough, and the more classy, incisively flavoured, fractionally off-dry Riesling Marlborough. There is also a vigorous, tangy, strongly wooded Riesling Oak Aged. Bone-dry, with a firm acid spine, the penetratingly flavoured, estate-grown Riesling Extra Dry is an intriguingly austere and steely style that demands to be served with food.

Apart from Riesling, Chardonnay is the other key white-wine variety in the Giesen range. The lower-tier, partly barrel-fermented Marlborough Chardonnay is full of savoury, citrusy, crisp flavour and offers fine value. The Reserve Chardonnay – in some vintages based on Canterbury fruit, in others sourced from Marlborough – is entirely barrel-fermented and given a full malolactic fermentation. The latest releases have been powerful and chewy, with rich, succulent, toasty flavours in a very upfront style and a long, buttery-soft finish.

The Giesens' charming winery shop is lined with German wine bottles; outside, oval German wine casks (foudres) also lend a distinctly German feel. Not surprisingly, apart from Riesling the Giesens produce other traditional German varieties like the pale, plentifully sweet Müller-Thurgau; deliciously weighty, rich and honeyish, oak-aged Botrytised Müller-Thurgau; dryish, easy-drinking, softly flavoursome Pinot Gris; and the floral, fine, very Riesling-like Ehrenfelser.

Red wine has traditionally played a minor role in the Giesen range, but the launch of a trio of top-flight Pinot Noirs from 1994, grown in Marlborough and Canterbury, bodes well for the future. Estate-grown, the Reserve Canterbury Pinot Noir 1994 is a very classy wine with concentrated cherry/oak flavours, complex and rich.

Down a West Melton driveway lined with English lavendar and vines and across a footbridge lies the two-storeyed, forest green Langdale Cafe and Wine Garden. Rough-sawn rimu beams and a double-sided fireplace create a warm atmosphere, with French doors opening to raised flower beds, covered seating areas and the vineyard. The menu features 'French and Italian country style' dishes, washed down, of course, with Langdale's selection of Canterbury and Marlborough wines.

Langdale's first vines were planted in 1989, followed by the first experimental wines in 1992 and 1993 and the first commercial vintage in 1994. Langdale is owned by a group of about 25 shareholders, including manager Lew Stribling.

Stribling, a former arts student at Canterbury University, worked in horticulture in Whangarei before he came back to Christchurch in 1989 to plant grapevines on the West Melton property he had purchased two years earlier. 'I developed an interest in wine going around the West Auckland vineyards,' he recalls. 'I was intrigued by the way the winemakers there were able to follow through the full creative process.'

Langdale Wine Estate

Langdales Road, West Melton

Owners:
Lew Stribling and shareholders

Key Wines:
Estate Riesling, Breidecker Medium, Breidecker Dry, Chardonnay, Pinot Noir; Marlborough Riesling, Chardonnay

The 4.5-hectare estate vineyard is planted principally in Pinot Noir, Riesling and Chardonnay, with smaller plots of Breidecker, Pinot Gris, Merlot and Cabernet Sauvignon. Grapes are also purchased from Canterbury and Marlborough growers.

Langdale's small output of wine, not made on-site, although a winery is planned, is mainly sold at the cellar door, in the restaurant or by mail-order. The initial releases of Breidecker, Chardonnay, Riesling and Pinot Noir have been of varying quality, but the lightly wooded Estate Chardonnay is attractive with its fresh, lively, green apple flavours.

Langdale, like many Canterbury 'wineries', is a restaurant operation as well as a wine producer.

Rosebank Estate – named after the 500 roses which flourish in its surrounding gardens – lies just off the main highway at Harewood, near Belfast, 15 minutes' drive north of Christchurch. Rosebank is as much a restaurant as a winery: during summer up to 400 people come for Sunday lunch. About half the wine is sold on-site.

Rosebank's founders, Brian and Margaret Shackel, previously ran a meat distribution company supplying hotels, restaurants and caterers throughout the South Island. Grant Rimmer, who gained his winemaking experience in the Hunter Valley and later at Villa Maria, made the initial 1993–95 vintages but departed in early 1996.

Unlike some of its competitors, Rosebank does not insist on growing all of its grapes in Canterbury. Far from it. The home vineyard, planted in 1991, is tiny: half a hectare of Chardonnay, Pinot Noir and Bacchus, manicured with lawn mowers and electric hedge trimmers. Grapes and wine have been drawn from everywhere – Akaroa, Waipara, Marlborough, McLaren Vale and the Barossa Valley.

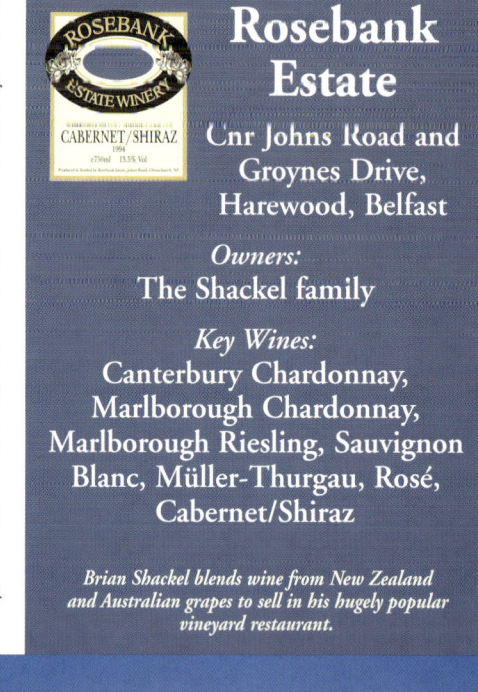

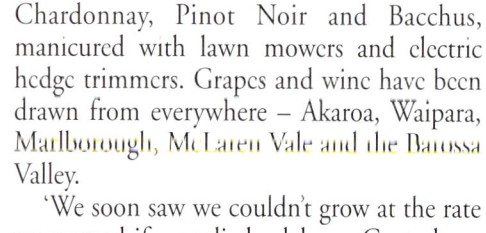

'We soon saw we couldn't grow at the rate we wanted if we relied solely on Canterbury fruit,' recalls Rimmer. 'As a winemaker, I didn't want to be shackled by Canterbury's marked vintage variations. Too many Canterbury wineries struggle to grow because they're reliant on their own fruit.'

The original buildings on the property – previously a dairy farm – have been converted; Rosebank's wine shop was formerly a two-car garage and the function centre was a hay barn. A drainage camber in the floor of the restaurant serves as a vivid reminder that this building, erected a few years ago, was at first intended to be a working winery, until a shortage of local grapes encouraged the Shackels to have their wines produced in Marlborough and at other Canterbury wineries.

Of Rosebank's annual output of about 4000 cases, the most talked-about wine to date is its Cabernet/Shiraz. An odd but workable marriage of Marlborough Cabernet Sauvignon and Barossa Valley or McLaren Vale Shiraz, this is a full, fresh and fruity red with pleasantly intertwined berryish, spicy and herbal flavours and soft, easy tannins. The South Australian Shiraz is used to give the wine extra body and structure.

Rosebank Estate Pinot Noir has also blended Marlborough fruit with a splash of Barossa Valley Shiraz. With its deep, youthful colour and fragrant raspberry/strawberry aromas, this is a fruity, firm but simple wine, lacking the flavour delights of fine Pinot Noir, but priced right.

Rosebank Marlborough Riesling is a full-bodied, off-dry wine with good depth of citrusy/limey flavour and racy acidity. The Müller-Thurgau is delicately flavoured, with an appetising sugar/acid balance. The Rosé, based on Müller-Thurgau with a splash of Cabernet Sauvignon, is berryish, soft and slightly sweet in a smooth, undemanding style.

Chardonnay is one of the highlights of the Rosebank Estate range, with the typically weighty, strong-flavoured, barrel-fermented Marlborough version joined recently by a deliciously fresh-scented, appley, nutty, crisp Canterbury Chardonnay grown at French Farm on Banks Peninsula.

Rosebank Estate

Cnr Johns Road and Groynes Drive, Harewood, Belfast

Owners:
The Shackel family

Key Wines:
Canterbury Chardonnay, Marlborough Chardonnay, Marlborough Riesling, Sauvignon Blanc, Müller-Thurgau, Rosé, Cabernet/Shiraz

Brian Shackel blends wine from New Zealand and Australian grapes to sell in his hugely popular vineyard restaurant.

Beefsteak and Burgundy are a magical match at dinner tables around the world. Rossendale, a family-owned farm, vineyard, winery and restaurant on the southern outskirts of Christchurch, is the first firm in New Zealand to export wine and beef grown on the same property and marketed under the same brand.

Rossendale, the closest winery to the centre of the city, only 12 kilometres from the Square, lies close to the Port Hills, on the edge of Halswell. Brent Rawstron manages the 166-hectare property, named after the area in Lancashire that his paternal grandparents came from, on behalf of the owners, Brent and his brothers Haydn and Grant. After cultivating crops during the late 1970s and early 1980s, a decade ago the Rawstrons diversified into beef and in 1987 the first vines sank root in their silty, sandy soils.

Ginger-bearded, with a strong marketing bent, Brent Rawstron graduated with a BA in education from Otago University, then took over the running of the family farm in 1976. He and his wife, Shirley, a GP, have both gained a postgraduate diploma in viticulture and oenology from Lincoln University.

Pinot Noir and Chardonnay (the noble varieties of Burgundy) are planted in the five-hectare estate vineyard, which is sheltered by the hills from cooling easterly winds. 'Our grapes typically ripen before those at West Melton but after North Canterbury's,' says Rawstron. White-wine grapes are also purchased from Marlborough growers.

The first 1993 and subsequent vintages have been made in the on-site winery by Dr Grant Whelan, who also produces wine under his own label (see Kaituna Valley). Production is planned to climb gradually from the current level of 1000 cases to around 3000. Much of the wine is consumed in Rossendale's 121-year-old restaurant, originally a gardener's lodge at the entrance to the Lansdowne homestead of Edward Stafford, Premier of New Zealand for over eight years between 1856–61 and 1866–69.

'Most of the wines are produced in a fruit-driven style for lunch-time consumption,' says Rawstron. 'The reserve styles are more complex and long-lived.' The Müller-Thurgau, grown in Marlborough, is a full wine with strong, citrusy, limey, rather Riesling-like characters. The Marlborough Chardonnay is impressively full, soft and creamy. The voluptuous Barrel Selection Chardonnay is very classy, with deep, toasty, mealy, soft flavours. The Pinot Noir is appealingly fragrant, delicately flavoured and supple. These are scarce, stylish wines.

Rossendale Wines

150 Old Tai Tapu Road, Halswell, Christchurch

Owners:
Brent, Haydn and Grant Rawstron

Key Wines:
Barrel Selection Chardonnay, Marlborough Chardonnay,

Much of Brent and Shirley Rawstron's consistently stylish wine is consumed in their 121-year-old restaurant, once a lodge occupied by Sir Edward Stafford's gardener.

St Helena no longer bestrides the Canterbury wine scene the way it did a decade ago, when its gold medal Pinot Noirs put the region firmly on the New Zealand wine map. The light but attractively scented and supple Pinot Noir is still the company's best known wine, but the Chardonnay, Riesling, Pinot Blanc and Pinot Gris are of equal quality.

Canterbury's oldest commercial winery was founded by brothers Robin and Norman Mundy. After nematodes rendered their potato farm unprofitable, they early took heed of the results of Lincoln University's pioneering viticultural research. By 1978 St Helena's first vines were planted at Coutts Island, near Belfast, 20 minutes' drive north of Christchurch. In late 1994, however, Norman Mundy withdrew from the venture (although he still owns vineyards leased to St Helena), leaving Robin and his wife, Bernice, as St Helena's proprietors.

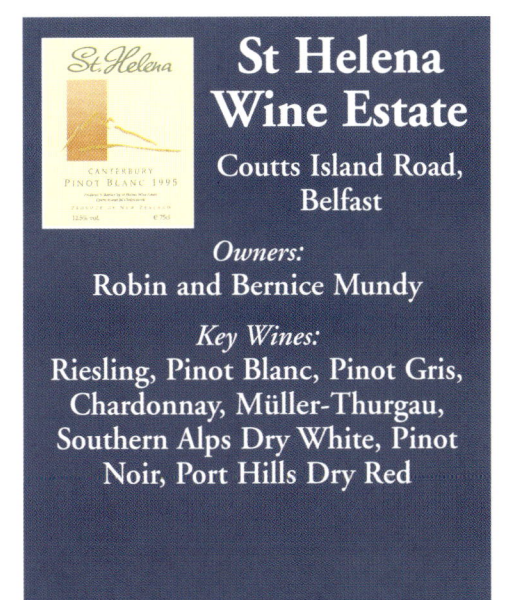

Bounded by branches of the Waimakariri River, the vineyard needs no irrigation because of its high water table. The river flow also encourages air movement, reducing but not eliminating the risk of frost damage to the vines. There was no 1987 Pinot Noir: three weeks before the expected harvest, an extreme, -10°C frost defoliated the vines, leaving the grapes with no chance of ripening. Today when frost threatens a helicopter is hired at $1000 per hour to hover over the vineyard creating a downdraught of warmer air.

The 20-hectare vineyard, planted in free-draining, high fertility soils, is established principally in Pinot Noir, Chardonnay, Pinot Blanc, Pinot Gris, Riesling, Müller-Thurgau

St Helena Wine Estate

Coutts Island Road, Belfast

Owners:
Robin and Bernice Mundy

Key Wines:
Riesling, Pinot Blanc, Pinot Gris, Chardonnay, Müller-Thurgau, Southern Alps Dry White, Pinot Noir, Port Hills Dry Red

St Helena, owned by Robin and Bernice Mundy, produces good wines from Chardonnay and Pinot Noir, supplemented by a fine value Pinot Blanc.

and Bacchus (for blending). 'We're putting a lot of effort into reducing vine vigour,' says winemaker Petter Evans. St Helena's premium varietal wines are wholly estate-grown, but some grapes are bought from other growers for the lower-tier wines.

With winemaker Danny Schuster at the helm from the first vintage, 1981 until 1985, St Helena achieved gold medal status with its 1982 and 1984 Pinot Noirs. His white wines, as a rule, were full-bodied and austere. Mark Rattray, the winemaker from 1985 until 1990, produced more commercial, fractionally sweeter and softer white wines.

Petter Evans, a Roseworthy College oenology graduate, joined St Helena in early 1991. A Cantabrian, Evans gained his early winemaking experience at Cloudy Bay and Limeburners Bay and has also worked at Château Remy in Victoria and in Germany. Evans significantly sharpened the wine quality at Pleasant Valley in Henderson between 1988 and late 1990.

The brick fronted, insulated aluminium winery was erected in 1981. St Helena produces 10,000 cases of wine in an average year, which the province has seen few of lately. The bargain-priced, briefly oak-aged Pinot Blanc (which sells well in the UK) is a hearty dry white with a subtle bouquet and pleasing depth of savoury, earthy flavour. 'Pinot Blanc is the most underrated grape in the country for a good dry white,' says Mundy. 'It crops almost twice as heavily as Chardonnay, and at five years old can taste quite Chardonnay-like.'

The Riesling displays fresh, slightly sweet, green-apple flavours in a light, delicate, tangy style. Southern Alps Dry White is a mild, lemony, drink-young blend with a sliver of sweetness to balance its lively acidity. The barrel-fermented Chardonnay varies in quality according to the vintage but can be top-flight; at six years old the 1989 Chardonnay was superbly rich-flavoured and sustained.

The briefly oak-aged Port Hills Dry Red is a chunky, flavoursome red that offers no-fuss, well-priced drinking. For Petter Evans, however, 'Pinot Noir is the big challenge. I'm spending much of my energy on the Pinot Noir. There are so many levels of quality – to get the extra is the hard part.'

The 1982, 1984, 1985 and 1988 vintages of St Helena Pinot Noir were powerful, deep-hued and supple, but of late the wine has grown markedly lighter. This is now a good, but not outstanding, wine, appealingly fragrant, raspberryish, spicy and smooth.

Sandihurst Wines

Main West Coast Road, West Melton

Owners: John and Joan Brough

Key Wines: Gewürztraminer, Gewürztraminer Reserve, Pinot Gris, Pinot Gris Reserve, Chardonnay, Breidecker, Riesling, Patio Red, Pinot Noir

---

'Gewürztraminer is where we'll make a name for ourselves,' predicts John Brough, proprietor of this fast-growing West Melton winery. I agree. With its mouth-filling body and strong surge of crisp, dry, peppery, persistent flavours, Sandihurst's aromatic Gewürztraminer Reserve is a very classy wine.

Named after the sandy knolls (hursts) that are a feature of the district, Sandihurst lies 25 kilometres from Christchurch near the township of West Melton, on the inland Christchurch-to-Arthurs Pass highway. John Brough and his wife, Joan, planted their first vines on these windswept plains in 1988.

Brough worked in the Christchurch-based fishing industry for 33 years, owning a boatyard, fishing boats and a fish-processing factory. In 1987, when he sold out of fishing, 'there was a fair bit of hype in the papers about the success of Canterbury vineyards'. Today the Broughs' own 16-hectare vineyard is planted principally in Chardonnay, Pinot Gris, Riesling and Pinot Noir, with smaller plots of Gewürztraminer and Breidecker. After failing to flourish, Merlot, Cabernet Sauvignon and Sauvignon Blanc have all been 'flagged away'.

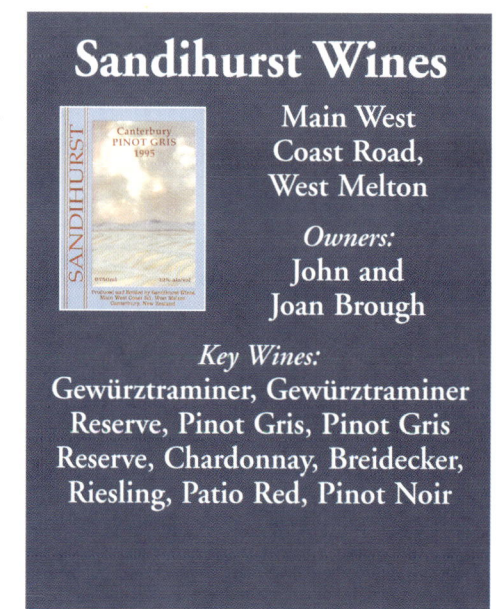

Wind is a key force in the vineyard; shelter belts are essential. Warm, dry nor'-westers reduce disease problems but the cool nor'-easters slow the grapes' ripening. 'Lincoln University reported that the heat summation here is ideal for Alsace and Burgundy varieties,' says Brough.

In a three-bay implement shed converted into a winery, winemaker Tony Coakley produced Sandihurst's first vintage in 1992. Coakley, a Cantabrian, has a graduate diploma in viticulture and oenology from Lincoln University and has previously worked at Neudorf, Merlen and in Oregon.

Coakley shares Brough's enthusiasm for Gewürztraminer. '"Gewürz" doesn't like a hot vintage. We pick it at around 21 brix [sugar level], so it's not too fruity, with good acidity.' Robust, dry and firm, the Gewürztraminer Reserve is a 'serious' wine in a powerful and deep-flavoured style.

The fractionally off-dry Pinot Gris and richer, drier Pinot Gris Reserve both show clearcut varietal character. The distinctly medium Breidecker is a light, vigorous wine with lemony, green apple-like flavours and tense acidity. The Chardonnay, a lightly oaked blend of Marlborough and Canterbury grapes, is citrusy and steely in a slightly austere, cool-climate style.

Patio Red, a light, easy-drinking wine based principally on Pinot Noir, is fresh, crisp and berryish; I'd serve it chilled as a decent dry rosé. The Pinot Noir is also a light style, with a Beaujolais-like charm in its youth.

Tony Coakley (left) and vineyard manager Mark Ludemann are starting to produce deep-flavoured wines from Gewürztraminer and Pinot Gris.

With three Pinot Noirs in his range, there's no doubt about Dayne Sherwood's specialty. 'We're looking for a longer-lived style of Pinot Noir,' he says. 'We want bigger, heavier wines with well-structured tannins.'

With its steep-pitched roof and colour of natural wood, Sherwood Estate's winery at West Melton is one of the most handsome in Canterbury. Sherwood and his wife, Jill, who oversees the company's administration and restaurant, planted their first vines in 1986. In free-draining silt loams over a gravel riverbed base, six hectares of Chardonnay, Pinot Noir (the two principal varieties), Riesling and Müller-Thurgau have been established. Grapes are also purchased from growers in Canterbury and Marlborough.

Dayne Sherwood is a Cantabrian who, after graduating with a BA in business administration and history, initially worked for an accountancy company and a bank. After spells at Torlesse and Hunter's, and gaining a post-graduate diploma in viticulture and oenology from Lincoln University, in 1990 Sherwood made the move into full-time winemaking. 'It all started from drinking the stuff,' he recalls, 'and then wanting to know more about it.

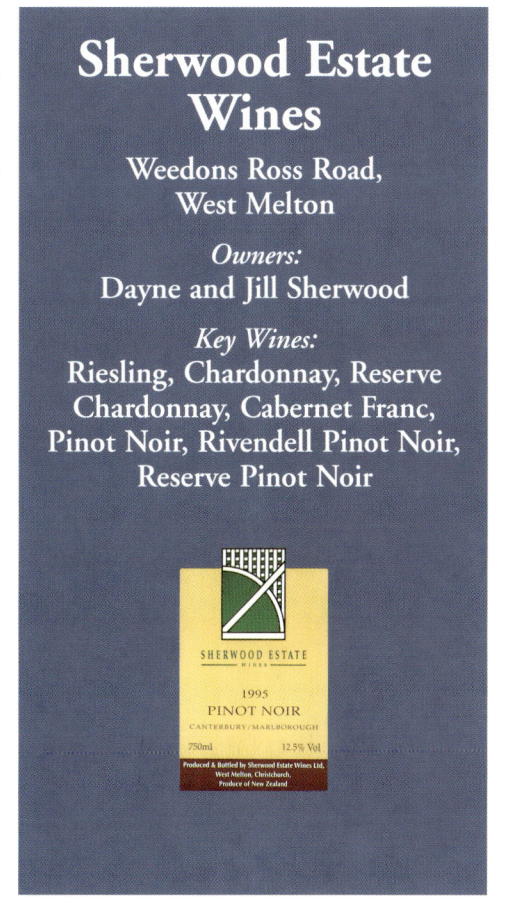

Sherwood Estate Wines

Weedons Ross Road,
West Melton

Owners:
Dayne and Jill Sherwood

Key Wines:
Riesling, Chardonnay, Reserve Chardonnay, Cabernet Franc, Pinot Noir, Rivendell Pinot Noir, Reserve Pinot Noir

Now it's a lifestyle and a business.'

Sherwood is a fan of Canterbury grapes, which he says produce wines with 'taut, tight structures and piercing fruit characters'. Easterly winds during flowering can be a problem, reducing yields, and irrigation is needed to prevent the vines becoming excessively water-stressed, but Sherwood reports having 'never been hit by frosts, and no problem getting sufficient heat to ripen the grapes.'

The first 1990 Riesling was produced at the Gatehouse winery, but the wines are now all made on-site. At first the Sherwoods planned to produce about 1500 cases of wine per year, but the output has climbed steadily and is expected to reach 7000 cases by 1997. Much of the wine is consumed in the vineyard restaurant, where the luncheon food ranges from small snacks of olives and cheeses to chicken vol-au-vents and home-made salmon pies.

The Pinot Noirs, typically, though not always, a marriage of Marlborough and Canterbury fruit, ascend from the fruit-driven style labelled simply Pinot Noir, to the barrel-matured Rivendell Pinot Noir (named after the Rivendell vineyard in

Dayne and Jill Sherwood are carving out a national reputation for their sturdy, strongly flavoured Pinot Noirs.

Marlborough), and finally to the hand-harvested, more heavily new oak-influenced Reserve Pinot Noir. My favourites are the bargain-priced, chunky, vibrantly fruity, almost sweet-tasting Pinot Noir and the robust, slightly meaty, rich-flavoured and firmly tannic Reserve Pinot Noir.

Sherwood Estate's white-wine selection features a pale, appley, tart Riesling and vigorous, slightly austere, rather Chablis-like Chardonnays. The Reserve Chardonnay, predominantly estate-grown and French oak-fermented, is an impressively weighty and full-flavoured wine, savoury, citrusy and nutty, with mouth-watering crispness.

Sherwood works six to seven days per week but enjoys the lifestyle. 'We've produced something from nothing – a piece of dirt used for grazing sheep – and are now making an income,' says Dayne. 'I'd do it all again.'

Silverstream Vineyard

Giles Road, Clarkville

Owners:
Peter and Gesina Todd

Key Wines:
Chardonnay, Pinot Noir

Most tall people would feel short standing next to Peter and Gesina ('Zeke') Todd, owners of the tiny Silverstream winery. 'We're the biggest winemakers in Canterbury,' grins Peter.

Silverstream, at Clarkville, near Kaiapoi, takes its name from a local, spring-fed stream where – on rare breaks from their seven days per week toil – the Todds go fishing. After losing most of their first 1988 vine plantings in a drought, and replanting in 1989, their first, silver medal-winning Silverstream Pinot Noir flowed in 1992.

Born in Holland, Zeke Todd came to Canterbury as a child and first crossed paths with Peter in London. Dark and strongly built, Dr Peter Todd was born to an Italian mother and English father: 'I consider myself more Italian than English,' he says. After gaining a PhD in molecular genetics from Leiden University in Holland, he worked as a research scientist and then came to New Zealand with Zeke in 1981. He still works part-time as a medical writer and editor of Japanese medical texts.

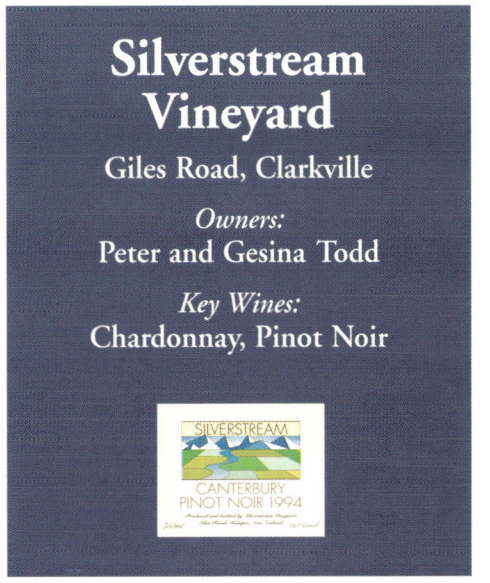

What prompted the Todds to make wine? 'We lived for a while in Collio, in north-eastern Italy, and used to go around the vineyards there, observing the differences in their grapegrowing and winemaking. The hills and plains of Canterbury reminded us of Italy, and St Helena had shown what could be done.'

The four-hectare vineyard, established in high fertility, alluvial silt loams, is planted two-thirds in Pinot Noir, one-third in

Chardonnay. The Todds do most of the work themselves: 'Peter does the tractor-work and makes the wine; I do most of the rest,' says Zeke.

The wines are 100 per cent estate-grown. 'Site is important,' says Peter. 'That's where our wines' distinctive features come from. We feel very strongly about that.'

The Todds produce about 1000 cases of wine each year in their on-site winery, and plan to grow to about 3000 cases. The Chardonnay is soft and rich, with rewarding depth of leesy, complex, buttery flavour. The deliciously perfumed, fleshy, ripe-flavoured 1992 Pinot Noir has been a hard act to follow, but this is a consistently characterful and sharply priced red.

Other Producers

French Farm

The handsome winery and restaurant at French Farm Bay, on Banks Peninsula, produced its first wines in 1991, based on Canterbury and Marlborough grapes. However, production ceased in 1994; the three-hectare estate vineyard and winery were leased to winemaker Mark Rattray and the restaurant to Peter and Jayne Thornley. The wines now sold in the popular restaurant under the French Farm label are purchased from Canterbury winemakers. The first 1994 crop off the home vineyard yielded a sturdy, full-flavoured and flinty French Farm Banks Peninsula Chardonnay and an auspiciously fragrant, stylish and supple French Farm Banks Peninsula Pinot Noir.

Kaituna Valley

Dr Grant Whelan, winemaker at Rossendale, and his wife, Helen, who also has a PhD, produce a trickle of fine quality Pinot Noir under their own label. Graeme Stean's vineyard, planted in 1979 on a north-facing slope in the Kaituna Valley on Banks Peninsula, is the source of the grapes. When the first 1993 vintage won a gold medal and trophy at the 1995 Liquorland Royal Easter Wine Show, it was the first New Zealand gold awarded to a Canterbury Pinot Noir since the St Helena 1984.

Waipara Estates

Marlborough winemaker Allan Scott (who was raised in North Canterbury) and his wife,

Dr Peter and Zeke Todd produce a characterful Chardonnay and Pinot Noir, full-flavoured and well-priced.

Catherine, have formed an equal partnership with Tony and Helen Willy, owners of a Waipara vineyard established in Sauvignon Blanc and Cabernet Sauvignon. Future plantings will focus on Chardonnay, Riesling and Pinot Noir. The 1995 Waipara Estates Chancellor Sauvignon was a good debut – fresh, aromatic, full-flavoured and zesty.

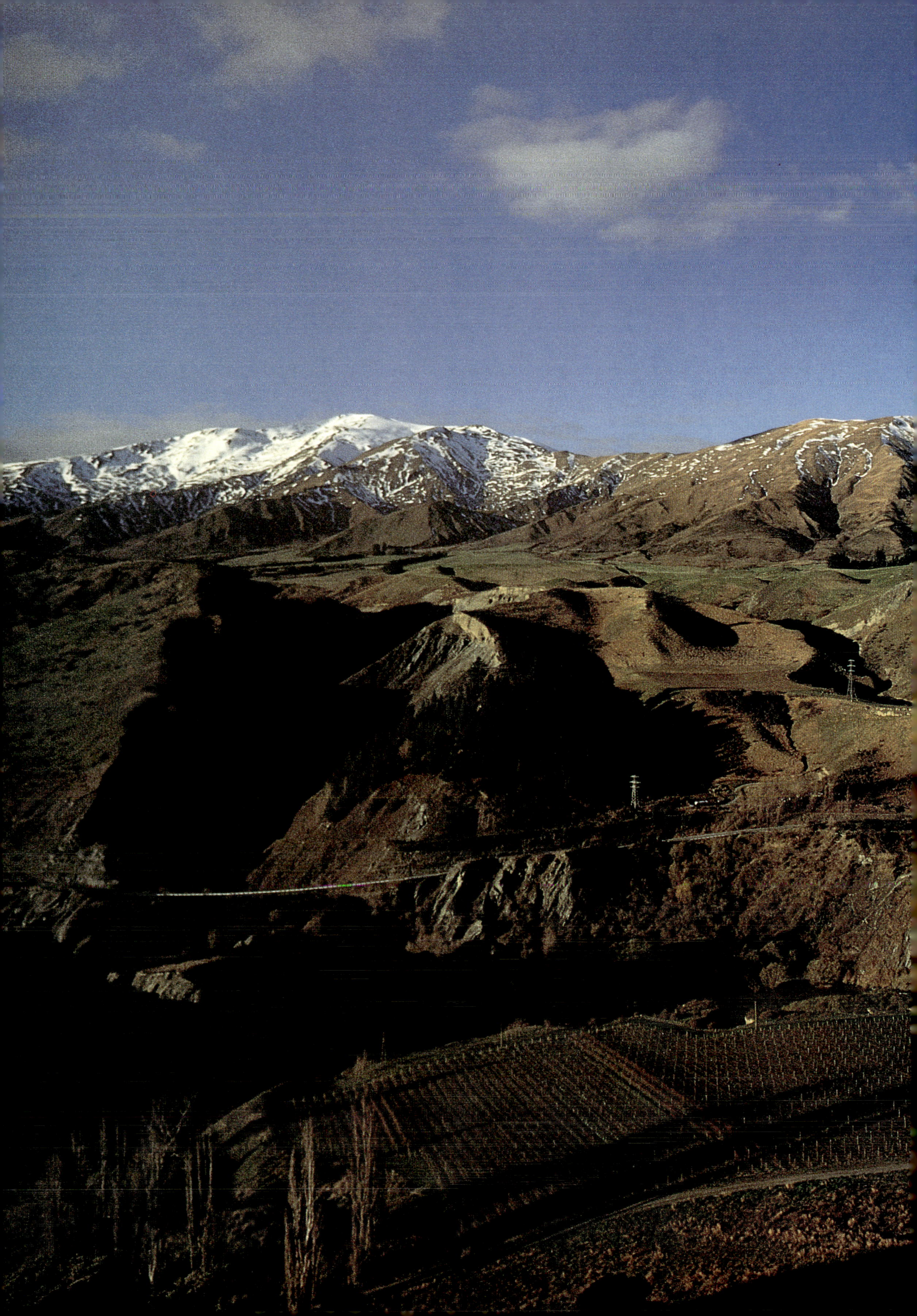

OTAGO

PRODUCERS

Black Ridge Vineyard
Chard Farm Vineyard
Gibbston Valley Wines
Kawarau Estate
Omarama Vineyard
Rippon Vineyard
William Hill Vineyard

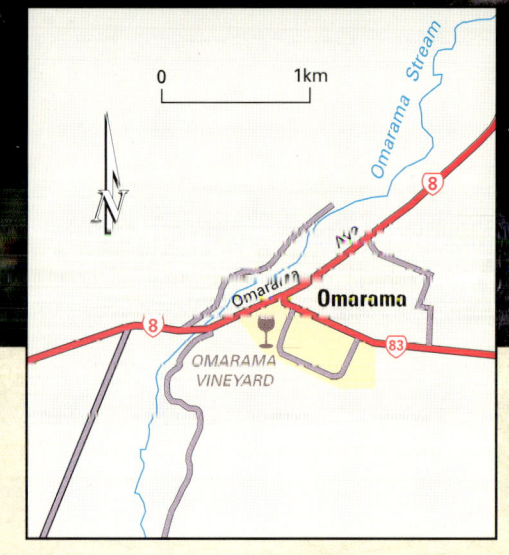

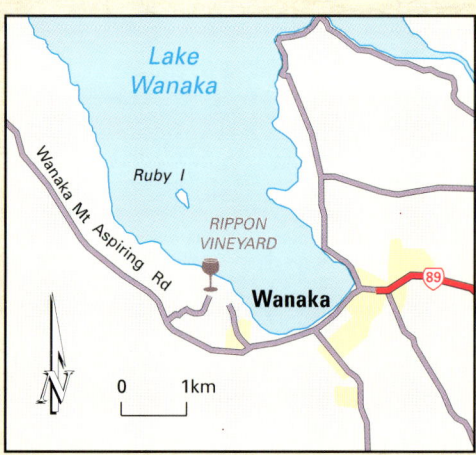

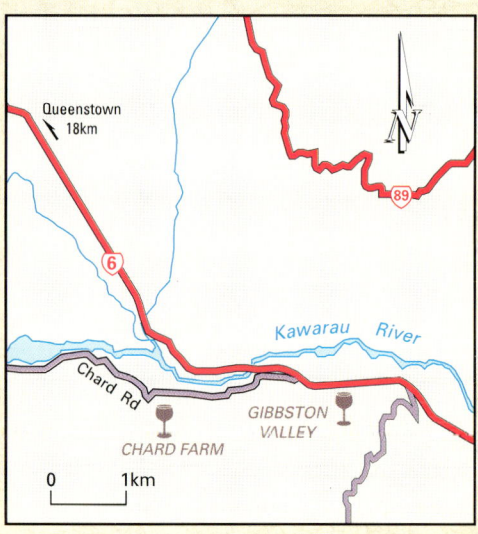

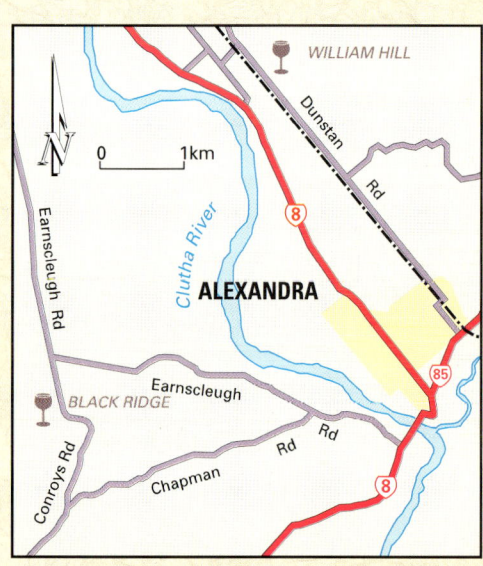

OTAGO

In early summer, grape flowers bloom along the narrow, north-facing strip of land on the south bank of the tumbling Kawarau River, between Cromwell and Queenstown. Wine fever is abroad in Central Otago. 'In the late 1980s, about 10 people would attend meetings of the local grapegrowers and winemakers' association,' recalls pioneer Alexandra winemaker, Bill Grant. 'Now we get over 100.'

Central Otago is further inland than any other wine region in New Zealand. This is a region of climatic extremes: the country's highest and lowest temperatures were both recorded near Alexandra. Summer is typically hot, autumn short and winter icy-cold.

The crunch question has been whether this region is sufficiently warm to support commercial wineries. To properly ripen, grapes must receive a certain amount of heat during the growing season. Meteorological readings confirm that the region's climate is extremely marginal for viticulture, cooler even than Germany, the most hazardous of European wine countries – and the source of its most elegant white wines.

Frosts pose another danger, threatening tender spring growth as well as the ripening bunches in autumn. Taramea, a tiny vineyard and winery established in 1982 on the valley floor at Speargrass Flat, near Coronet Peak, has in recent vintages been decimated by frosts. In such a relatively cool viticultural region, a sunny, elevated, north-facing vineyard site with a low frost risk is essential.

Being so far south, however, the hours of sunlight are long. 'On a warm day it stays above 10°C, for a long time, so the fruit carries on ripening,' says Rob Hay of Chard Farm. Dry autumn weather is another of the region's viticultural assets, encouraging the winemakers to leave their grapes late on the vines, into May or even June, ripening undamaged by autumn rains. Due to the lack of humidity, 'noble rot' is rare.

If you ask Rob Hay about the most important climatic influences on grapegrowing in Central Otago, the first factor he mentions is altitude. 'We're over 300 metres above sea level, which has a cooling effect. We're at a latitude of 45 degrees south, which is equivalent to Bordeaux and Burgundy, and we're inland. All those factors give you cool nights and suit grapes like Pinot Noir and Chardonnay that like to ripen slowly.'

A cluster of 10-hectare vineyards have recently been planted in the Gibbston Valley, protected from marauding rabbits by plastic guards and net fences. The principal new area of expansion, however, is an old goldmining settlement near Cromwell, where visitors are welcomed to 'Bannockburn, heart of the desert'. The vines at Bannockburn, which boasts Central Otago's warmest sites for grapegrowing, are irrigated with water delivered from old goldmining water-races.

With 152 hectares of vines planted in 1995, Otago ranks as New Zealand's seventh largest wine region, ahead of Nelson and Waikato/Bay of Plenty. Pinot Noir and Chardonnay are the predominant varieties (accounting for over 60 per cent of all plantings) followed by Sauvignon Blanc, Riesling, Gewürztraminer and Pinot Gris.

The finest wines flowing from Central Otago are its deep-scented, intensely varietal Pinot Noirs, but the Gewürztraminers and Chardonnays are also brimful of promise. The naturally high acid levels of the region's wines also suggest a strong future in bottle-fermented sparklings.

Black Ridge Vineyard

Conroy's Road, Alexandra

Owners:
Verdun Burgess and Sue Edwards

Key Wines:
Riesling, Gewürztraminer, Select Chardonnay, Earnscleugh Rise, Pinot Noir

Black Ridge is a vineyard blown out of rock. Bulldozers carved the dramatic, rock-strewn landscape to allow pockets of vines to be established, before each post hole was blasted with a stick of gelignite. Where grapes cannot grow, the wildly shaped schist outcrops are left to the wild thyme and the rabbits.

The southernmost winery in the world lies on a north-facing slope at Conroy's Gully, near Alexandra. The Old Man, Dunstan and Hawkdun ranges, which can be draped in snow even in mid-summer, provide a panoramic view from the vineyard.

Verdun Burgess and his partner, Sue Edwards, planted their first vines in 1981. Born in Invercargill, Burgess came to Alexandra as a builder, but when the Clyde dam was finished, work dried up. Grapegrowing looked to be 'the most economic thing to do with the land', so in 1989 he moved into wine on a full-time basis.

Tall, rugged, moustachioed, pipe-smoking, extroverted – Burgess is a forceful personality. 'We're cowboys around here,' he grins. 'I love shooting rabbits. They're good fun and they don't shoot back.'

The seven-hectare vineyard is planted in a few centimetres of topsoil overlying a layer of clay, with a hard, almost impenetrable rock subsoil. For Burgess, this 'rough, rocky terrain has a particular beauty I love.' A visiting wine merchant took one look and labelled it a 'hero's vineyard'.

Burgess believes the schist flavours the wine. 'Riesling has a very tough root system. It can squeeze water out of a stone, and it sucks minerals out of the rock. Black Ridge flavours are especially pronounced in the Riesling.'

Riesling, Gewürztraminer, Chardonnay, Breidecker and Pinot Noir are the featured varieties at Black Ridge. Cabernet Sauvignon is planted on the top slope, where, Burgess says, 'it's too hot for anything else'.

Only a trickle of wine flows from Black Ridge – about 1000 cases per year, starting to climb to 2000 cases. Since 1992 Mike Wolter (who is also the winemaker for other small producers) has worked in an on-site winery that, says Burgess, 'will be under construction for many extensions yet'.

Black Ridge Riesling is pale lemon-green in hue, with a fresh, citrusy, appley bouquet. The palate displays light citric and apple-like flavours, spine-tingling acidity and an appealing, Mosel-like delicacy. Gewürztraminer, the earliest-ripening variety, yields a big, dryish, peppery wine with pronounced varietal character.

The Select Chardonnay is a satisfyingly weighty and complex style with lots of savoury, appley, nutty flavour and a cool-climate steeliness and vigour. Earnscleugh Rise, a slightly sweet blend based principally on Breidecker, is floral, light and mild in a very undemanding style.

Recent vintages of Black Ridge Pinot Noir have demonstrated that a good red wine can be coaxed from the lowly rated (except for sparkling wine) Bachtobel clone. This is a fleshy, richly coloured and perfumed red with a restrained touch of oak, firm tannins and oodles of cherry, plum and spice flavour, deliciously fresh and vibrant.

During summer in Verdun Burgess' and Sue Edwards' Alexandra vineyard, temperatures are often still hovering around 30°C at 6pm.

Chard Farm Vineyard

Chard Road, Gibbston

Owners:
Rob and Greg Hay

Key Wines:
Riesling, Riesling Dry, Judge and Jury Chardonnay, Closeburn Chardonnay, Southern Lakes Chardonnay, Gewürztraminer, Sauvignon Blanc, Pinot Gris, Pinot Noir, Bragato Reserve Pinot Noir

Chardonnay and Pinot Noir have been the greatest successes at Chard Farm. 'When we started planting vines a decade ago, most of the talk was about Central Otago being suited only to German varieties,' recalls Rob Hay. 'But it's warmer here than people think. We took a punt on Burgundian varieties – and that punt has been successful.'

On a north-facing ledge 70 metres above the Kawarau River, with a riveting view across the gorge to the snow-draped Cardrona Range and Coronet Peak, Rob and his brother, Greg, have planted one of the country's most stunningly beautiful vineyards. 'We picked the site solely with quality wine in mind,' says Rob, 'not for its tourist potential – which is what many people think.'

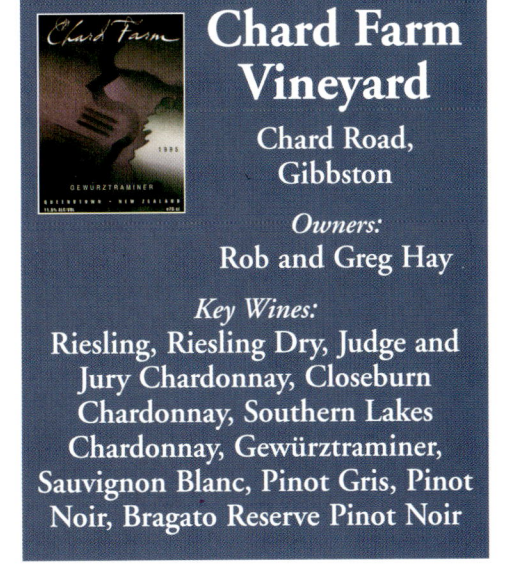

Chard Farm lies just off the main highway, 20 kilometres east of Queenstown. The precipitous access route to the vineyard, skirting sheer bluffs with a steep plunge to the river for the unwary, was once the Cromwell–Queenstown road; Chard Farm starts at the cattle-stop.

The land was originally worked by Richard Chard in the 1870s as a market garden, supplying food to the miners heading for the goldfields. Later, Chard Farm became a dairy farm and a stone-fruit orchard. The Hays uprooted the fruit trees before they planted their first vines in 1987.

Born in Motueka, Rob Hay graduated from Otago University with a BSc, and then embarked on a three-year study and work course in Baden and Wurttemberg. After

Brothers Rob (left) and Greg Hay have built Chard Farm into one of Central Otago's largest and most respected wineries.

working at Babich and Ruby Bay, in 1986 Hay came to the deep south. 'I could feel it would be good,' he recalls. 'I looked at the temperatures and tasted Alan Brady's grapes – the proof of the potential was there on the vines.'

Greg Hay, a marketing graduate, is Chard Farm's vineyard manager while Rob oversees the administration and winemaking. In moderately fertile silt loams with some clay bands overlying shingly sub-soil, the Hays have planted 12 hectares of vines. Pinot Noir and Chardonnay together cover two-thirds of the vineyard, with the rest devoted principally to Riesling, Gewürztraminer, Pinot Gris and Sauvignon Blanc. A few kilometres away at Lake Hayes, another vineyard was planted on a joint venture basis in 1992, and since 1994 grapes have also been purchased from Bannockburn.

The 1989 to 1992 wines were produced along the road at Gibbston Valley, but Chard Farm's own large steel winery, capable 'with a few extra tanks' of producing 18,000 cases, was erected for the 1993 vintage. With its current annual production level of around 10,000 cases, Chard Farm ranks alongside Gibbston Valley as one of Central Otago's largest producers.

The wines are marketed under two brands: Chard Farm and Southern Lakes. The top-tier, Chard Farm label is reserved for Central Otago, although not necessarily estate-grown, wines. The wines labelled Southern Lakes are grown outside the region or blended from Central Otago and other grapes.

Three Chardonnays are marketed. The premium Judge and Jury Chardonnay (named after prominent outcrops of rock across the gorge) is a blend of estate-grown and Bannockburn fruit, fermented in all-new French oak barriques. Fleshy and toasty, with lots of mealy, citrusy, buttery flavour and a rich, flinty finish, it flourishes with cellaring; the 1991 vintage is currently at the peak of its powers. Both the middle-tier, cask and tank-fermented Closeburn Chardonnay and Southern Lakes Chardonnay are full, subtly oaked, vibrantly fruity wines with a touch of complexity and strong drink-young appeal.

The Rieslings (both a medium Riesling and a Riesling Dry are made) are a copybook cool-climate style, in top vintages piercingly fragrant, flavourful and zesty. The Gewürztraminer is crisp, fresh and clearly varietal; the Sauvignon Blanc is racy, with very good depth of gooseberry/capsicum flavour.

Rob Hay predicts a bright future for Pinot Gris at Chard Farm. 'In a good vintage, by using older oak and lees-stirring, we should be able to make a decent food wine – an alternative to Chardonnay at Sauvignon Blanc prices.' This is a weighty, crisp, earthy wine with rich stone-fruit flavours.

Chard Farm Pinot Noir abounds with fresh, vibrant, cherryish fruit flavours, spicy, slightly smoky and deliciously forward in their appeal. The Bragato Reserve Pinot Noir has in the past not quite matched Rippon Vineyard's and Gibbston Valley's, but in its youth the 1995 vintage showed markedly more concentration and flavour richness.

The rust-red Gibbston Valley winery and restaurant attracts 50,000 visitors per year and is just along the road from another major tourist attraction, the old Kawarau Gorge railway bridge, now swarming with bungy-jumpers. The locally grown Pinot Noir is consistently classy, and for a fee you can tour the winery and sample young wines from the barrel in Gibbston Valley's new, 76-metre long underground cellars.

'My dream is an unbroken wall of vines along the Gibbston Valley,' says Alan Brady, the bearded, Irish-born founder. Brady purchased his briar-covered, craggy property, 25 kilometres from Queenstown, in 1976, and in 1981 and 1982 planted 350 grapevines to 'prove they would grow'. The first vintage of Gibbston Valley wine was bottled in 1984.

Gibbston Valley Wines

Queenstown-Cromwell Highway, Gibbston

Owners:
Alan Brady and shareholders

Key Wines:
Central Otago Pinot Noir, Pinot Gris, Sauvignon Blanc, Riesling, Chardonnay; Marlborough Riesling, Chardonnay; Waitiri Dry White, Ryecroft Red

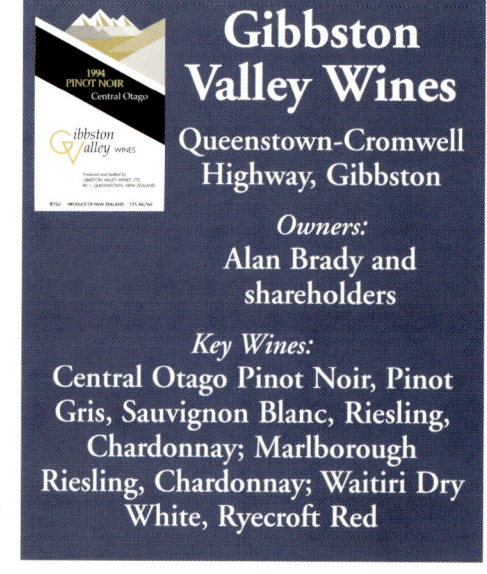

After coming to New Zealand as a 23-year-old, Brady worked on the *Evening Standard* and *Otago Daily Times*, became a television news editor in Dunedin, and later freelanced as a journalist, producer and director. In early 1990, after taking in partners ('I've never had any dynastic intentions regards the company,' he says) Brady plunged into wine on a full-time basis.

On a north-facing schist ledge at the foot of rocky bluffs, the three-hectare estate vineyard flanking the winery has been close-planted in Pinot Noir, Riesling, Pinot Gris and Sauvignon Blanc. Winery shareholders own other vineyards in the Gibbston Valley, and fruit is also purchased from growers in Central Otago and Marlborough. Of

Gibbston Valley's 1996 output of 12,000 cases of wine, 80 per cent was grown in Central Otago.

Wine has always been a hobby for winemaker Grant Taylor. Raised in North Otago, after graduating from Lincoln University with a Diploma of Agriculture, from 1980 to 1985 he was assistant winemaker at Pine Ridge winery in the Napa Valley, then chief winemaker at Domaine Napa from 1987 to 1993. Taylor joined Gibbston Valley in 1993 because the area's pioneering spirit appealed to him. 'In California I was one of a thousand winemakers. Here there are very few of us and we are still learning how to capture Central Otago's character in a bottle.'

The 1990 vintage of Gibbston Valley Pinot Noir – along with Rippon Vineyard's – first proved that Central Otago can produce top-flight wine. Both Brady and Taylor have a passion for Pinot Noir. 'Every winemaker wants to make a good red,' says Taylor. 'There's so much more work goes into it, shovelling out tanks of skins and so on; whites are just a warm-up. And Pinot Noir gets winemakers excited. Every year I like it more and more; it's a love affair that lasts.'

Gibbston Valley Central Otago Pinot Noir is stylish, mouth-filling and rounded with subtle, cherryish, spicy flavours, French oak complexity and a ripe, lingering finish. Ryecroft Red is a non-oaked, fresh and vibrantly fruity, drink-young style based on Marlborough Pinot Noir.

Grant Taylor has a hunch that Pinot Gris may emerge ultimately as Gibbston Valley's top white wine. 'Chardonnay ripens here with very high acid levels; Pinot Gris may prove better in that respect. But everyone likes Chardonnay and you express your region through Chardonnay.' Pale and aromatic, the Central Otago Pinot Gris offers plenty of peachy, earthy flavour, a distinct splash of sweetness and lively acidity. The barrel-fermented Central Otago Chardonnay, launched from the 1995 vintage, is delicious in its youth – fragrant and full, with rich, peachy, toasty, complex flavours.

Gibbston Valley's partly oak-aged Central Otago Sauvignon Blanc is tangy and briskly herbaceous. The Central Otago Riesling varies according to the vintage, but at its best is fresh, incisively flavoured and springy.

Waitiri Dry White is a light wine based on Marlborough Müller-Thurgau and Riesling, slightly sweet and mild. The Marlborough Chardonnay, part barrel, part tank-fermented, and Marlborough Riesling are both of a consistently high standard, with a delicious depth of fresh, vibrant fruit flavours.

Carved in 1995 into a steep bluff behind the winery, a dimly lit, 50-metre long tunnel leads to two side caves and a large chamber with a five-metre high vaulted ceiling. In Central Otago's climate of extremes (from 35°C in summer to -10°C in winter) the caves provide a stable year-round environment of 12–13°C, ideal for the storage of bottled wine and (eventually) over 400 casks of maturing Pinot Noir, Chardonnay and Sauvignon Blanc.

Alan Brady, one of the leading pioneers of Central Otago wine, became a Member of the New Zealand Order of Merit in the 1996 Queen's Birthday honours list.

Otago's vineyards are spreading beyond Central. Rob and Joan Watson's Omarama Vineyard is North Otago's first commercial wine venture.

In a north-facing basin alongside the main highway at Omarama (half way between Mt Cook and Cromwell), a decade ago Watson – a farmer and musterer – planted his first, experimental vines. Pinot Gris performed well in the silty, gravelly soils and today the one-hectare, irrigated vineyard is planted in four varieties: Pinot Gris, Morio-Muskat, the Geisenheim crossing GM312-53, and Müller-Thurgau.

The 1994 Pinot Gris, made at the Black Ridge winery, was sold at $5 per glass at Omarama Vineyard's vineyard shop and café, which opened in early 1995. This was a good debut: clearly varietal with plenty of peachy, earthy flavour and a slightly sweet, mouth-wateringly crisp finish. Don't look for it at Liquorland – the total production was 140 bottles.

Omarama Vineyard

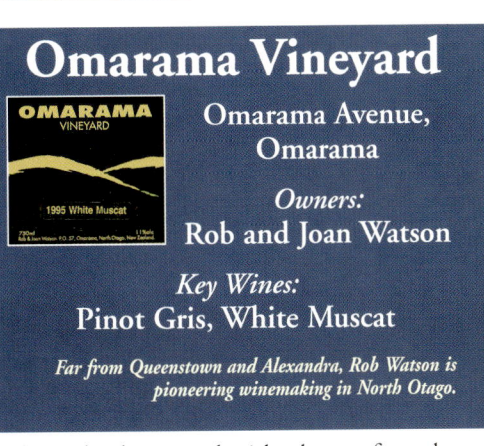

Omarama Avenue, Omarama

Owners:
Rob and Joan Watson

Key Wines:
Pinot Gris, White Muscat

Far from Queenstown and Alexandra, Rob Watson is pioneering winemaking in North Otago.

Rippon Vineyard
Mt Aspiring Road, Wanaka

Owners:
Rolfe and Lois Mills

Key Wines:
Pinot Noir, Selection Pinot Noir, Gamay Rosé, Osteiner, Gewürztraminer, Sauvignon Blanc, Riesling, Chardonnay, Hotere White

Rolfe and Lois Mills produce an exceptional Pinot Noir in one of the country's most breathtakingly beautiful vineyard settings.

The first classic wine to have emerged from Central Otago is Rippon Vineyard's exceptionally rich-flavoured Selection Pinot Noir. That status and the achingly beautiful view aren't Rippon's only claims to fame. 'We're New Zealand's closest vineyard to the sun,' says proprietor Rolfe Mills. 'At 310 metres above sea level, I believe we are the highest.'

Rippon Vineyard runs down a gentle schist slope to the shores of Lake Wanaka. The blue-water view to the majestic snow and cloud-capped peaks of the Buchanan Range at the head of the lake is glorious, but for Mills and his wife, Lois, it is wine that is 'all consuming'. The Mills' small winery sits at the crest of the slope, their house in the middle, and their little wine sales building down by the lake-shore.

Rolfe Mills planted his first vines, Seibels and Albany Surprise, at Wanaka in 1976. White-haired and gentlemanly, he is the grandson of Sir Percy Sargood, who once owned Wanaka Station. After a career as the sales director of the family clothing and footwear company, Sargoods, Mills came to Wanaka not knowing what he wanted to do.

'My only link with wine was drinking it. I'd been to Portugal and seen land in the Douro Valley that looked like the family land at Wanaka. I knew vines would grow here, but didn't know if they would ripen fruit.' The first, tiny batch of Rippon Vineyard wine flowed in 1984, produced by Rainer Eschenbruch at the Te Kauwhata research station.

The Mills' have planted their 13-hectare, north-facing vineyard in a glacial moraine. 'We have terrific drainage – all that gravel beneath us, covered by good soil brought down by erosion,' says Mills. Pinot Noir, Chardonnay, Riesling, Gewürztraminer, Sauvignon Blanc, Müller-Thurgau and Osteiner are the principal varieties, with a small plot of Syrah.

Clotilde Chauvet, scion of a French Champagne-producing family, produced the 1993 to 1995 vintages. Axel Rothermel, who graduated from an agricultural college in Ettlingen, Germany in 1985, and gained his practical experience in various vineyards and wineries in the Rheingau, now holds the winemaking reins.

Rippon's annual production is about 3000 cases and growing. The drink-young wines include New Zealand's only Osteiner – a crossing of Riesling and Sylvaner which yields a light, slightly sweet and mild, Müller-Thurgau-like wine; a tangy, grassy, medium-dry blend labelled as Hotere White; and a pink, fresh-scented, berryish Gamay Rosé, brimming with flavour and character.

The barrel-fermented Sauvignon Blanc is full-flavoured, grassy and buttery with a freshly acidic finish. The Gewürztraminer is gently aromatic, with a delicate, persistent spiciness. Shy in its youth, the Riesling has fresh, delicate lemon/apple flavours and spine-tingling acidity. The Chardonnay is the most Chablis-like in the country, with flinty, appley flavours in a slightly austere and steely style.

Rippon Vineyard Pinot Noir is an enticingly fragrant red, bursting with buoyant, raspberryish, cherryish flavours, rich, supple and sustained. Its more oak-influenced and subtle big brother, the Selection Pinot Noir, is Rippon's and the region's greatest wine.

RIPPON VINEYARD SELECTION PINOT NOIR

Alluring in its youth, with a delicious depth of vibrant, sweet-tasting raspberry/cherry fruit, Rippon's top Pinot Noir also blossoms with cellaring; the bold 1991 vintage is currently magnificently rich, savoury and complex.

Compared to its lower-priced stablemate, labelled Pinot Noir, the top wine is clonally selected (with a higher proportion of clones 5 and 6 and less 10/5), held longer on its skins before and after the fermentation, and matured in a higher percentage of new oak casks.

The densely spaced vines are pruned hard to yield a light crop of around seven tonnes per hectare of concentrated, flavour-rich grapes. Hand-harvested in cool (5–8°C) temperatures in May, the grapes are crushed by bare feet. Whole-bunch fermentation of about one-fifth of the fruit was introduced in 1993. Held on its skins for up to a month after the fermentation to boost its tannins, the young wine is then matured in half-new French oak barriques.

Reflecting its cool-climate origins, Rippon Vineyard Selection Pinot Noir is a wine of floral, supple richness and enduring freshness.

Frosts, birds and wasps caused heartaches during the establishment years, but now William Hill Vineyard is in expansion mode, with a new winery up and running for the 1995 vintage and new vineyards coming on stream.

For several years, Bill Grant produced only a trickle of Alexandra wine: 'A few thousand bottles a year, sold in a couple of months at my back door. I just wanted to prove it could be done; those who come after me can expand it.'

William Hill Vineyard lies on a sandy terrace above the Clutha River, on the western edge of Alexandra. Grant – whose full name is William Hill Grant – was raised in Dunedin and for many years was a schoolteacher. Stone quarrying and building have been his major activities in Alexandra. While travelling in Europe, however, he became convinced there are climatic parallels between the Rhine and Alexandra.

Grant planted his first two rows of vines in 1973. 'I waited for everyone else to do something, then when I heard Ann Pinckney was going ahead at Taramea [near Queenstown], I thought I'd better get cracking too.' By the early 1980s his vineyard had expanded to a half-hectare. After the first, experimental wines had been 'either drunk or disposed of', William Hill's first 'commercial' wines flowed in 1988.

The seven-hectare vineyard is planted principally in Chardonnay and Pinot Noir, with a smaller amount of Gewürztraminer. Riesling struggled to achieve full ripeness, but Pinot Noir 'ripens well, even in a bad season, with good crops, good colour, good everything,' says Grant.

The early vintages were processed at Rippon Vineyard and Black Ridge, but William Hill's new winery, capable of crushing 300 tonnes, is large enough to handle grapes for other Alexandra producers. Dhana Pillai, who owns the nearby Leaning Rock vineyard, is the winemaker.

Bill and Gillian Grant's son, David, recently took over as managing director of the winemaking venture. David also heads the family company, Alexandra Stone. 'I'll co-ordinate things around the place and be able to concentrate more on the vineyard,' says Bill.

The William Hill range is dramatically packaged in very tall, slender bottles with vertical labels running their full height. These are uniformly light, clean wines, delicately perfumed and flavoured. The Gewürztraminer is pale and fruity, with a touch of sweetness and spiciness. The Chardonnay, a non-wooded style with plenty of weight, is tart and appley. The ruby hued Pinot Noir, which is barrel-aged, displays fresh, floral aromas and light, buoyant, raspberryish flavours.

William Hill Vineyard

Dunstan Road, Alexandra

Owners:
Bill and Gillian Grant

Key Wines:
Pinot Noir, Chardonnay, Gewürztraminer, Riesling

Twenty-three years after his father, Bill, planted the first vines, David Grant has assumed control of this small Alexandra winery.

Other Producers

Kawarau Estate

With its excitingly perfumed and weighty, bone-dry, intensely spicy Morven Hill Gewürztraminer 1995, this fledgling company served notice it will be a force to be reckoned with. Charles Finny, Wendy and Geoff Hinton, and Nicola Sharp own two vineyards: the five-hectare Dunstan Vineyard, north of Lowburn, and the 2.5-hectare, steeply sloping Morven Hill Vineyard at Lake Hayes. Both vineyards were awarded full Bio-Gro status in 1996. A sales facility opened at Lowburn in 1996 and by 1997 the company plans to be producing 1600 cases of Gewürztraminer, Sauvignon Blanc, Chardonnay, Pinot Noir and Merlot.

Adams, Grant, 70
additives, 13
Airfield label, 63
AKARANGI, 94
ALLAN SCOTT, 144–145
ALEXANDER, 129
Allan, Claire and Mike, 156
ANTIPODEAN, 35, 36, 37
Appellation Vineyards, 80, 145
ASPEN RIDGE, 77
ATA RANGI, 117
Ata Rangi Pinot Noir, 117
Atkins, Annette, 128, 128
Auckland wineries, 65–71

Babich, Joe; Josip; Peter, 49–50
BABICH, 49–50
Baker, John and Michelle, 173
Bauer, Rudi, 174–175
Bay of Plenty wineries, 78–81
Bazzard, Charles and Kay, 39
BAZZARD ESTATE, 39
Beetham, William, 8, 116
Bellamour winery, 58
Belsham, John, 163
Benfield, Bill, 118
BENFIELD AND DELAMARE, 118
Bennett, Michael, 106
Berriman family, 95
Berry, Keith and Ruth, 171
Binnie, Phil, 155
Bird, Don; Robbie, 98
Bird, Robert, 9, 98
Bird, Steve, 80
Bish, Tony, 113, 158
BLACK RIDGE, 185
Blick, Brian and Sheryl, 45
Bloomfield, David; Eric; Pamela, 118–119
BLOOMFIELD VINEYARDS, 118
Blowers, Hazel and Michael, 170
BLUE ROCK VINEYARD, 119
Botrytis, 12
Bowen, Rob, 126
Bowling, Richard, 161
BRADSHAW ESTATE, 113
Brady, Alan, 186–187
Bragato, Romeo, 8–9, 116
Brajkovich
    Mate; Melba; Milan;
    Paul; 41–42
    Michael, 12, 41–42
Brink, Bill and Sally, 129
Brooke-Taylor, Paula and Rex, 163
BROOKFIELDS, 94–95
BROTHERS, 163
Brough, Joan; John, 178–179
Brown, Daphne and Murray, 145
Brown, Willie and Lea, 125
BROWNLIE BROTHERS, 113
Buchanan, Neil, 152
Buck, John, 108–109
Buffalora family, 64
Burgess, Verdun, 185
Buring, Chris, 127
Busby, James, 8

C.J. PASK WINERY, 95
Cabernet Franc, 24
Cabernet Sauvignon, 24–25
Cadwallader, Ian and Rachel, 105
CAIRNBRAE, 146
Cameron, Alec, 89
Campbell, Claire, 123
Campbell and Ehrenfried, 66
CANADORO, 129
Canning, Chris and Pamela, 75
Canning, Strat, 128–129
Canterbury wineries, 164–181
CELLIER LE BRUN, 146–147
Chambers, Bernard, 8, 108
Chan, Nick, 56, 101
Chan, Stanley, 77
CHARD FARM, 185–186
Chardonnay, 12, 13, 18–19

Chasselas, 12
Chauvet, Clotilde, 188
Chenin Blanc, 13, 19
Chifney, Rosemary and Sue, 120
Chifney, Stan, 116, 120
CHIFNEY WINES, 120
Chignell-Vuletic, Michelle, 37
Christchurch wineries, 172–181
Church Road label, 68, 110–111
Clark, Beverley; Jenny and Nelson, 119
Clarke, Jeff, 67
CLEARVIEW ESTATE, 96
Clearview Estate Reserve Chardonnay, 96
CLIFTON ROAD, 113
climate, 16–17
CLOUDY BAY, 147–148
Cloudy Bay Sauvignon Blanc, 148
Coakley, Tony, 178–179
Coats, Terri, 113
Coleraine Cabernet Merlot, 110
Collard, Brian; Bruce; Geoffrey; John, 50
    Lionel, 50
COLLARD BROTHERS, 50–51
Collards Hawke's Bay Chenin Blanc, 51
Coltart, Andy, 101
Compton, Mark, 75
CONDERS BEND, 149
Coney, John and Alison, 80–81
Cooks/McWilliam's, 53
COOPERS CREEK, 39–41
Corban
    Alex; Najibie; Wadier, 52
    Alwyn, 104
    Assid Abraham, 9, 52
CORBANS, 9, 52–54
Corporate Investments Ltd, 66–67
Cottage Block label, 53–54
Covell, Bob and Des, 79
COVELL ESTATE, 79
Cowley, Peter, 109
CRAB FARM, 97
Craike, J.O., 108
Crawford, Kim, 39–40
Crone, Keith, 113
CROSS ROADS, 97
Culley, Neill, 49

Dalmatian immigrants, 9, 28, 32, 33, 48
Daniel Le Brun Vintage Méthode Champenoise, 147
DARJON VINEYARDS, 173
Dashwood label, 161
DB Group, 52
DE REDCLIFFE, 75
Delamare, Sue, 118
Delegat, Jim and Rose; Nikola, 55
DELEGAT'S, 10, 55–56
Delegat's Proprietors Reserve Chardonnay, 56
Deutz Marlborough Cuvée, 68
Direct Capital Ltd, 45
DOMAINE CHANDON, 163
Donaldson, Christine and Ivan; Edward;
    Matthew, 169
Douglas, Mark, 37
Draper, Robin and Tom, 127
DRY RIVER, 120–121
Dry River Pinot Noir, 121
du Fresne, Andy, 139
du Fresne, Viggo, 132, 139
Duke, Gary, 153
Dunleavy, John; Paul; Terry, 64

Edmonds, Grant and Sue, 113
Edwards, Sue, 185
Elliott, Gillian; Martin, 106
Elspeth label, 79
Erceg, Michael; Millie; Mijo, 57
ESK VALLEY, 70, 98–99
ESKDALE, 99
Evans, Mary, 36
Evans, Petter, 178
Everling, Edel, 155
exports, 11

Fabris, Anne and Gary, 170
Fenton, Barry and Meg, 64
Field, Kaar, 100
Finn, Judy and Tim, 132, 134–135
Finney, Charles, 189
Fistonich, Andrew; George, 70
Foley, Warwick, 155
Forest Flowers label, 71
Forrest, Brigid; John, 149–150
Forrest, Jane, 162
FORREST ESTATE, 149–150
fortified wines, making, 15
FOXES ISLAND, 163
FRAMINGHAM, 163
Fraser, Roger, 129
Fredatovich, John and Peter, 56
FRENCH FARM, 181
Fromm, Georg and Ruth, 150
FROMM WINERY, 150

Gambitsis, 155
Gass, Craig; Jane, 149, 163
Gatehouse
    Carol; Desmond; Esma; Phillip;
    Stephen, 173
    Peter, 173
GATEHOUSE WINES, 173
Geoffory, Richard 163
Gewürztraminer, 12, 20
GIBBSTON VALLEY, 186–187
Giesen, Alex; Marcel; Theo, 174–175
GIESEN, 174–175
Gillan, Terry and Toni, 151
GILLAN ESTATE, 151
Gisborne wineries, 82–89
GLADSTONE, 122
Glazebrook, Garry, 104
GLENMARK WINES, 167
Glenvale winery, 70, 98
Glover, David; Penny, 133–134
GLOVER'S VINEYARD, 133–134
Goldwater, Gretchen; Jeanette and Kim, 62
GOLDWATER ESTATE, 62
Goldwater Estate Cabernet/Merlot, 62
Gould, Belinda, 171
Government Viticulturalists
    Bragato, Romeo, 9, 116
    Lindeman, B. W., 9
Graham, Anne, 163
Grant, Andrew; Beverley, 171
Grant, Bill; David; Gillian, 189
Great Barrier Island, 64
Green, Tina; W.H., 101
Greenhough, Andrew, 136
Greenmeadows Mission Trust Board, 102
Greenmeadows Vineyard, 8
GROVE MILL, 151–152
grower labels, 144
GUNN ESTATE, 113

Hadfield, Errol and Kaye, 163
Hamilton, Anne and Doug, 63
Hancock, Jeanette and Peter, 139
Hancock, John, 80
Hansen, Glenys, 127
Harrey, Cheryl and Jon, 139
Harris, Alix; Tim, 47
Harrison, Sir Richard, 113
Harrison, Wayne, 113
HARVEST WINE COMPANY, 89
Hassall, Julia and Tony, 81
HAU ARIKI, 129
Hawke's Bay wineries, 92–113
HAWKESBRIDGE, 163
HAWKHURST ESTATE, 113
Hay, Greg and Rob, 185–186
Henderson wineries, 48–60
Hendry, Andrew and Cyndy, 39–40
HERON'S FLIGHT, 36
Hillerich, Horst and Wendy, 77
Hinton, Geoff and Wendy, 189
Hitchcock, Kerry, 12, 45
Hladilo, Rado, 60
Hoey, Alan, 157–158

Hogan, Allen and Joyce, 160
Holland, David, 129
Holmes, Caroline, Chris and Douglas, 163
Hooper, Tony, 152
Hoskins, David, 36
Hotel du Vin, 75
HOUSE OF NOBILO, 45–46
Huapai wineries, 38–47
Hubscher, Peter, 66–68
Huntaway label, 54
Hunter, Ernie, Jane, 153
HUNTER'S WINES, 153–154
Hunter's Sauvignon Blanc, 154
HUTHLEE ESTATE, 100

Ibbotson, Judy and Neal, 159
Inkersell, Sarah, 58
Irongate Chardonnay, 50
Irwin, Denis, 86
ISABEL ESTATE, 163
Ivicevich, Anthony; Sue, 60

JACKSON ESTATE, 154
Jardine, Hamish; James, 97
Jelich, Stipan, 9, 57
Jensen, Geoffrey and Robina, 158
Jewelstone Chardonnay, 103
JOHANNESHOF CELLARS, 155
Johnson, Allan, 126
Jones, Philip; Sheryl, 138–139
Jordan, Tony, 153, 163
Judd Estate Chardonnay, 44

KAITUNA VALLEY, 181
Kalberer, Hatsch, 150
KANUKA FOREST, 81
KAWARAU ESTATE, 189
Kemble, John, 100
KEMBLEFIELD ESTATE, 100
Kernohan, Christine and David, 122
KINDALE, 163
Knight, Aran, 105
Knight, Bev; Monty, 34
KUMEU RIVER, 41–42
Kumeu River Chardonnay, 42
Kumeu wineries, 38–47

LAKE CHALICE, 155
LANDFALL WINES, 86
LANGDALE, 175
Larose Cabernets, 64
Laurenson, Alan; Jetta, 43
Lawson, Angus (Gus) and Ian, 108
Lawson, Barbara; Ross, 156
LAWSON'S DRY HILLS, 156
Le Brun, Daniel, 146–147
Lee, Devon and Estelle, 100
Levet, Charles, 8
licensing, 8, 9
LIMEBURNERS BAY, 43
Limmer, Alan, 107
LINCOLN, 56
Lindeman, B. W., 9
LINDEN ESTATE, 101
Lintz, Chris; Doris; Harold and Uni, 122–123
LINTZ ESTATE, 122–123
LOMBARDI WINES, 101
Longbush label, 86
Longlands label, 108
Longridge, 53–54
LONGVIEW ESTATE, 33
Lorenz, Almuth, 156–157
Loughlin, John and John; Kathryn, 112–113

MacFarlane family, 163
MacLennan, Ross, 111
MacMillan, Saralinda, 139
Malbec, 25
Marchbanks, Jenny and John, 139
Margan family, 43
MARGRAIN, 129
MARK RATTRAY, 167–168

INDEX

Marlborough wineries, 140–163
Marris, Brent, 55–56, 163
Marsden, Steve, 120
MARTINBOROUGH, 123–124
Martinborough Vineyard Pinot Noir, 124
Masfen, Peter, 67
Mason, David and Mark, 105–106, 113
Masters, Oliver, 117
Matakana wineries, 35–37
MATAWHERO, 86
MATUA VALLEY, 43–44
Mazuran, George, 9, 60
MAZURAN'S, 60
McCallum, Dawn, 120
McCallum, Neil, 114, 120–121
McCaskey, John, 167
McCauley, Brian and Shelley, 168–169
McDonald, Tom, 9, 93, 111
MCDONALD WINERY, 110–111
McKenna, Larry, 123–124, 126
McKissock, Alister, 77
McWilliams, Allan, 157–158
McWilliam's Wines (N.Z.), 9, 93
Mellars, John, 64
Mere Road Selection label, 79
MERLEN WINES, 156–157
Merlot, 25–26
Milicich, Ivan, 77
Mill Creek label, 158
Mill Road label, 81
Mills, Lois and Rolfe, 188
MILLS REEF, 79–80
Millton, Annie and James, 88–89
MILLTON VINEYARD, 88–89
Milne, Derek; Duncan, 116, 123
MISSION VINEYARDS, 92, 102–103
MISTY VALLEY, 60
Molloy, Hugh, 162
Molloy, Tony, 69
MONTANA, 10, 66–69, 110–111
Montana Marlborough Sauvignon Blanc, 69
Montgomerie, Ian, 70
Montgomery, Elise, 111–112
Mooney, Paul, 102, 103
Moore, Bruce; Jill, 171
Moore, Christine and David, 136–137
Moorlands Vineyard, 53
Morris, Michael, 108–109
MORTON ESTATE, 80–81
Morton Estate Black Label Hawke's Bay Chardonnay, 81
MOUNT LINTON, 163
MOUTERE HILLS, 139
MUIRLEA RISE, 125
Müller-Thurgau, 10, 12, 20
Mundy, Bernice and Robin, 177–178
MURDOCH JAMES, 129
Muscat Dr Hogg, 21

NAUTILUS, 157–158
Negociants New Zealand, 157
Neill, Rod, 139
Nelson wineries, 130–139
Neudorf Chardonnay, 135
NEUDORF VINEYARDS, 134–135
New Zealand Viticultural Association, 9
NGA WAKA, 125
NGATARAWA, 104
Northland wineries, 32–34
Nobilo, Mark, Nick and Steve; Nikola 45
NOBILO, 45–46
Nooyen, Nelda and Pieter, 77

O'Brien, Lester, 97
OHINEMURI ESTATE, 77
OKAHU ESTATE, 34
Old Masters label, 71
OMAKA SPRINGS, 158
OMARAMA, 187
OMIHI HILLS, 168–169
organic viticulture, 79, 88
Osborne, Morton; Vivien, 94
Otaka Holdings (NZ) Ltd., 75
Otago wineries, 182–189

Oyster Bay label, 55
Ozich, Davorin and Miro, 59

PACIFIC VINEYARDS, 57
Pain, Alistair, 129
PALLISER ESTATE, 126
Palomino, 21
Panorama, 60
PARK ESTATE, 113
Parker, Phil, 87
PARKER MÉTHODE CHAMPENOISE, 87
Parkinson
    Carol and Roger, 125
    Gordon and Margaret, 125
Pask, Chris, 95
Paton
    Alison, 117
    Clive, 116, 117, 129
Pattie, Phyllis, 117
Pearce, David, 87, 152
Pecar, Steve, 60
PEGASUS BAY, 169
PELORUS, 136
Penfolds Wines (N.Z.), 9, 67
PENINSULA ESTATE, 63
Pharis, Dick and Vivian, 170
Phillips, Andrew, 71
Phoenix brand, 57
Pickering, Martin, 62
Pillai, Dhana, 189
Pinot Gris, 21
Pinot Noir, 26–27
Pinotage, 26
PLEASANT VALLEY, 9, 57
POMONA RIDGE, 139
Ponder, Dianne and Michael, 159
PONDER ESTATE, 159
Porter, Rolf, 66
POUPARAE PARK, 89
Preston, Melissa; Tim; Warren (Paddy), 79–80
Prichard, Tony, 110–111
PROVIDENCE, 37

Radburnd, Kate, 95
Rainbow Ridge label, 60
Rapaura Vintners, 43
Rattray, Mark; Michelle, 167–168, 178, 181
Rawstron
    Brent and Shirley, 177
    Grant and Haydn, 177
Rayner, Kim, 170, 171
RED METAL VINEYARD, 113
red wines, making, 14
Reeves, Malcolm, 97, 113
Reid, John, 162
Revington, Mary Jane; Ross, 86, 87
REVINGTON VINEYARD, 87
RICHARD HARRISON, 113
Riddiford, Richard, 126
Riesling, 22
RIPPON, 188
Rippon Vineyard Selection Pinot Noir, 188
RIVERSIDE WINES, 105
Robard @ Butler, 53
Roberts, Dennis, 122
Robertson, Mark, 43–44
Robertson, Peter, 94–95
Robins, Greg and Lesley, 129
ROCKWOOD CELLARS, 113
RONGOPAI, 76
Rose, Chris; Phil, 162
rosé wines, making, 14
ROSEBANK ESTATE, 176
Roseworthy Agricultural College, 12
ROSSENDALE, 177
ROTHBURY (NZ), 163
Rothermel, Axel, 188
RUBY BAY, 136–137
Russell, Gordon, 98–99

SACRED HILL, 105–106
SAINT CLAIR ESTATE, 159

Salmond, Rebecca, 57
Salonius, Kim and Trish, 99
SANDIHURST, 178–179
SAPICH BROTHERS, 60
Saunders, Janet, 118
Sauvignon Blanc, 13, 22–23
Scanlan, Noel, 53
Schultz, Russell and Sue, 123
Schuster
    Danny, 168–169; 178
    Mari, 168
Scott, Allan and Catherine, 144–145, 181
Seagram, 66–67
Seibel, Norbert; Silvia, 58
SEIBEL WINES, 58
Seifried, Agnes; Hermann, 132, 137–138
SEIFRIED ESTATE, 137–138
Selak
    Ivan; Michael 46
    Marino; Mate, 46
SELAKS, 46–47
Selaks Sauvignon Blanc/Sémillon, 47
Sémillon, 13, 23
Seppelts, 111
Shackel, Brian; Margaret, 176
Shackleton, Andrew, 127
SHALIMAR ESTATE, 88
Shanks, Brian, 89
Sharp, Nicola, 189
Sherwood, Dayne and Jill, 179–180
SHERWOOD ESTATE, 179–180
Shingle Peak label, 44
Shiraz (Syrah), 27
SILVERSTREAM, 180–181
Simpson, Diane and Gary, 113
Smith, Steve, 70
soils, 16–17
Soler, Joseph, 8
Soljan
    Rex, 35, 58
    Tony, 58
SOLJANS WINES, 58
South Auckland wineries, 65–71
Southern Lakes label, 186
sparkling wines, making, 14–15
Spence, Bill and Ross; Rod, 43–44
Spencer, John, 70
SPENCER HILL ESTATE, 138–139
St Aubyns label, 71
St Niege Vineyard, 53
ST GEORGE, 106
ST HELENA, 177–178
ST JEROME, 59
ST NESBIT, 69
Steinmetz, Bartholomew, 111
Stitchbury, John; Warwick, 154
STONECROFT, 107
Stonecroft Syrah, 107
Stoneleigh Vineyard, 53
Stoneleigh Vineyard Rhine Riesling, 54
STONYRIDGE VINEYARD, 63
Stribling, Lew, 175
Stuart, Alec and Kerryanne; Helen, 88
Swamp Reserve Chardonnay, 41
Syrah, 27

TAI-ARA-RAU, 89
Tairawhiti Polytechnic Wine Industry Certificate course, 89
Tarring, Steve, 128–129
Taylor, Grant, 187
TE ARAI POINT, 37
TE AWA FARM, 108
TE HORO ESTATE, 129
TE KAIRANGA, 127
Te Kauwhata Viticultural Research Station, 9, 74, 76
TE MANIA, 139
TE MATA ESTATE, 8, 92, 108–110
TE WHARE RA, 160
Tenuwera, Tom, 152
Theedom, Tina, 119
Thomas, Alison and Thomas, 139
Thomas, Glenn, 160–161, 160

Thorp, Kim, 101
Thorpe, Bill; John, 86
Tiffen, Henry, 8
Tiller, Michael and Robyn, 163
Todd, Gesina (Zeke) and Peter, 180–181
Tomlin, Andrew, 170
TORLESSE, 170
TOTARA, 77
Trembath, Ian, 56
Tubic, Steve, 57
TUI VALE, 113
Turner, Ross, 128–129
Turvey, Tim, 96, 96
TWIN BAYS, 64
Twin Islands label, 157–158
Twin Rivers label, 110–111

van Dam, Faith and Tom, 76
van den Berg, Helma, 96
van der Linden, John, Stephen and Wim, 101
VAVASOUR, 160–161
Vavasour Reserve Chardonnay, 161
Veal, Judy and Mike, 163
VICTORY, 139
Vidal, Anthony, Cecil, Frank and Leslie, 111
VIDAL, 70, 111–112
Vidal Reserve Cabernet Sauvignon, 112
Vidal Reserve Cabernet Sauvignon/Merlot, 112
VILAGRAD, 77
VILLA MARIA, 10, 70–71, 98–99, 111–112
Villa Maria Reserve Barrique Fermented Chardonnay, 71
vine area, 11, 18
vine uprooting, 10
Voss, Gary, 128, 128
VOSS ESTATE, 128
Vuletic, James; Petar, 37–38, 37
Vuletich, Mario; Mate, 33

Waghorn, Simon, 162–163
Waiheke Island wineries, 61–64
WAIHEKE VINEYARDS, 64
Waihirere Vineyard, 9, 66–67, 84
Waikato wineries, 72–77
WAIMARAMA ESTATE, 112–113
Waimauku wineries, 38–47
WAIPARA DOWNS, 171
WAIPARA ESTATES, 181
WAIPARA SPRINGS, 171
Waipara wineries, 166–171
Wairarapa wineries, 114–129
WAIRAU RIVER, 162
WAITAKERE ROAD, 47
WALKER ESTATE, 129
WALNUT RIDGE, 129
Ward, David and Betty, 96
Watson, Joan; Rob, 187
Weaver, Sam, 163
WEST BROOK, 60
Wheeler, Jenny, 136
Whelan, Grant and Helen, 181
White, Greg and Sue, 162
White, Stephen, 63
white wines, making, 13
WHITEHAVEN, 162–163
Wi Pere Trust, 89
Wichman, Ron, 155
WILLIAM HILL, 189
Willy, Helen and Tony, 181
Wine Institute, 10–11
wine regions, 28–29; see also individual regions
Winemaking Industry Committee, 9
WINSLOW WINES, 128–129
WITHER HILLS, 163
Wohnsiedler, Friedrich, 9, 84
Woolley, Darryl, 46–47

Yelas, Stephan, 57
Yokoi, Shin, 152
Young, Chris, 158
Yukich, Frank, Ivan and Mate, 66–67

Bibliography

Beaven, D., Donaldson, I. and Watson, G., *Wine – A New Zealand Perspective*, 2nd ed., 1988.

Brimer, R., *Boutique Wineries of New Zealand*, 1993.

Brooks, C., *Marlborough Wines and Vines*, 1992.

Campbell, B., *New Zealand Wine Annual 1996*, 1995.

Cooper, M., *Michael Cooper's Buyer's Guide to New Zealand Wines*, 4th ed., 1995.

Cooper, M., *Michael Cooper's Pocket Guide to New Zealand Wines and Vintages*, 1990.

Graham, J.C., *Know Your New Zealand Wines*, 1980.

Halliday, J., *James Halliday's Pocket Companion to Australian and New Zealand Wines*, 1995.

Halliday, J., *Wine Atlas of Australia and New Zealand*, 1991.

MacQuitty, J., *Jane MacQuitty's Pocket Guide to New Zealand and Australian Wines*, London, 1990.

Reynolds, T., *My Side of the River: Tales From a Marlborough Vineyard*, 1995.

Saunders, P., *A Guide to New Zealand Wine*, 18th ed., 1995.

Scott, D., *Winemakers of New Zealand*, 1964.

Scott, D., *A Stake in the Country: A.A. Corban and Family 1892–1977*, 1977.

Stewart, K., *The Fine Wines of New Zealand*, 1995.

Stewart, K., *The New Zealander's Guide to Wines of the World*, 1994.

Talmont, R., *New Zealand Wineries and Vineyards 1996*, 1995.

Thorpy, F., *Wine in New Zealand*, 1971, revised ed., 1983.

Williams, V., *The Penguin Good New Zealand Wine Guide*, 4th ed., 1995.

ISBN 1-86958-297-7

© 1996 Text: Michael Cooper
© 1996 Photographs: Hodder Moa Beckett Limited

First published 1984
Second edition 1986
Reprinted 1987
Third edition 1988
Reprinted 1989
Fourth edition 1993
Reprinted 1994

Published in 1996 by Hodder Moa Beckett Publishers Limited
[a member of the Hodder Headline Group]
4 Whetu Place, Mairangi Bay, Auckland, New Zealand

Editor: Brian O'Flaherty
Cartography: Maps produced by Department of Survey and Land Information
Map Licence No: TL098898/7 Crown Copyright Reserved
Photography: All photographs in this book are by John McDermott except those attributed otherwise below:
page 21 Pinot Gris photo (Robin Morrison Estate) page 9 historic photo (Dick Scott, from *Winemakers of New Zealand*)

Cover photo: Montana's Brancott Vineyard, Marlborough

Printed in Hong Kong, through Bookbuilders Limited

All rights reserved. No part of this publication may be reproduced or transmitted in any form or
by any means, electronic or mechanical, including photocopying, recording, or any information
storage and retrieval system, without permission in writing from the publisher.